Preface

In his acceptance speech at Oslo
for the 1971 Nobel Peace Prize,
Chancellor Willy Brandt of the
Federal Republic of West Germany
called for an end to the abuses of
nationalism. "I say here what I say
in Germany: A good German cannot
be a nationalist. A good German
knows that he cannot refuse a
European calling. Through Europe,
Germany returns to itself and to the
constructive force of its history. Our
Europe, born of the experience of
suffering and failure, is the
imperative mission of reason."

"The imperative mission of
reason"! Willy Brandt spoke well
and he had the support of men
of good will everywhere. There is
little doubt of his sincerity as
well as that of other leaders in the
contemporary world who speak
rationally about cooperation,
consultation, and the common
problems of mankind. Again and
again statesmen and scholars speak
of nationalism as an archaic
phenomenon now in process of
decline in the presence of a rising
internationalism.

Unfortunately, the wish is father to the thought. Men of reason know well that it is utterly wrong to base a world society on so flimsy an edifice as nationalism, but they fail to see that they are dealing with a highly emotional and often illogical historical force. The fact remains that the whole machinery of nationalism works blindly on all over the globe—west and east, north and south. While the leaders of the world speak grandly of growing cooperation, they invariably place their own nation foremost in any list of priorities. Indeed, they are judged by their people on how well they succeed in enhancing the national image and protecting it from assaults from outside and inside the country. As *Realpolitiker* they must regard national power as the key essential to existence in a dangerous world—and a plague on any moral judgments of history.

The problems of contemporary society are many—varying political ideologies, the cold war, the race for nuclear supremacy, inflation, overpopulation, ecological disaster. High among them is the continuing problem of nationalism, which has an importance far beyond divisions of ideology or civilization. In the words of James Reston, "the bawling demands of nationalism are louder than ever."

Understanding nationalism is not an easy task. Only a comparative study can do justice to this subject in all its bewildering manifestations and allow us to understand its similarities and differences. What began in its modern form as a European libertarian movement, has spread to all corners of the world with its early liberal quality transformed into aggression and hostility. A modernizing force in societies seeking unity and independence, nationalism becomes a force for oppression once nationhood is won. Nationalism wears a cloak of many colors.

It is the purpose of this book to suggest some answers to the many questions incited by nationalism. What is the meaning of the terms "nation," "nationality," and "nationalism"? What are the differences between nationalism and patriotism? Is there any validity to the concept of national character? What is the history of nationalism from the eighteenth to the twentieth century? In what ways did nationalism contribute to the outbreak of the two World Wars? How has nationalism changed since 1945? What alternatives are there to nationalism in contemporary society? And finally, what can be said about the probable future of nationalism?

Each of these questions is bathed in controversy, but each merits consideration. The goal is to construct a set of criteria, pose the questions, and illustrate possible answers. The task is a formidable one and no pretense is made here of reaching final solutions. John Ruskin spoke about "masked words," terms which appear to have a scientific or rational and precise, well-documented meaning when they are, in fact, no more than terms of rhetorical abuse. "Imperialism" would lead the parade today. Nationalism,

Varieties of Nationalism: A Comparative Study

Varieties of Nationalism: A Comparative Study

Louis L. Snyder

Holt, Rinehart and Winston
New York

To the memory of Hans Kohn and Carlton J. H. Hayes, Pioneer scholars of nationalism; guides, philosophers, and cherished friends.

Published simultaneously in Canada by
Holt, Rinehart and Winston of Canada,
Limited.

Library of Congress Catalog Card
Number: 73-2097
ISBN: 0-03-018206-9

Printed in the United States of America
10 9 8 7 6 5 4 3 2 1

In all [a] great array of elaborate, statistically supported serious futurology mingled with free fantasy, there took place one movement which dominated much of the nineteenth century, for which no significant future was predicted, a movement so familiar to us now, so decisive both within, and in relationships between nations, that it is only by some effort of the imagination that one can conceive of a world in which it played no part. . . . This movement is nationalism.

Isaiah Berlin

with all its shades of meaning, comes close to this category. Hence it is necessary to use a broad canvas and pay close attention to language, communication, habit, propinquity, psychology, and myth.

In the long run, however, any satisfactory discussion of nationalism leads most often to the political arena. Nationalism must often be treated in its strict political sense. Some may regard this as nationalism narrowly conceived, but the alternative is a multivolume study with such titles as "The Psychology of Nationalism," "The Paradoxes of Nationalism," and "The Myths of Nationalism."

Nationalism has occupied the attention of the most highly regarded thinkers of our times. Albert Einstein spoke for many when he expressed his opposition to nationalism because it is an outgrowth of the aggressive peculiarity of human beings. "It is beyond me," he said, "to keep secret my international orientation. The state to which I belong as a citizen does not play the least role in my spiritual life; I regard allegiance to a government as a business matter, somewhat like the relationship with a life insurance company."

Einstein may have regarded nationalism as a business matter, but unfortunately many millions of his fellow "masters of creation" have accepted it as a more dominant aspect of their daily lives. For that reason it is essential that we give much more attention to this powerful political and psychological force that one day might help to make this earth uninhabitable.

As in all my previous work, the assistance of my wife in the organization and production of this book has been indispensable. My thanks go to her for repeated rescues from the pitfalls of grammar and style.

I would also like to thank Ray Ashton, my editor at Dryden; Steve Rapley, who designed the book; and Jo Anne Naples, who took charge of the proofreading during the final stages of production.

Louis L. Snyder,
Princeton, N.J., January 1976

Contents

Varieties of Nationalism: A Comparative Study

1

Approaches to the Omnipresent Ism

Political nationalism has become for the European of our age the most important thing in the world, more important than humanity, decency, kindness, piety; more important than life itself.

—Sir Norman Angell

A Pageant of Complexities

On June 5, 1968, the night of California's primary election, a wild-eyed young Jordanian forced his way through a crowd of victory celebrants and pumped a staccato of bullets into the head of Robert F. Kennedy, brother of assassinated President John F. Kennedy. When questioned after the assassination, Sirhan B. Sirhan struck a pose of patriotic innocence and exclaimed: "I did it for my country!" Palestine terrorist organizations soon claimed the pathetic assassin as one of their own freedom fighters.

On July 1, 1969, in the midst of royal pageantry at Caernarvon Castle for the investiture of Charles Philip Arthur George Windsor, 20-year-old heir to the British throne as Prince of Wales, an angered Welshman hurled a fire bomb into a truck and killed a military policeman. The day before the investiture, two other Welshmen, carrying explosives, mistakenly blew themselves up in the name of Welsh nationalism.

Several weeks later, on July 20, 1969, after a 500,000-mile journey from the earth, two astronauts, Neil A. Armstrong and Edwin E. Aldrin, Jr., stepped from the lunar module of *Apollo 11* and planted the American colors on the surface of the moon. It was the American flag and not the "spider emblem" of the United Nations—a needless offense to the ghosts of the Pole Copernicus, the German Kepler, and the Englishman Newton. The project, costing between 20 and 40 billion dollars, was fantastically successful, even if it was born in part of injured national pride in the cold war between the United States and the Soviet Union.

When Brazil won the World Cup soccer championship in the summer of 1970, the whole country erupted into an orgy of celebrations in which scores of persons died and thousands more were injured by fireworks, gunshot wounds, and traffic accidents. The euphoria was triggered by an automatic if illogical confusion of football wizardry with a sense of national superiority.

On July 31, 1970, the forty-third anniversary of the formation of the Chinese People's Liberation Army, three major newspapers in Peking printed this charge: "Not for a single day has the Soviet Union relaxed its preparations to attack China. . . . If the enemy should dare to intrude into any part of our great motherland, we shall resolutely destroy him and bury him on the spot."

On the surface, there seems to be no relationship between these diverse incidents and countless other similar ones, but through all of them runs the current of a dynamic force in human affairs today. It is that sentiment described by Arnold Toynbee as a tribal minded nationalism responsible for creating "a Boyg-like smog of impersonal relations." (In Ibsen's *Peer Gynt* the great Boyg is a shapeless cloud "neither dead nor alive; all slime and mistiness.")

This time the provocative Professor Toynbee was accurate: nationalism indeed is surrounded by a thick, almost impenetrable intellectual smog. Few historical phenomena are so suffused with paradox, inconsistency, and contradiction. An adaptable sentiment, it takes on different characteristics, depending upon time and space. Its variations do not reflect any fixed motives. It may be associated with liberalism and democracy no less strongly than with authoritarianism and totalitarianism. Its psychological roots are to be found in the special need of human beings for security, but so complex are its workings that it may reveal itself in any combination of political, economic, social, or cultural forms.

There is no absolute formula to be applied to nationalism. There is nothing "natural" about it: its building was as artificial as the construction of the Panama Canal. There is little "rational" about it: it is not necessarily a predestined way of life for the human animal. It is an ism covered with confusion thrice compounded.

Nationalism is no exception to the rule that there is scarcely any subject in history that has not inspired directly opposing analyses. Oswald Spengler spent a lifetime gathering evidence for his cyclical interpretation of history, only to be attacked by other scholars in criticisms ranging from satire to insult. Historians Hugh Trevor-Roper and A. J. P. Taylor, in the classic British style, can hurl thunderbolts at each other on the origins of World War II and then retire gracefully to tea. Nationalism, too, is a force whose complexities are so great that it may be approached and interpreted in different ways. It is a complicated subject for which there are no instant clarifications.

Methodology: Comparative Analysis

Yet complexity should not discourage investigation. After all, we are dealing here with one of the most important subjects in history. Nationalism in the West was an outgrowth of that revolution of modernization beginning in the sixteenth century and coming of age in the French Revolution. From the West it moved in a series of waves to all parts of the earth. One area after another was subjected to nationalistic impulses. Wherever it appeared, nationalism took on characteristics of its European forms. There were local, regional, and continental differences in space and time, but the overall identity was much the same.

What is the best way to study nationalism without being overcome in a haze of conflicting interpretations? The way of the comparative historian seems to have some value. The aim is to find either common denominators or differences in the characteristics and developments of nations and their leaders. The procedure has much in its favor: it examines by comparison and contrast the historical experiences of people to find why they act as groups. In the comparative recognition of similarities and differences there is a chance for understanding this elusive historical phenomenon.

Comparative analysis helps to evaluate not only the broad characteristics of nationalism in diverse areas but also causal relationships. The value of the comparative approach was suggested in the mid-nineteenth century by John Stuart Mill, who believed that one of the most fertile methods in empirical science is to compare two objects or situations which are completely alike except in just *one* respect. Any observed differences revealing themselves in the course of time may be attributed to this differential factor. Though Mill referred specifically to the pure sciences, his judgment holds as well for the social sciences. Causal factors, more precise in the pure sciences, tend to be extremely complex in the social sciences, but that is no reason to disregard them.

At the same time it should be admitted that the comparative approach is by no means a magic formula, clarifying all that needs to be known about nationalism. This procedure is no substitute for the vast amount of empirical research by scholars who study nationalism in every country from Finland to Tanzania, Uganda, and Zambia. Stated concisely, comparative history can test problems across time and space in ways in which more static methods (sociology, anthropology, etc.) cannot do.

The comparative method must rely on the evidence of individual studies. The gathering of data by specialists enables the comparative historian to deduce some generic principles of cause and effect common to several nationalisms existing in similar settings at the same time. Thus Latin American nationalisms, each of which retains its own special character, take on similar qualities based on common language and historical experience. The comparative historian uses the facts supplied by the specialist; if these facts prove to be faulty, the comparison loses its validity.

A Multidisciplinary Accent

This leads us to another important approach. Closely allied with comparative methodology is the multidisciplinary or interdisciplinary examination of the meaning and characteristics of nationalism. In its differing manifestations nationalism is of interest to all the social sciences: to the historian (origins and development), the political scientist (nationality), the sociologist (nation), the psychologist (national consciousness), the anthropologist (national character), and the economist (economic nationalism). Unfortunately, there is little liaison between the various disciplines. Historians know little about the tools and procedures of psychology, yet nationalism in its essence is a feeling largely stimulated by psychological drives. On the other hand, psychologists and social psychologists seem to be unaware of those time and space factors which attract the attention of historians. Teamwork is lacking in this special pursuit of knowledge.

This failing may be attributed in part to the high degree of scholarly specialization. Inductive studies among several disciplines are indicated, provided that the results are compared and correlated with the goal of making accurate generalizations. Psychologists and sociologists especially, to whom the study of nationalism would seem to be of major interest, have produced relatively little work on nationalism and its related phenomena. By far the greatest activity has been shown by historians who have devoted attention to every conceivable phase of nationalism.

The situation is not hopeless, for efforts are beginning to be made to harness all the relevant disciplines in the social sciences to study nationalism and its corollaries. There is a new emphasis upon such areas of research as the contexts in which nationalism operates, different magnitudes of the variables, the role of geography (proximity to hostile neighbors), the significance of national resources, and a call for consistency in the use of terms. Comparative studies in varied disciplines seek basic differences in nationalisms but seek even more for common principles. The search is for more reliable propositions, especially in ascertaining the complex psychological motivations animating the behavior of nations.

In this respect there is a path-breaking effort in the work of two Dutch scholars, H. J. C. Duijker and N. H. Frijda of the University of Amsterdam, with the support of UNESCO.[1] In examining every phase of national character and national stereotypes from the viewpoints of all the major disciplines of the social sciences, this study provides an excellent starting point for further research along multidisciplinary lines.

The Scientific Access to Nationalism

What about the possibility of using techniques of computerization to throw light on nationalism? In an age devoted to the enthronement of science, some social scientists are attracted by the quantitative method as a means of clarifying historical phenomena. In 1953 Karl W. Deutsch published a pioneer study designed to utilize the resources of the exact sciences to promote a better understanding of nationalism and its effects on world history.[2]

Deutsch was dissatisfied with the traditional study of nationalism. He admitted that there was some value in the older direct approach which yielded a wealth of data for recognizing the qualitative aspects of nationalism, the configuration of its symptoms, and the typical sequences of nationalistic behavior. Nevertheless, he questioned such procedures because they have not yielded quantitative measurement nor have they permitted accurate prediction. He called for a new set of tools which could open a new channel in the drive to make sense of nationalism.

Inspired by the scientific materialism of Hobbes and the empiricism of Locke, Deutsch presented three steps of a different method: (1) an examination of existing social sciences for another set of concepts and for other methods of investigation, (2) a search for a new set of structural concepts, and (3) an analysis as to whether such concepts might suggest more specific and more realistic views on nationalism.

After examining the disparate and often contradictory viewpoints on nationalism, Deutsch attempted to resolve the confusion by emphasizing the role of social communication. His study of the nature of political power led him to believe that it is dependent upon the highly uneven distribution of social communication facilities and of economic, cultural, and geographical interdependence. He defined a people as a crucial unit within a cluster of intensive social communications. The important factor in determining nationality and the nature of nationalism is to be found in the communicative facilities of society. These include a socially standardized system of symbols (language) and any number of auxiliary codes, such as alphabets, systems of writing, and calculating. Added to these is information stored in living memories, associations, habits, and preferences of the society's members, and in national facilities for the storage of information, such as libraries and statutes. The communicative facilities permit a common history to be experienced as common. Membership in a people consists essentially in the ability of an individual to communicate more effectively and over a wider range of subjects with members of his own language group than with outsiders.

Thus the Deutsch formula holds that the most important aspect of the unity of a people is the complementarism or relative efficiency of communication among individuals. It is something which might be called "mutual rapport," but on a larger scale. This complementarism of individuals, especially their assimilation and differentiation within the group, can and should be tested. According to Deutsch, tests and measuring devices can supply a quantitative analysis of nationalism and even allow for some predictions, even if cautious ones. The key is cybernetics, the comparative study of electronic calculating machines and the human nervous system, a discipline conceived originally by Norbert Wiener, late mathematician at the Massachusetts Institute of Technology. The testing should be interdisciplinary: the findings of social psychology, sociology, and anthropology should be related closely with those of history, economics, and the social sciences in general.

In the good scholarly tradition, Deutsch called for more research, better tools, more complete data, more realistic assumptions, and attention to refined mathematical techniques. He admitted that his projected tests were but crude indicators and that more sophisticated methods should be devised before any predictions about nationalism could be made. His commendable contribution was opening the study of nationalism to new measurement techniques. This is the sort of investigation which might explain why economic growth in certain areas led to national unification while in others it resulted in greater diversity.

Critics of Deutsch concentrate their fire on his predictability thesis. Nationalism, they say, concerns the psychology of human behavior, but it is essentially a historical phenomenon and as such takes on the quality of the historical process. In both history and nationalism, spiritual and accidental factors do not lend themselves easily to predictability. The critics say that such factors cannot possibly be measured. They say further that students of nationalism have not been successful in their quest for objective criteria of causes, values, and influences.

The results of Deutsch's formula are inconclusive. There has been little research on the quantitative aspects of nationalism since the appearance of his brilliant study. Meanwhile, his guideline is there, waiting to be used in the continuing struggle to make sense of a baffling historical force.

Nationalism and the Territorial Imperative

Still another approach to the study of nationalism takes the observer stumbling into the midst of the unresolved fracas between champions of either heredity or environment. In the past several years the attention of anthropologists, biologists, and sociologists has been directed to a motivating force in human affairs called "the territorial imperative." This is defined as an instinct by which animals regulate the distances among their members and stand aloof from other species. According to this theory, the ownership of land is not a human invention but rather one that has existed and exists widely among such animals as lions, wolves, eagles, ringtailed lemurs, seals, gorillas, and many other species who set aside a portion of the world's surface as their private property and fight to the death against any invaders who would take it from them. The territorial propensity is revealed in remarkable uniformity as, by means of evolutionary trial and error, species incorporate a zealous regard for territory into their general behavior complex. The instinct is said to be innate and to be even stronger than the sex drive. What it does is give the species security from the predator as well as access to a vital food supply.

The idea of the territorial imperative is applied to the human species on the assumption that man is a higher form of animal and, despite his greater brain capacity, lives and acts according to similar motivations that influence the lower animals. It is claimed that when human beings form social groupings to defend their title to the land or the sovereignty of their country, they are doing it for reasons no different and no less innate than those of the lower animals. Thus man's territorial expression is a human response to an imperative affecting both men and Norway rats (lemmings) with equal force. It follows that the nation-state is merely an invention of man to indicate the territory of his in-group. By this reasoning, nationalism becomes a sense of consciousness leading man to protect his territory against those who would take it from him.

This point of view was presented in highly provocative fashion by a onetime playwright and film scenarist who was so entranced by the disciplines of biology and anthropology that he decided to invade their sacred precincts. In a book published in 1966,[3] Robert Ardrey presented his case for an innate xenophobia which not only knits a society but defines it. His style is flowing and attractive. Following is a brief précis of the main thesis.

According to Ardrey, man's territorial expressions are but human responses to an imperative acting with equal force on lower animals and men. The territorial imperative is no less essential to the existence of contemporary man than it was to the small-brained proto-men millions of years ago. The biological nation is a social group holding an exclusive possession of a continuous area of space, which isolates itself from others through outward antagonism. The social principle always remains the same.

Ardrey contends further that the continuity of human evolution, from the world of the animal to the world of man, ensures that a human group in possession of a social territory will behave according to the universal laws of the territorial principle. Whether we like it or not, the territorial imperative is as much an ally of our enemies as it is of ourselves and our friends. Ardrey sees the territorial imperative as one of the evolutionary forces playing upon our lives—a biological law on which we have founded our edifices of human morality. "Our capacities for sacrifice, for altruism, for sympathy, for trust, for responsibilities to other things than self-interest, for honesty, for charity, for friendship and love, for social amity and mutual interdependence have evolved just as surely as the flatness of our feet, the muscularity of our buttocks, and the enlargement of our brains, out of encounter on ancient African savannahs between the primate potential and the hominid circumstance. Whether morality without territory is possible in man must remain as our final, unanswerable question."[4]

Response from the invaded disciplines was loud, angry, and caustic. Ardrey was denounced as "a popularizer of data he does not understand," as an amateur "not to be taken too seriously," and as "a fallible guide." His "layman's version of science" was described as "distorted, shallow, even downright erroneous'' and "shot through with ambiguity.'' It is irrational, said his critics, to allow him "to propagate false doctrine on the ground that it is provocative and controversial." He was accused of being master of the kind of statement that contains so many possible interpretations that "literally any position may be said to have been asserted."

Defenders of Ardrey called this criticism "the usual academic bellyache." One angered letter-writer-to-the-editor spoke for amateur scholars: "So many of our pompous pedants, reared upon an unvaried diet of predigested pap dribbling from 'accepted' sources, clinging to the shelter of 'recognized' authority so their togas will not be sullied by association with unapproved surmises, forget that today's dogma was yesterday's conjecture. The Gospel According to Scott, Foresman is not Holy Writ to the eager, inquiring mind. Through the ages, the Tree of Knowledge unfolds one leaf at a time; thus each generation of pedagogues has a new blanket of Ultimate Truth with which to smother the minds of their helpless charges."[5]

To the myriad scholarly complaints Ardrey blandly replied that he did not seek the confession box. "I recognize, of course, that no school of thought prevailing today on any continent will inform you that my proposition is correct."[6] Undaunted, he reiterated his theory of a dominantly innate instinct that leads man as well as animals to defend their territory. In a successor volume,[7] he revised his theory slightly by admitting that the territorial imperative is somewhat less than imperative, because it could include social and psychological space and status seeking, as well as physical space. Moreover, the territorial imperative could be expressed in retreat and accommodation as well as aggression. But Ardrey stayed with his original proposition: he continued to ignore the gap between animals and men and was unwilling to admit the uniqueness of man.

What does Ardrey's concept mean for the study of nationalism? Undoubtedly, a new dimension is added: what we call nationalism, by Ardrey's reasoning, becomes a calculable force which, released by a predictable situation, will animate man in a manner no different from other territorial species. Patriotism becomes not something we are taught in our environment—it is biologically innate. Ardrey points to Pearl Harbor as a basic laboratory experience and as a clinching argument: his own response to the Japanese surprise attack, like that of other Americans, was instant, voluntary, and an expression of a universal reaction by his social partners. It was a command "of genetic origin," an inheritance from the experience and natural selection of tens of thousands of generations of human and hominid ancestors. If this remarkable uniformity were not innate, he asks, by what processes of social conditioning had Americans been instilled with such love of country as to guarantee that when challenge arose they acted as one?

Nationalism and Modernization

Another approach to nationalism is to consider its nexus with modernization, the rapid revolutionary transformation of man's thinking and activism
from the traditional to the modern. The process of modernization began in
Western Europe and eventually was extended throughout the world. In its
course, the more advanced countries influenced the less developed peoples
in a whole complex of economic, technological, political, and cultural
conditions.

Among the historical institutions affected by modernization was nation
building. Nationalism exerted an enormous appeal in the politics of modernization. The building of modern states took place in an atmosphere of deep
national consciousness transcending all other interests.

In their early stages, nationalism (considered as an urge for security) and
liberalism (the drive for independence and unification) were closely associated. Both nationalism and liberalism were hotly desired by the up and coming
bourgeoisie, the middle class conscious of its place in society. The bourgeoisie wanted to be free from the traditional restraints of monarchy, nobility,
and clergy. It identified itself with the nation—what was good for the middle
class was considered to be good for the nation. Under bourgeois auspices the
home, family, school, and society were all imbued with nationalism, with
love for the fatherland, and with a corresponding contempt for any dissenting
ideology that denied the supremacy of national unity. God, flag, country were
the approved watchwords. Disloyalty to the national idea was suppressed:
treason became the most abominable crime of all. In bourgeois eyes, a
Europe based on national lines, in a system of free nations, would be more
desirable than one in which subject nationalities continued to live under alien
control.

The middle class was not alone in building the nation-state nor did it have
exclusive control of the national idea. Without a broad mass base, nationalism could not have turned out to be the all-powerful historical force that it
actually became. By a kind of socio-cultural osmosis, a sense of national
consciousness filtered down from the middle class to both workers and
peasants. Such was its strength that nationalism appealed to each major
group in the social order.

For centuries before the era of modernization, European peasants hewed
closely to the line of tradition, especially to customs favored and promoted
by ecclesiastical authority. They gave their support to dynasty and religion.
A profound change began during the French Revolution, when the peasants
began to abandon these traditional loyalties. They were astonished when
their old masters—members of the royal family and privileged aristocrats—went to the guillotine. Their faith in the authority of the Church

declined. In this revolutionary situation large sections of the French population, and later peoples throughout Western Europe, were deprived of the old authorities—dynasty, nobility, and clergy—to which they had turned for centuries for psychological nourishment.

Meanwhile, affected by the economic drives of the Industrial Revolution, peasants moved in a mass migration from their villages to the towns and cities. In the process of urbanization they took with them some of their old traditions, but they needed a new source for security. The idea of the national state, already advocated by the bourgeoisie, was immensely attractive. There was safety in group membership. In this way the national state became a new repository for the needs of the masses. Nationalism was the strong emotional bond giving Europeans a sense of community, a tradition to replace older loyalties, and a motivation for political activity.

Originally the cult of liberal-democratic ideologues, nationalism underwent a major change in the nineteenth century. Gradually, over the course of the century, what was once a liberating force became more conservative in outlook, opposed to reform, and dedicated to the status quo. At one time a force for freedom and independence, nationalism took on qualities of narrow arrogance, xenophobic hatred, rampant jingoism, and frenetic chauvinism. Integral nationalism opposed any cosmopolitan ideology, be it Christianity with its value system for people of all nations or socialism with its international commitments. This kind of nationalism helped ignite the world catastrophes of 1914–1918 and 1939–1945. What was formerly a historical force generating the unity of nations became an end in itself. Nationalism was a prime factor in the atavistic bestiality of Germany's Hitler, in the clown-buffooning of Italy's sawdust Caesar, and in the cold brutality of Soviet Russia's Stalin. It was responsible for severe economic decline, political loss of civil rights, social maladjustments, and psychological frustrations. It has progressed to such a point that even countries sharing the same ideology bolster their borders in fear of "alien" aggression from their comrade ideologues.

Unfortunately, modernization does not mean that the fruits of science have brought sublime benefits to the inhabitants of this planet. Under the restraining impulse of nationalism in the modernization process, science has been used to perfect more and more powerful weapons of destruction to "defend" the fatherland against "aggression." Integral nationalism in modern times is not a concept recommended by logical minds, but it is a way of life with which we are condemned to live.

Intellectual Precursors and Charismatic Activists

No matter what the approach to nationalism, attention must be given to the men who gave it direction. These individuals fall into two categories: the intellectuals who prepare the groundwork and give meaning and content to nationalism and, second, the men of action who implement the ideas of their intellectual predecessors. The historical process is well known. For example, the French Revolution received its initial impetus from the work of such pioneer *philosophes* of the Enlightenment as Rousseau, Voltaire, and Montesquieu but it was given direction by such activists as Danton, St. Just, and Robespierre.

In the same way, nationalism has its own combination of intellectual apostles and militant activists. The intellectuals supply content by glorifying the mother tongue, elevating the fatherland, and emphasizing national history, customs, and traditions. The activists utilize the resulting spirit of national consciousness either for liberation from oppression, for national unification, for territorial expansion, or for a combination of two or three of these goals. There are many examples. Early nineteenth-century German nationalism owes its tenor to such intellectuals as Fichte, Herder, Kleist, Schleiermacher, Turnvater Jahn, the Schlegel brothers, the Grimm brothers, and List, each of whom contributed in his own way to the rising sense of German national consciousness. All prepared the path for such *Realpolitiker* as Bismarck (from Prussian to German nationalism); William II (national aggressiveness: colonies and the Big Navy); and Adolf Hitler ("Today Germany, tomorrow the world!"). A similar process may be noted wherever nationalism appears, both in the old established states and in the emergent nations.

In comparing nationalisms we shall see a major pattern: the activists who promote nationalism usually reveal a quality of charisma that separates them from other leaders. There may be exceptions, such as the late Antonio Oliveira Salazar, dictator of Portugal for more than three decades. An unlikely autocrat, scholar, recluse, and shunner of publicity, Salazar made few speeches or public appearances and rarely traveled outside his country. ("The state does not pay me to lead a social life.") But he was the exception. Most activist nationalists exhibit qualities compounded of mysticism, arrogance, and eccentricity. Charisma, that special quality of leadership that captures the popular imagination and inspires unswerving allegiance and devotion, is the common denominator.

What is the nature of this psychological power exercised by men who as individuals personify their nations? There is a discernible pattern: from collective uncertainty rises a leader whose person incarnates and mobilizes his people. He gives the masses a sense of identity. He tends to bypass the conventional power structure of the old elite to appeal directly to the common people. Made to appear by propaganda as larger than life, he bullies and exhorts and inspires the masses. Because he incorporates in himself so much of the state, he encourages his followers to surrender their responsibilities. He is determined to give his people a sense of identity. He is always ready to proclaim the national unity, to denounce all enemies, to lead the nation to a place in the sun.

The leader who is touched with charisma must possess two essential ingredients for his post: he must be able to manipulate national pride and he must exert a magical appeal on the masses. Above all, he must radiate the type of confidence which can awaken and embody national consciousness and ambitions. If he has the special quality of a flamboyant actor always on stage, so much the better. He has the choice of a gallery of prototypes—the deadly dignity of a Napoleon, the classic arrogance of a Bismarck, the chest-thumping boldness of a Mussolini, or the screeching hysteria of a Hitler.

Included among the charismatic activists is the late Gamal Abdel Nasser, who was worshiped by the Egyptians even after the six-day war with Israel, when he incarnated defeat as completely as he had represented the nation. Added to the category are Nikita Khrushchev, contemptuously banging his shoe on the podium of the United Nations; the self-confident Castro of Cuba, strutting like a peacock; the exiled Peron of Argentina, dripping remote pity for the shirtless ones; and Mao Tse-tung of the People's Republic of China, swimming with the tide while uttering pearls of wisdom to be caught forever in little red books. Such is charisma in action.

The quintessential nationalist, suffused with charisma, was the late General Charles de Gaulle, whose life was constructed on the mystical conviction that he was predestined to save France. "France is not herself unless she is in the front rank," he wrote in the opening paragraph of his war memoirs. France could not be France without greatness. He admitted that he was inspired by sentiment as well as reason. "The emotional side of me naturally imagines France as the princess of the fairy tales or the Madonna of the frescoes, as though dedicated to a lofty and exceptional destiny." To the day of his death de Gaulle regarded it as his destiny to restore the shattered self-respect of a defeated people, to persuade them that they had indeed rebuilt their pride in France as a great nation.

Most charismatic nationalists, especially those in the Third World, created the inevitability of their own downfall. Regarding themselves as supermen, as indispensable Simon Bolivars without whom the nation could not exist, they began to believe in their own miracles and in their own infallibility. Often they were taken in by their own propaganda. The late Kwame Nkrumah, who made the mistake of leaving Ghana for Peking in 1966, learned to his dismay that his charisma had vanished and his country had had enough of him. Even the great de Gaulle, certain that his people had to choose between himself and chaos, threatened to resign if the people rejected a relatively unimportant referendum on the regional structure of France. Taking him at his word, the

French electorate did just that, and the stooped old father figure within hours was on his way back to Colombey. There is something evanescent in the typical charismatic nationalist.

From Periphery to Center

Each of these approaches represents a prismatic face of nationalism and each throws some light on a phenomenon overwhelming in its complexity. The best chance for enlightenment comes through comparative analysis with attention to multidisciplinary approaches. The quantitative method recommended by Karl Deutsch might yield results one day, but thus far we are apt to find clarification through attention to qualitative aspects. Robert Ardrey's territorial imperative may be a new path. What is basic in understanding nationalism is the fact that it is an offshoot of modernization, originating in Western Europe and then extending throughout the world. An invention of the human mind, nationalism combines the thought of intellectual forerunners and charismatic activists.

Such guidelines are most interesting and each deserves a book-length study of its own. But they remain at the periphery of the subject and it is necessary to move to the center. So that our perspective may not become distorted, let us start with first things first and turn to the problem of meaning.

Notes

[1] H. J. C. Duijker and N. H. Frijjda, *National Character and National Stereotypes: A Trend Report Prepared for the International Union of Scientific Psychology* (Amsterdam: North Holland Publishing Co., 1960), vol. 1 of *Confluence: Surveys of Research in the Social Sciences,* ed. by the International Committee for Social Science Documentation in cooperation with the International Social Science Council and with the support of UNESCO.

[2] Karl W. Deutsch, *Nationalism and Social Communication: An Inquiry into the Foundations of Nationality* (New York: Wiley, 1953).

[3] Robert Ardrey, *The Territorial Imperative: A Personal Inquiry into the Animal Origins of Property and Nations* (New York: Atheneum, 1966).

[4] *Ibid.,* p. 351.

[5] Marshall L. Levin of Fort Lauderdale, Florida, in *Saturday Review,* November 7, 1970, p. 35.

[6] Ardrey. *The Territorial Imperative,* p. 232.

[7] Robert Ardrey, *The Social Contract: A Personal Inquiry into the Evolutionary Sources of Order and Disorder* (New York: Atheneum, 1970).

2

In Search of Meaning

By nationalism I mean first of all the habit of assuming that human beings can be classified like insects and that whole blocks of millions or tens of millions of people can be confidently labelled "good" or "bad." But secondly—and this is much more important—I mean the habit of identifying oneself with a single nation or other unit, placing it beyond good or evil and recognizing no other duty than that of advancing its interests.

—George Orwell

The Tyranny of Words

Mark Twain put it bluntly—the difference between the right word and the almost right word is the difference between lightning and the lightning bug. The humorist saw words as forming the fabric of transmission belts by which people communicate with one another. Allegiance to words is, indeed, a necessary part of human existence. Throughout the course of history, people have found it difficult to respond to one another across rooms, streets, nations, and continents, often with deplorable results. Neighbors have come to blows and nations have gone to war by misunderstanding words. Too often words take on such a bewildering variety of meanings that it becomes dangerous to use them without adequate definition.

Socrates recognized the problem as early as the fifth century B.C. when, partly to avoid the acid tongue of his spouse, he hastened daily to the safety of the Athenian marketplace. There he was appalled by the way in which his fellow citizens used precious words without the least understanding of what they meant. Using a dialectic of his own, Socrates demanded that such words as "honor," "love," "faith," "justice," and "truth" be defined before they were used as weapons in argument. In this way he was able to bring discussion to a more rational plane, even if he had found a sure road to unpopularity.

The line is continuous from Socrates to speakers in the forum of the United Nations. Early Christians came to blows at the Council of Nicea in 325 A.D. over the meaning of a single word—as to whether the Holy Ghost proceeded "from" or "through" Father to Son. Today's Communist semanticists expropriate the clear-cut word "democracy" (from *dēmos*—people; *kratein*—to rule) and use it confidently, if erroneously, to describe a nation under a party dictatorship. Clearly, then, words have an infinite capacity for causing mischief.

Problem of the Isms

By some linguistic quirk, the use of the suffix "ism" has led to obfuscation and confusion. Seemingly simple words are given three additional letters and are thereby propelled into the region of the obscure. The words seem innocent enough in print—capitalism, imperialism, racialism, fascism, internationalism, socialism, communism, nationalism—but each is capable of causing trouble in human affairs. The isms represent significant historical movements in modern times, yet each one has been hidden in a fog of miscomprehension.

Use of the word "capitalism" is an example. Is it that system which Marx and Engels excoriated in the *Communist Manifesto* of 1848, or is it the far different ism of the twentieth-century world? Today, in much of Western society, capitalism is regarded as an evolving, controlled system based on the profit motive; in the Soviet Union and in Communist China it is damned as a tongue-soiling evil responsible for many ills in contemporary life. On the one hand, capitalism means the possibility of a prosperous society based on liberty, equality, and the pursuit of happiness; on the other hand, it denotes a dog-eat-dog system bringing huge wealth to the few and the agony of poverty to the many.

Much of the difficulty lies in the misuse of words. Thus the able journalist Winston Churchill, noted for his talent in selecting precisely the right word, consistently referred to a nonexistent British "race." Ex-President Richard M. Nixon said in a commencement address to the United States Air Force Academy on July 4, 1969: "When a nation believes in itself, as Athenians did in their Golden Age, as Italians did in the Renaissance, that nation can perform miracles." The American President (or perhaps his speech writer) was unaware that neither the Athens of the fifth century B.C. nor the Italy of the sixteenth century A.D. was a "nation." Athens was a city-state and Renaissance Italy was a collection of warring principalities, both existing long before the modern ideas of nationhood and nationalism emerged.

Similar confusion surrounds all the isms, especially the nationalism whose meaning we seek to extract. We shall see that this catch-all term ensnares historical allusions and that, like a chameleon, it can adapt itself in different countries in varied forms. It can be either unifying or disruptive; if we choose to apply value judgments, it can be either blessing or curse.

Tantalizing Core—The Nation

Nationalism comes from the root word "nation," itself an ambiguous term. "Nation" is derived from the Latin *natio*, signifying birth. Originally it meant a social grouping based on real or imaginary ties of blood. Such closely related words as "cognate" or "innate" convey the same idea of birth. There were varying applications of the term in the early Middle Ages, when *natio villae* was used to designate a kinship group in the village. In the later Middle Ages students of the University of Paris were divided into "nations" according to their places of birth.

In early modern times there arose the tendency to apply the term "nation" to the population of a country without regard for racial unity. By this time the word began to take on confused meanings. In his *Faerie Queen,* Edmund Spenser spoke of "a nation of birds," and Ben Jonson referred to physicians as "a subtile nation." With the three partitions of Poland and the French

Revolution in the late eighteenth century, the word "nation" began to be used interchangeably with "country."

It was at this time, too, that emphasis began to be placed on the abstract meaning of nation. Because one could not see the nation, it came to be regarded as a kind of mystical reality, whose unity of character could be sensed by faith rather than by sight. The nation came to be defined as "a congeries of wills, acting through centuries." This was based on the supposition that the individual is a single will acting in the space of a lifetime, while a nation is the sum total of all such individuals. Ernest Renan's definition became famous:

A nation is a grand solidarity constituted by the sentiment of sacrifices which one has made and those that time is disposed to make again. It supposes a past, it renews itself especially in the present by a tangible deed: the approval, the desire, clearly expressed, to continue the communal life. The existence of a nation is an everyday plebiscite.[1]

Historians today distinguish the nation from a race, a state, or a language. A nation is not the same thing as a church, even though nations today may owe much of their character to religious influences. What becomes important in the modern sense is that the occupation of a given area is essential for the existence of a nation, because it is through holding territory that a nation has its special *raison d'être*.

Above all, the conception of a nation implies a common political sentiment. J. Holland Rose used "nation" as a political term, designating a people which "has attained to state organization." Hans Kohn described the distinguishing characteristic of modern nations as "the political doctrine of sovereignty." Carlton J. H. Hayes pointed out that the word "nation" has been used since the seventeenth century to designate the population of a sovereign political state, regardless of ethnic or linguistic unity. All agree on the essential *political* connotation of "nation."

Historians Grope for Meaning

There is no one simple definition of nationalism. Carlton J. H. Hayes presented four shades of meaning. First, nationalism may be an actual historical process by which nationalities are established as political units or modern national states constructed out of tribes and empires. Second, nationalism may be the theory, principle, or ideal implicit in the actual historical process. Third, nationalism can be regarded as the activity of a political party, thus combining the historical process and political theory (Irish or Welsh nationalism). Fourth, nationalism can mean a condition of mind among the members of a nationality in which loyalty to the ideal of, or to the fact of, one's own national state becomes dominant over all other attachments, and in which pride is shown in the intrinsic excellence of, and in the mission of, the national state.

Hans Kohn saw nationalism as "first and foremost a state of mind, an act of consciousness." Man, he said, is subject to both ego and group consciousness. With the growing complexity of civilization, the number of groups increases. Within these pluralistic kinds of group consciousness there is generally one that is recognized by man as supreme and most important:

The mental life of man is as much dominated by ego-consciousness as it is by group-consciousness. Both are complex states of mind at which we arrive through experiences of differentiation and opposition, of the ego and surrounding world, of the we-group and those outside the group. The collective of group consciousness can center around entirely different groups, of which some have a permanent character—the family, the class, the clan, the caste, the village, the sect, the religion, etc. . . . In each case, varying with its permanence, this group-consciousness will strive toward achieving homogeneity within the group, a conformity and like-mindedness which will lead to and facilitate common action.[2]

Other historians echoed Kohn's concern for the psychological implications attached to the meaning of nationalism. Crane Brinton saw nationalism as, at bottom, no more than the important form the sense of belonging to the in-group has taken in our Western culture. Nationalism, he said, is one of the facts of life that no scientist can neglect, and a sentiment that can be most fully understood by the social psychologist. George P. Gooch defined nationalism as the "self-consciousness" of a nation. J. Holland Rose described it as "an intolerant and aggressive instinct."

Other historians sought to unravel the mysteries of nationalism by distinguishing between two possible meanings. Max Hildebert Boehm pointed to the broad and narrow meanings: in its broad sense, nationalism is an attitude ascribing a high place to national individuality (similar to patriotism); in its narrow meaning, it has a tendency to place an excessive, exaggerated, and exclusive emphasis upon the value of the nation at the expense of other values. Herbert Adams Gibbons described nationalism in its concrete sense as a particular way of manifesting national spirit (history, traditions, language) and in its abstract form as an idea controlling the life and actions of a nation (consciousness of solidarity).

This is a bare sampling of the concern historians show for the meaning of nationalism. Keeping in mind the pitfalls of semantics, let us now turn to the task of constructing a definition—not as the last word on this complex subject but as a useful tool in clarifying the nature of nationalism.

Building a Definition

The editors of Webster's *Unabridged Dictionary* made a valiant effort to reduce the intricacies of nationalism to manageable proportions in slightly more than one inch of space (in the original entry):

NA'TION·AL·ISM (năsh'ŭn·ăl·iz'm;-'l·iz'm;59), n. 1. National character, or tendency to it; nationality.
    2. An idiom, trait, or character peculiar to any nation.
    3. Devotion to, or advocacy of, national interests or national unity and independence; as the *nationalism* of Ireland or China. Cf. INTERNATIONALISM, 2; New Nationalism.
    4. Zealous adherence to one's own nation or to its principles; patriotism.
    5. A phase of socialism advocating the nationalizing of industries—essentially the same as *collectivism*. *Chiefly U.S.*
    6. *Theol.* The doctrine that the people of a certain nation or nations are God's chosen people.

It is an interesting if inconclusive attempt. Unfortunately, the breakdown into six special meanings serves to confuse the term rather than clarify it. It is not enough to identify nationalism with national character, nationality, or patriotism—each of which requires its own definition. In the search for meaning, it is easy to fall into Gertrude Stein's trap of "a rose is a rose is a rose." More light can be thrown on the isms by the expedient of emphasizing characteristics rather than seeking simple definitions. Yet there is need for a sharp demarcation in the study of the meaning of nationalism.

Perhaps the best approach is to build a definition inductively by attention to those factors which make nationalism (territory, language, traditions, history, customs, and a psychological community of interests) and then combine them in a simple statement. Throughout the search, understanding hinges upon the word "common." The essentials for the growth of nationalism are to be found in common territory and in a common history composed of triumphs, achievements, memories, and sufferings. It is something more than a spontaneous explosion of an exalted spiritual idea; rather it is the creation of a sentiment through the trials of historic circumstance. Nationalism rests on historical traditions which have been fashioned, often fortuitously, then preserved and synthesized by a combination of intellectual apostles and charismatic activists.

The following elements for our proposed definition all fall within the realm of the general. There are exceptions to each one.

The We-Group. Nationalism is the sentiment of a we-group fused by long social relationship and forming a nation. Let us dispose immediately of any identification of nation with race. The we-group need not be of common stock: more often than not it is a combination of different ethnic elements. Most people find it difficult to conceive of a close social unity without a physical bond, and they tend to regard the intimate fraternity between members of a nation as a kind of relationship between members of a family. The conception is incorrect: the distinguishing core of the we-group need not be essentially racial.

Common Territory.   The we-group inhabits a set territory and defends it against outsiders. Attachment to the common land gives a sense of security ("This is my own, my native land!"). The territory may be either compact or noncontiguous, yet it is significant that nationalism may prosper even in the absence of territory. The classic example is that of Poland, which disappeared after the three partitions of 1772, 1793, and 1795. In this famous case of international banditry, hostility to Polish nationalism formed a common bond between the Russian, Austrian, and Prussian governments throughout the nineteenth century. An independent Poland was reconstituted in 1919 by the Treaty of Versailles as a concession to Polish nationalism.

Common Language.   A third component of nationalism is a single language or closely related dialects. In the search for security, people who speak the same language are irresistibly drawn to one another. The tendency is to regard the nation as an extension of the family unit and the sentiment of nationalism as the binding factor between people who speak the same language. There may be family quarrels and feuds, but these are sublimated when there is danger from the outsider who does not speak the common tongue. Language became a prop for national kinship for those who were proud of their loyalty to the fatherland or motherland.

A common language may well be the main feature of a common historical experience, and then again it may not. There are examples in which states that are multinational are held together by religious or other beliefs. In fact, state boundaries only rarely coincide with a linguistic community. There may be several languages inside a national state. The best example is the Swiss people, who have their own sense of nationalism, but accept four languages as a matter of historical necessity: German, centering in Zurich; French, in the region of Geneva; Italian, in the Lugano area; and Romansch, a Romance dialect spoken in the easternmost cantons.[3] Swiss nationalism reflects geographical and historical realities.

At this point we must pause for a peripheral attack on the problem of definition, for nothing concerned with nationalism is simple and clear-cut. In the opening stages of our argument the first three elements of nationalism concern the we-group, common territory, and common language. Immediately there appears a serious obstacle: the difference between territorial nationalism and linguistic nationalism may be so great that they cannot be used in the same definition.

According to Lewis Namier, the British and Swiss concepts of nationality are primarily territorial, because here the state created the nationality and not vice versa. The historical process of British nationality operated within a geographically determined framework. Neither within the island nor in the English-speaking world outside could language be the criterion of nationality. The island character produced a rare entity, a real and not merely nominal nationality. Similarly, the geographical factor is obvious in the rise and development of Swiss nationality, even though the frontiers of Switzerland are by no means preordained.

The situation was quite different in Central and Eastern Europe, where it was not the state which molded nationality but a preexistent nationality which postulated the state. Thus the German nationality is linguistic and "racial" rather than political and territorial. It finds its final expression in the idea of the *Volksdeutsche,* holding that anyone of German "race" and language owes allegiance to the German fatherland. This concept of nationality became dominant on most of the Continent.

As an important by-product of this argument Namier saw freedom as safest in the self-contained community with a territorial nationality, such as that of Britain with its Parliament at Westminster representing citizens rooted in British soil. The unpolitical Germans, on the other hand, more than any other nation, emptied the territorial state of its communal elements and set up a sheer dynastic property ready to absorb territory and people of any language or race.

The revolution of 1848 was the watershed:

The year 1848 marks, for good or evil, the opening of the era of linguistic nationalisms shaping mass personalities and producing their inevitable conflicts: a nation which bases its unity on language cannot easily renounce groups of co-nationals intermingled with those of the neighbouring nation; and an alien minority within the State, or an intensely coveted *terra irredenta,* are both likely to distort the life of the nation, and impair the growth of its civil liberty.[4]

This brief peroration indicates that no monistic definition of nationalism is useful. Even Namier admits that he must not press his argument about British territoriality too far: in the next island there was a similar combination of Celt, Anglo-Saxon, and Norman, but the mixture failed to evolve an Irish territorial nationality.

Religion. The religious element of nationalism causes additional trouble. There may or may not be a religious content to nationalism: religion may be a positive factor in helping to keep the nation together or it may induce a negative sentiment turning with violence to the outsider. Religion becomes an element of nationalism when it contributes a sense of likemindedness and social homogeneity to a we-group.

One of the main distinctions between the medieval and modern eras hinges on religious change from an ecclesiastical to a secular society. The government of medieval Europe was a combination of *imperium* (the imperial power) and *sacerdotium* (the ecclesiastical power), fused and resistant to any tendency to break apart. The international Roman Catholic Church, with its structured hierarchy, was the repository of power. In the early sixteenth century, under the impulse of the rising national state, the great edifice was fractured in the Reformation (Luther, Henry VIII, Calvin, Knox). The causes were complex, but in most cases, especially in England, the national issue was decisive.

Once the currents of the Reformation and the Counter Reformation subsided, European states began to take their modern form. Some nations remained dominantly Catholic (France, Spain, Italy, Poland); others became primarily Protestant (England, Holland, the Scandinavian countries); still others kept both religions (notably the Germanies). It was a kind of religious hodgepodge with varying effects. Germany had a fairly even split, and that became a factor of some importance in the history of German nationalism. To make the French nation viable, governments since the eighteenth century recruited hard from the 10 percent Protestant minority. On the other hand, the 10 percent English Catholic minority remained politically passive from the time of Mary Tudor to that of Elizabeth II, save when spurred from the outside.

In this upheaval Roman Catholicism retained much of its strength almost everywhere, but the point is that the international structure was breached. Cracks widened in the edifice until church and state were finally separated at the time of the French Revolution, the point for the emergence of modern nationalism.

Religion became an element of nationalism when it contributed a sense of likemindedness and social homogeneity, but the pattern varies in the interplay of nationalism and religion today. Contemporary Italians see nothing unusual in regarding themselves as an amalgam of nationalist, Communist, and Catholic elements. To be an Italian without being a Catholic would seem to them preposterous: they attend Marxist meetings during the week, and speak the language of dialectical materialism, but on Sundays they go to Mass and echo the liturgy. Their nationalism is closely associated with religion. Comparably, in the United States, where many religions exist side by side, American nationalism attributes a minor role to religion.

Common History, Traditions, and Customs. According to Ernest Renan, what constitutes a nation is not speaking the same tongue, or belonging to the same ethnic group, but having accomplished great things in common in the past and wishing to accomplish them in the future. This feeling of common traditions forms one of the most important components of nationalism. A people who has lived together, fought against real or fancied enemies, and recorded great deeds in national history tends to transfer a sense of nationalism from one generation to another.

Common historical traditions and customs are bolstered by such symbols as a national flag and a national anthem, both of which reflect the pride taken by the citizen in his native land. The sight of the flag waving in the breeze or the familiar strain of the national anthem brings tears to the eyes and lumps to the throat of the patriot. Such reflexes are environmentally conditioned: no human being is born with knowledge of either flag or anthem.

Traditions become a part of national sentiment. Attention is given to "our forefathers" who unselfishly constructed the national state. Stories are passed from generation to generation in folk song and history text. Those who would depart from the old traditions must endure the hostility of their compatriots.

At the same time, on the nexus between common history and traditions, it is of some importance to recognize that there are, indeed, many instances of invented nationalism—a mythology created for the moment. It is possible for such invented nationalisms to assume the same importance as realities. Real nationalisms exist side by side with invented ones.

National Heroes. Of special import in the molding of nationalism is the making of national heroes. The pattern is as old as society itself: individuals as selected by the group as leaders (Lincoln) or are able to propel themselves into the seat of power by a combination of ambition and good fortune (Caesar, Napoleon). Covered with charisma, they are venerated in song and slogan.

Will to Unite. Added to these elements is a decisive psychological factor that forms the cement of nationalism—a common urge to union. This is the critical part of the formula, the catalytic agent bringing together the varying attitudes composing the nationalist urge. This state of mind is seen by the psychologist as *group consciousness* and by the sociologist as the *we-group*. The individual, with his own ego consciousness, is attracted to membership in the large group with its own symbols and traditions. He submerges his own ego inside the group because consciously and unconsciously he wants security for his own person and for his family. Where there are conflicts between group loyalties (and the nature of society is such that there may be many groups competing for the loyalty of the individual) the citizen usually selects one to which he can give his supreme loyalty.

These are the elements which are to be fused into a basic meaning. Because it is impossible to project the perfect definition, let us settle for one that is least objectionable. (But a caution: any one or more of these elements may be lacking without affecting the validity of the definition.)

Nationalism is that sentiment of a group or body of people living within a compact or a noncontiguous territory, using a single language or related dialects as a vehicle for common thoughts and feelings, holding a common religious belief, possessing common institutions, traditions, and customs acquired and transmitted during the course of a common history, venerating national heroes, and cherishing a common will for social homogeneity.

This definition reflects a process of what is sometimes called social mobilization, by which the commitment of the individual is transferred from the local to the national level. The individual becomes aware that his interests go beyond his local community to the national sphere. From every point of view—economic status, political loyalty, social dependence, cultural form, and psychological drive—the individual turns from a local society to a national community. This kind of social mobilization, though it may differ in details from country to country, forms the essence of nationalism.

Notes

[1] Ernest Renan, *Qu'est-ce qu'une nation?* (Paris: Calmann-Levy, 1882), p. 27.

[2] Hans Kohn, *The Idea of Nationalism* (New York: Macmillan, 1944), pp. 10–11.

[3] In 1938 Romansch was recognized as the fourth "national" language of Switzerland, but not as an "official" language. This meant that it could not be used in communications addressed to the federal authorities, nor could it be utilized in the texts of federal laws. Approximately 45,000 Swiss speak Romansch.

[4] Lewis Namier, "Nationality and Liberty," in *Vanished Supremacies: Essays on European History* (London: Hamish Hamilton, 1958), p. 53.

3

Clarification through Classification

While English and American nationalism was, in its origin, connected with the concepts of individual liberty and represented nations firmly constituted in their political life, the new nationalism, not rooted in a similar political and social reality, lacked self-assurance. . . . The quest for its meaning, the musing about a national "soul" or "mission," the discussion of its relationship to the West, all these became characteristic of the new nationalism.

—Hans Kohn

Meaning through Typology

Nationalism may be a myth, as Francis Delaisi described it, but even myths deserve clarification. The search for meaning continues in kaleidoscopic variety. Another approach, in addition to building a workable definition, is to classify or break down the ism into types, with accent on special characteristics of each variant. The method depends on the discipline: the social psychologist will search for psychological factors, the historian will think in terms of origins and development.

Two historians, Carlton J. H. Hayes and Hans Kohn, have done pioneer work in the typology of nationalism. Every study of nationalism must take their views into account. The Hayes vertical conceptualization follows roughly a chronological pattern from the appearance of modern nationalism in the eighteenth century to its recent forms. The Kohn formula, while recognizing the importance of chronology, prefers a horizontal comparison of Western and non-Western nationalisms. Each view complements the other. A brief comparison of the two classifications reveals how the historical mind can judge the same set of facts and come to differing conclusions.

Vertical Conceptualization—The Hayes Formula

The late Carlton J. H. Hayes was fascinated by all aspects of nationalism. He saw political nationalism as capping the economic and cultural nationalisms of our day and giving shape and direction to them. There was nothing new, he said, in the division of the world into separate political states, but political nationalism was a comparatively recent phenomenon in which peoples accepted the principle of nationality and were inspired with supreme devotion to it.

Hayes traced the evolution of modern nationalism in successive stages, to each of which he gave name and description. This typology remains a valuable compendium of what we know about the development of nationalism as a historical force.[1] In each case the type corresponds to the historical temper of the time.

Humanitarian Nationalism. The first systematic doctrine of modern nationalism emerged during the eighteenth-century Enlightenment. As the name implies, humanitarian nationalism was motivated by tolerance and regard for the rights of others. Every nationality was entitled to its own development, consonant with its own peculiar genius. Each nation would attend to the business of its own national development and each one would have only the kindest sentiment toward other peoples striving for a similar goal.

Jacobin Nationalism.   Under the impact of the French Revolution, humanitarian nationalism, which had not yet crystallized into a dogma, separated into several distinct types. The democratic form, preferred by Rousseau, became known as Jacobin nationalism, after the revolutionary Parisian club dedicated to republicanism and democracy. The idea was "to safeguard and extend the liberty, equality, and fraternity that had been asserted and partially established under humanitarian auspices in the early days of the Revolution." Jacobin nationalists, intolerant of opposition of any kind, relied upon force to achieve their ends. Fanatical in their determination to succeed, they were imbued with missionary zeal to bring to others the justice of their cause.

Traditional Nationalism.   Another form of humanitarian nationalism, Bolingbroke's aristocratic type, emerged after the revolutionary era as traditional nationalism. Conservative critics of the Jacobins were quite sure that "the quiet happiness of humanity could be assured less by the masses than by the classes." Opposed to "revolution" and "reason" as motivating factors in national development, they turned to "history" and "tradition." Nationality and the state had just evolved: it was idle to discuss how they began—perhaps by social contract.

Liberal Nationalism.   Midway between Jacobin and traditional nationalism was liberal nationalism, a form neither democratic nor aristocratic but possessing some of the characteristics of each. Mainly the creation of an Englishman. Jeremy Bentham, liberal nationalism first appeared in England, the country of perpetual compromise and acute national self-consciousness, and later spread to the Continent. It advocated the absolute sovereignty of the state, but it was careful to emphasize the principle of individual liberty. To eliminate war, Bentham proposed a program of universal peace which included a world organization, disarmament, and an international court.

Integral Nationalism.   As rivalries sharpened among states, nationalism assumed a form decidedly hostile to humanitarianism and liberalism. Integral nationalism, as the name implies, was dedicated to the exclusive pursuit of national policies, the absolute maintenance of national integrity, and the constant increase of national power. It placed national interests above those of the individual and, indeed, above all humanity. The nation became an end in itself. Every consideration was subordinated to the demands of nationalism. In domestic affairs, integral nationalism was illiberal and tyrannical; in international relations it refused cooperation with other nations.

The Hayes formula saw nationalism as an idea which was transformed from libertarianism to enhancement of national egoism. Loyalty to the national state was elevated above all other loyalties—with destructive results.

Other scholars are not altogether satisfied with Hayes's classification. Some express confusion about "humanitarian nationalism," in that they find nothing enlightened or human about the attitude of the people of one nation to those of another. Others find trouble with the concept of "traditional nationalism" on the ground that it is an imprecise term that does not quite cover the concept of property in states (the divine-right dynastic principle). They prefer Lewis Namier's distinction between "territorial" and "linguistic" nationalism. And "liberal nationalism," they say, was really based upon the simple presumption that self-determination was a good thing, equally appropriate for individuals and nations (1848 proved that it did not work).

Horizontal Interpretation—The Kohn Dichotomy

One of the merits of the historical approach is the possibility of observing the same set of facts from a different angle and deriving from them an equally valid conclusion. Thus Hans Kohn applied a horizontal measuring rod and presented an interpretation quite as enlightening as that of Hayes.

Kohn, like Hayes, saw nationalism as the outcome of a long historical process. It takes its character from the political climate as well as the historical conditions in which it is engendered. One type of nationalism, therefore, need not be the same as another. From this premise Kohn went on to present a major dichotomy in typology. He pointed to two socio-political environments in which modern nationalism made its appearance. One was the Western world, including England, the British colonies, the Netherlands, and Switzerland. The second was the non-Western world, which included Central and Eastern Europe and Asia. In each of these two areas there was a centrifugal tendency which gave a distinctive coloration to nationalism. There are dangers in generalization, for there are exceptions to any principles set up as a standard, but the Kohn prescription was nicely formulated and convincing. This was comparative history at its best.

Kohn organized his analysis along four lines: origins, historical motivation, characteristics, and development. Without attention to details, let us look at these elements of the Kohn formula.[2]

Here Kohn held views similar to those of Hayes, but he made a distinction between the origins of nationalism in the Western and in the non-Western worlds. In the West, the emergence of nationalism was primarily a political occurrence; it was preceded by the formation of the future national state or coincided with it. This is in contrast with the experience of the non-Western areas, where nationalism arose much later and also at a more backward stage of socio-political development. Nationalism in the non-Western world was a kind of spontaneous protest against the existing state pattern. Cultural contacts provided the original stimulus, and remained secondary to political exigencies.

Kohn paid close attention to historical motivation. In the early modern history of the Western world, at a time when the roots of national sentiment were being nourished, the Renaissance and the Reformation were enormously vital movements that extended far beyond either cultural or religious changes. Middle-class entrepreneurs rejected the Holy Roman Empire and all its medieval trappings, and substituted for it a society based on the needs of a national state and its prime defenders, the patriotic bourgeoisie. Nationalism in the Western world was thus a product of indigenous forces that came to fruition in the eighteenth century.

In the non-Western world, notably in Central and Eastern Europe and in Asia, the Renaissance and the Reformation did not result in profound changes. In the German states the two great movements of early modern times were more precisely scholarly and theological in nature, although there were some politico-economic overtones. But the Russian Empire, the Near East, and Asia remained virtually untouched by the Renaissance and the Reformation. The old division between Roman Catholicism and the Greek Orthodox Church, between relics of the Western and Eastern empires, still persisted. A kind of ephemeral universalism, closer akin to the Middle Ages than to modern times, remained in the non-Western world.

Kohn thus revealed a cleavage between the experiences of the Western and non-Western areas. He bolstered this view with an analysis of the characteristics of nationalism in the two worlds. His analysis of the nature of nationalism in Europe was much the same as that of Hayes. His argument can be understood best by this brief comparative chart:

The Western World

Open Society. Western nationalism was the product of the Age of Reason—the Enlightenment, *Illuminé*, or *Aufklärung*. This meant the ideas of liberty, equality, and fraternity, as well as the concomitants of constitutionalism, parliamentarianism, liberalism, democracy, tolerance, and free speech. This was the *pluralistic* or *open society*.

Reality. Nationalism in the West emphasized political reality. It responded to the challenge of building

The Non-Western World

Closed Society. Here the elements of the Enlightenment were rejected as unreasonable, even foolish. Nationalism meant not freedom but the duty to serve the state. This was the *authoritarian* or *closed society*.

Ideality. The non-Western mind was absorbed not by reality but by an eternal search for the ideal fatherland.

nations without too much regard for the past. The nation itself was regarded as a real, vital, existing thing. Political integration was sought around a rational goal.

This form of nationalism was characterized by myths and dreams of the future, and not by any immediate connection with the present. The newborn nation always looked to the past and to nonpolitical and history-conditioned factors.

Union of Citizens. Western nationalists saw nations as unions of citizens joined by a common will expressed in the social contract and other covenants and plebiscites. The people were to work together for a common future.

Folk Community. Non-Western nationalists regarded the nation as a political unit centering around the irrational, precivilized folk concept. The rallying point was not a free and rational order but the folk community. Emphasis was placed on the diversity and self-sufficiency of nations.

Individualism. Western nationalists approved a legal and rational concept of citizenship. Individual rights were regarded as sacred. All men were to be regarded as fundamentally alike as individuals, no matter what their social class or historic nationality.

Collectivism. In the non-Western world the decisive appeal was not to individual but to collective rights, to peculiarities of race or class. The idea of citizenship was left purposely vague, thereby lending itself more easily to exaggerations of imagination and to the excitation of emotions.

Self-Assurance. Western nationalism, reflecting the confidence and optimism of the *philosophes* of the Age of Reason, was self-assured and positive about its virtues.

Inferiority Complex. Non-Western nationalism, without any real roots in socio-political reality, lacked self-assurance. Often enough its sense of insecurity was overcompensated by overconfidence and aggressiveness.

Bourgeois Support. Western nationalism was supported by the politically and economically powerful bourgeoisie.

Aristocratic Base. Non-Western nationalism received its main support from a combination of aristocracy and the masses, both conservative minded.

Kohn, too, was criticized on the ground that his typology was far too favorable to the Western world. He was accused of cleansing Western nationalism of tribal impurities and of disregarding any manifestations of anti-democratic or non-Western nationalism in the Far East. Again, the criticism is unreasonable. Kohn never described Western nationalism as a complete blessing and the non-Western form as a total curse. He carefully pointed to non-Western nationalisms that accept Western forms. He gave his attention to unattractive features of nationalism in the West as well as in non-Western nations. Nowhere did he intimate that the open society is perfect or foolproof, although he did regard it as preferable to the closed society.

Both Hayes and Kohn saw nationalism as an originally humane, libertarian, and creative force which eventually was transformed into an oppressive, aggressive, and expansionist ism. They understood the excesses of integral nationalism and they called for its curb so that the liberating elements could function once again. Both defended that type of nationalism that combines love of country and national tradition with a sense of individual dignity.

Classification in Other Disciplines

Scholars of other disciplines follow their special interests in projecting classifications of nationalism. Political scientists emphasize the political nature of nationalism. Max Sylvius Handman presented this breakdown:[3]

Oppression nationalism: This form of nationalism exists among peoples exposed to a definite regime of disabilities and subordination (Jews, Irish, Poles in Germany and Russia, Greeks and Armenians in the old Turkish Empire).

Irredentist nationalism: Peoples who demand liberation from the domination of others (Rumanians, Serbs, Bulgars, Italians).

Precaution nationalism: A type of nationalism which responds to the stimulus of competition among modern nation-states and which identifies commercial expansion with national security. Always impelled by agitated concern for the life and honor of the group, this form of nationalism is often indistinguishable from imperialism.

Prestige nationalism: A form of nationalism stressing the glorious history of a people's past and demanding greater respect *(Action Française,* Oswald Mosley's British Fascists).

In classifying the types of nationalism, psychologists stress the real or imaginary working of the mind, group acceptance of ideas and symbols, and community behavior. Thus Gustav Ichheiser presents two forms:[4]

Conscious nationalism: In this form members of a community profess national values in a vociferous way, consciously strive toward national goals, glorify their real or imaginary peculiarities.

Subconscious (or unconscious) nationalism: Members of a national group, even though they do not formulate their national ideas, are nevertheless so influenced by naturally prejudiced concepts that they, without being aware of it, see and judge everything from a national point of view.

In their classifications, sociologists generally regard nationalism as a sentiment reflecting group behavior. Louis Wirth based his categories on profound social conditioning and group power struggles:[5]

Hegemony nationalism: A national group is motivated by the urge to derive advantage from consolidating smaller principalities into larger and more dynamic units (unification of Italy and of Germany).

Particularistic nationalism: Based on the secessionist demand for national autonomy, the first aim of this form is divisive in character but is succeeded by union with a more satisfactory group. Particularistic nationalism begins with striving for cultural autonomy and then takes on political significance (the potential nationalities in the Austro-Hungarian, German, Russian, and Turkish empires before 1914).

Marginal nationalism: This type exists in frontier regions between two states, among peoples who have a mixed culture. Marginal peoples are likely to adhere to traditions of their motherland (such border people as those in Alsace, Lorraine, Silesia, Schleswig, the Saar, and the Rhineland).

Nationalities in the Minorities: Minorities everywhere strive for recognition of their own traditional nationality and attempt to maintain their own culture while inside another nation.

The sociologist Konstantin Symmons-Symonolewicz presents a classification which takes careful cognizance of historical considerations.[6] Defining nationalism as "a series of stages in the struggle of a given solidarity group to achieve its basic aims of unity and self-direction," he presents a comparative typology of nationalist movements. His categories distinguish between two major kinds of nationalist movements: minority and liberation. Among minority movements he makes a distinction between perpetuative-segregative (the imperial Ottoman millet system) and the perpetuative-pluralistic (new countries of post-Versailles Europe). In the category of liberation movements he includes restorative nationalism (nineteenth-century Poland), revivalist nationalism (Flemish or Catalan movements), ethnic nationalism (Latvian or Somali forms), autonomist-secessionist nationalism (Latin America), and anti-colonial nationalism (Zaire, Indonesia). His final category is nativist movements (Riff mountaineers against Spain). Symmons's sociological formula is based on the assumption that the aims of all movements concerned with exclusive loyalty to a given group are essentially similar.

The Economics of Nationalism

In his classification Hayes touched upon economic nationalism only briefly, yet in any typology this facet merits closer examination. Economic nationalism underwent a change from mercantilism to laissez-faire to neo-mercantilism. The seventeenth-century economic policy known as mercantilism, a counterpart of *étatism,* was designed to bring all phases of economic life under royal control. In search of power, the state attempted to control all economic enterprise inside the country as well as commerce with all other peoples. At the same time, mercantilism was a national economic policy.

Mercantilism arose in Europe as a successor to medieval feudalism and manorialism. Its goals were varied: acquire bullion as a measure of wealth; develop agriculture and manufacturing; seek a favorable balance of trade; set up trade monopolies; create a merchant marine; and, above all, maintain economic enterprise under state control. This combination of policies transformed European society into an aggregation of national states, each one imbued with the mercantilist's simple presumption that economic gain could be made only at the expense of others.

The apostle *par excellence* of mercantilism was Jean Baptiste Colbert. The chief minister of Louis XIV, Colbert cleaned up the financial administration, eliminated profiteers, reduced the public debt by canceling questionable bonds, and increased both direct and indirect taxation. He encouraged industry and commerce, set up such great trading organizations as the East Indies Company and the West Indies Company, constructed model factories with state money, standardized and regulated domestic production, instituted high protective tariffs, improved roads and canals, established the French merchant marine, and expanded the royal navy. Behind all this economic activity were the goals of safeguarding the position of royalty and enhancing the prestige of the national state.

Colbert and his fellow mercantilists regarded it as highly necessary to promote both national interest and national consciousness. Directing their onslaught against the medieval combination of universalism and particularism, they aimed to destroy provincial, guild, and municipal restrictions on farming and industry. They would unify their own economic activities and simultaneously separate the interests of their own country from those of other nations. The nation must be strong; in contrast, other nations must be weak. Nationalism and economics were to be combined in close nexus.

Mercantilism successfully defended the idea of the national state at a time when foreign trade was comparatively ill organized. Unfortunately, mercantilism turned out to be a factor promoting war. All competing states could not possibly achieve a favorable balance of trade; and those left behind in the competition could resort to war as a means of achieving a place in the economic sun. Mercantilists by their very nature were inclined to show contempt for religion and ethics. They were often ruthless in their opposition to human and humanitarian needs. They gravitated toward traditional methods of coercion.

Profound economic change was obvious by the end of the eighteenth century. The now powerful bourgeoisie resented state interference in its economic affairs. It demanded freedom of action. It would have protection for its rights of property and contract, and simultaneously it insisted upon freedom from interference. It saw in the new idea of natural law a perfect response to its need—a body of doctrine attacking mercantilism and proving that capitalism and nature were in complete harmony. Nature, it was argued, meant the businessman to be entirely free in his search for profits. Any attempt to destroy that freedom was a violation of the laws of nature.

The new economic liberalism extolled capitalism, individual liberty, and natural law. Adam Smith took these fragmentary ideas and in his *Wealth of Nations* arranged them into an organized system of economics. Laissez-faire became the watchword of free-traders in what was now regarded as an international or non-national economic system. England, site of the First Industrial Revolution, was also the home of this non-national classical liberalism.

Adam Smith's classical liberalism was non-national. One of the first to revolt against his doctrines was Alexander Hamilton, Secretary of the Treasury of the infant American republic. Detesting the disorder and weakness he saw around him from 1775 to 1789, Hamilton in office called for an efficient, vigorous federal authority. In 1790 he issued two reports on public credit, one calling for a higher standard of national honor in money matters than the prevalent popular principles and the other favoring the establishment of a national bank. In 1791 he transmitted to Congress a *Report on Manufactures*, in which he presented arguments for a well-balanced national economy. In his famous *Report,* obviously directed against the ideas of Adam Smith, Hamilton proposed a systematic fostering of manufactures by protective tariffs, including bounties to agriculture. Moderate tariffs, he said, would help develop national industries.

The effect of Hamilton's measures was immediate and striking. They placed the credit of the new national government on a solid foundation; they served to stimulate industry and commerce; and they brought propertied men to the support of the national government. Actually, Hamilton used economic nationalism as a necessary prop to strengthen the Union. His *Report on Manufactures* was used thereafter as an argument for American protectionism, often to countenance a more extreme tariff policy than Hamilton had ever envisaged. It also served later as an inspiration for Friedrich List, father of the *Zollverein* and an equally enthusiastic supporter of a system of national economy.

Further economic change was generated by the middle of the nineteenth century. Under the impact of the New Industrial Revolution, both liberalism and nationalism were transformed. British classical liberalism declined as industrialization spread to other nations, which were no longer content to trade on British terms. Adam Smith's free economy was no longer able to satisfy the needs of an expanding commerce. Nations competing for world markets encouraged a neo-mercantilism calling for high tariffs to protect national industries, for subsidization of exports, for bounties to encourage local production, and for accent on a favorable balance of trade. Revived in an era of change in human behavior to irrationalism, violence, and aggression, this trend was to have serious consequences early in the next century.

The new economic nationalism had its first impact on agriculture. European landlords and farmers, angered by the importation of cheap grain from the United States and Russia, demanded higher tariffs. Business interests followed suit. Both the United States and Germany, leaders in the New Industrial Revolution, would shelter and protect their own national interests. The new economic nationalism worked at three levels: national governments were judged by their ability to protect agriculture and industry; landlords and manufacturers, as in the days of the Commercial Revolution, depended on governments to protect their interests; and the individual peasant or worker began to feel that it made a difference to what nation he belonged. As always, nationalism was reflecting the time in which it existed.

Liberalism and nationalism, formerly in merger, were now in conflict. The creed of liberalism held that any increase in the wealth of one nation meant advantage for all nations. It saw economic activity as profiting all peoples. Any increase in world trade would lead to peace because it tended to make nations dependent on one another. Nationalism tended to depart from these ideas. It regarded economic activity as a means to increasing the strength and prestige of the nation. In nationalist ideology, economics took on a quality of domination through force. Nationalists accepted the neo-mercantilist doctrine that one nation could grow wealthy only at the expense of another; there was a set amount of trade available, and what one nation appropriated of that commerce was lost to others. They rejected the liberal idea that trade and industry could prosper only in the presence of elementary morality. They were in favor of excluding morality as a necessary condition of economic prosperity.

This transformation in economic thinking took place in an atmosphere of hostility and hatred. In the process, economic nationalism merged almost imperceptibly into imperialism. In the last quarter of the nineteenth century the advanced countries of the West partitioned most of the earth among themselves. This kind of economic nationalism, dedicated to domination, monopoly, and exploitation, became a force for war.

Clarity through Description

Some of the fog surrounding nationalism can be dissipated by the expedient of observing how it works in its historical framework. The Hayes formula, with its chronological approach, and the Kohn dichotomy, with its comparative analysis, present most useful classifications. Other disciplines observe nationalism through the spectacles of their own specialties. Each, in its own way, sees one side of the geometrical prism that is nationalism. Though nationalism most often expresses itself in the political arena, deep underneath are motivating economic factors which give it content and direction.

Notes

[1] Carlton J. H. Hayes, *The Historical Evolution of Modern Nationalism* (New York: R. R. Smith, 1931), *passim.*

[2] Condensed from Hans Kohn, *The Idea of Nationalism,* op. cit., pp. 329 ff., 349 ff., and 573 ff., and *The Twentieth Century* (New York: Macmillan, 1949), pp. 19–32.

[3] Max Sylvius Handman, "The Sentiment of Nationalism," *Political Science Quarterly,* 36 (1921): 107–14.

[4] Gustav Ichheiser, "Some Psychological Obstacles to an Understanding between Nations," *Journal of Abnormal and Social Psychology,* 36 (1941): 427–32.

[5] Louis Wirth, "Types of Nationalism," *American Journal of Sociology,* 41 (1936): 723–37.

[6] Konstantin Symmons-Symonolewicz, "Nationalist Movements: An Attempt at a Comparative Typology," *Comparative Studies in Society and History,* 7 (January 1965): 221–30.

4

Patriotism: The "Last Refuge of a Scoundrel"?

I have always been opposed to extreme nationalism. The people of no one nation are superior to those of any other—different, yes, but superior, no. Extreme nationalists believe they have the right to dominate other nations. Patriotism is something wholly different; love of one's soil is deep in the nature of man.

—Pablo Casals

The All-encompassing Emotion

When in 1790 Nikolai Karamzin returned to his native land, he was overcome with happiness:

Kronstadt Coast! Motherland! I bless you! I am in Russia and in a few days I shall
be with you, my friends! I stop everything I meet. I ask questions only to speak
Russian and to hear Russian people!

In 1802 Robert Emmett, enthusiastic Irishman, engineered an uprising.
The idea was to seize Dublin Castle and hold the lord-lieutenant as a hostage.
But the insurrection was ill planned; the small group of revolutionaries
committed such crimes of violence that its brokenhearted leader fled. He was
captured, tried for treason, and hanged at the age of 25. His last words in the
courtroom became sacred to Irish patriots:

I am asked if I have anything to say why sentence of death should not be
pronounced upon me. . . . My lord, I acted as an Irishman, to deliver my country
from the yoke of a foreign tyranny, and the more galling yoke of a domestic
faction. It was the wish of my heart to extricate my country from this doubly
riveted despotism, to place her independence beyond the reach of any power on
earth, to exalt her to that proud station in the world which Providence has fitted
her to fill.

In 1809 Ugo Foscolo, Italian poet who led the way to the *Risorgimento,*
was appointed to the chair of "Italian Eloquence" at the University of Padua.
His inaugural address included this panegyric to his country:

Italy! O lovely land! O Temple of Venus and of the Muses! How thou art portrayed
by travelers who make a show of honoring thee! How thou art humiliated by
foreigners who have the presumption to master thee! But who can depict thee
better than he who is destined to see thy beauty all his life long?

In April 1816, in a toast given at Norfolk, Virginia, Stephen Decatur
expressed the sentiment without excess verbiage:

Our country! In her intercourse with foreign nations may she always be in the
right; but our country right or wrong!

No country has been immune from the powerful sentiment. The theme was
expressed in 1911 in this passage by Carl Reim, describing a goal for German
youth:

Love of country is a treasure imbedded in the heart of man by God. . . . Our
Fatherland is a holy land. Our ancestors preserved it with their blood. . . . This

land, fertilized with the blood of heroes, is a holy heirloom, not one foot of which shall be robbed from us. We are worthy of the fathers.

Belgians as well as Germans considered themselves "worthy of the fathers." On Christmas Day 1914, the first Christmas after the outbreak of World War I, Désiré Joseph Mercier, Cardinal of the Roman Catholic Church, enjoined loyalty to the Belgian government only and incurred the wrath of the German authorities by proclaiming patriotism a sacred thing:

And this profound will within us is patriotism. . . . Family interests, class interests, party interests, and the material good of the individual take their place, in the scale of values, below the ideal of patriotism, for that ideal is right, which is absolute. Furthermore, that ideal is the public recognition of right in national matters, and of national honor. Now there is no absolute except God. God alone, by His sanctity and His sovereignty, dominates all human interests and human wills. And to affirm the absolute necessity of the subordination of all things to right, to justice, and to truth, is implicitly to affirm God.

When, therefore, humble soldiers whose heroism we praise answer us with characteristic simplicity, "We only did our duty," or "We were bound in honor," they express the religious character of their patriotism. Which of us does not feel that patriotism is a sacred thing, and that a violation of national dignity is in a manner a profanation and a sacrilege?

Strange indeed were these words coming from a prince of that Church whose early believers rejected patriotism on the argument that man's obligations are to God, and after that to all humanity. But it was a time of war, and even high ecclesiastics were drafted to proclaim "the religious character of patriotism." Poets joined the chorus with their own special musical words. In 1915 Rupert Brooke, who was destined to die of septicemia at the Dardanelles at the age of 27, caught the prevailing spirit of selfless patriotism of British youth on the verge of sacrifice:

> If I should die, think only this of me:
> That there's some corner of a foreign field
> That is forever England. There shall be
> In that rich earth a richer dust concealed;
> A dust whom England bore, shaped, made aware,
> Gave, once, her flowers to love, her ways to roam,
> A body of England's, breathing English air,
> Washed by the rivers, blest by suns at home.

Both in time of war and peace, cardinals and poets, classes and masses, elite and ordinary, teachers and students—all are infused with this most powerful emotion. Textbooks in every country are devoted to its preservation. In 1926 Blanche Désiré had the pleasure of seeing her textbook, *Histoire de France, Cours élémentaire,* go into its 256th edition with this concluding "Moral of History":

Children, you have read the history of your country, the recital of its victories and defeats, its prosperity and adversity. Love your country as citizens and soldiers. As citizens you will fulfill all your duties and remain attached to the institutions which the Republic has founded. As soldiers you will perform with zeal your military service and, if the Fatherland appeals to your devotion, you will be ready to shed your blood for it. Thus France will follow the path of its glorious destiny if all citizens are united in the same sentiment, love of the Fatherland.

In World War I France mobilized a force of 8,410,000 men, only to suffer 6,160,800 casualties. In World War II, as if to accent Blanche Désiré's call to arms, France had a peak strength of 5,000,000 men and lost 210,671 killed within a few months. Patriotism was at a highwater mark in all the belligerent countries. It was expressed in many ways, including the statement in 1942 of heavyweight champion Joe Louis, who served in the U.S. Army because "what's wrong with my country ain't nothing Hitler can fix."

The examples are endless—these and many others testify to the potency of patriotism as a human sentiment. For most men the feeling is as normal as breathing, as expressed in Sir Walter Scott's lines:

> Breathes there the man with soul so dead
> Who never to himself hath said,
> This is my own, my native land!

Americans revere Nathan Hale, who on the gallows said: "I only regret that I have but one life to lose for my country." At the same time they reserve anathema for Philip Nolan, the chief figure of Edward Everett Hale's *The Man without a Country* (1863). J. M. Synge, in his *Autobiography,* put it this way: "Patriotism gratifies man's need for adoration and has therefore a peculiar power upon the imaginative sceptic."

Patriotism is so strong that the traitor to his country is regarded as far worse than a murderer. When William Joyce, the turncoat Lord Haw-Haw of German radio during World War II, was sent to Wormwood Scrubs prison in 1945 before his trial for treason, he had to be protected against the rage of fellow prisoners. Despite their social shortcomings, the convicted criminals were most anxious to show that they were not lacking in patriotism.

The Meaning of Patriotism

The simple definition of patriotism is love of country. The word is derived from the root word for father, indicating a sentiment based upon loyalty to the parent. The French *patriote* is from the late Latin *patriota,* "a fellow countryman," from the Greek *patriotes,* from *patrios,* "established by forefathers," from *patēr,* "father." The use of "patriot" to denote a fellow countryman is now obsolete.

Unfortunately, definition of the isms refuses to remain simple. The term "patriotism," like nationalism, is complicated by many shades of meaning. Patriotism may refer to (1) an affection (love of country; contentment with the physical features of the land and the characteristic speech, manners, and institutions of one's countrymen); (2) pride (from love of country flows pride, the belief that the native land is good and even superior to other countries); (3) an act of service (the urge to serve the country as the best proof and test of one's love for it); and (4) a wish (the hope that one's own country be civilized, wealthy, and powerful). The term "patriotism" may be applied to any of these meanings.

Patriotism and Nationalism: A Comparison

General Charles de Gaulle had no doubts about the plain difference: "Patriotism is when love of your own people comes first; nationalism is when hate for people other than your own comes first."

Most people do not possess the analytical shrewdness and sense of absolute certainty revealed by the late great French patriot, and hence far too often use the words "patriotism" and "nationalism" interchangeably, as if they are one and the same thing. Yet, despite the close relationship of the two terms, there are fine distinctions.

1. Land and People.   Patriotism is derived from *patria,* referring to a fatherland or a country. Nationalism comes from *nation,* literally a group of people having common historical traditions. Patriotism is concerned with the people's love for a *country;* nationalism refers to the historical sentiment of a *people.*

2. Country and Nation.   Patriotism is a psychological emotion that impels the individual to serve his country, the object of his loyalty. Nationalism, on the other hand, not specifically a psychological term, concerns itself mainly with the independence and unity of that social unit known as the nation.

3. Chronology.   Patriotism in one form or another has existed from the early days of social organization in the clan, gens, or sib. Not only was it present among primitive tribes, it also exists among primitive peoples today. It has appeared throughout the course of history. Nationalism, however, is a relatively recent phenomenon.

4. Defense versus Aggression. Patriotism is by nature culturally and militarily defensive. In the popular mind, the great patriot is the man who sings praise to his country in time of peace and who defends it in time of war. Despite the recent tendency toward denigration of the sentiment, the most respected patriot is the selfless hero who earns the Victoria Cross, the Congressional Medal of Honor, or the Iron Cross, First Class, in the fury of combat while *defending* his father's land.

Nationalism, in contrast, is inseparable from the notion of power. A malleable force, it may be used either to justify the use of power to forge the union of a nation or it may be applied to condone a mission for expansion. In either case nationalism, as compared with defensive patriotism, takes on a quality of aggression that makes it one of the prime causes for wars since the days of the Napoleonic campaigns.

5. Patriotism Replaced by Nationalism. In our contemporary age, with its vast improvements in techniques of communication, patriotism has a tendency to be replaced by nationalism. Patriotism, based on residence, appeared at the earlier stages of social and economic mobilization. As mobilization progressed and came to bring huge masses of the population into more intense competition, patriotism was replaced more and more by nationalism. One of the main reasons for this transformation, as pointed out by Karl W. Deutsch, is that nationalism is based on the far more intimate and slow-changing personal characteristics and communication habits of each individual.

Patriotism as a Part of a Conditioned State of Being

German infants are not born goose-stepping for the fatherland nor do Russian babies appear in the world squalling odes to the motherland. If we accept John Locke's dictum that the mind of an infant is a *tabula rasa,* a blank tablet on which the experiences of life are written anew, then patriotism takes on a strong psychological quality. From this point of view, patriotism is not an "innate" idea because the human mind, before any ideas are present in it, is a blank tablet.

Heredity or environment? Scholars have long debated the implications of this confrontation. The issue has never been solved successfully, and only intellectual con men hew to the line of a monistic preference for one side or the other. The truth probably lies somewhere in between. Certainly in patriotism there is an element of heredity involved in the disposition of the human to seek some element of security. But by far the greater force is the environmental conditioning induced by practices, artificial rather than natural, invented by man in setting up and maintaining his social order. In this respect, patriotism may be regarded as part of a conditioned state of being. Even Pavlov's dog can be trained to howl a reasonable facsimile of a national anthem or salute the national flag.

We have seen that nationalism is not actually a psychological term, but its political, social, and economic attributes stem from the psychological state of patriotism. In essence, patriotism is subjective. For that reason psychologists are concerned with the function served by well-established patriotism. Unfortunately, the discipline has not yet contributed adequate data on the growth of patriotism in children.

Some attempts, however, have been made by psychologists to trace the development of patriotic judgments among the young. From such admittedly insufficient studies they have derived generalizations such as that by Mussen et al.: "In the same way that the child becomes identified with his parents and his social class he also learns to identify with other subcultural groups (ethnic, religious, racial) to which they belong."[1] Other psychologists conclude that the learning of patriotism is a slow, gradual process and, like prejudice, may be derived from secondhand or socially determined experiences.

On the limited data available, Leonard Doob deems it reasonable to assume that infants at a very early age learn to perceive distinctive attributes in an object or person. Adults in this milieu significantly affect the learning process because children are strongly and emotionally identified with them. Originally, the identification was not patriotically motivated, but eventually it facilitates the learning of patriotism. "You love your mother for reasons best known to you, you love your teacher because he or she is kind and gentle, and then you love your country because they whom you love urge you most subtly to do so."[2]

In the learning process, therefore, parents, teachers, and peers become intentional or unintentional instructors. The idea is epitomized in the question of a six-year old girl reported by Gordon Allport: "Mother, what is the name of the children I am supposed to hate?"[3]

The results of learning patriotism at an early age are not allowed to disappear in our fragmented society. Love of country, conditioned in the child, becomes a way of life with adults. Their surroundings—literally their country—become of vital significance to them, and they readily accept the words and symbols that remind them of that nexus.

There are many examples of how patriotism becomes part of a conditioned state of being, how it becomes a habit in the lives of men. James Morris, in his *Pax Britannica,* speaks of the quality of British patriotism at the time of Queen Victoria's Jubilee in 1897, the moment of dazzling climax of the British Empire. To much of the world, Kipling's "white man's burden" was fearful hypocrisy, but not to the British. They saw themselves sometimes as masters of the world, but sometimes as servants—public servants, like policemen or schoolmasters. Queen Victoria's definition of the imperial mission was "to protect the poor natives and advance civilization." Morris described this conditioned patriotism in an accurate passage:

> And there was one more stimulus to splendour: patriotism, kind and guileless—not arrogant, vicious or greedy, not Jingoism, but simply love of country, like love of family, or love of home, in an age when soldiers unquestioningly fought for their country right or wrong, because they did not think it could be wrong, and there breathed few men who ne'er had said this was their own, their native land. The British were among the most patriotic people of all. They were immensely proud of their country, trusted it, and believed it to be a force for good in the world. The stronger England was, the safer and sounder the world would be. If there were peoples who opposed her dominion, they were probably led by wicked men, or knew no better.[4]

Patriotism in History

The regard for a special piece of land, translated into love of country, has been a compelling motive in human affairs. Early man was accustomed to direct his taboos against the stranger, the outsider of another tribe, who was supposed to stay on his own plot of land. The idea of patriotism flourished in ancient times; both the Egyptians and successive peoples in the Mesopotamian Fertile Crescent owed their loyalty to the state.

As civilization edged westward along the shores of the Mediterranean, the idea of patriotism maintained its hold. In the series of internecine struggles between Athens, Sparta, and Thebes, the citizen regarded his attachment to his city-state as a supreme obligation. One of the most successful techniques both in the consolidation of the Italian peninsula in the Roman Republic and in the formation of the conglomerate Roman Empire was the granting of citizenship to conquered peoples. The acquired peoples had the privilege of saying "I am a Roman citizen," while at the same time accepting the responsibilities of paying taxes and serving in the Roman army. Patriotism in the ancient world was both a consolidating and a disintegrative force. Arnold Toynbee attributes the death of both the Greek and Roman civilizations to *patriotic* wars between city-states, as well as to the failure to establish a system of international law.

After the decline of the Roman Empire, Western Europe settled into the divisive form of society based on feudal-manorial relationships. Medieval peoples directed their sense of patriotism toward the village, town, or petty feudal province in which they were born and in which they died. The Breton peasant or the Florentine craftsman was proud of his locality. His religion was Christian, but his political faith was determined by his place of residence.

He looked upon his immediate neighbors as like himself and as different from foreigners.

A more acute sense of patriotism was revealed during the later Middle Ages. Frenchmen and Germans, Englishmen and Italians, saw each other for the first time on crusading expeditions to the Holy Land and they were not especially attracted by what they saw. French and English patriotism was intensified during the Hundred Years' War; Teutons and Slavs became more conscious of patriotism in their fifteenth-century conflicts. Meanwhile, in the rise of vernacular national literatures the patriot-hero was venerated as the highest type of citizen, who was willing to sacrifice his life for the security and glory of the fatherland.

The nationalism that emerged in the seventeenth century was consolidated in the eighteenth, gained strength in the nineteenth, and became the most potent political force in the twentieth century. Similar to primitive tribalism, and calling for supreme loyalty, nationalism absorbed into its marrow that sense of patriotism that had existed through the course of history. Despite centuries of denunciation by those who are alienated by its tendency to stimulate irrational hatreds, patriotism today is just as important as ever. Peoples everywhere are stimulated by patriotic symbolism, veneration of national heroes, optimistic faith in the future of "our native land." Patriotism fills a deep psychological need.

Patriotism is capable of sudden transformation from a quiescent to an active stage. The United States on December 7, 1941, was a divided nation, puzzled by the European conflict. Then came the overwhelming shock of Pearl Harbor, followed by the greatest outburst of patriotism in United States history. The sentiment was activated in successive waves of reaction—outrage at the loss of American lives, crystallization of a sense of common danger, and an angry resolve to smash Japan, this tricky enemy.

Patriotism and War

Patriotism usually takes on highly emotional overtones during any war or warlike situation. The masses become convinced, rightly or wrongly, that their homeland is in danger, that their very existence is threatened by the enemy, and that their only choice is between victory or annihilation. They enshrine the patriot and condemn the traitor as the most despicable of creatures. Their patriotism is the ultimate expression of that nationalism engrained during the long years of peace and preparation.

The classic statement of patriotic fervor in time of war was expressed by Ernst Moritz Arndt, poet of the War of Liberation. This famous passage, written in 1813 to record the great outpouring of enthusiasm against the Napoleonic yoke, was reprinted again and again in German textbooks for the next 132 years to give impressionable young people the proper guideline for love of country. The practice was never specifically German—parallel passages may be found in the textbooks of virtually all nations.

Fired with enthusiasm, the people rose, "with God for King and Fatherland." Among the Prussians there was only one voice, one anger and one love, to save the Fatherland and to free Germany. The Prussians wanted war; war and death they wanted; peace they feared because they could hope for no honorable peace from Napoleon. War, war, sounded the cry from the Carpathians to the Baltic, from the Niemen to the Elbe. War! cried the nobleman and landed proprietor who had become impoverished. War! the peasant who was driving his last horse to death. . . . War! the citizen who was growing exhausted from quartering soldiers and paying taxes. War! the widow who was sending her only son to the front. War! the young girl who, with tears of pride and pain, was leaving her betrothed. Youths who were hardly able to bear arms, men with gray hair, officers who on account of wounds and mutilations had long ago been honorably discharged, rich landed proprietors and officials, fathers of large families and managers of extensive businesses—all were unwilling to remain behind. Even young women, under all sorts of disguises, rushed to arms; all wanted to drill, arm themselves and fight and die for the Fatherland. . . .

The most beautiful thing about all this holy zeal and happy confusion was that all differences of position, class, and age were forgotten . . . that the one great feeling for the Fatherland, its freedom and honor, swallowed all other feelings, caused all other considerations and relationships to be forgotten.

Not everyone was impressed by Arndt's description of the "holy zeal and happy confusion" of beautiful patriotism. There were many critics who attacked patriotism as the most dangerous of human ideas. In 1894 Leo Tolstoy wrote a long essay, *Christianity and Patriotism*, in which he presented the two as diametrically opposed concepts. "It is a terrible thing to say," he wrote, "but there is not, and never has been, a combined act of violence by one set of people upon another set of people which has not been perpetrated in the name of patriotism." He denounced the sentiment that led to such deplorable results. The masses, he said, were deceived by leaders who were preparing the most fearful calamities for them. At the same time he expressed his sorrow for "the good-natured foolish people, who, showing their healthy white teeth as they smile, gape like children, naively delighted at the dressed-up admirals and presidents, at the flags waving above them, and at the fireworks, and the playing bands." He predicted that long before the misguided people would have time to look about them, there would be neither admirals, presidents, nor flags, but "only the desolate wet plain, cold, hunger, misery—in front of them the slaughterous enemy, behind them the relentless government, blood, wounds, agonies, rotting corpses, and a senseless, useless death." It was a perfect preview for the Russia of 1917.

Tolstoy's advocacy of nonviolence and his polemical criticism of patriotism had worldwide repercussions among small groups of concerned pacifists, but his attitude had little effect upon the mood of the masses. For them, patriotism was a way of life, and if need be, a beacon to death.

Hyperpatriotism: Chauvinism and Jingoism

Patriotism can easily be exaggerated into an extreme form. When combined with militarism and imperialism, it takes on a vainglorious mood of mission and conquest. There are many variations of the theme, among them chauvinism, jingoism, and 100 percent Americanism (or 100 percent Italianism et al.).

Chauvinism is derived from the French surname of Nicholas Chauvin of Rochefort, who served in the armies of the First Republic and the Empire and who nourished a blind idolatry for his hero, Napoleon. Throughout the nineteenth century, French chauvinists called for a regeneration of the spirit that had electrified the Napoleonic armies. In 1882 Paul Déroulède published his *Poèmes militaires,* patriotic verses which enjoyed enormous popularity throughout France. Déroulède saw only the justice of his cause:

> We yield it now to duty's claim,
>   And freely pour out all our store;
> Who judges, frees us still from blame;
> The Kroumirs' muskets war proclaims;—
>   In answer let French cannon roar!
>
> Good fighting! and God be your shield,
>   Our pride's avengers, brave and true!
> France watches you upon the field.
> Who wears her colors never yield,
>   For 'tis her heart ye bear with you!
>
> French blood!—a treasure so august,
>   And hoarded with such jealous care,
> To crush oppression's strength unjust,
> With all the force of right robust,
>   And buy us back our honor fair. . . .

The British version of this kind of exaggerated patriotism took on the name Jingoism, used originally to praise Disraeli's action in sending a fleet to Turkish waters in 1878 to block Russia's drive to the warm water of the Mediterranean. The term came from a popular music-hall song:

> We don't want to fight, but by Jingo, if we do
> We've got the ships, we've got the men, we've
>   got the money, too!

Such hyperpatriotic boasts were used in England to mobilize group tensions instantly for defense or attack. Among the more assertive British Jingoists in the pre–World War I era was J. A. Cramb, professor of modern history at Queen's College, London. In May, June, and July 1900 Cramb delivered a series of lectures on the origins and destiny of imperial Britain in which he attempted to give Englishmen a vivid impression of their greatness. He saw the task of British expansion as one on behalf of civilization and against barbarism. "Every year, every month that passes, is fraught with import of the high and singular destiny which awaits this realm, this empire, and this race." He warned that the nations of the earth pondered British actions, "and by our vacillation or resolution they are uplifted or dejected." He called upon the witness of the dead:

And lo! gathering up from the elder centuries, a sound like a trumpet-call, clear-piercing, far-borne, mystic, ineffable, the call to battle of hosts invisible, the mustering armies of the dead, the great of other wars—Brunanburn and Senlac, Creçy, Flodden, Blenheim and Trafalgar. *Their* battle-cries await our answer—the chivalry's at Agincourt, "Heaven for Harry, England and St. George!," Cromwell's war-shout, which was a prayer, at Dunbar, "The Lord of Hosts! The Lord of Hosts!"—these await our answer, that response which by this war we at last send ringing down the ages, "God for Britain, Justice and Freedom to the world!"[5]

Chauvinism and Jingoism were matched by "100 percent Americanism." At the turn of the century Alfred Thayer Mahan urged Americans to "Look Outward!" It was advice taken seriously by Albert J. Beveridge, Senator from Indiana, who was certain that God had selected the American people "as His chosen nation to finally lead in the regeneration of the world." In a speech before the Senate on January 9, 1900, he spoke emotionally of America's elemental mission:

God has not been preparing the English-speaking and Teutonic peoples for a thousand years for nothing but vain and idle self-contemplation and self-admiration. No! He has made us the master organizers of the world to establish a system where chaos reigns. He has given us the spirit of progress to overwhelm the forces of reaction throughout the earth. He has made us adept in government that we may administer government among savage and senile peoples. Were it not for such a force as this the world would relapse into barbarism and night. And of all our race He has marked the American people as His chosen nation to finally lead in the regeneration of the world. This is the divine mission of America, and it holds for us all the profit, all the glory, all the happiness possible to man. We are trustees of the world's progress, guardians of its righteous peace.[6]

This sort of hyperpatriotism was denounced by Mark Twain and other dissenters, who held with Abraham Lincoln that "no man is good enough to govern another man without that man's consent." Under the impact of such criticism, the United States relinquished its hold on Cuba and the Philippines. After the wave of patriotism in World War II, American superpatriotism reappeared in the neurotic 100 percent Americanism of Senator Joseph R. McCarthy, whose disciples for a time gave a bad odor to American patriotism.

Apostles of exaggerated patriotism appeared in every country, from Ireland to Afghanistan to Spain. The motivations were similar: all spoke of the glory of the fatherland, all praised the national heroes, all wept in the presence of the flag and within hearing of the national anthem. The sentiment was expressed bombastically by the Italian patriot Gabriele D'Annunzio: "The enemy has pierced into the flesh of Italy, because Italy is not in those who live on her, trafficking with her and slandering her shamelessly, but in those who live for her alone, and suffer for her alone and for her alone are ready to die." To D'Annunzio, to die was not enough: "If to die means to cease fighting, then we may not die."

Such overblown patriotism can approach the bizarre. On November 25, 1970, Yukio Mishima, a Japanese novelist and serious contender for the Nobel Prize, took his life at the age of 45 in a ritual *hara-kiri* to demonstrate his love for his country. In real life Mishima recapitulated his own short story, called "Patriotism," about a young lieutenant who committed *hara-kiri*. To some Japanese this was an act of madness, but others regarded it as a classic statement of style, sincerity, and honor, an act of patriotism *par excellence*.[7]

In Germany, hyperpatriotism also took on a militaristic cast. The argument was presented before 1914 by Friedrich von Bernhardi: "War is a biological necessity of the first importance, a regulative element in the life of mankind which cannot be dispensed with, which excludes every achievement of the race, and therefore all real civilization." This justification of war reflected a new irrationalism that had been infecting the German mind since the impact of Romanticism in the early nineteenth century. In this kind of thinking the word *Vaterland* took on an odd and extravagant connotation, as witness this strange paean in a speech by Adolf Stoecker, Christian-Socialist court chaplain to William II in imperial Germany, who performed the feat of using the word "Fatherland" nine times in one sentence:

Ten years ago much blood was spilled to win freedom and unity for the Fatherland; one cannot think enough of the Fatherland, and it is inspiring when young men give their Fatherland more than themselves, and give their blood and lives for the Fatherland; but when one makes a repulsive idol of the earthly Fatherland, when there is no heavenly Fatherland above the earthly Fatherland, then the spirit of the Fatherland remains dark; in many souls today a wrong idea of the Fatherland exists.[8]

Patriotism as a Noble Art

Like nationalism, its alter ego, patriotism can be either a blessing or a curse. In its mild form, patriotism can be an ennobling virtue, representing a deep attachment to a particular way of life regarded as the best in the world. This kind of patriot has no wish to interfere in the affairs of other peoples and recognizes that others have the right and duty to love their own country. His patriotism may be compared to the faith he has in his own religion. It takes on the quality of a religious duty, illustrated in the union of veneration and awe expressed in the phrase "For God and Country."

Patriotism in this benign sense is the logical emotional outcome of a psychic identification process. The infant attaches himself to his parents; when he reaches adulthood he accepts the community impulse of patriotism. Asked to fight and perhaps die for his country, he is urged to defend a social organization deriving its emotional appeal from early obedience to his parents. Patriotism in this form becomes a substitute need for security, an attitude psychologically rewarding and socially recognized. Frederick the Great expressed it succinctly: "I love my country ardently. It is to her that I owe my education, my fortune, my existence, my all. Had I a thousand lives, I should with pleasure sacrifice them all, if I could thereby render her any service and show her my gratitude."

The attitude is as old as human association. In the late eighth century B.C. the legendary blind poet Homer described a supreme virtue when he said that "for our country 'tis a bliss to die." Mazzini, the nineteenth-century Italian hero, saw patriotism as a necessity for the service of humanity. Just as the family created the citizen, he said, so the nation created men, conscious of their past, critical of their present, and hopeful of their future. The nations should be looked upon as the families into which God has chosen to divide His people. "You are citizens," he told his compatriots; "you have a country in order that in a given and limited sphere of action, the concourse and assistance of a certain number of men, already related to you by language, tendencies, and customs, may enable you to labor more effectively for the good of *all men,* present and to come; a task in which your solitary effort would be lost, falling powerless and heedless among the immense multitudes of your fellow beings." Mazzini was aware that in practice the nation might fail to produce servants of humanity and suffer from "a more or less enlarged egoism," but he felt that even the perversion was better than the total absence of the bond.

In 1961, at a time when patriotism seemed to be going out of fashion, John F. Kennedy awakened much of the old tradition for Americans in his inaugural address: "Ask not what your country can do for you—ask what you can do for your country." And more: "Let every nation know, whether it wishes us well or ill, that we shall pay any price, bear any burden, meet any hardship, support any friend, oppose any foe to assure the survival and the success of liberty."

Overwrought Patriotism as an Evil

Criticism of patriotism in its evil form ranges from head shaking to fiery denunciation—from Albert Schweitzer's call for "a noble kind of higher patriotism which aims at ends worthy of the whole of mankind" to Dr. Samuel Johnson's aphorism about patriotism being the "last refuge of a scoundrel." The skeptical Voltaire was sure that "the greater the Fatherland, the less one can love it." Tolstoy described patriotism as "an immoral feeling, because instead of confessing oneself a son of God, as Christianity teaches us, or even a free man guided by his own reason, each man under the influence of patriotism confesses himself the son of his Fatherland and the slave of his government, and commits actions contrary to his reason and conscience." Lord Hugh Cecil, apparently impressed by Dr. Johnson, also saw patriotism as "the convenient cudgel of the scoundrel to batter critics dumb." Others of lesser eminence called patriotism "a stupid doctrine" and "the passion of fools."

Added to the denunciation by litterateurs was the attack by social psychologists who rejected the idea that patriotism is an innate instinct. While admitting that patriotism may reflect a human need for security, they see adverse neurotic and psychotic factors in it which can cause much trouble. It has been demonstrated time and time again, they say, that in periods of war crisis, patriotism almost always changes from harmless love of country to a contagious epidemic of mass irrationalism. Patriotism then becomes a means for the projection of hostility and aggression, as well as a manifestation of a psychic defense against fear and anxiety. Far from being a healthy emotion, it easily passes over into the abnormal and becomes the cause for much mischief in human affairs.

Even more vociferous was dissenting youth. After World War II German teenagers, appalled by the excesses of their elders in the Nazi generation, adopted an attitude of *"Ohne mich!"* ("Without me!"). The Yippie and Hippie culture, from Amsterdam's *Leidseplein* to New York's East Village, damned the patriotic impulse as "square" and outmoded. The relatively mild Julian Bond, a young member of the Georgia legislature, defined his own black nationalism:"First and foremost, we are black nationalists—black people who reject the stupid notion of patriotism that has made us first in war, last in peace, and never in the hearts of our countrymen." Although vigorous, these dissenting assaults on patriotism have not struck a wide response or generated a mass movement.

To all its critics, exaggerated patriotism, or "pooled self-esteem," is a deep-seated disease which cannot be healed by incantation. They point to a vicious circle—patriotism breeds nationalism, nationalism nurtures militarism, militarism encourages imperialism, and imperialism stimulates rebelling nationalism in the very peoples whom it subjects to its control. Worst of all, they say, patriotism is dangerous because it engenders hatreds leading inevitably to war. It mistakenly teaches citizens that they are a world unto themselves, that they are a "Chosen People" whose prime loyalty is based on love of country and not on their status as human beings. It generates a spirit of exclusiveness grounded on ignorance, smugness, and pride, instead of on intelligence, reason, and decency. In short, the critics see overblown patriotism as a deplorable emotion, just as they regard nationalism as a mischievous doctrine.

The critics say that it is of the utmost importance that contemporary human beings rid themselves of idolized patriotism and substitute for it a warm regard for a common civilization. It is absolutely necessary, they say, to think of a world community as the starting point of the social adventure. No part of this community would have the right or power to act as its own will deems best warranted, without regard for the will of other parts. The state must be prevented from hindering the needs of the world community from being realized.

Along with this suggestion of a viable global order with a world patriotism, the critics of the present phase issue a warning: the excesses of national egoism revealed in patriotic ardor and the social pressure of national patriotism are so dangerous that, unless curbed, they will destroy civilization.

Notes

The aphorism "Patriotism is the last refuge of a scoundrel" is attributed to Dr. Samuel Johnson by Boswell in his *Life of Johnson* (10 vols. [London, 1835], vol. 5, chap. 9). Such apothegms have a way of being easily garbled. For example, Martin Kilson, reviewing a book on pan-Africansim for the *New York Times Book Review* (March 12, 1972, p. 28), introduced this variation: "A scoundrel, in the sense that Dr. Johnson had in mind when he quipped that patriotism *or nationalism* is the *first* refuge of *the* scoundrel." (Italics mine.)

[1] Paul Henry Mussen, John Janeway Conger, and Jerome Kagan, *Child Development and Personality* (2d ed.; New York: Harper & Row, 1963), p. 409.

[2] Leonard Doob, *Patriotism and Nationalism: Their Psychological Foundations* (New Haven: Yale University Press, 1964), p. 126.

[3] Gordon W. Allport, *The Nature of Prejudice* (Cambridge, Mass.: Addison-Wesley, 1954), p. 307.

[4] James Morris, *Pax Britannica: The Climax of an Empire* (New York: Harcourt Brace Jovanovich, 1968), p. 128.

[5] J. A. Cramb, *The Origins and Destiny of Imperial Britain and Nineteenth Century Europe* (New York: Dutton, 1915), p. 239.

[6] Albert J. Beveridge, in the *Congressional Record,* vol. 33, pt. I (January 9, 1900), p. 705.

[7] See ch. 13 for a more detailed discussion of the Mishima case.

[8] Adolf Stoecker, *Christlich-Sozial: Reden und Aufsätze* (Bielefeld and Leipzig, 1885), p. 106.

5

National Character: Reality or Illusion?

There is, or there may be, a bewildering difference between national character as it appears in individual specimen, and national character as it appears in the conglomerate body of the whole nation.

—Ernest Barker

The Contamination of Lay Stereotypes

All Turks are stoical, obedient, and without imagination.
All Germans are militant and find pleasure in theories.
All Frenchmen are passionate and pragmatic.
All Englishmen are polite and class conscious.
All Italians are emotional and loud.
All Spaniards are proud and dignified.
All Russians are melancholy and frustrated.
All Americans are naive, materialistic, and violent.

These are among the common stereotypes that have passed into everyday speech. In all-embracing generalization, the people of one nation are endowed with a set of common, permanent qualities said to distinguish them from other peoples. Far too often the designations are wrapped in hostility in order to denigrate "the others" as being different and less richly endowed. For the music hall or television comedian specializing in dialect humor, the amateur sociology of stereotypes may be bread and butter: he ridicules the "typical" Scotsman, who is too frugal to go to the seashore and instead buys a herring which he waves in his living room to bring sea air to his family. Or the performer may seek audience response by imitating the proud bearing, the sense of *dignidad,* of the Spanish bullfighter.

Stereotypes are wildly exaggerated versions of what may bear an element of truth. They are used indiscriminately to describe everyone within a national group without regard for individual exceptions and in a way that admits no contradiction. Yet recognition of stereotypes is so widespread that they cannot be cast aside as of no consequence. The very fact of their acceptance gives them important historical value.

The study of national character is a field much contaminated by lay stereotypes about groups and nations. But it would be wrong to ignore such stereotypes completely or to deny their relevance. Something would be lost if the area of interdisciplinary investigation of stereotypes and closely related national character were to be abandoned because of criticism of the more ambiguous uses. Artificial stereotypes may well be exaggerated, sometimes even irrational, but this does not mean that inquiry into national character should be abandoned.

Behind the stereotypes may be a very real set of cultural characteristics, as pointed out by Herman Kahn, mathematician, games theorist, and think-tanker (RAND Corporation, Hudson Institute):

There is a remarkable degree of accuracy in many of the clichés people use about their own nation and about other nations. The latter are usually unfriendly stereotypes, but if you get behind them you begin to see that there are qualities which give rise to these clichés.

I don't think national characteristics are genetic; they are generally formed before you are 10 or 12, but everything reinforces them from that point on at least as long as you are in the same milieu. You can take an Italian boy of 12, bring him to America and so transform him that, if he goes back to his native village when he is 20, he will be thought of as *the* American for the rest of his life.

The specificity of a nation is a lasting and stubborn quality, and while it changes, it changes very slowly; and a political scientist would be doing himself a disservice if he left these characteristics out of account. Many otherwise intelligent people do not like to admit that, taking a cross-section of a population, there are differences of taste, temperament and ability among nations. There is a fear, which is perhaps exaggerated, that the implications of recognizing such differences may prove politically explosive. But you can't wish these problems away by denying their existence.[1]

In these down-to-earth phrases Kahn expressed conclusions on national character that have also been reached by many scholars. It is easy to underestimate the witty stereotypes applied to the people of different nations on the ground that "all human beings are alike." Yet at the root of the comical clichés is a serious combination of cultural characteristics along national lines. Ridiculing their existence is intellectually and politically dangerous business.

The Meaning of National Character

Closely associated with both nationalism and patriotism, national character may be defined as the totality of traditions, interests, and ideals that are so widespread and influential in a nation that they mold its image, both in the minds of the people concerned and in the beliefs of others. It refers specifically to those environmentally produced qualities of a people bound together by a sense of nationalism. The anthropologist Geoffrey Gorer spoke of national character as "the ideal image of themselves in the light of which individuals assess and pass judgment upon themselves and their neighbors, and on the basis of which they reward and punish their children, for the manifestation or non-manifestation of given traits and attitudes."[2]

The assumption is that where human beings form communities such as tribes, villages, cities, or nations, they also create distinctive social characters. Social character (of which national character is one facet) is a set of traits (attitudes about the nature of the world and notions about how to solve the many problems of living) that the members of a group come to share with one another over and beyond their individual differences.

It follows that this specific concept needs empirical investigation. Yet the idea is surrounded by so many inconsistencies, contradictions, and ambiguities that scholars often decide to steer away to safer waters. The study of national character becomes vitally important in hot and cold wars: during such confrontations men become more self-conscious as citizens who differ from other nationals. It would be unreasonable to confine the study of national character only to wartime and then only as a means of defeating the enemy. The more national character is understood the more is it possible for human beings to overcome their own narrowness and petty parochialism.

The Case for National Character

Before the great national revolutions the *philosophes* of the Enlightenment were fascinated by the idea of national character. In his *The Spirit of the Laws* (1748), Montesquieu admitted that, even though human nature is universally the same, in fact it presents a most variable mien. He attributed this to unique combinations of local circumstances operating on universal human nature. Men are influenced by various factors: by climate, by religion, by laws, by maxims of government, by precedents, morals, and customs—"whence is formed a general spirit of nations." As human beings respond to differential situations, "the characters of the several nations are formed of virtues and vices, of good and bad qualities."

A few years later the Scottish philosopher David Hume, in his *Essays and Treatises on Several Subjects* (1753), added content to the pre-revolutionary conception of national character. According to Hume, the human mind is imitative: the propensity to company and society is so strong in all rational creatures that their passions and inclinations run as a contagion through the whole club or knot of companions. Just as there is a personal character peculiar to each individual, so is there a national character among a number of men who are united into one political body. Their close relations, along with the same speech and language, lead to a resemblance in their manners.

Hume admitted that although nature produces all kinds of temper and understanding in great abundance, it does not follow that she always produces them in like proportions. In every society the ingredients of industry and indolence, valor and cowardice, humanity and brutality, wisdom and folly will be mixed in the same manner. Whatever it be that forms the manners of one generation, the next must imbibe a deeper tincture of the same dye. Hume asserted that men, being more susceptible of all impressions during infancy, and retaining these impressions as long as they remain in the world, then all national characters, where they depend not on fixed *moral* causes, proceed from such accidents as these, and that physical causes have no discernible operation on the human mind.

Hume saw this "contagion of manners" as more significant throughout the course of history than the influence of either air or climate. His thinking was clear cut, as witness this précis:

1. Where an extensive government has been established for many centuries, it spreads a national character over the whole empire. Thus the Chinese have the greatest uniformity of character imaginable, though the air and climate in their vast dominions admit of very considerable variations.

2. In small contiguous countries the people may have a different character as distinguishable in their manners as the most distant nations. Athens and Thebes were but a short distance from each other, yet the Athenians were as remarkable for ingenuity, politeness, and gaiety as the Thebans were for dullness, rusticity, and a phlegmatic temper.

3. The same national character commonly follows a precise boundary, and differs on crossing a river or passing a mountain. The Languedocians and Gascons are the gayest people of all France, but whenever one passes the Pyrenees he is among Spaniards. Hume asked whether it is conceivable that the qualities of the air should change so exactly within the limits of an empire, which depend so much on accidents of battle, negotiations, and marriages.

4. Where any set of men scattered over distant nations have a close communication, they acquire similar manners, and have but little in common with the nations among whom they live.

5. If an accident such as a difference of language or religion keeps two people inside a nation from mixing, they will preserve a distant and even opposite set of manners. Thus, in Hume's estimation, the integrity, gravity, and bravery of the Turks form an exact contrast to the deceit, levity, and cowardice of the modern Greeks.

6. The same set of manners follows the nation and adheres to it all over the globe, as witness the Spaniards, English, French, and Dutch colonists.

7. The character of a people changes considerably from one age to another. Hume felt certain that candor, bravery, and love of liberty formed the character of the ancient Romans, as subtlety, cowardice, and a slavish disposition distinguish the modern Romans. The old Spaniards were restless, turbulent, and addicted to war, but it would be difficult to arouse the modern Spaniards to war.

8. When several neighboring nations have close communication, they acquire a similitude of manners. Thus all the Franks seem to have a uniform character in the Western nations.

9. There is a wonderful mixture of manners and character in the same nation. And in this particular the English are the most remarkable of any people that ever were in the world. Nor is this to be ascribed to the mutability and uncertainty of their climate, nor to any other physical causes, because all

these causes take place in the neighboring kingdom of Scotland, without
having the same effect.

Hume's early analysis of national character was projected at a time when
modern nationalism was coming into existence. Making no claim to objectivity, he expressed his dislike of certain peoples. Yet, on the whole, his
general concept of national character and his defense of it were quite similar
to views held by defenders of the idea who came after him. In his *Ancien
Régime et la Révolution* (1856), Tocqueville commented on the way national
revolutions brought on a new integration of social power:

Beneath the seemingly chaotic surface there was developing a vast, highly
centralized power which attracted to itself and welded into an organic whole all the
elements of authority and influence that hitherto had been dispersed among a
crowd of lesser, uncoordinated powers.[3]

Hegel, too, visualized national character as the mainspring of historical
change:

The definite *substance* that receives the form of universality, and exists in that
concrete reality which is the State—is the spirit of the people itself. The actual
State is animated by this spirit, in all its particular affairs—its wars, institutions,
etc.[4]

Twentieth-century thinkers took much the same line. Salvador de Madariaga spoke of the "fact" of national character which stares us in the face.
He did not see history, geography, religion, language, or even the common
will as enough to define a nation. He described a nation as "a fact of
psychology, that which is *natural* or *native* in it gives its force to the word
nation." Ernest Barker held that national character, in its formation and
manifestations, has its analogies with the character of the individual man.
Each human being, he said, undergoes a process of moral growth, starting
with the raw stuff of original nature, partly environmental, partly biological.
This raw stuff is then shaped into a settled form by submission to social
discipline. That settled form is character—the sum of acquired tendencies
built upon native bases. The individual develops a constant identity which
expresses itself in "expectable" action. The growth of a nation, Barker said,
recapitulates this process. In much the same way a nation begins its life with
the raw stuff of a material base. Again in the same manner, it builds a pool of
acquired tendencies. And then it settles into the "unity and permanence of
form" we call national character.

Barker recognized the objection that there is a vast difference between the
individual and the nation. One can see the individual as a single body and his

character can be judged by his actions. But can one see or objectively describe another nation? To this Barker replied that unity of character must be a matter of faith rather than of sight, and that one can experience even what he cannot see. National character is something which can never be explained scientifically in detail, but it must be accepted as a thing which is simply given.

Barker's somewhat shaky defense of national character admitted the impossibility of scientific proof. National character must be "experienced," but it cannot be described in a manner guaranteed to obtain universal acceptance. Even if the outlines are shady, even if there are differences between national character as it appears in the individual and in the nation, there are so many evidences of its existence that it must be accepted as a reasonable conclusion. Proponents of national character grant that it may be enveloped in prejudice, and that it may be expressed in stereotypes to deprecate the people of another nation, but they still contend that it exists as an identifiable concept.

Negative: National Character Does Not Exist

In contrast there is an equally strongly held contention that national character does not exist. In its extreme form this view rejects anything connected with national character as facile and fallacious and as a product of wishful thinking. National character is identified with false stereotypes and it is denounced as based on generalizations that simply do not exist, as a reflection of national pride and hence irrational. It is nominated for oblivion, as fit only for a category including the primitive belief in trial by ordeal and the idea of the divine right of kings.

Behind this thinking lies the conviction that a nation is not a natural combination, as is a herd of sheep or a pack of wolves, but on the contrary is a largely artificial unit carved accidentally without any rational or orderly process. It is claimed that a nationality can be changed without affecting the quality of a nation's inhabitants. A case is Alsace-Lorraine, which for a thousand years has been shifted from the German to the French side and vice versa as a result of war and conquest. Yet the transfers have had little effect on the character of the people who have lived in these provinces.

Critics of national character hold that there are no qualities that can distinguish any group, such as a profession or a society, any more than a nation. They are not willing to grant that all professors are genteel, all lawyers are aggressive, and all plumbers are impolite, nor do they place much stock in the similar traits of all Masons, Catholics, or Republicans. They charge that, as soon as an attempt is made to generalize about either small or large groups, the result inevitably is oversimplification or, more often, confusion.

Hamilton Fyfe, a British scholar, called the whole idea of national character an "illusion," a folly that has frequently tormented and devastated the
world:

It is an idea, which, so far as I can discover, has never been examined and
analyzed. It has been uncritically accepted as a fact, though actually it is as much a
fiction as the supposed flatness of the earth, the supposed traveling of the sun
around the earth, the separate creation of all forms of life, and the differentiation
between "the human and the animal kingdoms." All these beliefs, once universally
held, are now universally rejected as delusions.

They were allowed to pass for truth because no one challenged them, just as the
illusion of national character has been given credence for the reason that it has not
been questioned, dissected, exposed. Hardly one of the prominent authors of the
late nineteenth and early twentieth centuries doubted that war was a permanent,
unavoidable part of the world order. From this they deduced differences between
nations, which produced hostility. Certain nations (France and England, Russia
and Turkey) they regarded as "natural enemies"; thus they attributed to
conflicting temperaments or ideals among the masses what were in fact clashes of
material interest among rulers or ruling classes.[5]

Fyfe pointed to the lack of consistency in the argument for national
character. The thoughts and emotions of a people can be altered within a
short time by education, the press, and propaganda, or even by mysterious
techniques. For example, the reactionary elements in the army and the
Church condemned Dreyfus and drove Zola into exile, but within a few years
the French were honoring the great novelist as a lover of truth. Where in 1932
the Germans were relatively proud of Einstein, in 1933, they hated him so
much that they burned his books. Fyfe concluded: "Men and women who
easily change their minds, their sympathies, are said to be weather cocks, to
lack character. Apply the same reasoning to nations and it will be seen that,
since no nation can show a consistent line of action, none have national
characters."[6]

Added to the confusion, say the opponents of national character, is the fact
that what is presumed to be national character may be modified or largely
influenced by sectional ideologies. There are ordinarily many sectional
divisions, each of which interprets national traditions and customs in its own
way and pays little or no attention to what does not fit into its own character.
There may be many different qualities in the pattern. Thus national character, like that of the individual, may be a constellation of numerous forces or
functions with countless variables. The argument holds that it is impossible
to track down the variables. Character, it is said, is seldom based on strict
unity, but is rather a group of contradictory tendencies among which the
balance is always being changed.

How is it possible, ask the critics, to endow a nation numbering millions with a single character or will? Is it not true that precisely opposite characteristics can exist within the framework of one people? For example, is it not obvious that Germany's political divisions have been accompanied by cultural schizophrenia? Which national character does one select? On one face of the coin may be seen the transcendental idealism of Kant, the classic humanitarianism of Goethe, and the tolerance of a Lessing. On the other side is displayed the warmongering of Treitschke, the anti-Semitism of court chaplain Adolf Stoecker, and the irrationalism of Alfred Rosenberg. Which is the real German character? The critics reply that national character is incompatible with common sense and a rational approach.

Even more, opponents of the idea of national character claim that it is a popular myth with an infinite capacity for damage. They say that it is often used to appease the consciousness of guilt that goes along with aggression. The citizens of one nation are led to believe that by some chemical reaction they have become a "chosen people," appointed to dominate other people and seize their territory. It is always the neighbor who is denounced as "a bloodthirsty beast" and "an arrogant aggressor." It becomes a holy mission to smite down the enemy. Paeans of praise are sung to the virtues of one's own nation while at the same time the national character of others is disparaged.

The Theory of Limited Validity

Midway between the two extremes is the view that national character does have a limited validity. The existence of similar manners—the core of national character—is recognized without minimizing the difficulties involved in interpreting them. It is granted that values have been inculcated within cultures by responses to environment, traditions, and education. According to the historian Leopold von Ranke, the national spirit can be felt but not understood; it is "a spiritual air, permeating everything."

The theory of limited validity recognizes the survival and persistence of national traits. Each individual in the nation is exposed to the forces making up the idea of nationalism, and most citizens feel themselves identified with the fortunes of the entire country. Anything that affects the group is regarded by the individual as happening to himself. It is precisely this process of identification, partly objective and partly imaginative, that accounts for the intensity of group life. This does not necessarily mean that national character is the totality of the character of the individuals concerned. Most people in a country may be opposed to war, yet they may find themselves carried along by the war spirit when it appears. Large numbers in any society may fail to conform and may act atypically.

Those who accept the idea of limited validity reject two parallel concepts that have tended to confuse the issue.

National character is not the same thing as racial character.   Racialism, with its accent on "pure" races and "superior" races, is a fraud. Nor is there any justification for distinguishing *racial* character. Few if any scholars speak of national character as if it were inheritable, yet there has been a tendency to use the two terms "national character" and "racial character" as interchangeable. Many observers turn away altogether from the term "national character" because they feel themselves open to attack as unscientific no matter how carefully they distinguish between nationalism and racialism.

There is no such thing as a "permanent" national character.   The contention that national character is a permanent, stable entity was borrowed by Herder from Montesquieu. Herder's *Volksgeist,* which may be translated roughly as "national character," became so fixed a persuasion that it helped mold the destiny of nations. According to Herder, "Germany since the earliest times had a fixed national spirit in all classes, still has it at the present time, and according to the organization will have it everlastingly." Such historians as the Englishman Macaulay, the Frenchman Michelet, the German Sybel, and the American Bancroft were inclined to accept the concept of a permanent national character. The notion became persistent, backed as it was by scholars of impeccable reputation. "In the literature of any people," said Henry Morley, "one can see all contrasts of form produced by variable social influences of one national character from beginning to last."

Yet these assumptions of the fixity and permanence of national character, even by able thinkers, contradict the evidence of human plasticity. Historically, the unity of any group is changeable, and the "personality" of nations may be variable. Transformations can and do take place in the personality of peoples. At one time the English were said to be unruly and disorderly, only to appear later as a solid people who prided themselves on the stability of their institutions and their law-abidingness. The Germans of the Holy Roman Empire and the German Confederation were a relatively quiet, peaceful people, comfortable, petty, and bourgeois in their habits, only to take a widespread reputation late in the nineteenth century and at the opening of the twentieth as a warlike community bent on conquest or ruin. Frenchmen in the early eighteenth century were known as a stolid, peace-loving people, proud of their loyalty to the monarchy, yet by the end of that century they had a violent revolution and attempted to impress their special idea of liberty, equality, and fraternity upon the rest of Europe. Thus, far from being fixed or permanent, national character changes in response to varied stimuli. It is unreasonable to maintain a complete constancy of national character, even though single characteristics often show strong powers of survival.

Those who accept the idea of limited validity are unhappy with the term "national character," especially because it is confused with the well-known stereotypes. Some prefer to use the term "basic personality structure of nations" to indicate characteristics shared by individuals of a common culture. They claim that this new term goes beyond the superficial aspects of behavior, such as manners or morals, and turns instead to what they call the integrative process—the inculcation of a given set of principles for the governing of behavior. The approach is new, but the basic element remains—certain common patterns of functioning can be observed in individuals who comprise the nation, and these patterns will not be found among other peoples who live in a different set of cultural conditions.

The Duality of National Character

Salvador de Madariaga deemed it a curious thing that national character is usually summed up by the voice of universal opinion as a pair of features, one a quality, the other a defect. Thus a Frenchman would call Englishmen hypocrites with practical sense. Corresponding to this dogma are clearness-licentiousness for the Frenchman, dignity-cruelty for the Spaniard, vulgarity-vitality for the American. "It is as if, in this big village of the world, each individual nation has been sketched down by its neighbors to its fundamental features—more or less accurately understood—and in this operation a good and bad quality has remained, witnesses to the double origin of the human soul."[7]

Madariaga's "double origin of the human soul" and its corollary, the duality of national character, assume special meaning and poignancy in the case of Germany, homeland of Goethe's Faust and Mephisto. The outstanding fact of German history is a polarity of development that has never really been resolved. In the earlier days there was on the one side the vague, shadowy ideal of the Holy Roman Empire, on the other a divisive particularism. The Reformation left other nations either dominantly Catholic or Protestant, but in the German states both churches retained their influence. In the nineteenth century came the conflict between the idea of a *Grossdeutschland* under Austrian auspices and a *Kleindeutschland* under Prussia. Always there was dichotomy, division, duality. In the twentieth century, after the blood bath of World War I, the Treaty of Versailles set up the Polish Corridor, separating East Prussia from the rest of Germany, and thereby created a split that was bound to accentuate German nationalism. The tendency toward duality was aggravated again after World War II by the partition into the Federal Republic of Germany and Communist East Germany.

Little wonder, then, that Germany's political division should be accompanied by cultural schizophrenia, epitomized by the combination of Bach, Beethoven, and Brahms on the one side and Hitler, Himmler, and Hess on the other. This has been the tragedy of German history—a persistent oscillation between good and evil, between God and the devil. In the words of A. J. P. Taylor, " 'German' has meant at one moment a being so sentimental, so trusting, so pious, as to be too good for this world; and at another a being so brutal, so unprincipled, so degraded as to be not fit to live. Both descriptions are true: both types have existed not only in the same epoch, but in the same person."[8]

This ambivalence in the German experience indicates the limited validity of that concept of national character that has attracted the attention of many disciplines. The German national character has existed for more than a thousand years, not always in identical form but in a way that can be recognized. National character thus becomes a kind of shorthand by which the historian can identify and describe a community distinguished by geography, language, and socio-political beliefs and practices—provided that it is used objectively, without emotion and without the goal of proving some preconceived notion.

National Character in the Twentieth Century

In recent years there has been notable work in interdisciplinary examination of national character, especially in twentieth-century perspectives. Much of this interest was stimulated by the great confrontations of World War II and the subsequent cold war. It was motivated to a large extent by a desire to improve transnational understanding. Peoples everywhere became more and more self-conscious as nationals with similarities to and differences from other nationals. It was assumed that the more fully one people could understand its national character, the more it could overcome its sense of parochialism and devote its resources to the emergence of a more healthy form of nationalism within a viable world community.

A special issue of *The Annals of the American Academy of Political and Social Science*, published in 1967, is a valuable contribution to the interdisciplinary study of contemporary national character.[9] The following is a brief précis from *The Annals'* study on the nature of recent findings on national character. The quality of the contributions indicates that the concept of national character is, indeed, very much alive.

Geoffrey Gorer, British social anthropologist, finds historical evidence suggesting that the typical character of the English middle classes has been modified relatively little in the last two centuries, but that the typical character of the urban working classes has changed. There were two major modifications in the mid-nineteenth century, at a time when the invention of a nationwide, unarmed police force "presented a new model for the ideal character"; and again after the end of World War II, when, for the first time in recent British history, practically all the children in working-class homes have been nourished adequately. It may be expected, Gorer believes, that the new working-class generation will modify the national character when this new generation becomes dominant at the polls.

Similar changes may be noted in the French national character, according to the studies of Reino Virtanen, specialist in French literature and civilization. Virtanen sees France as developing a distinctive national character as early as the seventeenth century—a peasant, artisan, bourgeois type of character, social but not hospitable, settled, routinized. On the opposite pole was the aristocracy, privileged, entrenched, and hungering for glory. But modern conditions, Virtanen says, have made a return to the era of grandeur impossible. There are signs that the French national character is undergoing basic modifications. The old accent on status is changing gradually, and traditional French rationalism is becoming more flexible.

Pitirim A. Sorokin, sociologist, lists the essential characteristics of the Russian nation as enormous vitality, remarkable pertinacity, and willingness to sacrifice for survival. The people are undergoing extraordinary territorial, population, political, social, and cultural growth. Their character is subjected to additional peculiarities: racial and ethnic diversity, unity in diversity, comparatively peaceful expansion and growth, the fighting of primarily defensive wars, comparative orderliness, and high dedication. Since the end of the 1920s, Sorokin says, Russia has begun to display other traits: supplanting rude force by the rule of law, modification of totalitarianism in favor of economic and social democracy, and "the moral renaissance of the Soviet people." These views are challenged by other students of Russian national character.

David Riesman, social scientist, speaks of the fragmentary work on American national character. Some psychoanalytically oriented studies assumed that national character was formed in early childhood, but later studies stressed the effect of class and ethnic differences in child rearing. Other studies have emphasized the adjustments of immigrants and travelers to America and the adjustments of Americans traveling abroad. Riesman finds American character as differing from that of other societies in the expectations it places upon the sexes and in ethnic, religious, and social characteristics. He believes that American national character is influenced by important economic factors, the mass media, and education. There is resistance to prevalent national styles, but the vital factor is the extent to which resisters resemble purveyors and adopters of these styles.

There is increasing interest in the twentieth-century national character of the South American countries. Gilberto Freyre, sociologist, sees the core of Brazilian character as spiritual volition, adventurousness, and poetical vision, shared with Portuguese ancestors. Here, too, there has been significant change. The Old World heritage has undergone expansion, differentiation, and transmutation in "creative synthesis" with New World elements. Brazilians have always tended to harmonize idealism with response to reality, political independence with traditional political forms. There is polarity in all areas of Brazilian life, from cuisine to football. According to Freyre, this process of creative synthesis of old and new continues as Brazil meets its future.

In his investigations of Japanese national character, anthropologist Douglas Gilbert Haring sees Japanese personality as based on traditions of submission to the powerful and of duty as fixed obligation to statuses, not to individuals. The family hierarchy remains the model for social relations. Despite changes, obedience is still the highest virtue, and those who are clever use it to their own advantage. The syndrome of *amaeru* originates in a frustrated need for love from a powerful person. Distrust of happiness is traditional and amounts to what may be called "Japanese masochism." Crowded living stresses simple pleasures. Traditional *giri* (duty toward statuses) tends to deny individuality; the ethics of respect for the individual conflict with submission. In contrast with Japan's remarkable technological progress, revision of patterns of human relations proceeds slowly.

S. N. Eisenstadt, sociologist, regards Israeli collective identity as developing from some basic ideological-revolutionary premises. It faces many new problems. The central issue has been the extent to which commitments to broader values and to collective responsibility can be maintained in the wake of the weakening of specific ideological commitments and orientations. Eisenstadt points out that the changing Israeli identity has been able to absorb to some extent the tensions and problems developing from growing technologization and professionalization. The extent to which a continuous, peaceful transformation of Israeli identity will be able to overcome the eroding tendencies is the most crucial problem facing Israeli society.

There is one common denominator in all this growing scientific research on twentieth-century national character and its changes under the impact of new conditions. Technologization has led to important modifications in the basic qualities of peoples everywhere, from the already industrialized countries to the emergent nations seeking to adjust themselves to new economic situations. In addition, class and ethnic differences play an essential role in the major changes taking place in national character.

Added to the scientific studies are popular analyses which find a ready market. Inspired by the travel explosion, people visit other countries, but instead of becoming more internationalist they remain even more convinced nationalists than before. They are fascinated by popular treatises on the national character of others, such as Luigi Barzini on the Italians, Sanche de Gramont on the French, Adolph Schalk on the Germans, and Anthony Sampson on the British. A recent study concerned with the "presentments of Englishry" gives this odd mixture of stereotypes and salient traits: affection for vegetation and minerals; love for animals (horses and birds); apathy toward children; fear of intellectuals and experts; a passion for amateurs and committees; universal love of gambling; affection for the losers; and peculiar notions of sex.[10] The author calls his book "an essay in discovery."

Notes

[1] From an interview between Herman Kahn and the British scholar, G. R. Urban, in *The New York Times Magazine,* June 20, 1971, p. 22.

[2] Geoffrey Gorer, "National Character: Theory and Practice," in *The Study of Culture at a Distance,* ed. Margaret Mead and Rhoda Métraux (Chicago: University of Chicago Press, 1953), p. 57.

[3] Alexis de Tocqueville, *The Old Regime and the French Revolution,* trans. Stuart Gilbert (Garden City, New York: Doubleday, 1955), p. 8.

[4] G. W. F. Hegel, *The Philosophy of History,* trans. J. Sibree (New York: Wiley, 1944), p. 50.

[5] Hamilton Fyfe, *The Illusion of National Character* (London: C. A. Watts, 1940), p. 3.

[6] *Ibid.,* p. 9.

[7] Salvador de Madariaga, *Englishmen, Frenchmen, Spaniards: An Essay in Comparative Psychology* (London: Oxford University Press, 1928), p. x.

[8] A. J. P. Taylor, *The Course of German History* (New York: Coward-McCann, 1946), p. 13.

[9] Don Martindale (ed.), "National Character in the Perspective of the Social Sciences," in *The Annals of the American Academy of Political and Social Science,* vol. 270 (March 1967).

[10] Anthony Glyn, *The British: Portrait of a People* (New York: Putnam, 1970), *passim.*

6

Birth Pangs: The Libertarian Impulse in England and France

It became increasingly apparent [that] the French Revolution introduced new possibilities in the use of political power, and transformed the ends for which rulers must legitimately work. The Revolution meant that if the citizens of a state no longer approved of the political arrangements of their society, they had the right and the power to replace them by others more satisfactory.

—Elie Kedourie

The Dawn of Nationalism in Europe

Modern nationalism is not a brand new phenomenon: it is rather a revival and amalgamation of older trends. It existed in crude form in the tribalism of primitive peoples. Subsequently, tribal nationalism was submerged for the most part in metropolitanism (attachment to a city-state or cultural center) or to localism (loyalty to the village or region, akin to modern ruralism or regionalism). Ancient peoples held allegiance to their city-state, Athens, Sparta, or Corinth. Even so, there was a vague sense of national sentiment—Philip of Macedon had to prove his qualifications as a Greek before he could participate in the Olympic Games. Rome ruled a huge empire, and a patriotic impulse emanated from the central city.

Elements of nationalism existed in the Middle Ages among peoples with kindred tongues, customs, and traditions. Feudal lords gave their allegiance to king, not country, but even here there was a kind of national sentiment. After the loss of Normandy, King John's barons, almost all of whom had joint holdings, had to settle whether they were French or English. Those who stayed with John retained a strong sense of what they were. In the thirteenth and fourteenth centuries, Englishmen strongly criticized such "foreigners" as Gascon in-laws of the king.

Yet this sort of group cohesion was more closely related to localism than to what became modern nationalism. The sense of nationalism was crystallized in modern times as the nation-state emerged, when loyalty to country became the dominant political concern of all classes. The urge was there in medieval times, but the formation was modern.

A distinction should be made between the rise of national states and the emergence of modern nationalism. The formation of the national state was one of the factors that marked the end of the Middle Ages and the beginning of modern times. In this historical process the international Roman Catholic Church lost its preeminent position in the governing structure of Europe and was succeeded by a combination of units called nations. Politically, the transformation denoted the change from kinship to national state; economically, the change was conterminous with the Commercial Revolution; socially, the new course was parallel with the surge to prominence of the bourgeoisie; and religiously, the rise of national states was accompanied by the appearance of modern secular civilization.

Great events—the Renaissance and the Reformation among them—took place during the rise of national states. Though the movement was inchoate, it moved in a common direction. Europeans still maintained a sense of loyalty to town, village, or region. For centuries the man who was asked his identity would reply that he was a Christian, a member of the Catholic Church centered at Rome. If asked "Whose man are you?" he would answer: "I am a villein of Lord So-and-So,'' or ''I am a Breton farmer,'' or ''I am the King's officer.'' He adhered automatically to manor, town, district, or arrondissement: he was born and died within its confines and never considered anything other than a local loyalty. At some point he began to take on a sense of national consciousness.

There was nothing ''natural'' or ''preordained'' or ''inevitable'' about this pattern by which it became fashionable to say ''I am a Frenchman'' or ''I am a Belgian.'' It was, in fact, accidental, unplanned—it just happened that way. The building of modern nationalism was an artificial, man-made phenomenon. Man remains a single species and there is no scientific evidence that the kind of cleavage that distinguishes nationalism is normal or natural or even desirable. Yet political or diplomatic relations between peoples are often based on assumed national differences as well as fear of the outsider. Though men everywhere face similar life tasks and the same cultural goals, their sense of national consciousness leads them into confrontation, war, and barbarities. Nationalism of this kind has had tragic implications for the contemporary (and temporary) residents of this planet.

From Small Acorns: Beginnings in England

The roots of English national consciousness lay deep. Love of country was long an essential element of the English character. As early as the middle of the sixteenth century the sentiment had crystallized to a point where most Englishmen were imbued with a sense of national pride. Shakespeare recognized the spirit. In *Henry V* the King speaks to ''you, good yeomen, whose limbs were made in England,'' and urged the cry ''God for Harry! England! and St. George!'' In *Richard II* are the stirring words of ''This Blessed Plot'':

> This royal throne of kings, this sceptred isle,
> This earth of majesty, this seat of Mars,
> This other Eden, demi-paradise,
> This fortress built by Nature for herself
> Against infection and the hand of war,
> This happy breed of men, this little world,
> This precious stone set in the silver sea,
> Which serves it in the office of a wall
> Or as a moat defensive to a house,
> Against the envy of less happier lands,—
> This blessed plot, this earth, this realm, this England.

By the seventeenth century those elements, which in combination make up the marrow of nationalism, were present in England. The land had been united in the days of William the Conqueror. As feudalism on the Continent took on a disintegrated form, in England it was consolidated and civilianized and, therefore, more inducive to the formation of a territorially compact unit. A common language was molded, from *Beowulf* to Chaucer to Shakespeare, and a literature appeared in which the aspirations of the nation were expressed. There were common historical traditions and national heroes. The Reformation was a national issue. All these characteristics were bound together in a consciousness of nationalism that was to withstand the ravages of revolution.

There were religious, political, and social patterns in early English nationalism. The religious element was basic. The Anglican Church was cast in a revolutionary mold, quite unlike any other religious movement. It showed little interest in the Great Unknown of the other world. It was an intensely practical religion, independent, interested in whatever took place on English soil, especially such vital material pursuits as government, banking, and social welfare. The Bible-reading Englishman took pride in his social activism and he was certain that his stand against tyranny had divine sanction. He worshiped God but he also loved his country. Modern secularism had its roots in this essentially religious movement.

The second major quality of early English nationalism was enervated by its accent on political liberty for the individual. In the process by which popular loyalty passed from kingship to the national state, English nationalism took on the mantle of libertarianism. A scintillating beacon was John Milton's prose pamphlet *Areopagitica* (1644), a strong protest against restricting the freedom of the press. Milton beseeched the Lords and Commons to "consider what Nation it is whereof ye are, and whereof ye are the governors." It was not a nation slow and dull, "but of a quick, ingenious, and piercing spirit, acute to invent, subtle and sinewy to discourse, not beneath the reach of any point the highest that humanity can soar to." Milton saw this nation as chosen before any other to sound forth the first tidings and trumpet of the Reformation to all Europe. It was "the mansion house of liberty." Certainly it was a matter of national pride that freedom be maintained in this blessed of all nations. "Give me the liberty to know. . . ."

Milton's combination of national pride and individual liberty became a message that was to be transmitted to all corners of the globe as a gift of the English mind and as the essence of civilized life. The new and popular nationalism, dedicated to individual liberty, was promoted from several directions: by the seventeenth-century John Locke, Whig, and the eighteenth-century Lord Bolingbroke, Tory.

Locke and Bolingbroke were theorists who expounded the idea of a libertarian nationalism. But added to theory was a most practical political matter, the gradual evolution of English parliamentarianism. The process was slow and at times discouraging, but at bottom parliamentarianism reflected a deep desire for a free society. Indeed, on a comparative basis, the emergence of Parliament from the fifteenth century onward as a territorial, rather than a tribal assembly, was of tremendous importance in the course of English nationalism. Some observers of the British scene are inclined to give more credit to this very real historical phenomenon than to the theories of Locke and Bolingbroke.

Added to religious and political factors of early English nationalism was a social trend which imbued all classes with pride in being English, in speaking the English language, and in possessing English traditions. English kings, sensitive to the rise of nationalism, sought to maintain their power by cooperating with the rising middle class against both feudal lords and cosmopolitan ecclesiastics. The upper classes, retaining their strength in Parliament, considered themselves to be the true guardians of English nationalism. The aristocratic Englishman was inclined to identify his own well-being with national interests.

The middle class, too, was much concerned with the emergent nationalism. Since the days of the Tudor monarchy, the self-confident bourgeoisie had been the beneficiary of the churning new social forces unleashed by the Commercial Revolution, with its steadily developing capitalism. The middle class was agreeably affected by the expansion of trade. By the seventeenth century this energetic class had accumulated great wealth and was beginning to seek political power commensurate with its economic status. Like the aristocrats, the bourgeoisie tended to identify wealth with the welfare of the nation.

The masses, too, became absorbed by national identity. Here there was no conscious rationalization of the meaning of nationalism, as had been typical of the aristocracy and the bourgeois *nouveaux riches*. The English masses found it easy to accept the spirit of nationalism—flag, anthem, heroes, music-hall patriotism.

Thus all English classes, from villagers to Cockneys to aristocrats, wrapped themselves in the mantle of national dignity. It was by no means a trickle-down nationalism by which a sense of national consciousness was imposed from above and then permeated the triangular social order from top to bottom. Rather it was a widespread acceptance by all classes of Shakespeare's paean to "this realm, this England."

There were worldwide repercussions. By the eighteenth century England was an enormously prestigious global power, admired and envied everywhere as a forward-looking national state and as the great innovator of modern civilization. The English idea of nationalism within a framework of historic liberties was studied and copied throughout the world. In comparing and contrasting the course of nationalism in modern times the English experience remains of vital significance.

The French Revolution and the Awakening of Nationalism

The decade from 1789 to 1799, one of the great turning points in history, marked the culmination of dynamic forces that created a modern state out of an outworn, creaking structure. Both nationalism and democracy appeared in France in their modern form. Change was the keynote. Politically, the monarchy was abolished and the democratic state was placed on a national foundation. Religiously, the Roman Catholic Church lost its powerful position in French society and, as a price for its continued existence, was forced to serve national ends. Socially and economically, the privileges of the aristocracy and the clergy were abolished as the middle class won its way to a dominant position in the power structure. All these developments took place in a milieu of revolutionary fervor, to the stirring tune of the *Marseillaise* and in common with the watchwords "Liberty! Equality! Fraternity!" From the storming of the Bastille in 1789 to the guillotine execution of Robespierre the Incorruptible in 1794, events cascaded in a torrent of emotion.

As always in history, behind the fireworks of revolutionary activism was a decisive intellectual trend. French *philosophes* of the Enlightenment, consciously or unconsciously, prepared the way for the explosion at the barricades. Among the thinkers at work were the "big three"—Voltaire on the Church, Montesquieu on the law, Rousseau on socio-political structures. Dissatisfied with their society and environment, they denounced the stratified system of privileges supported by the Old Regime. Their call for a greater sense of justice and tolerance ran straight through the social structure. Even aristocrats toyed with the ideas of the *philosophes* in elaborately formalized salon conversation. The call for reform was easily translated into understandable language for the common man, who still had to pay the outmoded salt tax and who saw his supply of bread dwindling in a virtually bankrupt society. In towns and villages, local schoolteachers and priests combined to bring the printed work of reformers to illiterate townsmen and peasants.

Voltaire, authentic and inspired voice of the age in which he lived, epitomized the skepticism of the Enlightenment in his aversion to the "superstition" of the Church and the papacy. His sharpest darts were directed against religion, which he attempted to ridicule out of existence. In 1761 the Parlement of Toulouse, encouraged by the religious passions of the community, condemned the Huguenot Jean Calas to torture and death for the alleged murder of his son. Certain that Calas was innocent, Voltaire worked for three years to make the local affair a European *cause célèbre*, and eventually obtained a reversal of the verdict. His championship of Calas brought out the evils of religious intolerance. Voltaire's works became the main source of inspiration for the anti-clerical movement that was to play an important role in subsequent French history. He singlehandedly did much to stimulate the separation of Church and state as well as the enhanced spirit of nationalism that came with it. Neither he nor his followers wanted control from Rome.

In his *The Spirit of the Laws* (1748), Montesquieu noted a close connection between love of country and the republican form of government. The laws of education in every state, he said, ought to be maintained in relation to the principles of that government. He defined education as "that which is received in entering upon the world and not that of parents and of schoolmasters. In republics education ought to inspire a sentiment which is noble but hard to be maintained—namely, that disregard of one's own interest whence arises the love of one's country." He saw love of country as peculiar to democracies, for in democracies alone the government is entrusted to private citizens. "Now a government is like everything else: to preserve it we must love it."

Similarly, Rousseau rejected aristocracy in favor of democracy as the valued core of the nation. He urged every citizen to love his country. "It is not walls nor men," he said, "that make the Fatherland: it is the laws, the morals, the customs, the government, the constitution, the mode of existence resulting from all these things. The Fatherland is in the relations of the State to its members. When these relationships change or come to nothing, the Fatherland vanishes." In his *Letter to d'Alembert* (1758), Rousseau urged that citizens be trained by simple public spectacles, pageants, and folk games to become conscious of national unity. "The general effect of the theatre is to strengthen the natural inclinations, and to give a new energy to all the passions."

Rousseau wrote his *Considérations sur le gouvernement de Pologne* (1772) at the request of a Polish nobleman who wanted to know how national patriotism might be intensified. The tract was one of the first systematic expressions of a conscious and calculated nationalism. Rousseau pointed out that "national institutions . . . inspire the people with that ardent love of Fatherland based on ineradicable habits." He recommended that citizens be educated "from mother's milk to death" on the idea of the nation. He believed that the instilling of patriotism through education was an absolute necessity. The essay became a kind of guidebook for the new democratic nationalism.

Thus, in his own way, each of the big three of the French Enlightenment contributed to the rising sense of national consciousness. Their ideas were translated into action by revolutionaries. Just as in England the Puritans, with their zeal for a new material-spiritual life, left an indelible stamp on the course of English nationalism, so in France did the Jacobins, with their call for individualism and democracy, leave an imprint on French nationalism. There was a quickened sense of national unity in the dramatic days of the Revolution. The citizen building a new society was expected "to be born, to live, and to die for the Fatherland." "This delightful land which we inhabit," intoned the Incorruptible, "and which nature caresses with love, is made to be the domain of liberty and happiness." Citizens would be patriotic, free, and happy, or else Robespierre would send them to the guillotine.

The revolutionaries were so entranced by their new democratic nationalism that they were quick to offer their experience to all the peoples of Europe. Their own army, the *levée en masse,* would rise in all its pride and glory to defend the fatherland against the traitorous *émigrés*. The French sword would bring the blessings of "Liberty! Equality! Fraternity!" to all Europe. In December 1792 the National Convention expressed it by decree:

The French nation . . . will treat as enemies every people who, refusing liberty and equality or renouncing them, may wish to maintain, recall, or treat with a prince and privileged classes; on the other hand, it engages not to subscribe to any treaty and not to lay down arms until after the establishment of the sovereignty and independence of the people whose territory the troops of the [French] Republic shall have entered and until the people shall have adopted the principles of equality and founded a free and democratic government.

Napoleon—Disseminator of Nationalism

The ideals of the revolutionaries were precise, but the Revolution itself was chaotic. The French felt that they needed a strong man who could maintain the achievements on the barricades and at the same time provide the citizens with order and stability. In an age of individualism a powerful individual could assume the task of defending the frontiers of the young republic. Perhaps he could be found in the young officer corps.

Indeed, there he was—a young man who fancied himself a potential military genuis, diplomatic wizard, and masterful statesman, and who believed in his star of destiny. An opportunist, the officer was ambitious for himself, for his family, and for France, in that order. Napoleon Bonaparte was to rise to power, harness the dynamic forces of the Revolution, and give France a decade of glory, followed by humiliating defeat.

Napoleon had known patriotic sentiment as a Corsican lad, but it was a patriotism directed against France. As a young officer he abandoned this sense of localism and embraced the cause of revolution. Once in power, he considered himself the logical successor of the enlightened monarchs, but, unlike them, he regarded himself as the master and not the servant of the state. The complete individualist, he misunderstood both the meaning of liberty and national consciousness that had emerged in the Revolution. He had little use for nationalism as a popular force unless it could be directed for his own use.

The great man would have been astonished had he been told that he was the catalytic agent who would unconsciously plant the seeds of nationalism throughout Europe. He was interested in conquest, not in disseminating the new ism for the benefit of other peoples. He urged his troops forward in one campaign after another in the belief that they were conferring the blessings of the French Revolution on lesser breeds. Actually, what Napoleon conceived to be altruism was regarded by others as immoral and satanic.

Thus Napoleon's rule in the story of developing nationalism must be placed within the framework of his own character and personality. He was totally eclectic in his approach to power—he tried everything. Always conscious of his special audience, he was a Muslim sympathizer when in Egypt, a devout Catholic when conversing with the Pope, just the right skeptic when in polite society. For him, nationalism was merely another historical phenomenon to be used in his own drive for the acquisition and maintenance of power. He took the revolutionary nationalism, which had already become somewhat weaker under the Directory, infused strength into it under his Consulate, and began to sponsor "new nations" subservient to his will. As his power solidified, he went further into the family dynastic game, awarding high positions to his brothers and in-laws in the new European family of nations. His aged mother was, perhaps, more aware than he of the precarious nature of the Napoleonic structure: in the Tuileries, it was said, she would wring her hands and cry: "If this would only last!"

Wherever the conqueror went he left imprints of his heel. Europeans everywhere supported their own sovereigns to resist what they called "a revolution gone crazy" in the hands of the French leader. Not until Hitler appeared was any national figure so roundly hated as was Napoleon. Witness this ode by Southey (1810):

> Who counsels peace at this momentous hour,
> When God hath given deliverance to the oppress'd,
>   And to the injured power?
> Who counsels peace, when Vengeance like a flood
> Rolls on, no longer now to be repress'd:
>   When innocent blood
> From the four corners of the world cries out
>   For justice upon one accursed head?

Comparatively speaking, the French experience stands in contrast to that of the English. Under the Napoleonic regime, French nationalism became more identified with militarism than with liberty, a development different from English libertarian nationalism. In the process, the French found themselves losing that special political democracy and individual liberty that they had described as fruits of their precious Revolution. Instead, they were chagrined to find themselves clamped in a rigid military dictatorship. In place of their lost liberty they had to be satisfied with Napoleonic glory.

This was, in fact, the special meaning of Napoleon's career—he had set an example for the potentialities of force, a cult that was to find many adherents in extremist movements a century after his death. Advocate of the philosophy that strength is neither error nor illusion but "naked truth," Napoleon foreshadowed the twentieth-century totalitarians. After his death, for the remainder of the nineteenth century and during the twentieth century, liberal nationalism continued to exist side by side with the more militaristic form inspired by Napoleon. Would-be autocrats found inspiration in the career of the Corsican adventurer.

To the day of his death Napoleon remained unaware of his decisive role in the spread of nationalism. He encouraged national sentiment in Italy and Poland only because he saw it as a boon for his own empire and projected dynasty. As the new Caesar or Charlemagne, he demanded loyalty from conquered peoples: he had no intention of encouraging their nationalism for their own good.

In conversation with the Comte de Las Cases, who shared his exile at St. Helena, Napoleon reminisced about the meaning of his career. People, he complained, had always spoken of his love for war, but he had always engaged in self-defense. Did he not immediately make proposals for peace after each of his victories? He had held the helm with a vigorous hand, "but the fury of the waves was greater than any force I could exert in resisting them . . . . I was never truly my own master, but was always controlled by circumstances." What he really wanted to do was to bind the nations in a United States of Europe. It was his intention to incorporate thirty millions of French, fifteen millions of Spanish, fifteen millions of Italians, and thirty millions of Germans into one nation. "It would have been a noble thing," he said, "to have advanced into posterity with such a train, and attended by the blessings of future ages."

Napoleon thought himself worthy of this glory, of "this grand, magnificent spectacle," of "this perspective of power, greatness, happiness, and prosperity," but others did not. It never occurred to the great man that non-Frenchmen might prefer their own way of life to the blessings of his contemplated imperial presidency of the United States of Europe. They were just not interested in his grand design "to simplify their monstrous complications." Instead of unifying Europeans under his banner, the conqueror, without actually wanting it, gave impetus and strength to rising nationalism throughout Europe.

At the same time, Napoleon extended for France the principles inherited from the Revolution. These principles involved constitutions, a declaration of rights, elected assemblies, political participation, and—above all—a consciousness of national unity. The legal chaos of the Old Regime was supplanted by a uniform, centralized system of departments, prefects, courts, and trial by jury—all of which meant that France was a nation and no longer a loose collection of provinces. When the restored Bourbon Louis XVIII accepted the Constitutional Charter of 1814, he was "Louis, by the grace of God, King of France and of Navarre." He was "King of the Nation," and France became an enduring nation-state.

The Early Beacons

In summary, nationalism received its most powerful early stimulus in mid-seventeenth-century England, the first modern nation in which linguistic, political, economic, and religious patterns merged. From its beginnings, English nationalism was identified with that idea of individual liberty epitomized in the political philosophy of John Locke.

Historical movements, however, are seldom monistic. The English experience should be compared and contrasted with developments elsewhere. Added to the English Revolution of 1688 were the key dates 1776 and 1789—the great landmarks of the American and French revolutions. The American Revolution proclaimed the principle of sovereignty as residing essentially in the nation. The French Revolution asserted nationalism as a revolutionary force among a people who had enjoyed little political freedom. The French version of nationalism was to take on a missionary coloration in its travels through Europe.

7

Force for Unification: Germany and Italy

Where is the German's Fatherland?
Name me at length that mighty land!
"Where'er resounds the German tongue,
"Where'er its hymns to God are sung."
Be this the land,
Brave Germans, this thy Fatherland!

—Ernst Moritz Arndt

The Ism Takes Divergent Courses

It is an indication of the fluidity and chameleon-like quality of nationalism that it acts in different ways, according to the politico-cultural climate in which it operates. Nationalism can be both a force for unification and a mechanism for disruption. The comparative historian observes how it stimulated German and Italian unity, but it was a disintegrative factor in the conglomerate Austro-Hungarian Empire.

England and France made their appearance as consolidated national states in the early modern period and the process was intensified through the nineteenth century. But early in that century a sense of national identity escaped the Germans and Italians. There was really no Germany or Italy, but rather "the Germanies" or "the Italies," both geographical expressions and composed of feudal fragments. In each case nationalism provided the cement for unification several centuries after other countries had attained their unity.

The Role of Herder

In the last third of the eighteenth century, Johann Gottfried Herder, poet and philosopher, played a most influential role in the rise of nationalism, both in the West and in the Germanies. Although not a nationalist in the modern sense of the word, Herder, Rousseau's German disciple, projected an ideology which deeply affected nationalist thought. The key to his thinking is to be found in his idea of national life as an organic growth. He depicted the history of mankind as a series of national organisms, each holding its own characteristic society, language, religion, literature, and art. Each one, in its own way, enriched mankind as a whole. "Every nationality," he said, "bears in itself the standard of its perfection, totally independent of all comparison with that of others." He developed the theory of the folk spirit (*Volksgeist*) and the national spirit (*Nationalgeist*) and spoke of their roots in the long chain of history. The creative forces of the universal, he said, individualized themselves not in the single human being but in the collective personalities of human communities. Men were above all members of their national communities. As manifestations of the creative spirit, Herder pointed to folk songs and folk lore and urged that they be no longer neglected.

Herder, the enlightened humanitarian, was by no means a propagandist for the creation of a German national state, nor for German national unification. He showed no partiality toward the Germans: to him, each nation reflected the divine will and was, therefore, a sacred concept to be cultivated. But he did exhort the German people to cultivate their national characteristics and avoid imitation of any ancient or modern nationalities. His praise for the native and the nation made him the prophet and precursor of the Romantic movement.

Nations and fatherlands, said Herder, should think only in terms of peaceful coexistence. He had no use for princes and states which thought of war, politics, and power. True nationalism, he believed, would promote the cause of peace. He had no way of knowing that, under the impact of the French Revolution and the Napoleonic conqueror, the kind of cultural nationalism he espoused would eventually turn into the bitter, aggressive nationalism of the nineteenth century. Despite his own wishes, Herder was elected to that grand body of enlightened thinkers whose ideas became subjected to pathological exaggeration.

The French Conqueror and Early German Nationalism

It is one of those curious facts of history—in 1789 the Germanies were a combination of exactly 1,789 independent sovereign powers, consisting of 314 states and 1,475 estates. These varied in size from the kingdom of Prussia (a product of the shrewd Hohenzollern dynasty and the bellicose Junker class) to medium-size and tiny principalities, each of which maintained its own government, army, flag, and system of tariffs. Kings, dukes, and margraves squabbled among themselves in defense of their rights. Some drove their states to bankruptcy in the hopeless task of imitating Louis XIV's magnificent Versailles. Building a healthy national state out of this crazy-quilt pattern was a problem of the first magnitude.

The French Revolution sent a wave of hysteria through German courts. German rulers denounced the events in Paris as insurrection run wild, and they trembled in the knowledge that a similar storm might break out in their own lands. At first the exciting ideas from Paris enjoyed some popularity among the educated class, but most Germans were disillusioned by the Reign of Terror, its anarchy, and its disregard of life and property. The seeds of rationalism—constitutionalism, liberalism, cosmopolitanism—did not take firm root in German soil. Trapped between the ideals of the libertarian West and the authoritarian East, the Germans remained suspended in a fatal dichotomy.

The initial stimulus for German nationalism came from the outside. Napoleon, always working in his own interest, altered the map and set the boundaries of the South German states much as they would exist in the twentieth century. On the principle of *divide et impera,* he shored up the smaller states at the expense of the larger. The rulers of Bavaria, Württemberg, Baden, and Saxony, deeming it better to ally themselves with the devil rather than fight him, adopted a honeyed servility, which they believed would act to their advantage.

It was methodical interference. As early as 1803 Napoleon established a glorified real estate office in Paris with the aim of redistributing the German ecclesiastical states and free cities among the secular princes. He reduced the number of sovereign German states to about thirty. Next he united the German states which he had created or enlarged into a permanent Confederation of the Rhine (July 21, 1806), "forever separated from the territory of the Germanic Empire." A few days later he sent a tough message to the Imperial Diet announcing the end of the Holy Roman Empire. Francis II abdicated as Holy Roman Emperor, but retained the title of Francis I, Emperor of Austria. Thus, by Napoleonic interference, the old German Empire, in existence for almost a thousand years, vanished, and the independence of the states that had grown up on its territory was legally recognized. Napoleonic power had formalized the end of theocracy in the Germanies. The consolidation was to survive Napoleon's downfall and pave the way for national unification.

The shadowy old Holy Roman Empire was supposed to be ended by Napoleonic fiat, but at the same time, as A. J. P. Taylor has pointed out, there remained something of a Reich. It always included either too little or too much. The Reich itself was a problem in German nationalism, for it included non-Germans and left out Germans.

Whatever the disposition of the idea of a Reich, Napoleon nourished the germs of nationalism. The key factor was Prussia. In 1805 Napoleon went to war against England, Russia, and Austria, and won a great victory at Austerlitz. Prussia, despite violation of her territory by French troops, avoided entering the war against Napoleon, and even came to an understanding with him. The hitherto cautious Frederick William III allowed himself to be carried away by the war party in Berlin. The timid Teutonic poodle suddenly decided to attack the giant French mastiff. Napoleon was delighted—he now saw an opportunity for a reckoning with Prussia.

The ensuing conflict was short and decisive. Napoleon arrived in Franconia with 200,000 fervent warriors and inflicted disastrous defeats on the Prussians at Jena and Auerstadt (October 1806). The Prussians gave way in wild panic as the French surged into Berlin; they seized the Victory Monument on Brandenburg Tor and sent it back to Paris as a war trophy. Frederick William fled to Königsberg. Prussia lost half her territory and had to pay an enormous indemnity. It was the most humiliating defeat in Prussian history up to that time, but it was not a complete disaster. Out of it emerged a powerful sense of German nationalism.

The Regeneration of Prussia

Hatred of Napoleon was especially intense in Prussia. Here the vacillating Frederick William III finally came to the conclusion that the only way to match or defeat the French was to imitate them. Granted, the Revolution with its extraordinary reforms had brought a new vigor to the French people. The Prussians would seek a similar set of reforms, but they would change "not through a violent impulsion from within but through the wisdom of those in authority." Prussia would revise her whole social structure by a revolution from above.

At the fulcrum of the reform movement was Karl Freiherr vom und zu Stein, imperial knight of Nassau, whose contempt for "foreigners" had led him into service for the Prussian state. "I hate the French," he admitted, "as much as it is allowed a Christian to hate." He urged the complete overhaul of the Prussian bureaucracy. The king came to the conclusion that his assistant was "intractable, obstinate, and disobedient," and dismissed him, only to recall his "eccentric official" ten months later. In October 1807 Frederick William III, at vom Stein's urging, issued a key reform edict: "From Martinmas 1810 all serfdom shall end throughout our entire realm." The royal decree, cautious in tone, made it clear that most powers of the landed nobility would be retained under the king's protection. Together with Karl August von Hardenberg, vom Stein was responsible for a series of edicts eliminating medieval economic restrictions, establishing a new system of municipal self-government, and creating a more efficient bureaucracy.

Meanwhile, David van Scharnhorst, assisted by August Wilhelm von Gneisenau, reorganized the Prussian army and introduced military conscription and a reserve system. Karl Wilhelm von Humboldt inaugurated education reforms designed to increase the authority of the state.

All these reforms, though couched in the language of liberalism, were meant actually to make Prussia the most powerful German state. They were successful, but in preparing the way for German nationalism they also gave a special character to the Prussian system. Militarism was solidified and education was geared to service to the state. There were but few concessions to democratic egalitarianism. The Prussian way of life, distinguished by accent not on individual freedom but on the ideal of authority, *die Obrigkeit*, was later welded on Germany as a whole.

In this way German nationalism was born and nurtured, in the darkness of Napoleonic despotism. Ironically, it was an outside autocrat who was responsible for igniting the flame of German nationalism. By abolishing medieval rule in the Germanies, Napoleon, without wishing it, contributed to the rise of German national sentiment.

The Impact of German Romanticism

Closely allied with the rise of German nationalism was romanticism, a Europe-wide movement which had an especially strong effect in the Germanies. Conservative European intellectuals reacted against what they called "the self-evident dictates of pure reason," as well as against the excesses of the French Revolution. They began to use old ideas to fight the principles of 1789. Romanticism stressed the emotional side of human nature, exalting faith and intuition instead of the intellect. It issued a plea for the claims of the imagination, for individualism, for the national genius in all its aspects. Philosophical romanticism turned into transcendental idealism, always with accent on the emotions—ideals, spirit, and faith—and reflecting that same confidence the rationalists had bestowed on the intellectual faculties. By the end of the eighteenth century the terms "imaginative," "extraordinary," and "visionary" became more and more familiar in German literary and political life.

Romanticism found fertile ground in the Germanies. In the 1770s a youthful cult, called *Sturm und Drang* (Storm and Stress), represented a combination of the new tendencies: intuition and mysticism, return to nature, and love for the vague and mysterious. At the same time it denounced "sterile rationalism" (*Vernünftelei*) as an invention of the "pygmy French." In the early nineteenth century these interests were popularized in a political romanticism which represented a reaction against that democratic rationalism that was held responsible for the tragic immoderateness of the French Revolution. German romantics looked back with envy at the great past, to the days of order, security, and legitimacy. They longed for the happy times of the old Holy Roman Empire.

This was the special nature of German romanticism: politically, its interest in the past was linked with the rising sense of national spirit stimulated by hatred for Napoleon. German scholars turned to the study of national laws, institutions, and language to prove that German culture was rooted deeply in history. They would draw strength from German antiquity, from the German landscape, from German art forms. They contemptuously rejected their own age as barren in feeling and imagination, and steeped themselves instead in the obscure mysticism of the past. What they wanted was not French universalism and world citizenship but a new Germany, with its citizens valiant, truthful, pure, courageous—a kind of fanatical idealization of views originally presented by Tacitus. All this harmonized with the rising sense of national consciousness.

This advocacy of national genius led to romantic claims of Teutonic superiority. Later, in more blatant form, it was to become the theme of Hitler's National Socialism, distinguished by its perverted view of the Nietzschean superman, its romanticized myth of a "pure" Aryan race, its anti-rational emphasis on "thinking with the blood," its naive anti-intellectualism, and its glorification of militarism.

Outstanding among the legion of German romantics was the trio of Arndt,

Fichte, and Jahn. Ernst Moritz Arndt, born in 1769 (the same year as Napoleon), was raised in an atmosphere of freedom and abundance. In 1800 he became an instructor in the University of Greifswald, and was raised to the rank of professor within six years. Napoleon was the object of his contempt and hatred. In poems, pamphlets, and songs he attempted to arouse a crusading spirit against the French conqueror. He condemned German princes for "selling their souls into bondage" and demanded that all Germans unite to smash the French stranglehold. Forced to flee from French agents, he encouraged his countrymen from exile. The defeats of Jena and Auerstadt, he said, were not the last word in German destiny. "It is possible," he said, "to defeat Napoleon with his own weapons. His soldiers are ordinary mortals, and as soldiers, no less brave than Hungarians, Austrians, and Swedes. . . . German generals! Trust and believe in your men. They are firm, stout-hearted, loyal and courageous. When the final reckoning comes, they must be inspired by justice and the Fatherland!"

In 1807 Arndt issued this "Appeal to the Germans":

German man, feel again God, hear and fear the eternal, and you hear and fear also your *Volk;* you feel again in God the honor and dignity of your fathers, their glorious history rejuvenates itself in you, their firm and gallant virtue reblossoms in you, the whole German Fatherland stands again before you in the august halo of past centuries. . . .

No longer Catholics and Protestants, no longer Prussians and Austrians, Saxons and Bavarians, Silesians and Hanoverians, no longer of different faith, different mentality, and different will—be Germans, be one, will to be one by love and loyalty, and no devil will vanquish you.

A similar combination of nationalism and romanticism was expressed by Johann Gottlieb Fichte, a German philosopher of Swedish descent. Awarded the chair of philosophy at Jena in 1794, he won quick recognition for his brilliant lectures. After his appointment as rector of the new University of Berlin in 1810, he spent the rest of his life there. During the winter of 1807–1808, when German morale was at a low point after the Napoleonic victories, Fichte delivered fourteen "Addresses to the German Nation," in which he urged resistance. He told his audiences that just as their German forefathers had refused to submit to Rome, so must they oppose the French conqueror. The Germans alone, he said, were capable of the highest perfection and they deserved the cultural leadership of the world. Among all the civilized peoples of Europe, only the Germans spoke an original tongue; all others—English, French, Spaniards, or Italians—had damaged their intellectual life by using an adopted or derived tongue. All other branches of the human race, "those we now regard as foreigners but who are actually our blood brothers, are indebted to the Germans for their very existence."

German freedom, said Fichte, should be established on the highest moral basis. It was important that the Germans be called to national regeneration because they had a world mission:

Our present problem . . . is simply to preserve the existence and continuity of what is German. All other differences vanish before this higher point of view. . . . It is essential that the higher love of the Fatherland, for the entire people of the German nation, reign supreme, and justly so, in every particular German state. No one of them can lose sight of the higher interest without alienating everything that is noble and good.

It was heady stuff, and Germans listened in rapture. Fichte's addresses, according to Friedrich Meinecke, "have been published, read, and become famous as one of the greatest beacons of our new German history."

The third of this odd trio of German romantics was Friedrich Ludwig Jahn, an eccentric demagogue who sought solace in the great legendary past. He called for a rebirth of the shattered morale of his countrymen. The best way to do it, he said, was to pay strict attention to physical well-being. Too many Germans had been infected with "Gallic cosmopolitanism" and had become soft and effeminate. They must use old Swedish exercises to heighten their physical and moral powers and become strong, self-assertive, and self-confident. There were far too many lambs in the world—Germans must become tigers. In his *Das deutsche Volkstum* (1810), Jahn glorified the German people as a divine, creative force:

Volkstum is the common character of a people, its inner being, its rules and life, its power of development, its power of progress. All peoples have their own peculiar thoughts and feelings, loves and hates, joys and sorrows, hopes and yearnings, ancestors, and beliefs. German means national. Our feeling of nationalism, or Germanness, has been disappearing more and more because of our sins. We must return to the lost past and re-create Nation, Germanness, Fatherland.

There were others who took a similar line, among them the Grimm brothers, Jakob Karl and Wilhelm Karl, who called attention to indigenous national literature; Friedrich von Schlegel, who described the Rhine as "the all-too-faithful image of our Fatherland, our history, and our character"; Adam Müller, who saw the state as infinitely greater than the individual and as the fountainhead of all life. To these may be added Schleiermacher, Friedrich Ernst Daniel Schleiermacher, patriotic pietist; Johann Ludwig Tieck, director of the Dresden Theatre; Novalis (Friedrich von Hardenberg), mystic poet; Karl Theodor Körner, composer of stirring war songs, and killed at the age of 22; and Friedrich Wilhelm Joseph von Schelling, idealistic philosopher. Especially effective was the Brandenburger poet and novelist Ludwig von Arnim, who was devotedly attached to the soil on which he was born, and who collected old popular legends and songs while traveling through Germany.

All these romantics contributed in their own way to the sentiment for an organic folk community. Most of them began to think of the German nation as an entity rather than as various isolated, particularistic units. The duty to develop a *national* German consciousness was postulated again and again. The romantics saw in the rebirth of the German nation the only hope of relief from chaos and confusion. Indeed, some romantics were so distressed by the submission to Napoleon that they gave up the struggle: Heinrich von Kleist, the first important German dramatist after Schiller, died by his own hand on the shore of the Wannsee near Potsdam in 1811. Others were tougher and devoted their skills to the mighty cultural destiny of the new German nation-in-being.

Much of the thrust of German romantic nationalism was anti-French, but there were other qualities engrained in it. It was also anti-aristocratic, anti-cosmopolitan; on occasion, anti-effete intellectual snobs. Nor did its proponents operate on the same plane. Included in the hodgepodge of motivations were both the impact of Fichte's *Reden,* addressed to university crowds, and Jahn's gymnastics, directed to the boy on the streets. The appeal of nationalism more often than not cuts through all levels of the social order.

On a comparative basis, English romanticism, sparked by Wordsworth, Byron, Keats, and Shelley, also called for obeisance to the imagination, but their work was dominantly cultural and aesthetic. German romanticism, on the other hand, wanted to be something more than a poetic image: it took on political overtones and became a means by which a struggle could be maintained against the principles of the French Revolution. The supercharged emotionalism associated with later German nationalism was due in part to the special nature of German romanticism.

War of Liberation, 1813–1815

Invigorated by reform, Prussia made an alliance in 1813 with Russia against Napoleon. There was still no German political entity: the only "German" force was the *Freikorps,* a band of patriotic volunteers in black uniforms. The position of Prussia was vital. Frederick William III, hitherto weak and unimaginative, suddenly emerged as a dynamic leader of his people. His proclamation to the Prussian troops at Breslau on March 17, 1813 ("Appeal to My People"), took advantage of the new consciousness of nationalism:

Many times in the past you have expressed the desire to fight for the freedom and independence of the Fatherland. That moment has now arrived! . . . You must

doubly feel your holy duty. Be mindful of it on the day of battle. . . . He who
feels for the Fatherland must not think of himself. . . . Victory comes from God!
Show yourselves worthy of His high protection by being obedient and loyal. Let
courage, endurance, loyalty, and strict order be your glory! . . . We also fight the
great battle for the independence of the Fatherland. . . . Let faith in God,
courage, and endurance be our solution!

Like a groggy prizefighter responding to the bell, Napoleon attacked the
Russians and Prussians, but now he also had to face the Austrians, and soon
he was opposed by almost the whole of Europe. At long last, he was defeated
at Waterloo, where Prussian troops under Marshal Blücher played an important part.

Drive to Economic Unity: The *Zollverein*

Germans were now freed from the Napoleonic yoke, only to face the
Austrian Metternich, a reactionary genius of Europe who was determined to
set the political clock back. German youth demanded a free and united
country. Student fraternities *(Burschenschaften)* pledged themselves to oppose tyrants at home as well as abroad, and particularly demanded an end to
Metternich's meddling from Vienna. On October 18, 1817, during the jubilee
year of the Protestant Revolt, students held a celebration at the Wartburg,
during which they consigned symbols of tyranny to the flames. On March 23,
1819, a fanatical student murdered a reactionary journalist who was suspected of being in the pay of the Russian Tsar. In response to these "insurrections," Metternich drew up the Carlsbad Decrees, establishing a rigid
censorship, providing for the supervision of students, and paving the way for
the arrest of vociferous patriots. He had had enough of revolutionary,
radical-minded Young Germany.

This political activity was matched in the economic sphere by a new drive
for unity. The German states in 1815 were burdened by a bewildering variety
of water, inland, and provincial tolls. In a chaotic tariff system, some 2,775
articles were subject to duties, collected by an army of 8,000 officials. The
merchant who traded between Hamburg and Vienna, or between Berlin and
Zurich, had to cross ten states, familiarize himself with ten different customs
duties, and pay ten successive tariffs. Prussia had 67 different tariffs, as well
as a plethora of currencies.

Something had to be done to remedy this deplorable situation. Gradually,
between 1818 and 1834, the *Zollverein,* or customs union, was fashioned to
achieve economic reform. There is some difference among scholars on the
origins of the *Zollverein.* Some feel that it owed little to theorists but was
rather the work of small-minded Prussian bureaucrats who were primarily
concerned with efficiency and economy. Others, including the present

writer, see the idea as proposed originally by Friedrich List, a Württemberger economist, and appropriated by Prussia for her own benefit. One by one the German states were forced into the Prussian economic orbit. Eventually, the *Zollverein* included 18 states in an area of 162,870 square miles and a population of 23,000,000—all under Prussian control. For Prussia, the customs union meant economic power and political prestige. Even more, she regarded the *Zollverein* as a means of winning the influential middle class to the cause of national unity.

And what about the originator of the idea? During his lifetime, List was battered and bruised, the target of unappreciative industrialists and the prey of the Austrian secret police. To Metternich, opposed to anything that tended to promote either Prussian or German nationalism, List was "a heroic swindler" and "a tool of squealing manufacturers." Even his fellow Germans at first called him "a revolutionary Jacobin" and a "demagogue." The attitude changed after List's death, when it became obvious to his countrymen that he had performed a distinct service. He was revered as a great German patriot-hero, as "a great German without Germany," as an economic genius who embodied the best of Cromwell, Canning, Dr. Quesnay, Robert Peel, and even Aristotle. Admirers pointed to his goal of a "practical, diligent, thrifty, enlightened, orderly, patriotic, and freedom-loving democracy." It was a belated tribute to the first German to express the national concept at the economic level.

1848: The Revolution a Failure

The Revolution of 1848 in France and the flight of Metternich from Vienna had important effects on the course of German nationalism. Germans, too, flocked to the barricades to demand a constitution and a national parliament. A self-constituted body of liberals, the first really representative assembly in German history, met at Frankfurt to frame a constitution for a united Germany. But there were overwhelming problems for the advocates of unity, such as the multiplicity of sovereignties, antagonism between Protestants and Catholics, and differences between north and south.

The key issue at Frankfurt was the rivalry between Prussia and Austria. There were bitter debates between the advocates of a *Grossdeutsch* (Great German) solution under Austrian auspices and the *Kleindeutsch* (Little German) state under Prussian control. There was no encouragement from the monarch. When Frederick William IV, the Prussian king, was offered the crown of a united Germany by the Frankfurt Assembly, he refused it on the ground that it came "from the gutter." Ridiculed as a parliament of professors, unable to achieve any agreement, the assembly, prodded by the drawn swords of the king's army, dispersed.

German nationalists were grievously disappointed by the failure of 1848. They recognized now a huge gap between the political aspirations of German liberals and the actual liberal influence. Overwhelmed by power politics, the liberals showed themselves to be too weak in the struggle to attain national unity. In the words of A. J. P. Taylor, "For the first time since 1521, the German people stepped to the center of the German stage only to miss their cues once more. German history reached its turning point and failed to turn. That was the fateful essence of 1848."

It was a tragic year for the Germans. On the surface it seemed that the elements of rationalism—liberalism, democracy, social contract, egalitarianism, tolerance, constitutionalism—were at long last converging in a common stream. For a brief moment decision-making power was out of the hands of the autocratic princes and in possession of liberals, who sought unity through persuasion—only to fail miserably. When the wave of revolution receded, liberal nationalism was buried in the dregs, and the Prusso-German symbiosis was triumphant. From then on the drive for German unification was to depend upon cohesion through power as well as dependence upon Prussian traditions of discipline, authority, and efficiency.

The old slogan *"Einheit, Freiheit, Macht"* ("Unity, Freedom, Power") lost its impact when *"Freiheit"* died, between 1848 and 1866. The Germans were not alone in this kind of historical irony: comparatively, the French, for their part, spent several centuries trying to square *égalité* with *fraternité*.

Bismarck—Manipulator of German Nationalism

German national unity was achieved not by the professors at Frankfurt but by a Pomeranian Junker. Otto von Bismarck was originally a Prussian patriot and he retained his preference for Prussia throughout his life. It was only during the Foundation Years of the Second German Reich that he took into account the necessities of nationalism. Nor was he interested in the pan-German program calling for union of all German-speaking peoples in the Austrian and Russian empires, in Switzerland and Holland. He would settle for a German nation under Prussian control.

Scholars interpret Bismarck's nationalism in various ways. Some say that he changed from Prussian to German nationalist and that he epitomized the qualities of traditional nationalism. Others hold to the view that, as an enthusiastic Prussian, he was trying to fend off the patent implications of German nationalism. From this point of view he was really not a nationalist but a manipulator of nationalism. Others say that Bismarck perverted liberalism by splitting and corrupting it with nationalist glory. They admit that he was a master of political strategy, but that Germany and Europe paid a high price for these qualities. They charge that his solution of the German question left more problems than there had been before. The vulnerable structure of his empire left national emotions in a state of permanent uneasiness. Bismarck, they say, more Prussian than German, cynically sacrificed democratic rule on the altar of the German nationalism in which he never believed.

On September 30, 1862, shortly after his appointment as Minister-President of Prussia, Bismarck appeared before thirty members of the Prussian *Landtag*, the lower house, and warned them not to exaggerate their powers. He declared that the Prussian constitution did not give them the sole power of arranging the budget. The *Reichsrat*, the upper house, said Bismarck, as well as the Crown, had much to say in the matter. He ended his speech with a ringing exhortation:

Not by speeches and majorities will the great questions of the day be decided—that was the mistake of 1848 and 1849—but by iron and blood.

The final phrase was destined to spread, with the rhythm changed to "blood and iron." Despite criticism, Bismarck never repudiated his words, lamely explaining that all he meant by "blood" was "soldiers."

The words "iron and blood" set the pattern—unity by force and not by persuasion. After the *Landtag* refused to grant him the credits he wanted for army appropriations, Bismarck defied the constitution of 1850 on the ground that "necessity alone is authoritative." He proceeded to levy, collect, and spend money for the military without presenting either a budget or an accounting.[1] Despite violent opposition, he championed king and army against parliament and people.

Conservative, militarist, monarchist, Bismarck made it plain that he had no use for "phrase-making and constitutions." He defended all that was traditional in German history, especially the institution of monarchy. He was convinced that a united Germany needed the firm hand of the Hohenzollern dynasty. "Never did I doubt that the key to German politics was to be found in princes and dynasties, not in publicists, whether in parliament and the press or on the barricades." His conception of the national structure was a narrow one, more in line with "reason of state" *(Staatsräson)* than any other form of national idea. He was the classic *Tatmensch*, the man of action who manipulated the reins of power in his own way and who was responsible only to his conscience, certainly not to the people.

As in other matters, Bismarck had some positive ideas about German nationalism. In constructing his state he took into consideration the dynastic loyalty and the narrow patriotism of the various German peoples. He was sure that Germans could be goaded into action only by attachment to a dynasty or by anger, and it was clear to him that anger could never be of a permanent nature. The German, he said, gave proof of his special form of patriotism as a Prussian, Hanoverian, Württemberger, Bavarian, or Hessian, rather than as a German national. To Bismarck love of fatherland also meant attachment to a prince on whom the German could concentrate his loyalty. If all the German dynasties were to be deposed suddenly, in all probability national sentiment would not be enough to hold all Germans together. A dynastic bond, in Bismarck's view, was necessary to unite Pomeranians, Holsteiners, and Silesians.

Bismarck saw particularism as the curse of German history. It had always been a preponderant force working against German national sentiment. Particularistic dynastic interests were justified only insofar as they fitted in with common national-imperial demands. When dynastic interests threatened national impotence and disintegration, they must be brought to their proper level.

Bismarck was aware that Prussian particularism remained a powerful sentiment. But in his mind the important thing was that Prussia was destined to be the uniting power behind the new Germany. Once achieved, Prussian nationalism could be merged into the greater whole. This is exactly what happened. German nationalism was to be the end product of Prussian nationalism. Prussia made up two-thirds of united Germany, but Bismarck saw to it that the heart of the nation beat in Berlin. Prussia absorbed the rest of Germany and gave to it a nationalism colored by authoritarianism and militarism.

Similitude: The Italian Experience

From the vantage point of comparative history, Italian nationalism took a course similar to that in the German states. Just as Prussia played the dominant role in the drive for German unity, so did Sardinia, including Piedmont and Savoy, lead the way to Italian unification. The German and Italian *nations* had existed for a long time, but there had been no corresponding German and Italian *states*. Both were mired in confused disunity. The German Hohenzollern dynasty had its counterpart in the Italian house of Savoy; Bismarck of Prussia-Germany had his double in Count di Cavour of Sardinia-Italy. There was similarity here, not contrast.

In 1815, in the name of legitimacy, the Congress of Vienna returned the Italies to their former fragmentation. The Papal States in central Italy were given back to the Church; the kingdom of the Two Sicilies (Sicily and Naples) was reestablished in the south; the kingdom of Sardinia (Sardinia and Piedmont), to which Genoa was added, was restored; large and small duchies were awarded to their former rulers; and Lombardy-Venetia was given to Austria. In this hodgepodge of competing states the petty princes, angered nobility, and dissatisfied clergy, emulating Metternich, called for the suppression of all revolutionary activity. Reactionary Italians had little use for French liberty, equality, and fraternity.

Not all Italians looked to the past. Patriots were infuriated by Austrian interference in Italian affairs—French rule had been supplanted by Austrian surpemacy. At first there were mild calls for national unity, then the demands were orchestrated into a crescendo of protest. But there were many unsolved problems which added difficulty to the task: the existence of diverse sovereignties; deep-rooted differences between north and south; and the reluctant attitude of the Pope, who as a territorial prince refused to relinquish his dominions for the benefit of a united Italy. In the Italian peninsula, as in the Germanies, particularism was a traditional way of life and it was not easy to supplant it by national cohesion.

Risorgimento: **Role of the** Carbonari

The Risorgimento (Resurrection) was used as a literary term in the eighteenth century, but politically it denoted the movement leading to national unification in the nineteenth century. It prepared the way morally and intellectually for a united Italy. Among the more effective stimulators of the Risorgimento were the Carbonari (charcoal burners), a secret society organized originally to combat Napoleon and carried over into the period of Austrian domination. Among its members were patriots from the ranks of army officers, nobles, landlords, government officials, workers, peasants, and even priests

It was a dissenting movement and it was activist. The Carbonari aimed to free the country from foreign rule and to bring the blessings of liberty to the Italian people. The society was careful to use Christian and liberal phraseology in its pronouncements: "Carbonarism teaches the true end of moral existence, and gives rules of conduct for social life. . . . It is to the sacred rights of equality that the 'Good Cousins' must especially attach themselves." The society used a set of mysterious symbols designed to appeal to the masses, as well as a secret, impenetrable correspondence in which a private dictionary of terms used words referable to others.

Harried by the Austrian police, the Carbonari struck back in a kind of guerrilla warfare. In 1820, emulating the Spanish insurgents, they led a revolt, only to be suppressed. In 1821 another uprising in Piedmont was frustrated with Austrian aid. Again in 1831 there were rebellions in Parma, Modena, and the Papal States, all of which were crushed by Austrian troops. Members of the Carbonari were hunted down, imprisoned, tortured, executed, or exiled. Italy became, as Byron noted, "a graveyard." The overwhelming difficulty was that the Carbonari, lacking effective leadership, tended to promote isolated and sporadic rebellions that could be suppressed easily. The movement gradually faded and was absorbed in Mazzini's Young Italy.

Italian patriots were not discouraged by the failure of the *Carbonari*. Their goals remained: opposition to tyranny, support for popular sovereignty, elimination of clerical influence, and Italian independence.

Early Apostles of Italian Nationalism

At first Italian national sentiment was limited to a small minority of poets and peasants, but they were to prepare the ideological framework for unity. In the late eighteenth century Vittoria Alfieri, expert dramatist and lover, loudly demanded an end to French interference in Italian affairs. Italians, not Frenchmen, he said, were rightful leaders of civilization. His *Il Misogallo* (1799), a collection of polemics in prose and verse, expressed his hatred for all things French. He insisted that liberty was by no means an abstract principle but a simple necessity identified with national freedom. He pronounced himself the prophet of a future united Italy.

Added to Alfieri's voice was that of Ugo Foscolo, patriot-poet of the *Risorgimento*. In *The Sepulchre* (1807) he summoned the mighty dead from their tombs to witness the struggle for Italy. Appointed to the chair of "Italian Eloquence" at the University of Pavia, he urged his countrymen to use their literature for a national end. Angered by this display of the kind of nationalism to which he was opposed, Napoleon abolished all chairs of "National Eloquence" in Italian universities.

In the 1820s and 1830s Alessandro Manzoni and Giacomo Leopardi spoke out as poets of liberty and independence. The Piedmontese Vincenzo Gioberti, a progressive priest who was often in conflict with his ecclesiastical superiors, called for a federation of Italian constitutional states under the intellectual leadership of the papacy. For his pains, he was arrested on suspicion of political intrigue and banished without a trial.

All these literary patriots worked busily to produce moral arguments for liberty and unity. As always, ideas presupposed action. In Italy, as in other countries, the poets gave way to the activists—Mazzini, Garibaldi, and Cavour.

The Liberal Nationalism of Giuseppe Mazzini

He was a remarkable man, highly intelligent, exceptionally generous, kind and warm. In his lonely cell at the fortress of Savona, where he was imprisoned in 1830 as a member of the *Carbonari*, he became aware of the great "apostolate" of his life. It would be his mission to work for the liberation of Italy from both foreign and domestic tyranny and for its unification under a republican form of government. He would dedicate his whole being to this calling.

Mazzini pronounced the French Revolution negative, but he enthusiastically glorified the coming Italian revolution as pointing the way to a great future, not only for Italians but for all the world. Only the Italians, he said, were equipped to bring a positive message to the new age. First they would reestablish that unity that Rome had brought to mankind in the time of the Caesars and in the era of the great Popes. A third, and greater, Rome would emerge to bring leadership to Europe.

Disgusted by the inertia of the bourgeoisie, Mazzini turned his appeal to energetic youth. While in Switzerland in 1834, he founded Young Italy, *La Giovine Italia,* designed to replace the *Carbonari* as a revolutionary society. For well-educated young Italians of liberal leanings, Mazzini's mission became a holy cause. "The secret of raising the masses," Mazzini wrote, "lies in the hands of those who show themselves ready to fight and conquer at their head."

From 1830 to 1848, years of optimism and hope, Mazzini and his followers worked laboriously for their beloved Italy. For Mazzini nothing mattered except the cause. He never married and he seldom had any money. He worked all through the days and often all night, meeting other revolutionaries, collecting and distributing funds, reading and writing. This was the lonely nationalist in action.

Although Mazzini was a man outstanding in purity of purpose and moral fervor, his teachings contained some dangerous germs. As Lewis Namier pointed out, his heart was stronger than his head. He adhered to the tenets of a truly humanitarian liberalism and he often wrote of the "joint destiny of humanity." In other words, he saw Italian nationalism as a part of the greater humanity of mankind. However, at the core of his teaching was the national glorification of Italy and a claim for Italian moral superiority. He claimed a position of primacy for Italy; he assigned her a unique mission; he showed contempt for France and Austria; he denounced "moderates" and was intolerant of their lack of progress. "We demand independence, unity and liberty, for ourselves and for our fellow countrymen. . . . All are agreed in the cry of *'Out with the foreigner!'* "

Once Italy obtained her just reward, then other peoples, Mazzini felt, had the right to unification. His conscious thought, says Namier, "turned toward humanity and embraced the whole," but he was capable of denouncing "foreign barbarians."

It is reasonable, then, to place less stress than is ordinarily done on Mazzini's humanitarian motives and considerably more on his deep sense of Italian nationalism. Nor must his liberalism be exaggerated: the movement for the complete liberation of Italian soil would have to be directed, he said, "by a provisional dictatorial power, concentrated in the hands of a small number of men."

Mazzini's charisma gave vitality to the struggling aspirations of the Italian people. His services to the cause of Italian unity were to be of tremendous importance. Others carried the torch.

Romantic Rebel: Giuseppe Garibaldi

To Mazzini's voice was added the activism of Giuseppe Garibaldi. Born at Nice in 1807, the son of a seafaring captain, the young man worked his way from cabin boy to captain in the merchant marine. He joined a group of Saint-Simonians, who were exiled from France, and from them he imbibed a sense of revolutionary mysticism. The process was enhanced by membership in Mazzini's Young Italy. "Columbus," said Garibaldi later, "was not as happy at the discovery of America as I at finding a man actually engaged in the redemption of our country."

In 1836 Garibaldi left the Old World and its beckoning prisons and sailed to Brazil, where he found several like-minded Italian exiles eager for adventure in the name of freedom. He became an experienced guerrilla leader in Rio Grande and Uruguay, while maintaining a correspondence with Mazzini. He returned home upon receiving the news of incipient revolution in 1848, placing his sword at the disposal of the revolutionaries. His name was already well known.

To Garibaldi, republican nationalist, the reactionary Neapolitan monarchy in southern Italy was a monstrosity. Assembling a force of 1,062 Italians and five Hungarians, all of whom wore bright red woollen shirts and red hats, he set sail from Genoa on May 5, 1860, to conquer Sicily and Naples. Escaping Neapolitan ships, the motley band, after a month of forced marches on land, sleepless nights, and exposure to the weather, entered Palermo in triumph. An eyewitness described the reaction of the people:

Children were brought up, and mothers asked on their knees for his blessing; and all this whole time the subject of this idolatry was calm and smiling as when in the deadliest fire, taking up the children and kissing them, trying to quiet the crowd, stopping at every moment to hear a long complaint of houses burned and property sacked by the retreating soldiers, giving good advice, comforting, and promising that all damages would be paid for.[2]

From Palermo the triumphant Red Shirts set sail for Naples. At Volturno they defeated an army twice their size. In November 1860 Garibaldi resigned, after delivering his army to Victor Emmanuel, who had appeared with his

Sardinian troops in Naples. This was Garibaldi's greatest moment—the patriot-hero had done his work and was now ready to retire. He went back to his farm at Caprera "with a large bag of seed corn and a small handful of lira notes." He left a warning for his people: "The misfortunes of Italy arise from the indifference of one province to the fate of the others." He called for redemption from the moment that men of the same land ran to help their distressed brothers. "Let us put an end once for all to the miseries of so many centuries. Prove to the world that it is no lie that Roman generations inhabited this land."

These were the words of the complete patriot, one of the great masters of revolutionary war. To Garibaldi, all that mattered was national consolidation—he had no desire to be dictator. Subsequently, his career was to be marred by impetuous decisions because he believed himself to be slighted by the men he had brought to power.

George M. Trevelyan gave a vivid picture of the emotional patriot:

Garibaldi had, perhaps, the most romantic life that history records, for it had all the trappings as well as the essence of romance. . . . He never had education, either intellectual, diplomatic, or political: even his military training was that of the guerrilla chief; not, till he was past learning, did he experience the ordinary life of the settled citizen. . . .

The man who loved Italy as even she has seldom been loved, scarcely knew her. The soldier of modern enlightenment was himself but dimly enlightened. Rather, his mind was like a vast sea cave, filled with the murmur of dark waters at flow and the stirring of nature's greatest forces, lit here and there by streaks of glorious sunshine bursting in through crevices hewn at random in its rugged sides. . . .

[He had] above all the passion to be striking a blow for the oppressed, a passion which could not be quenched by failure, nor checked by reason, nor sated by success, old age, and the worship of the world.[3]

Cavour: Architect of Italian Unity

The third of the triumvirate of activists was Count Camille di Cavour, scion of an ancient noble family of Piedmont. One of the great figures of the *Risorgimento,* he organized it with great skill and conducted the negotiations needed to overcome obstacles in the way to Italian unity.

Cavour was respected but won little affection. Mazzini and Garibaldi disliked him intensely and he returned the sentiment. At every stage of his career—in the defeat of Garibaldi, in his exploitation of the French—he displayed a cynicism and realism comparable to Bismarck. Lacking the *Eisen und Blut* prop, he made up for it with stealth and shrewd diplomacy. He understood the fiery emotionalism of both Mazzini and Garibaldi, but unlike them he was quite willing to welcome foreign aid as indispensable in the task of uniting Italy. From his point of view, neither the Italian masses, nor the papacy, nor the Sardinian army was strong enough by itself, or even in combination, to assure the goal of unity.

The Italian historian Adolfo Omodeo sees Cavour as a moderate who opposed extremism, acquired prestige, and became a center of attraction. Knowing that history is a great improviser, Cavour set forth clear programs and well-defined aims and ideals. Through him, "history improvised Italian unity suddenly." Unlike Mazzini, he avoided mixing the national with the democratic and social problem. Surrounded by those who hated him, opposed by the democrats, disliked by the moderates as well as by Victor Emmanuel II, he nevertheless succeeded in consolidating his position and encouraging the Piedmontese to navigate against the reactionary currents in post-1848 Europe. He lacked demagogic qualities but he knew what was going on. His career was in effect a triumph of political realism.

Appointed Prime Minister of Sardinia in 1852, Cavour first fashioned a liberal government in his small kingdom as a preliminary step to national unification. An able administrator, he improved the finances, reorganized the budget, reformed taxation, introduced free trade (he was opposed to restrictive mercantilism), and lessened clerical influence. Under his urging, Sardinia joined England and France in the Crimean War, thereby bringing the Italian case for unity before the Great Powers at the end of the conflict. In 1858 he formed an alliance with Napoleon III, "that strong believer in the principle of nationality."

Cavour then drove straight to his objective—a settling of accounts with Austria. He instigated insurrections against Austrian rule, correctly surmising that the Austrians would once again seek to intervene in Italian affairs. Vienna sent an ultimatum, which was promptly rejected. Austria declared war on Sardinia in 1859. The combined French and Sardinian forces won victories at Magenta and Solferino. Then the suspicious Napoleon III, alarmed by the success of his small partner, decided to make a separate peace at Villefranca. Cavour was forced to make his own peace at Zurich, but he obtained Lombardy as his share of the spoils.

Impressed by Cavour's success in standing up to the Austrians, the states of Modena, Parma, Tuscany, and the Romagna voted to join Sardinia in 1860. The next year Victor Emmanuel II of Sardinia was made King of Italy, united now except for Rome and Venetia, both of which were added within a decade. In the process of consolidation several Italian-speaking areas were left out: Trieste, Istria, and the Trentino (Austria), Ticino (Switzerland) and Nice and Corsica (France). For still dissatisfied Italian patriots, these became Unredeemed Italy, *Italia Irredenta,* waiting to be brought into the Italian fold.

Nationalism the Binding Factor

In summary, in both Germany and Italy, national unity was achieved despite a crossfire of antagonized interests. A comparison reveals similar historical trends. In each case the multiplicity of sovereignties, the urge to particularism, and the apparently insurmountable differences seemed to militate against unity. But there were intellectuals to provide the theoretical content of a binding nationalism. The German Friedrich von Schlegel cried out: "Awaken Germans from stupor and shame and ignominy! Awaken and act for the sake of German honor!" The Italian Ugo Foscolo called upon the dead from the Italian past to rise from their tombs and carry on the struggle against the despised Austrians. Nobility, bourgeoisie, and proletariat rallied to the national cause. Bismarck and Cavour, *Realpolitiker* and men of action, completed the process. In both Germany and Italy, nationalism was the ultimate factor working for unification.

Notes

[1] On September 1, 1866, after the quick defeat of Austria, Bismarck appeared before the *Landtag* and in a witty mood asked for a bill of indemnity retroactively legalizing his actions in ruling unconstitutionally in financial matters from 1862 to 1866. He expressed his regret. By now he was so dominating, hypnotic, and successful that the indemnification was voted by a large majority.

[2] *The Times* (London), June 13, 1860.

[3] George Macaulay Trevelyan, *Garibaldi's Defence of the Roman Republic* (London: Longman Green, 1907), pp. 23–25.

8 Force for Disruption: Austria-Hungary

For my part, the question of nationality
is more important than liberty. Until a
people can exist as a nation, it cannot
make use of liberty. Liberty can easily be
recovered when it is lost, but not
nationality. Therefore I believe that in
the present position of our country we
must aim rather at the preservation of
our greatly menaced nationality and seek
only for the development of our
nationality.

—Nicolas Bălescu, Rumanian patriot

Comparative Dimensions

Nationalism is a two-edged sword. One side can be a force for unification (Germany and Italy), the other an energy for disruption (Austria-Hungary). Always it responds to the special historical circumstances of the time and area in which it appears. We can best judge its repercussions through comparison and contrast.

More often than not the rise of nationalism meant the formation of a nationally homogeneous people and the fusion of nation and state. But on a comparative basis this was never true of the old Austrian Empire, which was transformed into a nationally heterogeneous state, multinational, and embracing large and small bitterly opposed minorities. Nationalism here took on a different character, epitomized in such widely accepted concepts as pan-Germanism, pan-Slavism, South Slavism, and the all-Polish movement:

At the same time, the traditions of the old territorial states, the sovereign entities out of which the Habsburg power was developed in the course of so many centuries, have been kept alive in Austria. They have been basically preserved, reorganized, and promoted as full-fledged national movements, partly overlapping, partly running parallel to, and partly conflicting with the ethnic racial trends of the nineteenth century. These historical units, commonly referred to as the historicopolitical entities *(historisch politische Individualitäten)* were backed up and revived by national forces distinctly different from those promoting ethnic programs. No similar concepts exist otherwise in the history of eastern central Europe.[1]

Anti-Habsburg sentiment was strong in the polyglot empire. One component people after another laid claim to independence and freedom from the strangling hand of Austrian centralism. But each was unwilling to give to others that liberty which it demanded for itself. This turned out to be a kind of Parkinson's law of nationalism: "Never do unto others nationally what you demand for yourself."

Bonds of Union in the Conglomerate Empire

Paradoxically, the Austrian Empire was able to maintain its existence for many centuries, even though it seemed always to be on the verge of dissolution. What were the bonds holding together such heterogeneous peoples? First was a common economic structure. Geographically, the Danubian region formed a rough economic unity: agricultural Hungary was the breadbasket; Croatia and Slavonia produced domesticated animals; Bohemia was the source of coal and iron; Galicia had rich oil fields. Vienna was the financial and commercial hub of this Danubian complex, a free-trade area.

A second unifying force was the Catholic Church, which retained the loyalty of a large majority of Austrians, Hungarians, Slavs, and Italians. There was a Protestant minority in Austria and Hungary, and the Greek Church included Rumanians, Serbs, and Ruthenians. But the Catholic Church was by far the most influential religious community.

The fulcrum was the Habsburg dynasty. From the time Rudolf became Emperor in 1273, the house continued to supply Holy Roman emperors until in 1806, under Napoleon's insistence, the new empire was established and the title of Holy Roman Emperor changed to that of Emperor of Austria. In the nineteenth century, loyalty to the dynasty was a strong emotional force in the multinational empire, especially upon the part of bureaucracy and army. The government attempted to ease bourgeois antagonism by appointing to the bureaucracy representatives in proportion to the various nationalities. At the same time, the monarchy used divide-and-rule tactics to take advantage of antipathies among the nationalities.

Toward the end of the nineteenth century and into the twentieth, each component nationality began to regard national independence as a supreme goal, even if it had to be achieved at the expense of a neighboring nationality. The imperial government, secure in its Viennese citadel, failed to understand or appreciate the increasingly clamorous calls for liberation. There were disintegrating forces at work: the middle class called for a more democratic rule; the industrial laborers demanded better working conditions; the peasants insisted that reform was overdue. These were practical matters that might have been met with a series of reform measures. Perhaps the situation could have been saved had the monarchy supported a cohesive federation with strict attention to the equality of all nationalities. But apparently it did not quite understand, or perhaps underestimated, the power of nationalism in action.

Problem of the Nationalities

Unlike the pure sciences, with their ordered array of atoms, molecules, and precise mathematical formulae, history plays no favorites in its capacity for promoting confusion. The Austrian Empire had more than its share of political chaos and disorder. Constituted in 1804 and after 1867 known as the Austro-Hungarian monarchy, it was composed of numerous peoples who resisted unity. Austrians, Czechs, Slovaks, and Hungarians conflicted not only with the empire but with each other. Identical objectives created no real union.

The conflict between the Danubian nationalities in the polyglot empire was part of a broader struggle that engulfed Europe. But here it took on a special character in which the goal was fragmentation, not union or federation of like-minded nationalities. Each minority hotly demanded the right to have its own national government, and each showed little support or understanding for the right of other nationalities to obtain the same end.

Who were the Austrians? That question leads straight to the issue of master-subject nationalities. The Habsburgs moved restlessly between the two, almost invariably siding with the imperial aristocracy. It has been said that the most genuine Austrians were surely the Jews, for to be an Austrian meant to deny nationality.

At the beginning of the twentieth century the Habsburg Empire was truly a Slavic house with a German facade. There was a bewildering array of people in the polyglot empire:

Germans: The German-speaking Austrians made up only about a quarter of the population. Most Austrians lived in Vienna and the surrounding region, in the Tyrol, and a strong minority (against the majority Czechs) in Bohemia and Moravia. Bourgeois Austrians, educated and prosperous, controlled the dynasty, government, Church, schools, court, and army. They were dedicated to the task of holding other minorities in submission.

Hungarians: The Hungarians (Magyars) formed a core in the center of the country, with minorities in Transylvania and Slovakia. Originally, they were an Asian tribe who, under the leadership of Arpad (c. 870–907), pressed westward across the Carpathians in the ninth century, invaded the region called Hungary, caused great devastation in the process, but eventually settled down and embraced Christianity. The Magyar language, a branch of the Ugrian group of the Ugro-Finnish linguistic family, is one of the few in Europe unrelated to the Latin, Germanic, or Slavic tongues. The Hungarian gentry owned estates worked by the mass of poverty-stricken peasants.

Czechs: The most important subgroup of Slavs was the Czechs, who formed the majority in Bohemia and Moravia. Bohemia, with its rich coal and iron deposits, was the industrial center of the empire. Prosperous Czechs, literate and self-conscious, resented the German minority. Political-minded Czechs insisted that Bohemia, much like Hungary, formed a historic unity and, therefore, was entitled to independence or to an equal position such as that granted the Hungarians. Czech ambitions called for an Austro-Hungarian-Czech triadism to replace the old dualism. The Slovaks of Slovakia, mostly poor peasants who were closely related to the Czechs, similarly resented their Hungarian rulers.

Yugoslavs: In the south, the Yugoslavs were separated from their related Czechs by Austrians and Hungarians. Consisting of several connected groups (Serbs, Croats, and Slovenes), the Yugoslavs were also related to the adjacent Serbs and Montenegrins. Mostly peasants and herdsmen, the Yugoslavs were distinguished by a strong sense of nationality.

Poles: In Galicia, at one time part of the Polish kingdom, Slavic Poles formed the majority, alongside a Ukrainian minority. Though generously treated by the Habsburgs, the Poles supported the idea of a regenerated Poland, of which they would become a part. As in Hungary, landed magnates owned great estates worked by peasants. Again as in Hungary, commerce was carried on mostly by Jews, who considered themselves assimilated but who as "outsiders" were condemned to endure discrimination and oppression.

Ruthenians: The Ruthenians (their name is a latinized form of "Russia") also inhabited Galicia, northern Bukovina, and Transcarpathia. Their linguistic and ethnographic features were close to those of the neighboring Ukrainians. Ruthenians' sense of national consciousness was vigorous and zealous.

Rumanians: Settled in Transylvania and the Banat were the Rumanians, who had a strong sense of community with their fellow Rumanians across the border. There was also a Rumanian minority in Bukovina, alongside the Germans and Ukrainians.

Italians: Along the Adriatic coastline, especially in Trieste and Fiume, were many Italians, living alongside the southern Slavs. There were also Italians in the Alpine region of Trentino. For Italian nationalists, this was part of that "Unredeemed Italy" *(Italia Irredenta)* which belonged to a united Italy. The Habsburgs, of course, were not inclined to recognize such pretensions.

The bitterness of conflicting peoples of different origins and linguistic families was not confined to the Habsburg Empire. The entire Balkan area was subjected to this kind of rivalry. Serbians and Bulgarians, both of Slavic origin and Greek Orthodox faith, both objectors to Turkish rule, nevertheless found it impossible to unite in a common front. Instead, they fought viciously over parts of Macedonia, to which each made "valid historical claims." The Balkans deserved the appellation "the tinder box of Europe." Little wonder, then, that nationalism was a cause for disruption in this area of variegated, conglomerate peoples.

František Palacký, Czech "Father of the Fatherland"

It was to be expected that poets and patriots, theorists and activists, would function loudly in this maelstrom of ambitious nationalities. Outstanding among the pioneers of Czech cultural nationalism was the historian and politician František Palacký (1798–1876). Born in Moravia of a Protestant family, he settled in Prague in 1823. Here he made the acquaintance of Count Francis Sternberg, an enthusiastic Bohemian nationalist, who was determined to awaken Czech nationalism by a study of historical records. Under the sponsorship of Sternberg, Palacký became the first editor of *The Journal of the Bohemian Museum*. He was also made official historiographer of Bohemia, though it took a decade to obtain consent from Vienna.

Palacký published his master work, *The History of the Bohemian People*, in five volumes from 1836 to 1867. The study, covering the years up to 1526 (the date of the extinction of Czech independence), was based on research in the local archives of Bohemia. It promptly won a place as the standard work on the subject. Palacký presented a new interpretation: the basis for Czech democracy was fashioned by the late medieval Hussite movement with its "liberal" attitude. Austrian police censors, who were angered by Palacký's account of the Hussite movement, did what they could to hinder publication of the work.

The Czech cultural awakening now had its hero. Encouraged by Palacký, other scholars began to show a special concern for philology. They compiled dictionaries and grammars to "purify" what was widely regarded as a peasant language and to transform it into a weapon for national sentiment. Typical of the national literature of this movement was Jan Kollár's *Slavic Daughter of Slava*, which riveted attention to the unity of all Slavs and forecast a great future for their mission.

On March 6, 1848, the Vorparlament, or Preliminary Parliament, consisting of 500 former deputies of the German Diet, met at Frankfurt-am-Main to prepare the convocation of an elected German parliament. Because Bohemia was a part of the German Confederation, Palacký, a member of the Slav Congress at Prague, was invited to attend. But he declined to go to Frankfurt. His letter of refusal defined the Czech national point of view for the first time:

I am a Czech of Slav descent and with all the little I own and possess I have devoted myself wholly and forever to the service of my nation. That nation is small, it is true, but from time immemorial it has been an independent nation with its own character; its rulers have participated since old times in the federation of German princes, but the nation never regarded itself nor was it regarded throughout the centuries, as part of the German nation. The whole union of the

Czech lands first with the Holy Roman Empire and then with the German
Confederation was always a purely dynastic one of which the Czech nation, the
Czech Estates, hardly wishes to know and which they hardly notice.[2]

Despite the tone of independence revealed in his letter, Palacký at this time
favored a strong Austrian Empire, consisting of a federation of the southern
German and Slav states with adequate respect for minority rights. He
suspected that the delegates at Frankfurt were determined to undermine
Austria and make its existence impossible. "When I look behind the Bohemian frontiers, then natural and historical reasons make me turn not to
Frankfurt but to Vienna to seek there the center which is fitted and destined
to ensure and defend the peace, the liberty, and the right of my nation."[3]

Palacký was well aware of conditions in southeastern Europe. Along the
frontiers of the Russian Empire there were many peoples differing in origin,
language, history, and habits—Slavs, Rumanians, Magyars, and Germans,
as well as Greeks, Turks, and Albanians. None by itself was strong enough to
successfully resist the giant Russian neighbor to the east. It could do so only if
it was bound in firm ties with adjacent peoples who shared its contempt for
Russia. In Palacký's view, the vital artery of the Habsburg Empire, "this
necessary union of nations," was the Danube, and the focus of power should
never be removed from the river.

Palacký urged the Austrians to set up a strong and lasting federation, on the
principle that nature knows neither ruling nor subservient nations. The
central authority would provide a defense against any violations of equality.
Vienna should proclaim this fundamental rule of justice openly and sincerely,
"the *sacra ancora* for a ship in danger of floundering." "Every moment is
precious: for God's sake do not let us delay another hour with this!"

Palacký's views met with much Habsburg sympathy and he was even
offered a portfolio in the Austrian cabinet. However, in 1852 the federal idea
collapsed, and while union with the Hungarians was achieved in 1867, the
Czechs were ignored in the process. Discouraged, Palacký turned more and
more to the cause of Czech independence. He became leader of the Nation-
alist-Federalist Party in the Bohemian *Landtag* and began to call for the
establishment of a Czech kingdom which would include Bohemia, Moravia,
and Silesia.

Despite his activities for Czech independence, Palacký, throughout the
remainder of his life, believed that the Habsburg Empire would have func-
tioned well as a monarchical federation with equality for all its members.
Each state would develop its own autonomous national culture, and each
would cooperate in the common concern for security, peace, and progress.
Only political realities forced Palacký reluctantly to abandon this goal and
favor a strictly Slavic national program.

Other Czech nationalists refused to accept Palacký's idea of federation in any form. They drew from his teachings only the paean of praise to Bohemian history and traditions. They pronounced him "father of the Fatherland." They called him the master who brought recognition to Bohemian national history, who understood the place of the Slavs in Europe and the world, and who defined their own national objectives.

Here once again we see the strange working of our treacherously complex ism. Nationalism meant one thing to Palacký, another to his followers. He wanted a Czech nationalism within the framework of the Austrian imperial idea and hoped to see it work on a basis of equality. His followers were integral Czech nationalists who accepted his lead only part of the way and demanded Czech freedom, Czech independence, and Czech union—all attainable only by separation from the Habsburg Empire.

Louis Kossuth and Magyar Nationalism

Comparatively, the Slavic cultural awakening was matched by a similar development among the Magyars. The Hungarian Magyars had exhibited a sense of independence as early as the era of Turkish domination in the sixteenth and seventeenth centuries. The wealthy landowning Hungarian nobility (Estates) not only defended its class interests but also insisted that its national identity be maintained within the Habsburg Empire. In the nineteenth century, as the wave of nationalism began to engulf Central Europe, the Hungarian nobility joined the rising bourgeoisie to help promote a new linguistic nationalism. Magyars wanted their language to be used as the official tongue of administration and legislation in areas where they were predominant.

Language was not the only facet of this Magyar nationalism. Hungarian patriots began to demand a top-level place among the nationalities of the supranational Habsburg Empire. They wanted autonomy and they talked independence for themselves, but they were unwilling to grant equivalent rights to such non-Magyars as Serbs, Slovaks, Rumanians, and Ruthenians.

Magyar nationalism found its most fiery apostle in Ferencz Lajos (Francis Louis) Akos Kossuth (1802–1894), patriot and politician. Born to a Magyarized Slovak family of the petty Hungarian nobility, he began his career as a lawyer, practising with his father. Appointed by Count Hunyady to be his deputy in the National Diet at Pressburg (1825–1827, 1832), Kossuth sent a series of letters to his patron in which he presented arguments for constitutional reform, liberal legislation, and Hungarian independence. Despite the censorship, his letters were widely circulated. In 1837 Kossuth was arrested on a charge of high treason. After serving a year in prison, he was condemned to four more years. Metternich, guardian of the establishment, responded to public indignation by releasing Kossuth after he had served two years.

In 1841 Kossuth became editor of *Pesti Hirlop,* the newly founded organ of the Liberal Party. In its columns he called for the abolition of feudal burdens and for taxation of aristocrats. Not content with these limited objectives, he also attacked Austria in violent terms, while at the same time contemptuously denying the rights of Hungary's non-Magyar peoples.

Kossuth rapidly became the best-known popular leader of Magyar nationalism. The authorities stepped in to terminate his connection with his paper. In a personal interview, Metternich tried to satisfy the annoying Magyar patriot by offering to take him into government service, but Kossuth refused. He preferred to become leader of the extreme liberals in the struggle for Magyar nationalism.

When Paris sneezed, all the capitals of Central Europe broke into paroxysms of coughing. The signal came on February 24, 1848, when revolution erupted in Paris, after which riots broke out in major cities, including Budapest. Within a few days Kossuth was demanding parliamentary government for Hungary. He appealed to "our beloved Archduke Francis Joseph" to perpetuate the ancient glory of the dynasty by meeting halfway "the aspirations of a free people." Kossuth's impassioned speech was read aloud on the streets of Vienna on the day of Metternich's fall.

The Austrian authorities were perplexed. How could they handle this Hungarian firebrand? Panic-stricken, they promised a constitutional regime for Hungary and awarded Kossuth the office of Minister of Finance. It was an unimportant and inoffensive post, but Kossuth immediately took advantage of it to issue a separate Hungarian coinage.

After the abdication of Ferdinand I, the new Emperor, Francis Joseph, announced that he would "unite all lands and races of the monarchy in one great body politic." Francis Joseph revoked his predecessor's concessions and pronounced Kossuth a traitor. The Emperor knew that he could count on the support of Croats, Serbs, and Slovenes, all of whom were angered by Kossuth's contempt for their special national aspirations.

On December 15, 1848, when the Austrian commander Windischgratz advanced into Hungary to bring the Magyars into line Kossuth urged his people to rise up in self-defense. By the next spring the Hungarians were counterattacking successfully. In mid-April 1849 Kossuth issued a famous manifesto proclaiming Hungarian independence:

1. Hungary, together with Transylvania, and all parts, countries, and provinces appertaining thereunto, is and shall be a free and independent European State. The territory of the whole of this said Hungarian State is indivisible, and its integrity inviolable.

2. The House of Habsburg-Lorraine, by its treason, perjury, and armed aggression on the Hungarian nation, and further by the audacity which prompted it to divide the area of the country, to separate Transylvania and Croatia from Hungary, to annihilate the independent political existence of the country, and to raise an armed power for the purpose of murdering the nation—by these and many other gross crimes and enormities has the House of Habsburg-Lorraine broken the Pragmatic Sanction, and every other tie which joined the two countries of Austria and Hungary. In consequence of which, the perjured House of Habsburg-Lorraine is and shall be excluded, and deposed and banished, now and forever, from the dominion, sovereignty, and enjoyment of the territories of Hungary, as well as Transylvania, and all the parts, countries, and provinces thereunto appertaining.

And the said House is and shall be declared in the name of the nation to have forfeited the throne, and to be excluded and disowned and banished.[4]

Kossuth was now elected dictator. Despite heroic resistance, the Hungarians proved to be no match for the combined Austrian and Russian forces fighting to maintain the status quo. By August 1849 the revolt was crushed, the constitution annulled, and Hungary reduced to a dependency of the Habsburg crown. The angered Austrians sealed the defeat by executing fourteen Hungarian generals. Kossuth abdicated and went to Turkey, where he was interned. Liberated in 1851, he fled on an American man-of-war. The people of Marseilles greeted him as a Hungarian national hero, but Louis Napoleon, Prince-President, refused to allow him to cross France.

On October 23, 1851, Kossuth landed in England, where he was received with extraordinary enthusiasm. Carl Schurz, an eyewitness, described his entry as like that of a national hero returning from a victorious campaign. "He appeared in his picturesque Hungarian garb, standing upright in his carriage, with his saber at his side, and surrounded by an equally picturesque retinue. Speaking in classic English with a soft tinge of foreign accent, he aroused an enthusiasm which mocked all description."

Kossuth's eloquence was effective for the immense multitudes crowding the streets, but it was unable to induce the British government to take active steps against Russia and Austria on behalf of Hungary. The efforts of the Hungarian nationalist to arrange confidential talks with members of the Palmerston ministry came to nothing. The experience was repeated in the United States, where Kossuth was greeted as a patriot who had succumbed to the overwhelming power of the Russians, and as a prophet whose burning words had kindled the fire of liberty in the hearts of his countrymen. But official Washington was unwilling to abandon the traditional American policy of opposition to any intervention in affairs of the Old World. After all, another patriot-nationalist, George Washington, had warned about the implications of such conduct.

Kossuth returned to England, where he lived for the next eight years in close friendship with Italian nationalist Mazzini. Kossuth became embroiled in the usual squabbles among unhappy refugees. Other Hungarian nationalists accused him of arrogance and duplicity, and especially condemned his insistence on being called "Governor." During the Crimean War, Kossuth tried to form a Hungarian legion to assist the French, but his project fell through. Embittered by a Hungarian law depriving of citizenship all Hungarians who had been absent voluntarily from their homeland for ten years, Kossuth went to Italy.

During his last years, Kossuth began to see the unreality of his earlier opposition to other Hungarian minorities. Belatedly, he advocated a federation of nationalities on an equal basis. But the damage had been done.

The *Ausgleich* of 1867

The national struggles of 1848 in the Habsburg Empire were doomed to defeat. The consequence was a return to absolutism. However, an uncomfortable Francis Joseph, aware of the necessity for holding the loyalty of all the nationalities in his realm, attempted to satisfy them without weakening the central power. In the process, he tended to favor the Magyars in order to prevent another Hungarian explosion. There was also pressure from a victorious Bismarck, who was quite willing to interfere in an empire which could not find answers for itself.

Central to the new course was the *Ausgleich*, or Compromise, of 1867, an agreement between the Austrian government at Vienna and Hungarian politicians providing for the transformation of the Austrian Empire into the Dual Monarchy of Austria-Hungary. On the one side was what was officially called Austria (technically the kingdom and lands represented in the *Reichstag*, the imperial parliament) and on the other side the kingdom of Hungary. Both states were to have a common monarch, who controlled military and naval affairs, and there would be three ministers in common (army, foreign affairs, and finances). Each state would have its own prime minister and its own legislative body, but sixty members from each parliament would form the Delegations, a body summoned annually by the Emperor-King to meet alternately at Vienna and Budapest. Economic conditions were to be regulated by agreements to be revised every ten years; there would be internal free trade and a common currency for the entire state.

The Compromise of 1867 was a major concession to Hungarian nationalism. Francis Joseph conceded virtually all the Magyar demands excepting those for a separate office for the army and another for foreign affairs. Hungary had as many representatives in the Delegations as all the other provinces together. At long last, after centuries of rebellion, the Magyars had achieved equality in a dual state. They had won much, but they were still not satisfied. Almost immediately they tried to win greater independence for the Hungarian sections of the imperial and royal army.

It was to be expected that the scintillating success of the Magyars would stimulate the aspirations of other nationalities. The Hungarians were far less generous in the treatment of their own minorities. The Compromise left Croatia-Slavonia inside the kingdom of Hungary. In a settlement concluded in 1868, the Hungarians gave Croatia-Slavonia her own Diet *(Sabor)* and recognized linguistic rights, but they did not permit the existence of a responsible Croatian-Slavonian ministry. Instead, a local governor was appointed by the Hungarian authorities.

The Slavs at once began to call for a major Slavic unit in the empire. In 1871 an attempt was made by the Hohenwart-Schäffle ministry to enter into negotiations with the Czech leaders for a federal solution that would have given the German and Czech languages equal status. Francis Joseph declared that he would be willing to recognize the Bohemian kingdom and be crowned at Prague with the ancient crown of Saint Wenceslaus.

There were immediate protests from Germans and there were student riots in Vienna. Andrassy, the Hungarian leader, arriving in Vienna as an all-powerful arbitrator, quickly eliminated the plan for a Bohemian compromise by questioning Hohenwart: "Are you prepared to carry through the recognition of Bohemian state rights with cannon?" Francis Joseph succumbed to Andrassy's opposition. Negotiations were halted, the Hohenwart-Schäffle ministry was dismissed, and the plan for a Czech compromise was stifled.

Our Parkinson's law for nationalism was working to perfection: after the implementation of their own demands, Hungarian nationalists were not inclined to grant other minorities the rights they had won for themselves.

An Emperor's Impossible Task

For Francis Joseph it was a grievous dilemma. For the rest of his reign he worked to preserve the unity of his conglomerate empire. He regarded himself as an enlightened monarch devoted to his people, but his was an impossible task in a nation in which the two strongest nationalities were unwilling to give equal status to the weaker component parts.

It was a valiant but ineffective struggle. Francis Joseph favored the introduction of a general franchise, which would have improved the position of the oppressed nationalities, but the outbreak of World War I put an end to this mild proposal. He made it a practice to veto the laws of local diets or town councils when they were offensive to other nationalities, but instead of improving the situation, he succeeded only in arousing anger on all sides.

The Polish problem was a thorny one. Francis Joseph saw to it that a certain measure of autonomy was granted to the Poles in Galicia. The grateful Poles pledged loyalty to the Habsburg dynasty: they were often called "the only Austrian patriots." But the Poles claimed not only autonomy for themselves but also the right to dominate the Ruthenians in Galicia. Both nationalities were vigorously loyal to the monarchy, but they were at loggerheads in their own relations. Poles and Ruthenians could agree only on the hope that one day Austria would help liberate their brethren in Russia.

Francis Joseph understood and sympathized with the Czechs. Each time he was disposed to grant them some degree of autonomy, he aroused the violent opposition of the German minority in Czech territory. On each occasion Hungarians immediately supported the Germans. An effort to place the Czech language on a par with German in Bohemia and Moravia quickly foundered on the rock of German and Magyar opposition. Faced with criticism from Germans and Hungarians, three times as numerous as the Czechs, the Emperor was forced to postpone his plans to help the Czechs.

Added to the squabbling nationalities was the clash between pan-Germanism and pan-Slavism during the first decade of the twentieth century. The pan-Germans accused Francis Joseph of softness toward the Slavs and of allowing Austria to become "a Slav state." Pan-Slavs proclaimed Russia's historic mission to liberate the Slavs in both the Habsburg and Ottoman empires and promote Slavic union under Russian protection. The clash of these movements was among the causes leading to the outbreak of World War I.

In 1906 Prime Minister Baron Beck, at the urging of Francis Joseph, made still another attempt to resolve the nationalities problem by sponsoring electoral reform, including manhood suffrage. It was a valiant effort, but it was too late. The task of promoting the living together of different types, languages, and ethnic groups turned out to be an unmitigated failure. The "Empire without an idea" was well on the way to disintegration, a victim of disruptive nationalism.

The Power of Disruptive Nationalism

A motivating factor in modern history is not the legal idea of nationality but rather nationalism or the social force of national consciousness. The Austro-Hungarian Empire provides the classic case of how divergent nationalities inside a great state can contribute to dissolution as well as to unification. Some twelve nationalities lived side by side in the old Austro-Hungarian Empire, but few people in the Danubian basin ever spoke of an Austro-Hungarian *nation*. Despite varying degrees of loyalty to the Habsburgs, there was never a strict unity in the conglomerate state but rather a kind of federation of mutually hostile peoples, waiting patiently and sometimes impatiently for political change.

The story of the Austro-Hungarian Empire is one of violent struggle between warring nationalities. In Vienna it was believed that the combination of dynasty, Church, and economic bonds was too strong to make dismemberment possible. But the gentlemen of Vienna did not take into account the overwhelming growth and strength of irredentist movements. One could not call the Southern Slavs in the empire a national unit: they were in turn divided into three nationalities, Serbs, Croats, and Slovenes. Even in united Yugoslavia today, traditional hostility persists between Croats and Serbs.

The centralizing policy and the curbs on nationalities pursued by the Habsburgs were ineffective. In a war situation, the different nationalities were bound to work for the dissolution of the empire and constitute their own independent states. Here, then, was a striking example of how nationalism can function in a manner diametrically opposed to the familiar drive for unification.

Notes

[1] See Robert A. Kann, *The Multinational Empire: Nationalism and National Reform in the Habsburg Monarchy, 1848–1918* (New York: Columbia University Press, 1950), 1:33–37.

[2] Translated in Hans Kohn, *Pan-Slavism: Its History and Ideology* (Notre Dame, Ind.: University of Notre Dame Press, 1953), p. 65.

[3] *Ibid.,* p. 69.

[4] *Annual Register, 1849* (London, 1850), pp. 332–33.

9

Watershed: Nationalism and the Two World Wars

Millions of Frenchmen have entered this war with a fervor of heroism and martyrdom which formerly, in the most exalted epochs of our history, characterized only the flower of the combatants. Young or old, poor or rich, and whatever his religious faith, the French soldier of 1916 knows that his is a nation which intervenes when injustice prevails upon the earth, and in his muddy trench, gun in hand, he knows that he is carrying onward the *Gesta Dei per Francos.*

—Maurice Barrès
The Undying Spirit of France (1917)

To defend honor, liberty, and right; to offer up life, health, and property on the altar of the Fatherland, these have always been the joy of German youths. It is an honor to wear the King's coat. . . . Love of country is a treasure embedded in the heart of man by God. . . . Our Fatherland is a holy land. Our ancestors preserved it with their blood. . . . More national consciousness, much more than we now possess! That is the end to which we history teachers must help our youth.

—Carl Reim
German schoolteacher (1911)

The Multiple Causes of World War I

Historians, a notoriously testy lot, take great pleasure in annihilating each other's facts and interpretations. Yet few of them differ on the *immediate* causes of the two world wars of the twentieth century. In agreement they point to the sparks that set off the conflagrations. In World War I it was the assassination of Archduke Francis Ferdinand at Sarajevo on June 28, 1914. In World War II it was Hitler's invasion of Poland on September 1, 1939.

This pleasant harmony fades the minute the historian turns to the remote or fundamental causes for the two wars. Following each great conflict there was a lively revisionism challenging the conventional designation of responsibility. Two conclusions can be made without raising blood pressure among historians: (1) in both world wars there was a host of interrelated causes that prepared the way; and (2) in each case nationalism was one of the major forces leading to the abyss.

The drift to war was apparent for decades before 1914. Europe was in a precarious condition. After achieving Germany's national unification in 1871, Bismarck negotiated a set of alliances to maintain the delicate balance of power. The cornerstone of his diplomatic structure was the secret Triple Alliance (1882) between Germany, Austria-Hungary, and Italy, which for Germany meant a guarantee against French *revanche* as well as a means for "driving to the East" *(Drang nach Osten)*. To counter this alliance, Britain, France, and Russia formed the Triple Entente, a coalition providing for mutual assistance in the event of war. In this way an uneasy Europe was divided into two armed camps.

Behind the diplomacy was a generating economic conflict. The rapid industrialization of Europe had led to a struggle for markets, raw materials (coal, iron, oil), and fields for investment. Britain had long been the world's most powerful nation: her colonial empire was first in size, her industry advanced, her navy dominant on the seas. The trademark "Made in Britain" was recognized everywhere. Magnificent egoist, inflexible in his goals, the British trader was admired and envied as a master of technical progress and was often despised as a too successful entrepreneur.

Germany's economic expansion was remarkable for its rapidity and magnitude. Her isolation in the heart of Europe made her logically the leader of Continental trade. German efficiency and scientific genius, assisted by governmental paternalism, was an advantage in the race for economic supremacy. Germany's late start in industrialization was an additional asset because her factories could be equipped at the outset with modern machinery.

The zealous Germans faced serious economic barriers. Their merchants were blocked throughout the world by the Entente powers. Just before the outbreak of war, William II sent a message to President Wilson complaining that "all the nations of the world are directing the points of their bayonets at Germany."

At the same time, it is important not to use this "economic" argument as monistic, nor should we exaggerate its effects. Despite the rivalry, trade between Britain and Germany had much improved. Tensions were somewhat reduced: in the critical days of 1914, William II was away at sea. Those who oppose the theory of overwhelming economic compulsions ask: If economic interests had really directed affairs, would there have been a war with the total disruption of the delicate world market?

It is best to settle for a multiplicity of causes, of which the economic factor was one. What is very obvious is the fact that Europe on the eve of World War I was a camp of stubborn belligerents. Symptomatic of mutual distrust were military conscription, new instruments of warfare, and enormous military and naval budgets.

International Anarchy and Nationalism

Added to the diplomatic tangle, the economic clashes, and the rising militarism was a system which G. Lowes Dickinson called "international anarchy." While each nation maintained the peace within its own borders by constitutional and legal means, it recognized no equivalent restraining international organization for the family of nations. Internally, each government could act as it thought best. There was supposed to be an "international law" governing the relations between nations, but it was ineffective in the absence of any overall authority. Offenders were subject only to the judgment of mankind, and that was very vague at best. Diplomacy in this milieu became a labyrinth of trickery. Sworn allies were not necessarily loyal friends; on occasion, nations even made secret agreements with the enemies of their allies.

All efforts to construct some kind of international machinery were sporadic and ineffective. The first Peace Conference at the Hague, summoned by Tsar Nicholas II in 1899, was attended by representatives of twenty-six nations, but it was unable to do much to soothe national rivalries. Germany blocked efforts at the reduction of military armaments. The second Peace Conference at the Hague (1907), representing forty-four nations, could do little more. The Permanent Court of Arbitration, supposed to settle international disputes, could not solve any of the major problems brought before it. Large and small nations proclaimed their devotion to peace, but clearly they had no intention to abolish war. The peace movement collapsed ingloriously in 1914, when Sir Edward Grey saw the lights going out all over Europe.

It was a tragic state of affairs. The fluidity of the nationalist idea had made nationalism irreplaceable. No matter what the ideology attempting to usurp the function of nationalism—movements like pan-Germanism or pan-Slavism, supranationalism of all kinds, halfhearted attempts at international organization—all were found wanting. No twentieth-century nation was willing to sacrifice even a tiny portion of its national sovereignty for common global welfare.

Nationalistic Sore Spots in 1914

Nationalities were repressed and other nationalities wanted to be liberated. There were many sore spots on the map of Europe in 1914. Alsace-Lorraine had been the scene of Franco-German rivalry for a thousand years: on this issue Germans and Frenchmen could find no common ground. By the Treaty of Frankfurt (1871), a triumphant Bismarck had annexed Alsace and most of Lorraine despite French claims. For Germany, the provinces were vital economic assets, especially because of the iron mines. Politically, Alsace-Lorraine represented for the Germans the first conquest for the new empire *(Reichsland);* strategically, it was a buffer zone to protect the Rhine. To the cry of French nationalists that the provinces be restored, German patriots replied that the area had been stolen originally by Louis XIV from the Holy Roman Empire.

Equally dangerous zones in 1914 were the Austrian-held but dominantly Italian districts of Trentino and the cities of Trieste and Fiume. Italians angrily demanded return of their "lost provinces." There were 400,000 Italians in the Trentino–Alto Adige region belonging to the Austrian Tyrol. Trieste (Slovenian Trst) and Fiume (Rijeka), seaports on the northern Adriatic to the northeast of Venice, were regarded by the Austrians as their outlets to the sea. Both towns had substantial Italian populations and both were centers of Italian irredentism. Although Austria and Italy were supposed to be working partners in Bismarck's Triple Alliance (1882), they were at odds on the disputed seaports. Italian nationalists were enraged when the "secret" Treaty of London excepted Fiume from the territories that were to be awarded to Italy as the price of her participation in World War I.

Poland was another focus of trouble. There was no Poland on the map of Europe in 1914, but the idea of a revived nation was very much alive. Dismembered in the three partitions of 1772, 1793, and 1795, Poland had been reborn during the Napoleonic Wars, only to be divided again among Russia, Austria, and Prussia. But the flame of Polish nationalism was not extinguished. Adam Mickiewicz and other *émigré* poets spoke up for regeneration and urged their fellow Poles to reject humiliation and despair. Was not Poland "the Christ among nations, innocently crucified"? "Poland will rise again!"

The conglomerate Habsburg Empire was a boiling cauldron. Unhappy under Austrians and Hungarians, the Slavs and other suppressed nationalities demanded equality or independence. Francis Joseph did his best to hold the lid down. In 1908 the two Serbian provinces of Bosnia and Herzegovina, administered by Austria-Hungary since the Congress of Berlin (1878), were suddenly annexed by Austria-Hungary. Apparently the idea was to prevent the formation of a great Slavic state in the heart of the Habsburg Empire. The Slavic population of the two provinces reacted violently.

On June 28, 1914, came the critical spark. Archduke Francis Ferdinand, heir-presumptive to the Habsburg throne, and his wife were assassinated in Sarajevo, the capital of Bosnia, by Gavrili Princip, a fanatical Bosnian youth. That tragic incident led straight to war.

The whole Balkan region was seething with discontent. Greeks, Serbians, Bulgarians, and Rumanians all wanted a greater share of the disintegrating Ottoman Empire. Greek nationalists demanded southern Albania, Thrace, Constantinople, and parts of Asia Minor. Rumanian patriots pointed to Transylvania, Bukovina, and Bessarabia as indisputable parts of the Rumanian fatherland. Superimposed on these frustrated national ambitions was the clash between pan-Germanism and pan-Slavism. Added to the maelstrom of conflicting aims was Britain's effort to discourage German expansion through the Balkans (the Berlin-to-Baghdad Railway).

The Balkans swarmed with ultrapatriots, chauvinists, and jingoists. Poets produced fiery literature for "the cause." Liberators called for freedom; entrenched nationalists shouted "traitors" at their opponents. The invasion of Belgium on August 4, 1914, came almost as a relief to the assorted patriots, encouraged mightily by the sweet odor of coming victory.

Peacemaking: Wilsonian "Idealism" versus Reactionary Nationalism

The war itself did not erase the virus of nationalism. Nor were the postwar leaders and delegates at Versailles free of the infection. There had been grievous loss of life, enormous property damage, and ancient states had been shattered beyond repair. Now there was a serious threat of anarchy. The delegates at the peace conference were worried about the dangerous example of Communist Russia.

Versailles witnessed a clash between Wilson's rationalism and Clemenceau's fervid nationalism. The American President received an extraordinary welcome in Europe, as a messiah who had come to end the curse of war. The League of Nations, he was sure, would put an end to unrestrained nationalism. For his pains in supporting an eminently realistic position he was denounced by his enemies as an impractical idealist.

Wilson's loudest critic, Georges Clemenceau, "the Tiger," was a born polemicist who looked more like a walrus than a tiger. Clemenceau, "French father of victory," was contemptuous of the American do-gooder: "God Almighty had only Ten Points; Wilson has to have Fourteen!" Clemenceau demanded gruffly that Germany be punished for her sins and that France be made secure from further attack. His one interest was his beloved France—all else was trivial.

Britain and Italy had their own nationalists at Paris. David Lloyd George had pledged to "hang the Kaiser" and collect from Germany the costs of the war "shilling for shilling and ton for ton." He would have the German navy interned and German submarines and warplanes destroyed. Vittorio Emanuele Orlando, the Italian Prime Minister, desperately sought for the implementation of Italian national aspirations. Angered at what he deemed to be unfair treatment on Fiume, he walked out of the council, and was not invited to return. The Big Four became the Big Three.

Added to the major delegates were representatives of the smaller states, each clamoring for recognition of some claim: Venizelos of Greece, Smuts of South Africa, Bratianu of Rumania, Paderewski of Poland, the Emir Feisal of the Hejaz. The persistent cry was self-determination—for Ukrainians, Armenians, Finns, Balts, Persians, Egyptians, Zionists, Sinn Feiners, Albanians, and Lebanese.

The key issue at Versailles was the Fourteen Points versus the secret treaties. On January 8, 1918, Wilson had issued a statement of war aims, which made a deep impression on war-weary Germans, weakened their morale, and led them to believe in the possibility of a favorable peace. At Versailles the Fourteen Points came into conflict with the secret treaties, agreements by the Allies to award Constantinople and the straits of the Bosporus to Russia, portions of *Italia Irredenta* to Italy, Alsace-Lorraine to France, and other assignments of the spoils of war. After the November 1917 Revolution, the Bolsheviks published the secret treaties as a means of embarrassing the capitalistic victor powers. The Allies had come to Versailles with neither clean hands nor consciences.

The proceedings at Versailles took place in an aura of nationalistic bias. Each delegate had to take into account the reactions of his own people, parliament, and press. There were always pressures from home. In this milieu any projected parliament of man took second place to national interests. The problem was to make a new map in the presence of conflicting nationalisms, imperialistic designs, demands for strategic frontiers, postwar bitterness, desire for reparations, and the Bolshevik threat. It was a gigantic task. Far from being smothered at Versailles, nationalism emerged even stronger than before the war.

Nationalism and the Peace Settlements, 1919

At Versailles they called it "recognition of self-determination," but actually the preponderant sentiment in the territorial settlements was nationalism. What happened thereafter was much like building sand castles at the seashore—no sooner was the edifice constructed than it began to disintegrate. Solutions for national ills led only to the creation of more danger spots.

In the name of nationalism the "lost provinces" of Alsace-Lorraine were returned to France. The idea was to right the wrong done by Bismarck in 1871. Though they professed an older historical claim to the provinces, the Germans accepted the blow, at least for the moment. At the time, they seemed to be more angered by the award of Moresnet, Eupen, and Malmédy, three small districts, to the Belgians.

There were further irritations to German national pride. A part of northern Schleswig was returned to the Danes after a plebiscite. Clemenceau infuriated the Germans by insisting that the left bank of the Rhine be made a permanent autonomous state. This was, said the Tiger, the "natural" frontier of France. The plan was vetoed by Wilson in the interest of morality and by Lloyd George as a means of promoting Continental stability. But both Wilson and Lloyd George, as a substitute, had to guarantee French security against a German attack.

In the West the peacemakers did what they could to undo Bismarck's slights to nationalism. In the East they busied themselves with righting the wrongs committed by Frederick the Great against Poland.

The thirteenth of Wilson's Fourteen Points was explicit:

An independent Polish state should be erected which should include the territories inhabited by indisputable Polish populations, which should be assured a free and secure access to the sea, and whose political and economic independence and •
territorial integrity should be guaranteed by international covenant.

At long last Polish nationalism was recognized. A restored Poland was given an outlet to the sea by a "corridor" running through German territory, an award certain to stimulate German nationalism in the future. The port of Danzig, overwhelmingly German in population, was made a free city under mandate of the League of Nations. In this way one sore spot was eliminated, only to create another.

The Poles, reacting normally in the age of nationalism, immediately revealed an enormous territorial appetite. Not altogether satisfied with the restoration of their old state, and backed by the French, they made additional claims. Wilson and Lloyd George rejected the Polish demand for all of East

Prussia. In the settlement there were more Germans in Poland than Poles in Germany.

Italy, too, invoked the name of nationalism. She called for the entire Dalmatian coast of the Adriatic, including the port of Fiume. Irritated, Wilson insisted that Fiume be awarded to Yugoslavia as her outlet to the sea. A gang of embittered Italian patriots, led by Gabriele D'Annunzio, eccentric lyric poet, seized Fiume and declared that they would not leave, no matter what the conference decided. By the Treaty of Rapallo (1920, revised in 1924), Fiume was annexed to Italy, with provision for free commercial use of the port by the Yugoslavs.

There were parallel treaties with Austria (Treaty of St. Germain), with Hungary (Treaty of Trianon), with Bulgaria (Treaty of Neuilly), and with Turkey (Treaty of Sèvres). All were similarly designed to recognize the national claims of dissatisfied peoples in the shattered Austro-Hungarian and Turkish empires. Austria was reduced to a tiny land-locked republic with a population of 7,000,000. The new Hungary was one-third its prewar size, with districts ceded to Czechoslovakia, Rumania, Yugoslavia, and even Austria. Several million Magyars were intermingled with non-Magyars.

In the dismantled Ottoman Empire, most of Armenia went to the Soviet Union and large tracts in both Europe and Asia Minor went to Greece. The Treaty of Sèvres never went into effect: it was converted into a scrap of paper by militant Turkish nationalists. Mustapha Kemal led the Turks to war against the Greeks in Asia Minor and triumphantly negotiated the considerably more favorable Treaty of Lausanne (1923).

Thus the peacemakers, faced with conflicting national demands, did what they could in an impossible situation, but their best produced only unstable compromises and the seeds of future conflict. Each time a national issue was resolved, another arose in its place. There were new danger spots—the boundaries between Italy and Yugoslavia, between Italy and Austria, between Czechoslovakia and Germany. Nationalism was a Hydra-headed monster at Versailles.

The Big Three were defeated by an ism. Wilson hoped for the best: ''I think it will be found that the compromises, which were accepted as inevitable, nowhere cut at the heart of any principle: the work of the Conference squares, as a whole, with the principles agreed upon as the basis of peace as well as with the practical possibilities.'' Lloyd George was partially satisfied: ''It is a stern but just treaty.'' Clemenceau was ecstatic: ''Nine and forty years have I waited for this. The treaty is something fixed and final which settles the affairs of Europe forever.''

The French Tiger was far too optimistic. German nationalism was only temporarily quiescent. It still smoldered. ''What hand would not wither that signed such a peace?'' asked Philip Scheidemann, who had worked hard for a peace of reconciliation. "Do not expect us to be our own executioners,'' commented German delegate Matthias Erzberger, who signed the treaty and as a reward was assassinated in 1921 by fanatical nationalists.

Attempted Safeguards: The Minorities Treaties

For generations the European story was one of oppression by one nationality over another. Students of history are not surprised by this fact. Indeed, most of human history—the course of what is called civilization—is in part a record of oppression of one kind or another by individuals, groups, states, and nations. The Europe of post–World War I was no exception to this sad state of affairs.

The peacemakers of Versailles had to award spoils to the victors while at the same time scaling down the number of minority peoples. Theirs was a virtually impossible task and they succeeded mostly in redistributing hatreds. They placed several million German-speaking people in the new Czechoslovakia. They included several hundred thousand Germans in the boundaries of reborn Poland. They scattered other national minorities helter-skelter throughout Central and Eastern Europe. People who had belonged to dominant majorities before 1914 now became discontented minorities.

The number of national minorities was increased because of the criss-cross of new boundaries. The ethnic composition of East Central Europe had been so intermingled that it was now impossible to set up homogeneous states. The forced exchange of minorities (Turkey and Greece, Bulgaria and Greece) turned out to be highly unpopular for all the peoples concerned. Calls for federalization were rejected on the ground that it would lead to further disintegration.

With the reshifting of national boundaries, it became a matter of some importance to guarantee the human rights of minorities and to protect them against discrimination. The League of Nations was supposed to supervise special treaties for this purpose. The problem was especially severe in Poland, Yugoslavia, Czechoslovakia, Rumania, and Greece, all of which solemnly agreed "to protect the interests of inhabitants who differ from the majority in race, language, or religion." Any minority that felt itself aggrieved by its treatment was encouraged to submit its case to the League of Nations.

The phrases were glowing on paper but, unfortunately, they were not executed in good faith. The League was too weak to command respect. It was the old scourge of nationalism at work: once a minority achieved its independence and took control, it revealed the utmost reluctance to grant other minorities the status it had won for itself. "Liberators" quarreled with "treasonable secessionist agitators," meaning minority nationalists. An exception was the case of the Czechoslovaks, who were worried about their new national integrity but did what they could to satisfy the demands of the German minority in the Sudetenland. It was not enough—the Sudeten Germans later turned to Adolf Hitler to "liberate" them.

Resentful national minorities remained a source of internal weakness and external friction. The conglomeration of new sore spots was a contributory factor to the outbreak of World War II. Once again nationalism was showing its capacity for historical mischief.

Loss of Social Momentum: Nationalism and World War II

During the long armistice from 1919 to 1939 the politics and economy of Europe and the world in general languished in a kind of uneasy hibernation. The victor powers of World War I, hit hard by the depression of 1929 and fearful of new wars, settled into despondency. The momentum of change slowed down. Instead of seeking a new way of life freed from the old animosities, the diplomats of Europe turned once more to the bankrupt policies of the past.

Nationalism was as intense in 1939 as it had been in 1914. Versailles turned out to be a peace that ended peace. All attempts to create a viable internationalism were frustrated. At the core of this situation lay a paradox typical of the dangerous ism: most people realized that unrestrained nationalism had been largely responsible for World War I, yet they were only lukewarm in advocating the alternative of some form of internationalism. They were aware of a progressive worldwide cooperation in commerce, industry, and finance, but they were unwilling to abandon either their national flag or national anthem.

People everywhere were familiar only with the external aspects of forces moving them in any direction. To them, nationalism was confused with patriotism, and love of country was good. Most of them refused to accept the argument that internationalist movements would be less bellicose and disruptive, and possibly more humane and apt to produce a better world.

Similarly, most people, unaware of historical currents, did not realize that nationalism, a phenomenon arising in the eighteenth century, is associated with economic and demographic revolution. They did not know that nationalism evolved with the mass age, that it was becoming more abstract, messianic, dangerous.

German nationalism, temporarily driven underground in 1919, was revived in this atmosphere. Lewis Namier saw it as an example of recurrent historical phenomena:

The rise of a pathological nationalism ten or fifteen years after a national defeat seems a recurrent phenomenon, practically independent of the terms imposed on, or accorded to, the defeated country. It comes apparently when the children of the war period attain the age of twenty to thirty; adults may learn the lessons of war and defeat, but those who have experienced the passions of war and the bitterness of defeat while still incapable of critical understanding seem burdened with frantic, almost insane resentments, which break forth in afterlife and give a pathological turn to their politics.[1]

In other words, a wave of nationalist exasperation was bound to sweep Germany, even if she had been given more lenient terms at Versailles. Germans found it just as difficult to accept the loss of their dominant position in Europe as had the French after "the wounds of Waterloo."

Responsibility for the outbreak of World War I can be distributed among the leading personalities of the belligerent powers. But for World War II the critical human factor was Adolf Hitler, the kind of man who could only have been produced in the age of the masses. He alone made the vital decisions for starting the conflict at the moment of his own choice. The second fiddler in the process, Mussolini, was only an auxiliary troublemaker. Granting the thesis of the brilliant A. J. P. Taylor that the inefficiency of British and French statesmen contributed to the breakdown of the peace machinery, it is a distortion of history to place them on a par with the monomaniacal Nazi as instigators of the most terrible war of all time.

Nationalism revealed itself in its worst and most intolerant form in the mind of Hitler. The quality of this mind was caught in an extraordinary sentence by the British historian Hugh Trevor-Roper: "A terrible phenomenon, imposing indeed in its granite harshness and yet infinitely squalid in its miscellaneous cumber—like some huge barbarian monolith, the expression of giant strength and savage genius, surrounded by a festering heap of refuse—old tins and dead vermin, ashes and eggshells and ordure—the intellectual detritus of centuries."[2] This evil genius, convinced of his own destiny, succeeded beyond all expectations in brainwashing a gifted but apolitical people. Germany, he said, had the right to satisfy her need for expansion (Lebensraum) at the expense of any other country or combination of countries standing in the way. One surprising coup after another endeared him to the hearts of his people, who were deeply impressed by his special brand of nationalism. In relatively quick time he converted the German military machine, weakened during the Weimar Republic, into a juggernaut of destruction.

This does not mean that German nationalism should be singled out as the only single cause for the outbreak of World War II. It was, however, a triggering factor of great importance among a multiplicity of contributory causes. The pre-1914 political climate was still there. There was the same economic warfare to achieve self-sufficiency and a favorable balance of trade, the same drive for protective tariffs and managed currencies, the same cutthroat competition. There was the same kind of international anarchy when the League of Nations failed to set up a working system of collective security. An uneasy Europe was burdened by the traditional forms of alliance and alignments.

Something new was added to this explosive mixture by the charismatic personality of the Austrian ex-tramp who could screech louder than any other statesman performing at his top level. Adolf Hitler ridiculed the League as "a joint-stock company for the preservation of the booty won in the war." His advent as German Chancellor in January 1933, followed by the German walk-out in October, meant the end of the Geneva Disarmament Conference. The armaments race was resumed. Again the recurrent theme—each country suspiciously eyed the armed strength of its neighbors and in the name of preparedness began to strengthen its own military machine. Again came the game of power politics and the use of military threats to win diplomatic quarrels.

The peoples of Europe were gripped by fears, both rational and irrational. "Perhaps the worst factor of all is the sense of fatality that pervades Europe, the uncertainty about the future, the bewilderment about the present, the sense of having stood for two decades on shaky ground. [World War I] destroyed something in Europe which has never been restored. It might be called social stability."[3]

Men of good will had hoped that the peoples of the world, disgusted with periodic descents into barbarism, would turn at last to international conciliation. It was not to be: what was lacking was a willingness to accept the common interests of mankind as precious and desirable. To such a tragic pass had nationalism brought the peoples of the world in 1939.

Notes

[1] Lewis Namier, "Pathological Nationalisms," *Manchester Guardian*, April 26, 1933.

[2] From the introduction by Hugh Trevor-Roper to *Hitler's Secret Conversations, 1914–1944*, by Adolph Hitler (New York: Farrar, Strauss & Young, 1953), pp. xxix–xxx.

[3] Harold Callendar, "Europe Gropes for a Way Out," in *The New York Times*, March 31, 1935.

10

Divarication: The New Nationalism

The twentieth century is the first period in history, in which the whole of mankind has accepted one and the same political attitude, that of nationalism. Its rise everywhere implied an activization of the people and the demand for a new ordering of society.

—Hans Kohn

The Irreplaceable Sense of Belonging

Looking backward beyond the two world wars, we see that the twentieth century began on an optimistic note. Parliamentary democracy was on the march and a better world seemed to be in process of formation. But lurking in the background were critical unsolved problems, the most serious of which was the constant threat of war. There was little sense of morality among statesmen and diplomats—the great masters of diplomacy were those who could manipulate the big lie for their country. Nor was there any international organization capable of settling disputes between nations. Science had brought swift changes toward better living conditions but it had also introduced more terrible and destructive weapons. There was a vigor of a sort, but it was a vitality of fever, not health. Nationalism was one of the major forces which helped push this brave new world into the mire of World War I.

During the twenty years of the long armistice from 1919 to 1939 came the rise of communism and fascism, as well as the stunning impact of the Great Depression. World War II worked even greater havoc than the earlier war, including the introduction of genocide, that nadir of human depravity. After 1945 two great superpowers, the United States and the Soviet Union, confronted one another in a cold war. The possession of nuclear weapons changed the entire character of relations between nations.

In 1900 there seemed to be the bare possibility for the emergence of a unified humanity with a common design. By mid-century it became clear that the divisions between mankind were more pronounced than ever before. Only slowly did concerned people realize that the world structure had slipped into a dangerous whirlpool.

Two political trends gained momentum. On the one hand, the traditional nation-states that formerly had dominated the world were no longer able to compete with the two superpowers, the United States and the Soviet Union. On the other hand, as colonialism receded, dozens of small powers came into existence. Smaller and less experienced, they nevertheless imitated the older states. Nationalism was showing a surprising resiliency.

The "Newness of the New Nationalism"

Despite the milieu of paradox in which they operate, the isms accurately reflect historical change. The new nationalism, similar to the older form, mirrored the time in which it existed. It retained its basic nineteenth-century characteristic of being either a force for unification or for disruption, but something new was added. Contrary to the hope of internationalists, nationalism had become more prevalent as the twentieth century wore on. "Expectant peoples" through their elites led revolts against imperialist rule and set up their own independent states. The new nationalism took on racial overtones. Its proponents were often little conscious of their common interests and common culture.

What is new about the new nationalism? Some observers insist that it is merely a variation of the older form and hence is not new at all. Others say that although it remains fundamentally the same historical phenomenon that emerged in seventeenth-century England and eighteenth-century France, it has taken on new characteristics and hence should be distinguished from the early form.

A Global Ordering of Society

First and foremost in the quality of the new nationalism is its worldwide framework. The older nationalism was distinctly European in origin and development, while the new nationalism, a product of self-assertion throughout the world, has taken on a global aspect. For the first time in history the entire world has accepted one and the same concept as its most important political sentiment. The new nationalism has become a determining and dominating historical force among all the peoples of the earth.

As it entered its global phase, an always accommodating nationalism took on overall tendencies adapted to the special circumstances of each country. At first it recapitulated the European experience in calling for an open society on libertarian lines. Leaders of new nations spoke glowingly of independence, freedom, civil liberties, and social reform. Libertarian nationalism would be the panacea of all problems, including peace, prosperity, and security.

Unfortunately, the libertarian aspect, as in Europe, was not to endure. The new nationalism, much like the older form, tended to move in the direction of the closed society. One after another, the new nationalist liberators (Nkrumah in Ghana, Sukarno in Indonesia, Castro in Cuba) were transformed into arrogant nationalists. The fathers of the fatherland became authoritarian figures.

In theory, each new nation was to take its place as a viable unit in a working world society. In practice, liberation was followed by precious little freedom, peace, or security, and no disposition to relinquish national sovereignty in favor of global rule. The new nations became insecure and xenophobic. Those who demanded freedom from oppressors quickly became oppressors themselves. In the name of nationalism, Indians and Pakistanis, freed from British control, began to attack each other. Independent Nigeria, hailed as a new working democracy, slid into civil war with Biafra. There was chaos in the Congo. Political arguments over national borders became commonplace;

the economic life of many new states was crippled by internal and external hatreds; cultural and psychological differences were accentuated. The new nation-states did not act differently from their predecessors—they were just as little inclined to reject nationalism as an outmoded anachronism.

The course of the new global nationalism brings into focus a special problem concerning the new nations. A pertinent query is justifiable: Is freedom, as we are inclined to think of it in European and American society, actually compatible with any "emerging" society of the new order? Further, is it even (to use an awkward word) "relevant"? The emerging societies had no Renaissance, no Reformation, no Enlightenment—no sets of experiences which in common could provide them a framework of libertarianism. Little wonder, then, that most new nations bypassed the lake of liberty and headed straight for the shoals of nationalism.

Despite the urge for freedom in Western Europe, by far the greater part of the Continent was fragmented by nationalism. European fragmentation was followed by balkanization of the world. Global nationalism also meant rigid adherence to national sovereignty, to unrestricted economic isolation, and to cultural xenophobia. Wherever it appeared, the new nationalism consistently retained the worst features of the older form.

Technology and the New Nationalism

It was to be expected that the new nationalism would be affected by advances in technology, especially by changes in transportation and communication. The world has grown much smaller in the sense of vastly improved intercommunication. The old Mercator map has been replaced by the polar projection; sea power has given way to air power. It now takes less time to fly from New York to London than it took only a short time ago to travel by train from New York to Richmond. Coffee drinkers in Europe are unaware that they have much to do with the income of farmers in Brazil. American tariffs have an important effect on the livelihood of Japanese workers. Raises in the price of oil by Arab states sent waves of dislocation through the economic systems of every nation in the world. People everywhere are influenced by advertising campaigns originating in Madison Avenue offices. The physical interconnectedness of peoples all over the world has become a new fact in contemporary life.

This remarkable environmental transformation has had an effect on the course of nationalism. The old attachment to local patriotism is being replaced by a somewhat wider loyalty. Classical, narrow patriotism, looking primarily to home and hearth, is being succeeded by a more rigid nationalism looking outward to a hostile world. Although technology has brought national cultures closer together, at the same time it has tended to emphasize political differences. Thus another paradox: far from stimulating a workable internationalism, technology has actually contributed to the hardening of national lines. A new historical law is in process of formation: the greater the lip service to internationalism, the greater the desire to oppose any lessening of national sovereignty. Both the Alexandrian concept of the cosmos and Wendell Willkie's One World still appear across the horizon as a distant goal.

Technology not only hardened the political structure along national lines but it also affected national economies. Experimental economic combinations among nations, of which the Common Market is the best example, have enjoyed some success. However, most statesmen at the policymaking level stiffen when they hear suggestions for extending economic into political unity. This has led to a critical problem, described by Barbara Ward: "However violent the effort made at various times—for instance in the thirties—to insulate national economies from the force of change or development or collapse at work in world trade, the web of commerce has grown so strongly that today the nations appear to have only two choices: either to make the intricate system function or else to strangle in its tangled skein."[1]

Conformity to the Nuclear Power Structure

The announcement came from Washington on August 6, 1945: "The force from which the sun draws its power has been loosed against those who went to war in the Far East." It was, indeed, a great turning point in the history of warfare when the *Enola Gay* dropped the first atomic bomb over Hiroshima. That event changed the whole power base of world society.

After World War II there was a three-way split between the Communist bloc, an anti-Communist bloc, and a number of neutral, unaligned states. By far the most serious rivalry was between the United States and her allies and the Soviet Union and her allies in the so-called cold war.[2] Initially, this cold war was a predictable case of push and shove among the victorious powers, a very real expression of intense nationalism carrying over from World War II. At this time the Communists adopted an aggressive strategy, exploiting the weakness of unstable regimes and infiltrating nationalist movements everywhere. The early policy of the United States was containment, designed to halt the advance of world communism by constructing defensive alliances, helping weak governments, and blocking subversion.

Behind this conflict was the reality of atomic power. The United States exploded its first nuclear-fission hydrogen bomb in 1951, the Soviet Union in 1953. Both countries possess a missile system capable of giving the hydrogen bomb direction to its target. The cold war erupted into confrontation. The

Berlin crisis of 1961 and the Cuban missile crisis of 1962 brought home to both sides the futility of threatening one another with nuclear attack. President John F. Kennedy warned: "Powers must avert those confrontations which bring an adversary to a choice of either a humiliating retreat or a nuclear war." Premier Nikita Khrushchev agreed: "Only madmen can hope to further the cause of Communism by a nuclear war in which a million workers would be killed for each capitalist." This retreat from nuclear holocaust did not end the cold war, but it did cancel out a United States–Soviet Union hot war by mutual deterrence.

The new nationalism quickly adapted itself to the power base of nuclear weapons. The British exploded a hydrogen bomb in 1957, the Chinese in 1967, the French in 1968. Before his death, General Charles de Gaulle was determined to press ahead with a nuclear-weapon development program as proof of his restoration of *la gloire*. Even smaller nations were inclined to look to atomic energy as the great equalizer in a situation where they had to take a low second place to the great powers. Latecomers on the technological scene, they nevertheless dreamed of commanding respect through possession of nuclear striking power.

The fact of nuclear power would seem to generate a desire everywhere for a quick end to nationalism—for its burial. Unfortunately for the residents of this planet, that has not happened.

The Qualifying Factor of Populism

The new nationalism, functioning in a changing social structure, was modified by the infusion of a populist strain. Until the mid-seventeenth century the rural peoples of Europe owed their loyalty to hereditary princes and the nobility. Resentment against the privileged classes was fused into an explosive instrument in the French Revolution by the up and coming bourgeoisie, aware of its power and determined to use that strength for its own benefit. The bourgeoisie maintained its supremacy throughout the nineteenth century, despite challenges from below in the revolutions of 1830 and 1848 and the Paris Commune of 1871.

The twentieth-century pattern has varied throughout the world, but in general the workingman and the peasant—the "common man" below the bourgeoisie—have bettered their positions in society. They have seen the elimination of many old obstacles. There are fewer estates, castes, and civil privileges. When compared with the restrictions he endured a century earlier, the common man has made giant strides in what has been called "his" century.

This new status may be recognized in a variety of patterns, running all the way from the Scandinavian welfare state to the Communist society of Soviet

Russia. Every revolutionary movement of the twentieth century was both national and social, including the fascism of Mussolini and Hitler, both of whom boasted that they had combined the best elements of nationalism and socialism. The emergent nations took on not only the trappings of nationalism, but virtually all of them favored socialism in one form or another. Nationalism was the instrument by which they had freed themselves from colonial powers and with which they had satisfied their urge for security. Socialism was for them a device for assuring a successful modern technology.

The new nationalism, then, is no longer dominantly bourgeois, but a populist force geared to the socialization of national power. Indeed, this populist tinge helps distinguish the new nationalism from the earlier, conventional form. The blend varies in content: it exists in democratic countries as well as in Fascist or Communist dictatorships. Flags and anthems remain as national symbols, but added to them is a deep concern for the welfare of the masses.

India provides a good case. Throughout his career, during the thirteen years he spent in prison as well as during his activities after independence as Foreign Minister and Prime Minister, Pandit Jawaharlal Nehru displayed the most ardent sense of nationalism. India to him was not merely an image or an abstract notion but the homeland of millions of his fellow human beings who needed help. He would accept for his country neither the communism of the Soviet Union, with its heavy price in loss of freedom, work, and lives, nor the capitalism of the United States, which seemed to be working well for the masses but which operated with supplies of capital which India did not have. Instead, he recommended for his country a benevolent nationalism combined with democratic socialism. Like political leaders elsewhere, Nehru was anxious to exploit the current populist trend.

Common Denominators

No matter where it exists, nationalism retains similar basic qualities. Always it tends to reflect the historical circumstances of the areas in which it functions. This holds as well for the new nationalism, which tended to take on the characteristics of broad geographical regions. The patterns are by no means absolutely clear, and there are exceptions, but there are certain common denominators to engage our attention.

Fragmentation persists in the European cradle land of nationalism. It can be recognized at three levels: among the older, established nations (Britain, France, Germany, Italy, and Spain); among the succession and successor states (Yugoslavia, Czechoslovakia, Poland, and Russian-absorbed Latvia, Estonia, and Lithuania); and among the mini-nationalisms calling for liberation (Welsh and Scots in Britain, Catalans and Basques in Spain, Flemings in Belgium, and Bretons in France). The United States of Europe remains an unattainable ideal on a continent frustrated by balkanization.

The rise of black nationalism in Africa was predictable as a counterforce to European imperialism on that continent. Exploiting their new riches, the imperial powers held on to their African colonies as long as they could. The white man's burden was said to bring the blessings of civilization to backward natives, but this kind of altruism was considerably less real than the lure of copra, rubber, and diamonds. The process of decolonization began after World War II, when the exploiting powers began to drop their African colonies like so many hot potatoes. The process brought additional problems. Africa's new nations tried to adapt themselves to the old borders set up by the imperialist powers. The resultant clashes between the new African nationalism and the older traditional tribalism kept the continent in continuous ferment. Out of the chaos emerged a new black nationalism, dominantly ethnic and directed against the white man.

In similar fashion, the new nationalism in the vast spaces of Asia took on the common characteristic of hatred for the old colonialism. The role of the imperialist in Asia was as unpleasant as in Africa. British, French, German, and Russian entrepreneurs carved up the continent into spheres of influence, with little understanding of a culture and civilization that had even longer traditions than much of the Western world. Asian nationalism crystallized after 1945, and with explosive force. There was no unified action in the Asian countries: here as elsewhere, nationalism worked for fragmentation.

A politico-religious nationalism emerged in the Near and Middle East, the cradle land of three great religions—Judaism, Christianity, and Islam—which has never been free of religious impact. All three religions ultimately spread to other regions, but Islam retained its hold on the land bridge between Europe and Asia. Consciousness of Islamic affinity remained strong in the area; it was tempered eventually by political nationalism. However, intense rivalries between the various Islamic nations were far too deep to allow free rein to political ties. After World War II there was a closer relationship among the Arab states, due primarily to a common hostility to Israel. But even here, local patriotisms militated against effective Arab combination. Meanwhile a new Jewish nationalism came of age: after long exile and persecution, the Jews in 1948 realized their dream of a national homeland in Israel. Nationalism on both sides was exacerbated and led to bitter clashes.

The success of the American and French revolutions inspired unrest in Latin America. Simón Bolivar and José de San Martín led revolts against Spanish rule. Where North America went on to test democratic federalism, the Latin American states, finding it difficult to overcome their Spanish heritage, alternated between anarchy and dictatorship. This trend continued into the twentieth century, when Latin American nationalism was tempered by populism. The general pattern was complex and variegated: though most Latin American states were of Spanish origin, each preferred to go its own nationalist way. One of the few unifying sentiments was a common hostility to the Yankee colossus to the north.

From its beginnings, American nationalism exhibited a lick-all-creation spirit. This new melting-pot breed was certain that its own institutions were superior and that Europe was declining into senility. The two world wars boosted the United States into the position of the most powerful nation on earth. Americans still retained faith in what they regarded as a preeminent democratic society decidedly worthy of emulation. The goal had already been described by Ralph Waldo Emerson: "The office of America is to liberate, to abolish kingcraft, priestcraft, caste monopoly, to pull down the gallows, to burn up the bloody statute-book, to take in the immigrant, to open the doors of the sea and the fields of the earth." In the mid-twentieth century, Americans slid almost imperceptibly into a role as policemen of the world society, thereby stepping into the shoes of the once ubiquitous British redcoats. American G.I.s were sent to European posts, as well as to Korea and South Vietnam, to block the inroads of communism. Clearly there is such a thing as American interest abroad, and it was, in this instance, related to the extension of the cold war.

Equally obvious was the persistence of Russian expansionist nationalism. Both Tzarist and Soviet Russia were dedicated to expansion: the old Russian nationalism was countered by imperial Britain, the new form by the United States. Soviet Russia regarded herself as the standard bearer of Marxist-Leninist internationalism, only to adopt an ardent nationalism of her own. If the office of Americans was to liberate other peoples, then the intention of Russians was to free any number of smaller nations from what they denounced as capitalist exploitation and then bathe them in the wave of a future Communist world. Moscow found an annoying problem: Marxian internationalism foundered as the Communist world split into rigid national units.

A comparative analysis of all these major areas reveals some superficial differences in the working of the new nationalism. But underneath runs the same basic psychological drive, seeking security in the system of homelands, fatherlands, and motherlands.

Notes

[1] Barbara Ward, *Faith and Freedom* (London: Hamish Hamilton, 1954), pp. 208–9.

[2] For further discussion of the confrontation of American and Russian messianisms, see chapters 14 and 15.

11

Europe: Fragmentation and Mini-nationalisms

In general it must be emphasized that national self-determination is intended for nations and not for fragments of nations. It would certainly be absurd to allow every province or town of a State to claim the right of secession. This would lead to a paralyzing instability in everything and to political and social disintegration.

—Frederick Hertz

Balkanization and Socialization

After the appalling loss of life and property in World Wars I and II, it might have been expected that Europeans would be disgusted with nationalism and its tribal wars. Reasonable men believe that the old idea of separate, sovereign, autonomous states is an anachronism, an anomaly, an outworn force ready for the dustbin of history. But rational men far too often find themselves existing as ciphers among an indifferent majority. Disillusioned, they would like to see an end to perfervid nationalism and in its place a working United States of Europe. They grant that nationalism was born in Europe, that nations have existed for the longest time there, that peoples have wrought havoc on one another there. Let it end there.

Such is the dream of just and sensible men. Yet, despite changing institutions and differing forms of growth, nationalism on the European continent retains its life and vigor. It is fragmented, balkanized, and tinged with the urge toward secession, but it retains its force.

We have seen that there is one all-important difference between the new and the old—the interpenetration of nationalism and socialism. The fusion of these two isms, one of the most striking phenomena of recent history, is worldwide in scope but is especially evident in Europe. Despite the discredit nationalism has earned, its original attractiveness remains. It has attained more strength and has been morally justified by combining with the urge for social welfare. As national administrations become stronger, they become more socialistic in their aims.

The way in which nationalism and socialism blended in Europe varied from country to country. There are three major examples:

The Communist Version.   With Stalin's deadly triumph over Trotsky and the subsequent purge of the opposition, the Bolsheviks came to the conclusion that they could save communism only by nationalizing it. Even though nationalism was supposed to be a disintegrative force, it attracted Communists precisely because it was regarded as a means of self-preservation. Russian communism, hewing to its own version of the Marxian line, became more and more nationalistic.

The Fascist Paraphrase.   Fascism, among other things, was a product of the conflict (and the liberal dilemma) between liberty and security. In this confrontation, nationalism becomes an appropriate *Ersatz*. Among the numerous examples is the story of Germany from 1848 to 1866. In more recent times, Fascist dictators Mussolini and Hitler found that they could enlist the support of the masses by promising protection against poverty, unemployment, and insecurity. They knew that they could not function without the recognition and assistance of their people. It was no accident that Hitler called his movement National Socialism—an appeal to both nationalism and socialism. As it turned out, the dictators were considerably more attracted by national aggressiveness than by socialism; both presented the argument that their countries had been denied their historically justified *Lebensraum*.

The Democratic Amplification. Marxist ideas, geared to a more democratic plane, also gained influence in the more open societies. The way already had been prepared by the inauguration of universal suffrage, the growth of popular education, and systems of social security. Socialism in the democracies tended to lose much of its international coloring and to become sharply distinguished from communism. Parliamentary socialist parties became nationalistic in character: dedicated to socialist egalitarianism, they at the same time retained a sharp sense of national identity.

An excellent example of this fusion of nationalism and socialism can be found in the Scandinavian welfare states. Another case is that of Britain, well prepared by a long liberal tradition and by Fabian socialism, and inclined to extract the best of the fused isms in providing for social welfare. French administrators at the top level knew that their staying power depended on how well they could meet public demand for social reform. A similar situation may be noted among other democratic European states from Switzerland to Holland.

It is by no means an exaggeration to say that since the turn of the century communism and socialism have made progress only insofar as they identified themselves with nationalism. The beginning of World War I provides a crucial case in point. Socialists throughout Europe, with the exception of those in Bulgaria, voted for war credits. In December 1913 William II wrote to the retired Bülow: "First let us shoot down the Socialists, or behead them, or somehow make them harmless, then we can face an external war." He changed his mind on August 4, 1914, when the Social Democrats voted in caucus 96–14 in favor of war credits. Now the delighted Emperor could exclaim: "I know no parties any more, I know only Germans!"—a sentiment duly recorded on commemorative coins. Hugo Haase, Socialist spokesman, explained: "It is not up to us today to decide for or against peace, but to grant the required means for defense of our country." And soon from the front lines came these words from a Socialist *Reichstag* deputy who had volunteered for service: "To shed one's blood for the Fatherland is not difficult; it is enveloped in romantic heroism." Clearly, then, neither democratic Socialists nor totalitarian Communists can resist the appeal of nationalism. At one and the same time, but in differing degrees, they proclaim the virtues of internationalism but "recognize the right of every people to national independence."

Charles de Gaulle and the Revivification of French Nationalism

It is a fascinating spectacle—how one man, touched by charisma, could manipulate nationalism to lift his country from a second-rate level to equality with Europe's leading nations. In a process of historical legerdemain, Charles de Gaulle did more than any other individual to renew the core of nineteenth-century nationalism.

Above all, de Gaulle was distinguished by faith in his country, by love for the physical beauty of the land, and for its heritage, and by ceaseless struggle to restore France to a front-rank position in the community of nations. He was certain that, as head of state, he was surrounded by a "mythic aura" which excused his sense of arrogant autocracy and self-righteousness. He nominated himself, as did the "Good Prince" described by Machiavelli: it was his duty to protect the state and people against nefarious vested interests. He disdainfully brushed aside the accusation that he was turning the clock backward. For him, that was an achievement of the highest order.

De Gaulle regarded himself as the heir of the epic tradition of France. Belief in French grandeur was a part of his very being: it was not a matter to be discussed or argued. He transformed everything into symbols of French glory—even athletic events. When a French rugby team distinguished itself by defeating Cardiff, de Gaulle sat down to send a handwritten letter to the captain: "Dear Sir: That was a magnificent triumph, more beautiful and complete than that of last year. All Frenchmen will rejoice in your victory." The most important thing in the world for him was to keep the mystique of French grandeur afloat. He refused to accept the prevalent notion that France had lost her sense of mission and had shrunk to its Continental size, or that his country had become mission territory for such foreign ideologies as American capitalism and its opposites—Marxism, Maoism, and Marcusianism.

The whole life of de Gaulle was constructed on the premise that he was born to save France. Almost as imperious as Louis XIV, a problem child for his allies in war, a paternal democratic authoritarian in peace, he virtually singlehandedly infused new energy, pride, and dignity into a defeated, miserable people.

De Gaulle gave evidence of his genius as early as 1934, when he published his *Vers l'armée de métier,* designed to describe the army of the future. He advocated a small highly trained professional army of fast-moving armored troops. His views on the tactical employment of armor were contrary to the old military traditions of the Third Republic. French generals, unlike their German counterparts, were not inclined to listen to the pompous, arrogant colonel.

After Hitler's Nazis smashed France in 1940, de Gaulle fled to London, where he proclaimed himself leader of the French resistance and set up a national committee as the nucleus for a future French government. From this time on he was regarded with disdain by both Roosevelt and Churchill. At the Casablanca Conference, called in January 1943 to determine Allied military aims, de Gaulle claimed that he had at his disposal an army of 256,000 men (French Committee of National Liberation). France, he said, was once more a great power and he ought to be included in making any decisions affecting the postwar world. Roosevelt, unimpressed, labeled him a Joan of Arc. At Casablanca, de Gaulle never quite got over the shock of learning that "Roosevelt intended that the peace should be an American peace, and that in particular France should have him for savior and arbiter."

De Gaulle admitted that his emotional side tended to imagine France, like the princesses in the stories or the Madonnas in the frescoes, as dedicated to an exalted and exceptional destiny. "But the positive side of my mind," he said, "also assures me that France is not truly herself unless in the first rank." Only vast enterprises, he warned, could be capable of counteracting the divisive elements inherent in the people of France. "To my mind, France cannot be France without greatness."

De Gaulle was certain that in some mysterious way he was selected to be the incarnation of the spirit of France. He believed that he not only spoke for France, he *was* France. A call from the depths of history, he wrote, as well as the instinct of the nation itself, led him to bear responsibility for the treasure in default of heirs to assume French sovereignty. He believed himself to be the one destined to hold legitimate power. He would be the one to call the nation to war and to unity, to impose order, law, and justice, to demand from the world respect for the rights of France. "In this realm, I could not compromise in the slightest degree."

To this consummate egotist, Roosevelt and Churchill were seeking to relegate his beloved France to a secondary place. He had no intention of allowing this to happen. He was sure that "Germany's collapse, Europe's laceration, and Anglo-American friction" offered a miraculously saved France an exceptional opportunity for action. This would permit him to achieve the "grand design" he had conceived for his country.

What was de Gaulle's great plan? He would assure France's security in Western Europe by preventing the rise of a new Reich that might threaten her safety. As leader of the French, he would cooperate with East and West, and if need be, contract the necessary alliances on one side or the other without accepting any kind of dependency. He would persuade the states along the Rhine, the Alps, and the Pyrenees (Germany, the Low Countries, Italy, and Spain) to form a political, economic, and strategic bloc. He would establish this organization as one of the three world powers and, should it become necessary, he—the spokesman for France—would act as the arbiter between the Anglo-American and Soviet camps. Among his major premises was his belief that the United States and the Soviet Union, left to themselves, would lead the entire world to disaster. France (read *de Gaulle!*) must rescue this planet from that catastrophe.

There was no hint of gratefulness in de Gaulle's makeup. What was past was past. France had been saved by the courage and perseverance of the British in their finest hour, but this did not mean that de Gaulle would support Britain's application to enter the Common Market. The United States had given crucial aid to France in both world wars, but this did not prevent de Gaulle's assault on the American dollar. France came first! Gaullism sought, above all, the grandeur of a revived France. It was plainly and simply an act of faith to support the nation in exercising that major role she had played in Europe for a thousand years.

As the impeccable embodiment of French national consciousness, de Gaulle was hostile to the idea of European supranationalism. Nothing was to stand in the way of French sovereignty—not the United Nations, the North Atlantic Community, or the Common Market. France would not relinquish one bit of her hard-won sovereignty in favor of internationalism of any kind. France would remain the traditional guardian of European freedom. And when de Gaulle spoke, he would be speaking in the name of Europe and European civilization.

This was the inspiration de Gaulle pursued with singleminded intent. It is fair to say that the French turned to him after a dozen years of bumbling and catastrophic management under the Fourth Republic. Much of his work was successful.

In 1945 and 1946 he was unanimously elected Provisional President but resigned after leftist parties withdrew their support. He was recalled to power in 1958 at a time when the Fourth Republic was threatened with collapse as a result of the Algerian conflict. He set to work vigorously to put an end to the "disasters" the previous regimes had brought on France. His new constitution, providing for a powerful President, received an 80 percent vote of approval in a referendum. The President had the right to choose the Premier, dissolve the Assembly, and in times of emergency to govern by decree. Only 131 of the deputies of the preceding Assembly were reelected. To meet economic problems, de Gaulle sponsored a series of stabilization measures, froze the salaries of state employees, devalued the franc, increased taxes, and cut social security payments. He spoke contemptuously of European integration, but he made certain to remain inside the Common Market. He put an end to the Algerian war, and France found herself at peace for the first time since 1939. Annoyed by American power in Europe, he invited the

North Atlantic Treaty Organization to leave the soil of France. He would cease to take part in the NATO military structure, but he would be willing to remain in the political alliance.

All these actions on both domestic and foreign fronts were coldly deliberate. By his moves on the Common Market and NATO, de Gaulle was forcing his allies to undertake important reconsiderations of their strategy. Above all, by what others considered to be obstructionist tactics, he was calling attention to the importance of France as a vital link in the chain of Europe. This was his way of expressing the power of a resurgent France.

In the process of renewing French nationalism, de Gaulle brought a measure of security and order to a people whose delegates in the National Assembly had often sought to settle their differences by fist fights. The Gaullist regime received a severe test in the spring of 1968, when the country underwent the traumatic experience of a near-revolution. De Gaulle's government was opposed by a large section of the student population, the younger workers, and much of the general public. Behind the discontent was the feeling that the establishment—from the antiquated Sorbonne to substandard housing to outmoded business practices—was not adapted to the needs of a modern industrial society. Theoreticians and practitioners of violence seemed to be on the verge of victory in the streets, but the rebellion never gained momentum. De Gaulle, with typical dignity, risked his political life: he called for a national election and won it handily.

Despite this momentary triumph, deep damage had been done to de Gaulle's image as the personification of France. Eleven months later he threatened to resign if the people rejected a relatively unimportant referendum on the regional structure of France, but one which he regarded as significant. This time the electorate took him at his word and within a few hours the old warrior was on his way home to Colombey-les-Deux-Églises. The self-appointed father figure of the French nation became absorbed in writing his memoirs. But his countrymen had not forgotten his stubborn sense of independence, and his insistence on preserving strict French sovereignty.

De Gaulle's brand of nationalism was effective not only in France but had repercussions throughout Europe. His success in exploiting the idea of national greatness provided a kind of beacon for other Europeans. They shared his contempt for any kind of supranationalism that would tend to limit their own sovereignty. As a result, de Gaulle was the despair of Eurocrats as well as internationalists of every caliber. Others would seek to imitate his zeal for an archaic national grandeur. In thus pursuing the hegemonic aspirations of his beloved France, he was responsible for adding much strength to contemporary nationalism.

Nationalism in Postwar Germany

Germany in 1945 was a tragic example of what happens when nationalism goes berserk. For the second time in the twentieth century her dream of expansion was shattered. This time the cost was terrifying in its enormity: 6,000,000 lives lost; tremendous property damage; a great civilization in shambles. It was as if most of the country had been laid waste by a gigantic scythe. In virtually all cities of over 100,000 population, 90 percent of the buildings were wholly or partly destroyed. Berlin was heaped with mountainous piles of debris; Dresden was devastated by fire bombs. The system of transportation was in chaos: every bridge across the Rhine was destroyed and lying on the river bed; most of the railroad tracks were smashed and beyond repair. This was the national "rejuvenation" promised Germany by the little man of Berchtesgaden.

Stunned and bewildered, the Germans seemed unable to comprehend the disaster. There was no revolution: Germany was freed from its dictator by outsiders. With little psychological preparation, traditional German morality collapsed under the shock of defeat. If anything, Germans had had enough of nationalism and its evil consequences. German youth turned away in disgust from the symbols of national pride and honor.

Then came the economic miracle. Within a decade the West German economy achieved a recovery almost without parallel in history. A defeated people rose like a phoenix from the ashes. The economic accomplishments were extraordinary: production rose rapidly; the currency reserve was bolstered; public finances showed surpluses; unemployment was reduced. It was truly an astonishing performance.

By 1953 West Germany could boast of an industrial output 59 percent higher than in 1936. Now she was the most important creditor in the European Payment Plan, with an accumulated credit of nearly half a billion dollars. From 1951 to 1956 West German exports tripled in value and began to close in on second-place Britain and the first-place United States. In 1955 West Germany had a trade surplus of $286 million, at a time when Britain had a deficit of $985 million. In that same year German automobile exports increased to $331 million from $54 million in 1950. The small German *Volkswagen* began to appear in markets all over the world, and complete assembly plants for its manufacture were set up outside the homeland.

For the victor powers, mired in their economic difficulties, it was an almost unbelievable phenomenon. West Germany's success was due in part to American aid, but other countries received such help with far less spectacular results. Not the least significant factor was plain, simple, hard work. Indeed, as suggested by Rebecca West, the beaver-like activity of the West Germans may be attributed in part to a desperate attempt to forget their Nazi past and sublimate their guilt feelings by work, work, and more work. Strong constraints were imposed by trade unions on their rank and file (profits, incidentally, were by no means comparably reduced).

Whatever the reason, West Germany rose rapidly to the top of the European economic structure. German goods once again flowed in huge volume to the markets of the world, and the mark came to be recognized as one of the more stable hard currencies. The economic recovery was a classic case of the free-market economy operating with a limited number of selected controls.

Politically, the picture was not quite as bright. At Versailles in 1919 Wilhelminian Germany was split into two uneven parts by the Polish Corridor, a decision that was bound to fan the flames of German nationalism. Again in 1945, the defeated nation was divided into two estranged halves. West Germany, deeply committed to the West, became dependent on the United States nuclear umbrella and troop presence. The Bonn republic eventually became the strongest European power in the North Atlantic Treaty Organization, as well as in the European Common Market. East Germany was "adopted" by the Soviet Union as its most important partner. The regime, centering at East Berlin, became the foremost Communist power in Central Europe, as well as a key member of the Warsaw military pact.

In a sense, German contradictions became embodied in national division between West and East. In late November 1972 Chancellor Willy Brandt announced that negotiations between West Germany and East Germany on a basic treaty defining their relations were completed. The formula drafted for the treaty preamble took note of the differing views on the German national question between the two states, but at the same time declared that both sides proceeded "from the real situation in Germany." This represented a victory for the concept of one Germany, despite the postwar division into two states.

Once again, as on many occasions in their history, the Germans are faced with a dilemma. In the West they have an open society, free and democratic. In the East they have an authoritarian, closed society, which is labeled "democratic"—Communist style. Suspended in limbo between West and East, the Germans suffer from a sense of national frustration.

Aware of the unpopularity of earlier German regimes, pragmatic political leaders in Bonn sought to furnish the stability the German public seemed to need. At first, politicians of the Social Democratic Party managed to voice a good share of "way-out" nationalist oratory, but as they learned that they had to have the petty bourgeois vote, they began to temper their rhetoric. Together with politicians from the Christian Democratic Union, they avoided the excesses of polemics and, especially, an appeal to German national consciousness. They stressed German participation as a respected member of the European family. They turned to what might be called a restrained nationalism.

This toned-down approach left a vacuum for any movement dedicated to the resurgence of German nationalism. Into the breach in West Germany stepped the National Democratic Party (NPD), which announced itself as the standard bearer of the new German nationalism. The movement, neo-Nazi in some respects, now and then won some local successes, but thus far it has not amounted to much. Yet the NPD merits attention despite its current weakness and unpopularity, if only because of past experience: in the early days of nazism, Hitler was accepted (in 1919) as member number 7 of the then unimportant German Workers Party and went on to create a world-shattering dictatorship. Very few observers, however, expect a similar role for the NPD.

The NPD was originally formed from the fragments of a dozen right-wing splinter groups, the hard core of superpatriots, ultranationalists, and a cadre of fanatical young radicals. The platform appealed to the same elements that had supported the ultra right in the nineteen-thirties, but it clothed them in new dress. It denounced the division of Germany into two states and projected the slogan "Germany for the Germans—Europe for the Europeans." Most of its twelve "principles" were motivated by national sentiment:

Work for the recall of foreign troops on German soil, including the Americans.
  Get rid of the 1.3 million foreign workers in Germany.
  Put an end to the "one sided" war crimes trials so long as "in other countries millions of war crimes against German men, women, and children go unpunished."
  Destroy the lie about German responsibility for the war. It is necessary to give "a true picture of history."
  Put an end to money "extorted from our nation" as compensation. (The term "Jews" is not used.)
  "Germany claims the territories where Germans have lived for centuries." This refers specifically to the lands beyond the Oder-Neisse line, but party leaders interpret it also to include Austria as "German land."
  "We don't need America."

The NPD disavowed anti-Semitism, although in campaign speeches its candidates often made veiled insults against Jews and Israel. On occasion, speakers revealed the "inside news" that the notorious gas chambers had been constructed by American troops after the war in an effort "to blacken Germany." One speaker made a slight concession: "We are against compensation to any Jews in Israel—to German Jews, yes; to Israelis, no!"

The chief architect of the NPD was Adolf von Thadden. Bland and personable, he sought to give his movement an air of respectability. He had none of the ungrammatical eloquence of a shouting Hitler, nor was his approach to Germany's political problems beset with paranoia. In grass-root rallies over the country he preached the message of nationalism. War crime trials, "a national pollution," must be ended. All German veterans who had fought for the fatherland, including even those of the Nazi *Waffen SS,* must be rewarded with pensions. American economic and cultural influence must be eliminated. It was only reasonable that West Germany negotiate with the Soviet Union for reunification and the recovery of "pure" German soil. Thadden praised the Russians for "their creative use of nationalism."

To Thadden, nationalism was the magic means to restore the glory of Germany's past and realize the hope of her future. It was the essence of the German dream. This was precisely the sort of romanticism that had enticed the Germans in the past—with tragic results. Here it was again: nationalism would bring the new Germany her lost unity, discipline, and pride.

In state elections held in November 1966 the NPD returned 23 candidates in Bavaria and Hesse, polling 225,000 votes (7.9 percent) in Hesse and 390,000 votes (7.4 percent) in Bavaria. In Nuremberg, the site of Nazi rallies, the NPD received 13.1 percent of the total vote; in Bayreuth, home of Wagnerian traditions, it won 13.9 percent. In April 1967, 6.9 percent of the voters in the Rhineland Palatinate and 5.8 percent in Schleswig-Holstein cast their ballots for the NPD. In the national elections of November 1972, the NPD received only 0.06 percent of the vote (the Communist Party received 0.03 percent). Obviously, the new party was not making much headway. Certainly the situation at the present writing is different from 1933, when the Weimar Republic was plagued by millions of unemployed and was on the verge of economic disaster. But despite its prosperity, West Germany, even as other countries, remains good soil for the propaganda of a revived nationalism and for unfulfilled national ambitions. In this respect the NPD, though its influence should not be exaggerated, is playing an energizing role. It has a special appeal to army officers, older extremists, and hotheaded youth, as well as to disgruntled farmers, failing businessmen, the dissatisfied, and all those who are annoyed by the hesitant leadership of the Bonn republic. Its convictions are shared by those Germans who were angered by the catastrophe of 1945 and the subsequent splitting of the country. The argument is clear: if General de Gaulle has proved that nationalism in Europe is still "respectable," then Germans have as much right as Frenchmen to promote it for the national welfare. It remains to be seen whether the vigilant press and deep democratic values of the Bonn republic will be able to restrain the excesses of this kind of reborn German nationalism.

The Tribes of Europe

Most people are accustomed to thinking in terms of political and economic units that are national or supranational in scope. They are therefore much puzzled when reverse trends, smaller than national, begin to assert themselves. Yet this phenomenon has been taking place throughout Europe, even in countries with traditionally stable political conditions. It is a kind of European tribalism, a frenzy for assertive nationhood by small sectional groups distinguished by linguistic differences that are heightened by class and cultural distinctions. These mini-nationalisms add another level to the story of nationalism in Europe.

Mini-nationalisms are much encouraged by the recent emergence of new, small nations. National independence and its corollary—self-determination—have become political fads of our time. Since the end of World War II, more than sixty new states have declared their independence and started along the road of nationhood. Often unstable, and economically weak, many of these states face severe problems of adjustment. Most have been accepted as new members of the United Nations; others demand membership.

The appearance of many new, small countries has stimulated calls for independence among minority groups in the major European states. There is now real concern in nations that have taken their own unity as a matter of course and had previously regarded the idea of separateness as unattainable. The minorities present a logical argument: if Ghana, Algeria, and the Congo can win their freedom, why cannot the Welsh, with their own language, traditions, and history, similarly be granted the blessing of liberation? Tribal leaders become self-appointed Bolivars, Garibaldis, and Sukarnos and take on the mantle of instant Father of the Country. They accept the dictum of Manuel Luiz Quezon, the Filipino nationalist, who once remarked: "I prefer a government run like hell by Filipinos to a government run like heaven by Americans." What they accomplished is an intensification of nationalism all over the Continent. Europe remains the homeland of the persistent ism in still another form.

Both in Europe and elsewhere the cause of mini-nationalism was given a tremendous boost in October 1974 when the United Nations, by a vote of 105 to 4 invited the Palestine Liberation Organization (PLO), which claimed to be the sole representative of the displaced Palestinians in the Mideast, to participate in the November UN debate on Palestine. This was the first time any organization other than a constituted government had been permitted to address the General Assembly. The decision set a precedent for the dissident nationalisms to demand that they also be heard. The Ukrainians in the Soviet Union, the Basques in Spain, the Scots in the United Kingdom, all were encouraged to present their own demands for recognition. Until this decision all the larger nationalisms had regarded their dealings with minority groups as essentially an internal matter. Now, with the door open in the United Nations to the PLO, the larger countries could no longer make such a claim. There was a new impulse for mini-nationalisms and their urge toward fragmentation.

Flemo-Walloonian Friction in Belgium

One expects a sense of tribalism in Eastern Europe, beset as it is with political instability. Czechs and Slovaks have been quarreling since their union in the autumn of 1918. Serbs, Slovenes, and Croats live side by side in Yugoslavia, but with mutual antagonisms. This same kind of bickering also exists in Western Europe, where even established states are beginning to be worried about the implications of disintegrative nationalism.

The clash between Flemings (Dutch related) and Walloon (French related) mini-nationalisms in Belgium is an example. Behind it is a long historical controversy. The Congress of Vienna in 1815, seeking to remake the map of Europe without attention to national sentiment, joined Holland and Belgium together in the kingdom of the Netherlands. It was an unfortunate alliance of two communities, separated by centuries of linguistic and religious differences. Though the Belgians prospered under the arrangement, they were increasingly discontented by the suspicion that the Dutch language was being forced upon them. In 1830, responding to winds of change originating in Paris, the Belgians declared in favor of independence. The European powers agreed to the union of Flemings and Walloons in a single kingdom.

The new Belgium, with its antagonistic Flemings and Walloons, inherited a serious language problem. A kind of linguistic borderline between the two groups ran across Ypres, Courtrai, Brussels, and Liège. But the country as a whole prospered in the late nineteenth century: Flemings and Walloons were hard-working advocates of capitalism and both shared in the wealth of the country. Nineteenth-century Belgium was among the most industrialized Continental countries and had a rail network not far behind that of England.

The nationalism gripping most of the countries in Europe during the late nineteenth century never wholly conquered the Belgians, but the tribalism reflecting mutual Flemish and Walloonian hatreds proved to be the stronger force. The issue was aggravated after World War II by a population shift. Until then the French-speaking Walloons formed a majority of the Belgian population; since then a higher Flemish birth rate shifted the numerical balance. The Dutch-speaking majority began to feel slighted, and especially resented the preference given to the French language.

Relations between the two groups were exacerbated by religious and economic problems. The Flemings were predominantly Protestant, the Walloons mostly conservative Catholic. Between 1959 and 1969 more than a billion dollars in foreign capital was invested in Belgium, some two-thirds of it from the more than 750 "outside" companies that set up branches or affiliates in the country. Although most of these firms were American controlled and maintained their headquarters in Brussels, most of their plants were built in Flanders, to the distress of the Walloons.

In 1963 a law was passed shifting the linguistic frontier. In the process, the 543-year-old University of Louvain, the largest Roman Catholic university in the world, was placed seven miles inside Dutch Protestant Flanders. Flemish students, making up 55 percent of the enrollment, demanded that the university be split and that the French-speaking students be removed. Soon Flemish and Walloon students were battling in the streets, hurling bottles at one another and at the neutral police. When a board of bishops met to discuss the university's future, its members were divided along linguistic lines.

The clash at the University of Louvain was a microcosm of a countrywide phenomenon. Ramifications of the conflict entered deeply into every phase of Belgian life. "One only speaks Flemish to one's servants," said an aristocratic Walloon. Whenever the language issue emerged passion took over, followed by riots in the streets. It would have seemed wiser for both sides to rise above outmoded linguistic jealousies and arrange a mutually tolerant formula similar to the Swiss multilinguistic confederation. At the present moment, the Belgian Senate is studying constitutional reform proposals designed to end the unitary state and create regional autonomy. But the basic problem remains, with all its seething hatreds. This is the kind of European mini-nationalism that can lead to paralyzing instability.

"Gora Euzkadi!"—"Up with the Basque Nation!"

The mini-nationalist passion of Flemings and Walloons is by no means unique in Europe: it is more than matched by the Basques in southwestern Europe. Some 750,000 Basques live in the industrial heartland of northern Spain in four provinces (Vizcaya, Alava, Guipuzcoa, and Navarre) on the slopes of the Pyrenees. The Spanish Basques share with 150,000 French Basques in three neighboring provinces a vigorous sense of independence. In their early history they resisted all attempts by both Romans and Visigoths to assimilate them. At the beginning of the tenth century the Basques south of the Pyrenees were brought into the kingdom of Navarre, but they managed to retain self-rule in their *fueros* (assemblies). Their language—complex, guttural, related to no other—is a favorite of linguistic experts, who are fascinated by the task of ascertaining the origins of this consistently incorporative and agglutinative tongue.

From the late nineteenth century on, the Spanish Basques have made it clear that they prefer an independent state. During the Spanish Civil War of 1936–1939, the Basque provinces, forming an isolated Republican enclave, held out against the Franco forces, probably because the Republicans gave them autonomy at the beginning of the conflict. The Basque republic lasted just eight months. From 1940 to 1950, when the Franco regime was in its most repressive mood, the Basques, like their neighbors in Catalonia, suffered under Madrid's rule. They were punished by a removal of privileges or by restrictions on such symbols of Basque nationalism as language, education, press, song, and dances. On occasion, the provinces were declared to be in a state of emergency. The civil guard, drawn from non-Basques, was rougher on the Basques than on other Spaniards.

Sturdy and stubborn, proud and militant, the Basques reacted violently against suppression. Many gave up in disgust and went into exile, especially to Argentina, Mexico, and Cuba. Some 12,000 Basques now live around Boise, Idaho. Meanwhile, Basque nationalism was kept alive by the *émigré* government set up in Paris and by the Basque Nationalist Party (PNV) inside Spain.

The Basque revolutionary movement was split by a generation gap. Young activists, discontented with the almost conservative approach of the elderly *émigré* government and unwilling to wait much longer for independence, formed the *Euzkadi Ta Azkatasuna* (Basque Homeland and Freedom) in 1960. Young activists of the well-drilled, underground ETA raised money by raiding banks; made bomb attacks on town halls, Civil War memorials, and police stations; placed booby traps in the cars of Falangist officials; and dynamited deserted civil guard posts. Composed of young men from 17 to 21, the ETA represents the first generation of Basques who are free from the traumatic memories of the Civil War days. They look upon themselves as colonists living under a foreign yoke and therefore advocate an all-out war for freedom. Nationalism is their religion.

The older Basque nationalists were placed in a dilemma: if they condemned the activities of the young upstarts, they would be discredited in the eyes of their people. If, on the other hand, they remained silent, they would be regarded by the Madrid government as accomplices of the young revolutionaries and they would have to pay the penalty.

In the summer of 1968 Meliton Manzanas, the dreaded political-police chief of Guipuzcoa Province, was killed in daylight, apparently by ETA fanatics. He had been, said one young Basque nationalist, "the butcher of our people." "We set up our own tribunal, condemned him to death, and executed him. Our central committee has decided on further executions."

The Franco regime responded angrily with mass arrests, but without warrants or investigation. A state of emergency was declared and civil rights were suspended for three months. Six defendants, accused of complicity in the murder of Manzanas, were found guilty and condemned to face a firing squad. Workers in the Basque country immediately called protest strikes. But this domestic outcry was dwarfed by the reaction abroad. Virtually the entire world united in condemning the sentences and attempted to persuade Franco to be lenient. The governments of Sweden, Britain, West Germany, and Italy pleaded for clemency; Pope Paul VI was prepared to call Franco to ask for mercy; even the Soviet Union (herself under attack for harsh death verdicts against Jewish airplane hijackers) joined in the call for clemency for the Basque rebels. Franco responded to world outrage by commuting the death sentences to 30 years in prison.

Global public opinion had saved the lives of the Basque nationalists, but despite Franco's clemency there was a bitter aftertaste. Franco had shown once again who was master in Spain. But the repressive overtones of the trial awakened old Basque resentments. To Franco and the military, the Basques remained criminal terrorists and bandits with shadowy Marxist connections. For the Basque separatists, the trial and its outcome marked a temporary setback in the continuous drive for autonomy. Here, too, is disintegrative nationalism in its most energetic form.

The Red Dragon of Wales

Not even Britain, progenitor of the modern state, is free from the reverberations of mini-nationalism. Geographically, the British Isles form a small unit in Europe, but here, too, are evidences of tribal separatism, encouraged by language, culture, and special economic problems. Both Welsh nationalists and Basque revolutionaries are brothers, equally proficient in song and dance, but the Welsh version of contemporary mini-nationalism is considerably more gentlemanly and less inclined at the moment to depend upon explosives as an argument for autonomy. It exists side by side with the current near–civil war in Northern Ireland.

In July 1966 Gwnfor Evans, representing the Welsh Nationalist Party, *Plaid Cymru,* won the seat for Carmathan in the House of Commons by polling 16,179 votes, a considerable rise in his constituency. Announcing that "the Welsh people are on the march," Evans called for separation from England. Wales, he said, must have her own distinct foreign policy, as well as a seat in the United Nations. He would settle for no mere regionalism with a federal system analogous to that of the United States or West Germany, but only for complete autonomy. Two years later, in July 1968, Dr. Phil Williams, a young Welsh Nationalist, failed by just under 2,000 votes to win a seat in the Caerphilly by-election for the House of Commons, but he succeeded in cutting off some 19,000 votes from the Labor majority.

These elections indicated that Welsh separatist nationalism had become a factor of slightly more than minimal importance in British politics—certainly that Welsh autonomy was not merely a kind of August bank holiday silliness. In the past, knowing Londoners were convinced that Wales was so closely associated with the English economy that she would collapse if she tried to exist as a separate state. The feeling was widespread that every Welsh hill farmer would be bankrupted if he were denied access to British markets, and Welsh labor would be overwhelmed by unemployment. But such sentiments did not take into account the staying power of nationalist ideology.

The summer of 1968 saw another test of Welsh nationalism, when Charles Philip Arthur George Windsor, age 20, knelt on a slab of Welsh slate before the castle at Caernarvon and was invested with the title of Prince of Wales. The personable young man also assumed, along with the title, the 600-year-old Teutonic motto *Ich Dien* (I serve). More than 2,000 policemen, including Scotland Yard officers in bulletproof vests, joined 2,500 soldiers to protect the future King of England and titular head of the British Commonwealth. Obviously, it was necessary to take into account the bizarre reasoning of assorted crackpots—as well as a tide of Welsh nationalism that was running higher than at any time in this century.

The more militant Welsh nationalists saw to it that there were incidents. On the night before the investiture, two men were killed when a bomb they were planting exploded prematurely. As Queen Elizabeth rode to the castle in an open carriage, a young man threw an egg against the polished woodwork of the coach. After the ceremony, a British army truck suddenly burst into flame, killing a young soldier inside.

Behind the demonstrations was a deepening sense of separatism in Wales, a mountainous area of grim, often tragic coal mining valleys, about the size of Massachusetts. Its 2.7 million people are represented by some 36 seats in the British Parliament.

Though united with England since 1536, Wales has a history of its own. In 1282 the last native ruler, Llyelyn ap Gruffydd, was killed by supporters of King Edward I. Legend has it that Edward sought to appease his unruly Welsh subjects by promising them another prince who would be "born in Wales, could speak no English, and whose life and conversation nobody could stain." That promise was not kept, and resentment mounted.

At the root of the conflict is an ancient, tongue-twisting language. The Celtic language, related to Gaelic, Manx, Cornish, and Breton, is far older than English. Belonging to the Indo-European family of languages, it was spoken long before the Roman conquest, and survived eight centuries of opposition by English authorities. The Bible was translated into Welsh in 1588. Although today only one in four Welshmen can speak the old tongue, it remains the everyday language in rural villages, and all Welsh school children

get some instruction in the language. The deep veneration for Welsh was
expressed this way by Oxford scholar Sir John Morris Jones:

> The sweetest tongue in all the world
>   is on the lips of my love,
> Is on the lips of my love.

Each year the Welsh sense of identity and separateness is revived by the
National Eisteddfod, a social union and arts competition. The early eisteddi-
fods were restricted to sessions of the bards to discuss matters concerning
their craft, but in the nineteenth century the festival became an annual
patriotic event, devoted to competitive choral singing, poetry composition,
and Scripture recitations. Participants wearing colorful robes now take part
in hymn singing, dances, and semireligious rituals with traditional harp
accompaniments. Special honor is awarded the winning author of a poem of
alliterative verse in strict meter.

The purpose is always to preserve the Welsh tongue. The movement *Urdd
Gobaith Cymru* (League of Youth), founded by Sir Ifan ap Owen Edwards, is
meant "to protect the Welsh language." The Welsh actor, Richard Burton,
described the sentiment precisely: "Well, what's to do? I don't know. But I
do know that, tiny a nation as we are, and being no better and no worse than
other nations, I *do* know that we are different and that we want to remain so.
We don't want to have that hot rush of blood to the head when someone
mistakes us for English, or thinks that we are one of England's quainter
counties. We want to be uniquely ourselves and we want to keep our unique
language."

Added to the factor of language is the Welsh heritage of economic
suffering. Many Welshmen believe that Wales has been neglected far too long
by London. Derelict towns bear witness to the catastrophic decline of coal
mining, once a flourishing Welsh industry.

In the elections of October 1974 the Welsh nationalists gained one seat in
the House of Commons and a total of three. Most Welshmen still oppose
independence, but a majority have expressed a preference for a separate
Welsh Parliament. As long ago as 1948 Westminster rejected a proposal for a
separate ministry for Wales, and instead set up an Advisory Council with
vaguely defined powers. In 1959, as a concession to Welsh nationalism, a
separate Ministry for State Affairs was established.

Welsh militants, as is the way with nationalists everywhere, view these
concessions as half-measures. Under the banner of a red fire-breathing
dragon they carry on a kind of subdued guerrilla warfare against "English
rule." They are confident that their day will come. The attacks range from
moderate to extreme. Members of the Welsh Language Society splash paint

over signs with English place names. Terrorists use explosives to protest the flooding of Welsh valleys as water reservoirs for English cities.

Whether or not Welsh nationalism continues to be a cultural curiosity remains to be seen. The movement may or may not grow in size and strength and pass from the cultural sphere into the political. Meanwhile, in its present form it is symptomatic of the kind of mini-nationalisms that exist throughout the structure of Europe.

The Specter of Scottish Nationalism

Mini-nationalism, a once quixotic movement, has intensified and become more serious in Scotland. Here the strains of nationalism ran deep, even though the union with England dated from 1707. For the last half century Scottish nationalism was more of a lyrical liberation call than a movement for secession. Rival Gaelic language organizations, such as the older *Comunn na Canain Albanaich* and the new *An Comunn Gaidhealach*, sought to maintain Scottish cultural distinctions.

On a comparative basis, earlier Scottish nationalism was a kind of revolt with manners, modest in aims and lukewarm in attitude. It was not accompanied by the turbulence and violence of other mini-nationalisms. Moderate Scottish nationalists agreed that matters concerned with Crown, defense, and foreign affairs be left to Parliament in London, but called for exclusive control over Scotland's internal affairs, industry, public health, housing, education, and social insurance. The following resolution of a Scottish Convention on October 28, 1949, received 1,250,000 signatures within six months:

This National Assembly, representative of the people of Scotland, reaffirms the belief that the establishment of a Scottish Parliament with legislative authority over Scottish affairs is necessary to the national interest of Scotland, and in order to give the people an effective means of demonstrating their determination to secure this reform, the Assembly hereby resolves to invite Scots men and women to subscribe a Covenant in the following terms:

"We, the people of Scotland who subscribe to this engagement, declare our belief that reform in the constitution of our country is necessary to secure good government in accordance with our Scottish traditions and to promote the spiritual and economic welfare of our nation. . . with that end in view, we solemnly enter into this Convenant whereby we pledge ourselves, in all loyalty to the Crown and within the framework of the United Kingdom, to do everything in our power to secure for Scotland a Parliament with adequate legislative authority in Scottish affairs."

The mood thus far was not for complete separation from England. But meanwhile the Scottish Nationalist Party (SNP), which had been founded in

1928, began to call for complete independence instead of mere home rule. The nationalists rejected the concept of "loyalty to the Crown and within the framework of the United Kingdom," which they regarded as a spineless acceptance of the status quo. Motivated by patriotism, SNP members busied themselves with door-to-door canvassing, publication of leaflets, and intense electioneering. They also played the game of publicity. On Christmas Day 1950, Scottish nationalists managed to steal the Coronation Stone, or Stone of Scone, from Westminster Abbey, and deposited it inside the ruins of Arboath Abbey, several yards from the spot where the signing of the Scottish Declaration of Independence in 1320 was reenacted each year in a summer pageant. The stone was returned to Westminster Abbey several days later. For the nationalists this was more than a schoolboy prank, it was rather a symbol of Scottish liberation. To emphasize their goal, they refused to recognize the title "Elizabeth II" and regularly damaged pillar boxes bearing the Queen's cypher.

In recent years the sentiment for Scottish separatism increased dramatically. More and more Scots expressed dismay with the way they have been governed from London and have concluded that they can do the job better themselves. There is little rancor against Whitehall, little violence, and virtually no incivility. But there is a distinct and growing belief that England has become "over-centralized and fossilized." Many Scots now see England as a sinking ship foundering at sea and they believe it is best to set out in their own lifeboat.

Added to political difficulties are deep-rooted economic differences. Scottish nationalists point to the artificial state of their own economy controlled from London. Scotland is a country of 30,000 square miles, rich in minerals and agricultural products, with just over five million people. England, after Taiwan and Bangladesh, is the most densely overpopulated country in the world, with 910 persons per square mile. England is economically unbalanced, and a potentially rich Scotland must share her troubles. The Scots are angered by the concentration of wealth in the south and by the loss of their talented young to London. The economic issue was considerably aggravated by the discovery of sulphur-free petroleum under the Scottish sector of the North Sea. This oil, valued at billions, could make Scotland the richest nation per capita in Europe. British demands would exhaust these immense oil resources in 25 years, but the oil would last at least ten times as long if maintained under Scottish control.

The clash on oil resources was responsible in part for a quick rise in the fortunes of the Scottish Nationalist Party. Until the mid 1960's its drawing power was small and unimportant. It grew in voting strength from 2.4 percent in 1964 to 5 percent in 1966. Then all Britain was astonished when in the elections of October 1974 the SNP won 11 parliamentary seats and 30 percent of the Scottish vote. In the past the national psyche of Scotland had been permeated with the idea that she was in a permanent and necessary state of subservience to London—the source of all law, leadership, and subsidies. Suddenly, there seemed to be a coming end to Scotland's traditional role of inferiority.

There were evidences elsewhere of the intensification of mini-nationalism. Even in the Isle of Man there were calls for national status. A self-governing dependency of the British Crown, 227 square miles in area with a population of 49,300, the tiny island won the attention of the British press in the summer of 1968 when its executive council decreed that the union jack would not thereafter fly from public buildings on official occasions. Instead, the Manx flag would be displayed on such occasions as royal birthdays.

Behind Welsh, Scottish, and Manx mini-nationalisms was a persistent tribalistic sentiment. To the larger nationalist these are picayune, even amusing, movements led by local crackpots. But the mini-nationalist regards his cause as deadly serious business in which oppressed patriots are dominated by an alien Government. Each nationalist liberator regards himself as a model Mazzini calling for freedom from the yoke of outsiders.

Regional Chauvinism in Croatia

The existence of mini-nationalisms throughout Europe gives weight to the theory that nationalism is a two-edged sword: again and again we can see it as a force for disruption as well as unification. This tendency is illustrated by the recent history of Yugoslavia. Created after World War I and the dissolution of the Austro-Hungarian Empire, Yugoslavia survived World War II and emerged as a Communist state.

The old Austro-Hungarian Empire was undermined by calls for liberation by the conglomerate people who composed it. Among them were Serbs, Croats, and Slovenes, all independent-minded peoples whose sons and daughters now populate Yugoslavia, along with other major groups: Macedonians, Albanians, Bosnian Muslims, and Montenegrins. During the chaos of World War II, rivalries between these subgroups, especially between Serbs and Croats, became more and more intense. In 1943 civil war broke out between the Chetniks, a resistance movement headed by Serbian Draja Mikhailovich, and Communist partisans led by Croatian Josip Broz Tito. In 1944 Allied support was given to Tito, whose rise to supreme power, favored by Soviet Russia, was uninterrupted. In June 1946 Mikhailovich was tried as a German collaborator and executed.

Acting for the National Liberation Committee, Tito took action after the war to make Yugoslavia a totally Communist state. Unlike the pro-Serb Mikhailovich, Tito rallied all sections of Yugoslavia without distinction, calling only for political unity. He set up several republics, composed of Serbs, Croatians, Slovenes, Macedonians and Bosnians, each of which was given wide cultural independence. To keep his federated state under control, Tito was careful to make maximum concessions to local autonomy.

Tito's first and basic quarrel was with the Kremlin, which was anxious to include Communist Yugoslavia within its sphere of influence. Acting through the Comintern, Stalin called on Yugoslav Communists to depose their leader because he refused to be bound by Moscow's discipline. For five years, from 1948 to 1953, Yugoslavia's political and economic life was dominated by Tito's quarrel with Stalin. The Kremlin was unable to undermine the dissident Yugoslav leader. Tito had welded the peasants into a powerful guerrilla partisan army during the war and he retained his popularity with them, as well as with all classes in the country. The quarrel aroused national pride even among Yugoslavs who hitherto had been hostile to the centralized government. After the Russians began an economic blockade of Yugoslavia, Tito sought and obtained assistance from the United States, France, Britain, and the World Bank. He was thus able to assert his independence against Soviet claims and to inaugurate a policy of "national-communism." It was a bitter defeat for Stalin.

Victorious in his foreign policy vis-à-vis Soviet Russia, Tito was still faced with major difficulties on the domestic scene. There was still the problem of keeping his historically distinct peoples together. Of the Yugoslav population of some 20 million, the Serbs constituted 42 percent, the Croats 23 percent, the Slovenes nine percent, the Macedonians five percent, and the Montenegrins three percent; the remaining 18 percent was made up of Albanians, Hungarians, Turks, Slovaks, and Gypsies. To satisfy the component parts of his nation, Tito decentralized local government, industry, and agriculture. His revised constitution of 1953 provided for considerably greater local autonomy than had existed before.

Ethnically, the Serbs and the Croats, the two largest subgroups in the country, are closely related. Their languages are similar, although the Orthodox Serbs use the Cyrillic alphabet while the Catholic Croats write the Latin script. After the Napoleonic Wars, these two peoples developed their own national psychologies, reflecting the conflicts between Byzantium and Rome, between Habsburgs and Ottomans. Precisely because both the Serbs and the Croats enjoyed great freedom inside the Yugoslav state, they tended to stress their historical heritages. For the Croats, the Serbs remained "our ancient enemy."

Much of the rivalry was economic. In 1970 Serbian authorities in Belgrade announced the coming construction of a railway line from Belgrade to the Montenegrin seacoast—deliberately designed to avoid Croat territory. Croat leaders countered by planning a highway of their own, from their capital at Zagreb to the Croatian port of Split.

Such nationalistic manifestations revealed a widening cleavage between Serbs and Croats, and in recent years historic Croatian nationalism exploded in virulent form. Croatian intellectuals called for separation from a unified Yugoslavia and issued demands far beyond what even the liberal government in Belgrade could grant. They accused the central government of using the bonanza from tourism for assistance to non-Croatian regions. They asked for a separate army, a Croatian airline, and even membership in the United Nations. Most of them held important positions in *Matica Hrvatska,* the Croatian cultural association. Tito labeled these intellectuals "counter-revolutionaries" who were using legally recognized associations to prepare the overthrow of his system. He also accused them of being connected with Croation *émigré* organizations, in Moscow and elsewhere, as well as with foreign intelligence services.

The younger generation was especially attracted by Croatian mini-nationalism. To young Yugoslavs, Tito's guerrilla comrades had grown fat and lazy as parvenus attracted by the consumer society. They also attacked the "sandwich generation"—those between 30 and 50—as equally flabby and deadened by hypocrisy. There was a mounting tide of alienation among Croatia's university students. The ruling elite in Belgrade confronted young Croatians who were unresponsive to its stale revolutionary slogans.

In December 1971 more than 30,000 Croatian students went on strike and called for an end to Croatia's "colonial situation." Gathering in Republic Square in Zagreb, they chanted Croatian songs and taunted the police. Several dozen young nationalists were injured, 14 ringleaders were arrested, and 250 were detained by the authorities. The purge touched off even more demonstrations. The authorities placed the *Matica Hrvatska* under direct police control, and purged its editorial offices, as well as local Croation Communist Party organizations. All such measures only intensified Croatian alienation.

For Tito, himself of Croatian birth, the dilemma was painful. He admitted that factionalism among Yugoslavia's six constituent parts has been a pressing problem. He denounced nationalism as "a weapon for fascism and other reactionary interests that could tear us apart," while at the same time praising it because it meant Yugoslavia's independence from Moscow.

In Tito's mind national independence for Yugoslavia was the primary question—everything else, even economic problems, was secondary. During his first dozen years of power he had suppressed "bourgeois nationalism" of all kinds, only to find a new kind of mini-nationalism emerging among his Croatians. He had little faith in an equitable compromise of conflicting views in a democratic context. On the contrary, he deemed it necessary to cleanse the Augean stables. He wanted a return to the tight discipline of early Yugoslav communism. The *Stari* ("Old Man") was close to 80, but he had no intention of allowing "misled" Croatian nationalists to implement a "counterrevolution" from which only the Kremlin could benefit.

Indeed, the Soviet Union, long angered by Tito's "national communism," was encouraged by the deepening sense of Croatian mini-nationalism. The split of Yugoslavia into several mutually hostile nationalities would be to the Kremlin's advantage. Croatian *émigrés* in West Germany, Eastern Europe, and in Moscow call for an independent Croatia under Soviet protection. The stakes are high: an independent Croatian state, centered at Zagreb, would provide Moscow with strategic air and naval bases.

The unresolved quarrels inside Yugoslavia show that historic rivalries have a way of bubbling to the surface despite claims of a viable unification. Under a strong leader such as Tito, national yearnings of subgroups for "independence" could be suppressed for a time. The conglomerate peoples of Yugoslavia rallied together when threatened by Stalin's efforts in 1948 to dominate Tito, and by Brezhnev in 1968 and the Kremlin-led invasion of Czechoslovakia. Yet when the external danger from Moscow receded, the old nationalistic rivalries emerged in new forms. The Serbs could never forget that in World War II Croatian extremists, living under Nazi occupation, killed 100,000 of the Serbian minority inside their borders. Nor would the Croatians agree that the huge foreign income attracted by their coastal resorts should be drained off to the federation coffers in Belgrade to be used for development projects in other Yugoslav republics.

Tito once described "the unity we have attained among the nationalities" as his greatest achievement. In his old age he began to see that nationalism could work for disruption as well as unification.

The European Connection

In summary, the European continent, cradle land of nationalism in its modern form, still shows the scars of the stubborn historical phenomenon. A comparative analysis of European mini-nationalisms reveals similar trends. General de Gaulle's passion for France looked straight back into the nineteenth century and gave sanction to other nationalists. Germany, a major victim of the virus, seeks to cure the disease by doses of economic antibiotics and by supporting European unity. All other European states, Spain, Italy, Belgium, Holland, and Poland among them, are still subject to divisive nationalism. Throughout the Continent mini-nationalists claim the right of secession. Flemings and Walloons in Belgium, Basques in Spain, Welsh and Scots in Britain, Croatians in Yugoslavia—among other mini-nationalists, demand self-determination as a right for fragments of nations as well as for whole nations.

12 Nationalism versus Tribalism in Africa

Young African's Plea

Don't preserve my customs,
As some fine curios
To suit some white historian's tastes.
There's nothing artificial
That beats the natural way,
In culture and ideals of life.
Let me play with the white man's ways,
Let me work with the black man's
   brains,
Let my affairs themselves sort out.
Then in sweet re-birth
I'll rise a better man,
Not ashamed to face the world.
Those who doubt my talents
In secret fear my strength;
They know I am no less a man.
Let them bury their prejudice,
Let them show their noble sides,
Let me have untrammeled growth.
My friends will never know regret
And I, I never once forget.

—From *An Anthology of West African Verse* (1957)

Contrasting Structures: The Telescoping of History ~ 3

Human beings, whether in London, Lagos, or Ibadan, are more alike than different. No matter where they live, they are subject to the same material and psychological needs. Not the least of these necessities is the need for security from infancy to adulthood. The contemporary African may not give much of his conscious attention to nation making—often, like others else-where, he does not even understand the meaning of a nation—but he knows well that his personal safety is closely bound up with that of his peers. He senses automatically, without being reminded of it, that in union there is strength.

In this way African nationalism bears comparison with nationalism in Europe, the area of its origin. The critical factor remains the need for security. On a comparative basis, African nationalism, like its preceding European counterpart, was mounted on the same base, but it developed its own special characteristics. It was new primarily in the chronological sense.

In the process of nation building in early modern Europe, the cultural foundations—history, traditions, language, and literature—were laid first, and then came the political drive to nationhood. The procedure in Africa took exactly the opposite course. When the fever of rebellion was succeeded by national independence in the early 1960s, the political connotations came first: the selection, appointment, and self-assertion of national heroes, the franchise for autonomy, the structured legislative bodies. Soon the new country, no matter what its size, was sending its delegates to the halls of the United Nations. Then and only then came the careful buildup of cultural identity, the appeal to the great past, the competitions for prize-winning national anthems. It was a kind of telescoping of history in reverse form.

This was the main difference in the structure of nationalism in its European birthplace and on the African continent. There were also similarities as well as differences.

Speaking generally, differing ideologies and social forces masquerade under the common name of nationalism. European nationalism in the nine-teenth century was dualistic in nature, the result of contrasting historical experiences east and west of the Rhine.[1] On one side was the *state-nation* (England, France, the United States), in which the idea of the nation developed within the chrysalis of the state: a sense of nationhood transcend-ed ethnic differences. On the other side was the *nation-state* (Central and Eastern Europe), in which ethnic and political frontiers coincided: the idea of the nation developed within the core of the individual culture. Out of this came the special European dichotomy: the state-nation (nations formed by the state) and the nation-state (states formed from nations).

This distinction holds also for Africa, where both forms appear alongside one another, but the dominant type was the state-nation.[2] More often than not, the desire was for the already existing state under foreigners (the colonial territory) to construct the nation, not the reverse. There was an important difference in the time element. The building of nations in Europe took place over the course of centuries. In Africa, however, the new nation-building was a hurry-up process, taking not centuries or decades but a matter of years. Philip D. Curtin calls this type of state-nation only an embryo, "the aspirant state-nation." Within a comparatively short time the new African states adopted nationalism as their preferred mode of political behavior, including some of its more deplorable characteristics.

This does not mean that the nation-state type is lacking in Africa. It exists there in all its ethnic confusion. In fact, much of the strife now burdening Africa is due in part to the conflicts engendered by the two contrasting forms. Opposed to the state-nation's seeking its identity are the already existing nations, which Europeans call "tribes." These tribes, as we shall see, meet the definition usually applied to nationhood: common culture, territory, language, and traditions, as well as institutions to articulate these elements. An example is Biafran tribalism, which called for independence from Nigeria.

The Black Man's Burden

The most distinguishing feature of African nationalism is its ethnic coloration. When compared with European nationalism, the African form reveals a close affinity with its correlative racialism. This is understandable. For a century the great continent has been the scene of an ever-widening hostility between white and black men. White Europeans took upon themselves the "burden" of civilizing backward tribes in exchange for access to the continent's riches. The white man brought Western laws, a modicum of education, pots and pans, and syphilis to countless villagers. Only grudgingly did the white benefactor relinquish his control over the peoples of Africa.

With little preparation, the African built his new state on the haphazard boundaries created by the white man. Accepting the superiority of Western civilization, he tried to imitate its ways while retaining his own dignity and respect for his customary way of life. The difficult and complex process was marred by riot, rebellion, and bloodshed. Those Western observers who were quick to criticize the behavior of African "savages" forgot that their own nation building was by no means free of similar conflicts.

In Africa, distaste for the white man and his works is a unifying force of continental-wide proportions. This kind of ethnic hostility differs from the European experience. At no time was European nationalism a continental-wide unifying force operating as a unit against external enemies. In the African experience, black nationalism was directed against white exploitation.

Added to the motivation of black against white was a social variation between European and African nationalisms. European nationalism came of age in an era of mass education. In varying degrees, love for country was instilled among mostly literate Europeans at home and at school. African nationalism, on the other hand, made its appearance in a vastly different social order. Those Africans who were influenced by primitive voodoos and ancient taboos had little or no understanding of what national consciousness meant. At mid-century the African illiteracy rate was high, hovering around the 90 percent mark, and only a relatively small group had the advantage of higher education. Political power was captured and exercised by a small minority of educated elite, trained in Western colleges and universities. African nationalists had an ambivalent feeling, a kind of love-hate for their European and American teachers. They called for liberation, but at the same time they were willing (for the most part) to work with their former colonial rulers in the task of westernizing African civilization.

The emergence of nationalism in Africa brings to attention one of the salient characteristics of nationalism as a historical force. It reveals that the ism appeals even when it is perfectly clear, or as clear as anything can be, that material benefits flow the other way. The human disposition for group life, expressed in a need for association with compatriots, is a powerful one, no matter what its consequences. Loyalty to a flag can be most attractive, even if the symbol represents a poverty-stricken society. Indeed, the African experience indicates that the tribal and feudal antecedents of nationalism in Europe are probably more significant than hitherto realized.

African nationalism operated at two levels: (1) negatively and externally; in response to imperialism and colonialism, it asserted and won the right of black Africa to achieve freedom from white controls; and (2) positively and internally; it represented a desire to obtain the benefits of modernization.

On the external level, African nationalism was a reaction against alien domination. Africans had long been subjected to white power. When they broke away, they refused to accept the idea that all the world revolved around Western Europe. They opposed not only the idea of imperialism but also the concept of race supremacy of white over black. They did not feel inferior.

On the internal level, African nationalism revealed a desire on the part of the black man to obtain the benefits of twentieth-century advances. Both the educated elite and the illiterate masses were quite willing to recognize the advisability of many features of European life that they could see all around them. But they wanted reform on their own terms, without subservience of any kind. In this sense African nationalism represented the dignity of black men as human beings. They wanted to be relieved of the colonial mentality instilled in them by Europeans. They no longer desired to be victims of the white man, but his eye-level equal. They would regenerate the best of their own cultural past and combine it with the technological knowledge of their former masters to achieve the goal of a modernized society. It was a task of immeasurable difficulties, but the African was determined to attempt it.

African nationalists knew well the results of contact with Europeans. They protested that when the European came and appropriated African land, he took away not only their livelihood but also the material symbols that held family and tribe together. They resented efforts to "civilize" them, to "teach them the disciplinary value of regular work," and to "give them the benefit of European progressive ideas."

Granted, there were some progressive ideas among the Europeans—material prosperity, advanced medical knowledge, hygiene, and literacy. But that was not enough, according to Jomo Kenyatta, who later became Kenya's first Prime Minister. "So far [1938] the Europeans who visit Africa have not been conspicuously zealous in imparting those parts of their inheritance to the Africans, and seem to think that the only way to do it is by police discipline and armed force. They speak as if it was somehow beneficial to an African to work for them instead of for himself, and to make sure that he will receive this benefit they do their best to take away his land and leave him with no alternative. Along with his land they rob him of his government, condemn his religious ideas, and ignore his fundamental conceptions of justice and morals, all in the name of civilization and progress."[3] Kenyatta added, with that pride characteristic of African nationalists, that the African is conditioned—by the cultural and social institutions of centuries—"to a freedom of which Europe has little conception."

African nationalists resented that sense of inferiority proposed by the white man and accepted by many tribal elders. Tom Mboya, Kenya's Minister of Economics and Development, who was assassinated by a gunman in Nairobi on July 5, 1969, expressed the annoyance of the new African at this situation and proposed that Kenyan nationalism must overcome any feeling of inferiority:

I remember, when I had decided to become involved in KAU (Kenya African Union) in 1952, how not only my father but other elders in my tribe often told me: "We can never compete with the European. After all, he has aeroplanes, he flies about while we walk on foot. He has cars and he has guns."

I was virtually told we were beating our heads against a brick wall. But I did not find it strange, because I knew various District Commissioners who at Barazas (meetings) had told the people they could not compete with the white man because they had not learned to make a nail. To foster this spirit of inferiority among

Africans, the administration had identified everything good with the European and everything bad or inferior with the African. Thus first-rate maize or eggs or potatoes were designated "European-type maize (or eggs or potatoes)," and all inferior maize, eggs or potatoes or even cattle were described as African-type (*"Mahindi ya Kizungu"* and *"Viazi vya Kiafrika"*).[4]

The reaction of African nationalists against this kind of treatment is certainly understandable, even if it was emotional, intemperate, and on occasion vindictive. These qualities were plainly exhibited on June 30, 1960, by the new Premier of the Congo, Patrice E. Lumumba, in an Independence Day speech before the King of the Belgians and distinguished guests from all over the world. A combination of bitterness and candor, it accurately mirrored the sentiments of African nationalists:

. . . No Congolese worthy of the name will ever forget that independence has been won by struggle, an everyday struggle, an intense and idealistic struggle, a struggle in which we have spared neither our forces, our privations, our sufferings, nor our blood.

This struggle of tears, fire, and blood makes us profoundly proud because it was a noble and just struggle, an indispensable struggle to put an end to the humiliating bondage imposed on us by force.

Our lot was eighty years of colonial rule; our wounds are still too fresh and painful to be driven from our memory.

We have known tiring labor exacted in exchange for salary which did not allow us to satisfy our hunger, to clothe and lodge ourselves decently or raise our children like loved beings.

We have known ironies, insults, blows which we had to endure morning, noon, and night because we were "Negroes,". . .

We have known that the law was never the same depending on whether it concerned a white or a Negro: accommodating for one group, it was cruel and inhuman for the other. . . .

We have known there were magnificent houses for the whites in the cities and tumble-down straw huts for the Negroes, that a Negro was not admitted in movie houses or restaurants, or stores labeled "European," that a Negro travelled in the hulls of river boats at the feet of the white in his first class cabin. . . .

All that, my brothers, we have profoundly suffered.[5]

Background: Spoliation of the Dark Continent

The story of how European imperialists surged into Africa after the dramatic Livingstone-Stanley episode of 1871 is a familiar one. English, French, Spanish, Portuguese, Dutch, Italian, and German colonizers carved the great continent into subjugated territories. They drew the boundaries in accordance with their own economic interests and not in conformity with ethnic realities. Bored by the complex disparities among peoples, they made no attempts to organize the tribes into integrated units. Indeed, they built roads and railroads, but only to link the coastal cities and to assure communications with the homeland: the convenience and well-being of the natives seldom entered their minds. The tribes back in the bush were important only as a source of cheap labor to deliver gold, diamonds, rubber, ivory, copra, palm oil, cocoa, coffee, and a variety of timbers. Here again, as in the past, human greed was a factor of prime importance.

The Europeans who latched on to African soil and drained it of its wealth little dreamed that the 350,000,000 natives even considered the idea of independence. But in one way or another the Africans learned nationalism from their colonial masters. The movement was at first slow and then gathered momentum. Manifestations of native nationalism were rare before 1939, but pressures began to build up in the cauldron. During World War II, Allied leaders, determined to hold African support, began to throw out hints of eventual autonomy. Added to this gesture was a simultaneous decline in the white man's prestige because of reverses at the hands of the Axis, and particularly because of the loss of face suffered by the white man against the Japanese. The thousands of African troops who had served overseas returned home with different ideas about ethnic inferiority.

African nationalism matured quickly after the close of World War II. By mid-century the occupying powers were beginning to liquidate their African holdings. Thirty newly independent African states came into being within boundaries drawn in the chancellories of Europe late in the nineteenth century. These borders reflected the realities of imperialistic competition, not the desires of indigenous populations. Severe disruptions marked the emergence of a rambunctious African nationalism. There had been little preparation for the launching of these new national states. It was too much to expect that Africans could accomplish in a decade what had taken European and American states, supposedly possessing more political sophistication, several centuries. The record of the West in assuring national unity (unification of Germany and Italy and the American Civil War) was by no means free of bloodshed. Africans, too, learned by bitter experience that the road of nationalism is a thorny one.

It is generally accepted that African nationalism is a reaction against European domination, the natural consequence of the white man's exploitation as well as of the imperialistic urge to extract profit from the labor of the black man. According to this simplistic formula, African nationalism is closely connected with the existence of European imperialism and colonialism. But that is not the entire story. As always, the complexities of historical forces seldom can be reduced to simple terms. Elie Kedourie, a British scholar, refuses to accept the explanation that nationalism is simply a reaction to conquest and alien rule. In a closely reasoned argument, he gives his own conception of what there was in European rule to distinguish it from other alien dominations, something that goes beyond the "misleading" theory of economic exploitation.[6]

According to Kedourie, Europe was the origin and center of a deep radical disturbance that spread over the entire world in ever-widening ripples and brought unsettlement and violence to the traditional societies of Africa and Asia. It does not matter whether these societies did or did not experience direct European rule. It is this strong European influence that gives their common features and their family resemblance to nationalist movements in countries which did not know European rule or which have been ruled by Europeans for a relatively long time.

In describing the character of the disturbance that Europe has produced in the rest of the world, Kedourie says that European military might and administrative methods, much more powerful and technically superior to anything available to those traditional societies, had a more pervasive and drastic effect than previous conquests. "European administrative methods in particular, centralized, impersonal, uniform, undiscriminating in their incidence, had a leveling and pulverizing effect on traditional hierarchies and loyalties, traditional ties of dependence which, however capricious and oppressive in their general effects, did yet have about them a warm and personal quality which made power seem approachable and comprehensible to the humblest and most insignificant man."

Applied to African societies, European administrative methods had a destructive effect. The traditional tribes had hitherto been largely self-sufficient; now they found themselves linked to world markets. A social fabric that had existed for centuries was loosened and shaken, and it could offer scant resistance against attack from the outside. The African chieftain, whose authority had been undermined by Europeans, now found that his dignity had become mere show. "All this humanity could not but feel its familiar world suddenly or by degrees become alien, its traditional loyalties drained of significance, and its customary pieties hollow and meaningless." The result was a serious and distressing psychological strain.

The Kedourie analysis is an excellent one because it reveals how the ideas which traveled from Europe to the traditional societies formed an incoherent medley of European traditions, themselves also incoherent. These strands were passed on either by accidental transmission or because they were used in Europe. Nationalism was one such idea which, originating in Europe, was diffused throughout Africa, where its popularity became as great as it had been and is in Europe.

In Africa, however, nationalism as a doctrinal system immediately confronted the old traditional tribalism. Let us turn now to the struggle between these two isms.

The Clash between Tribalism and Nationalism

The term "tribalism" is derived from the Latin *tribus,* referring to one of
the three original ethnic divisions (Luceres, Ramnes, Tities) of the early
Romans. Today tribalism is defined as the sentiment of loyalty to an ethnic or
linguistic group. It has become customary to apply the term to African
peoples to imply the primitive, inferior, or savage. Yet a kind of tribalism
exists in the Western world (French-speaking Canadians, Dutch-speaking
Flemings, Basques) as well as in Africa.

African tribalism represents loyalty to early subgroups. The African
regards his tribe, not his nation-state, as the true object of his loyalty. He
feels a strong attachment to one of the more than 5,000 tribes scattered
throughout the continent. This gives him his identity—in the same way as a
medieval peasant was loyal to his village or the modern Frenchman is loyal to
his nation. The African feels a sense of union with his kinship group and he is
suspicious of any outsider. His xenophobia is one of his most elementary
characteristics. Along with his peers, he believes in magic, in the capacity of
his shamans, in good and evil spirits, in taboos. He gives close attention to the
traditional tribal rites governing birth, puberty, marriage, and death. To him,
his tribe represents strength and security in a hostile environment.

The able Kenyan nationalist, Tom Mboya, saw positive contributions in
tribalism. To him it represented the African structure of interdependence
within the community, where each man knows that he has certain responsibilities and duties and where there are sanctions against those who do not
fulfill expectations. For example, there is inherent generosity within a tribe.
From the time a child is born, he is virtually the property of the entire tribe or
clan, and not just of his father and mother. He is expected to serve all his
comrades, and also to receive help from everyone. As a young child he herds
cattle in a group with other children of the clan. Later he works with others to
build a hut for a comrade, without distinction of family. If as a youth he did
not make his full contribution to the community, he would not stand a chance
with the clan elders when he comes to marriageable age. If he is in need, his
demands might well be disregarded, and he would be told by the elders that he
deserves nothing better until he proves himself. This aspect of the African
tribal system provides discipline, self-reliance, and stability.

Against these positive aspects of tribalism described by Tom Mboya were
negative characteristics. Too often the man who lived completely within the
confines of his tribe tended not so much to revere its customs but to
discriminate against other tribes. Tribalism was responsible for a bewildering
variety of cultures and political unions, crisscrossing in a bizarre and often
incomprehensible pattern. Each tribe, possessing its own way of life, developed attitudes that made it difficult to live in peace with other tribes. One

tribe might deem it desirable to acquire gold or silver coins, while another judged wealth only in the number of women or cattle acquired by a member. There was constant intertribal warfare.

Colonial administrators, consciously or unconsciously, tended to build up tribal antagonisms. The ancient principle of divide-and-rule was used: it was easier to influence the natives if an amenable tribe could be found and used against another tribe that was hostile. Missionaries often taught Africans to despise their tribal culture on the ground that it was incompatible with modern civilization. Africans were told that European social behavior was superior to the black man's customs. The result was often a conflict in the minds of unsophisticated natives as to whether they should remain completely tribal or change to the European way of life.

Seventeen of black Africa's thirty-four countries marched to independence in 1960, followed by thirteen more as the continent was swept by change. In the process of nation making, one of the most difficult problems concerned the old boundaries set up by nineteenth-century colonial masters. Using a kind of gerrymandering manipulation, the early imperialists combined or separated tribes in helter-skelter fashion with little or no attention to tribal loyalties.

Almost immediately after independence there began a conflict between the new nationalism and the old tribalism. To build viable nations, it was necessary to weld the tribes into workable units, but almost everywhere the polyglot tribes remained fragmented. In the new hodgepodge, no state has frontiers based on either sound geography or ethnology.

Despite urbanization, industrialization, and increasing education, most Africans tended to retain a sense of loyalty to their tribes and to resist the infiltration of outsiders. It was not easy to eliminate the old tribal antagonisms and the nepotism that went along with them. On one side was the attempt by Western-educated African leaders to recapitulate the European experience—to unify a country and build a strong national economy. On the other side were the persistent tribal differences. Ambitious politicians took advantage of continuing tribalism by filling administrative offices with their fellow tribesmen, thereby creating even more friction.

The entire continent, with its approximately 700 tongues, was left in tribal chaos. In Kenya the minority Luo tribe was in deadly conflict with the dominant Kikuyu, and the situation was complicated by feuds between the Masai and Kikuyu, either for cattle or women, and by boundary quarrels between the Luo and the Kissii. In Ruanda-Urundi, a part of the old German East Africa, the giant Watusi people formed a ruling elite over the Bahutu, who comprised some 84 percent of the population. Violence spread as the numerically dominant, short-stature Bahutu cut the stately Watusi down to size by the logical expedient of chopping off their legs. With Ruanda a republic under Bahutu control, and Urundi a monarchy of the Watusi, it became impossible to weld the two into one nation-state. The United Nations trusteeship was terminated in 1962 and Ruanda-Urundi became two independent states, Rwanda and Burundi.

In this tribal kaleidoscope, Hausas were distributed in Nigeria, Mali, and Upper Volta; Woloffs in Gambia, Senegal, and Mali; Ewes in Ghana and Togo; Bakongo in Angola and both Congos. The divisive tribalism led to a growing list of coup-struck nations. Juntas were based on tribal support. One colonel after another, with Napoleonic pretensions, sought power without regard for the democratic process. There were coups in the Congo, Dahomey, Nigeria, Upper Volta, Ghana, and Sierre Leone. There was constant unrest as one regime after another was shaken by the power drives of rival tribes.

Case History I: Strife in the Congo

The combination of unmanageable tribal chaos and economic animosities produced explosions throughout the continent. Civil wars were fought with conscious brutality.

The Congo, formerly the Belgian Congo, consists of 905,328 square miles in the south-central heart of Africa. In addition to a rich agricultural basin, there are enormous mineral resources in Katanga Province in the southeast, including cobalt, copper, and uranium, which are mined by the Union Minière du Haut-Katanga, a Belgian company. In the Congo are more than 200 ethnic groups, divided into three major categories: Negroes (Bantu, Sudanese, and Nilotics), Hamites, and Pygmies. In 1959 the European population was 117,000.

The movement for independence gathered momentum in the late 1950s. In 1959 the Belgians, unwilling to face protracted guerrilla warfare, suddenly granted full independence to the Congo. Misjudging the mood of the Congolese, whom they believed to be contented under colonial rule, the Belgians had given little attention to preparing their African wards for freedom. On Independence Day, June 30, 1960, the new nation's first Prime Minister, Patrice E. Lumumba, let the Belgians know that they were no longer welcome. Several days later, the *Force Publique,* a rabble army, went on a rampage, killing, raping, and pillaging.

Soon there was additional trouble in the copper-rich south. Katanga, without which the new nation could not well survive, declared its independence. Moise K. Tshombe, a right-winger widely regarded as favorable to Belgian interests, became President. He hired British and Rhodesian mercenaries to train and lead his rebel army.

Meanwhile the country began to fall apart with intertribal strife. The *Force*

Publique was unable to maintain order, as tribesmen, Belgian citizens, and missionaries were assaulted in the streets. After the hard-pressed government at Leopoldville turned to the United Nations for help, a U.N. force of 20,000 men, from other African states, as well as such European neutrals as Ireland and Sweden, moved in to restore order. Funds were lacking for the enormous job, and Communist members of the United Nations refused to contribute to the common effort.

At this time a comic-opera dispute broke out between Joseph Kasavubu, a former bookkeeper who had been elected President, and Lumumba, the Prime Minister, whose party had won the most seats in the National Assembly. After each rival announced the "resignation" of the other, Colonel Joseph C. Mobutu, the Army Chief of Staff, dismissed them both and expelled Soviet diplomats and technicians from Leopoldville. The United Nations recognized the Kasavubu delegation as representing the legitimate government. Lumumba was handed over to his worst enemies, the Katanga rebels, and was murdered "while attempting to escape." A United Nations commission later pronounced Tshombe as directly implicated in the crime, and the dead Lumumba became a hero throughout Africa. Communists everywhere hailed him as a martyr in the struggle against "African neo-colonialism."

After heavy fighting between United Nations troops and Katanga forces, the secession was ended in the spring of 1963. The next year Tshombe, who had gone into exile, was invited to return as the Congo's new Prime Minister. In a new insurrection the Simbas, peasant rebels, gained control of half the country. The revolt was suppressed with the help of several hundred mercenaries and a contingent of Belgian paratroopers. In 1964 Tshombe was dismissed, and Mobutu again overthrew the Kasavubu government. Mobutu eliminated civilian politicians, tightened his control over the police, and instituted a federal system with a unicameral legislature. His government appropriated the assets of the Union Minière. Kasavubu died in March 1969, and in June Tshombe died, a captive in Algeria. On October 27, 1971, the Democratic Republic of the Congo took the name of Zaire, a variation of the African name for big rivers, specifically the Congo, whose basin lies almost entirely within the republic. The name was chosen as a means of returning to and accenting the nation's "traditional authenticity."

Zaire, the most populous African state after Nigeria, Egypt, and Ethiopia, was still beset by tensions arising out of tribalism and unequal distribution of wealth. It presents a typical case of nation building in Africa and elsewhere. Neither in Africa nor in Europe did reasonable men sit down at the conference table and work out the destiny of their country. Instead, they turned to force, power, might—the essential ingredients of integral nationalism—for inspiration in the making of new nations.

Case History II: Civil War in Nigeria

There were similar difficulties in Nigeria. On the western bulge of the continent just north of the equator, it was fashioned out of territories originally colonized by the British. The population of 62 million embraces a fifth of the black peoples of Africa. The country is well endowed with natural resources, including tin, lead, coal, and iron. It is estimated that many billion gallons of oil lie beneath its coastal waters.

Nigeria provides the perfect example of how colonial powers constructed frontiers without regard to ethnology or geography. It was the creation of a British colonial official, Lord Lugard, who combined three disparate areas in which three major tribes dominated nearly 250 tribal and linguistic groups. From the day it won its freedom the country has been struggling to keep the three regions together. Here again is an example of the confrontation of unifying nationalism and fragmentizing tribalism.

In the undeveloped north, more a part of the Sahara than of the tropics, lives the seminomadic Hausa tribe, forming roughly 60 percent of the Nigerian population. Speaking a language of their own, adhering to the Islamic faith, the Hausas regard themselves as the most important tribal unit and jealously guard their position. In the west, the country of cacao, live the urbanized Yorubas, a people with a highly developed social and economic life. In their capital at Ibadan, a city of 500,000, is an important college that is associated with the University of London. The restive Yorubas resent the northern Hausas. In the east, the country of palm products, live the talented, industrious, and assertive Ibo tribesmen. About 14 million when independence was proclaimed, the Ibos are individualistic and clannish, and are known for their unbending will and arrogance. They accepted Christianity in the early twentieth century, when the first missionaries penetrated the swamps and jungle of the Niger delta. It is probable that the Ibos migrated from the Nile Valley centuries ago: though most of these tribesmen are black, many others are light in color, with a reddish-tinted skin.

When the eastern region was linked with the rest of Nigeria, the ambitious Ibos spread through the cities and especially into Lagos, the capital of the federation and the main seaport. They became middlemen in the markets, clerks, engine drivers, station masters, bank tellers, mechanics, and salesmen. By the end of World War II more Ibos were studying in the United States than all other Nigerian tribesmen together. Wherever they went, the proud Ibos maintained a sense of loyalty to their village, family, district, and "the Ibo nation." They aroused the enmity of the Muslim Hausas in the north, who criticized the Ibos for "laughing at the Prophet." In turn, the Ibos regarded the Hausas as stupid and inferior because they could not speak English.

Added to the disparate characteristics of Muslim Hausas, animist Yorubas, and Christian Ibos were bitter regional differences between other minor
tribes. Living in the east, among the Ibos, were the Ibibios, Efiks, Ogioas,
and Ilwas, some of whom felt toward the Ibos the way the Ibos felt toward the
Hausas.

Tribal antagonisms exploded with independence in 1960. On January 15,
1960, the first Prime Minister, Sir Abubukar Tafawa Balewa, a Muslim
northerner, who wore the title *Alhaji* in recognition of his pilgrimage to
Mecca, was assassinated. To most Hausas the murder was clearly the
opening step in an Ibo conspiracy to take over the country. As official
corruption increased in the federation, a group of Ibo army officers staged a
coup in January 1966. The new government promised a unified state with
less tribalism, but the Hausas in the north were unimpressed.

There was no lessening of tribal instability. In 1966 a wave of violent rioting
swept through the north, in which as many as 50,000 Ibos were slaughtered.
Ibos from all over Nigeria began returning to their homeland. Meanwhile an
attempt was made to ease the situation when the military government
announced the creation of twelve ethnically based states to replace the
previous areas. It did not work.

The situation gradually degenerated to the stage of civil war. A new state
appeared in the east, Biafra. Named after the isle of Biafra, an arm of the Gulf
of Guinea, it included not only Iboland but areas whose tribes resented the
Ibos. The Biafran leader, General Odumegwu Ojukwu, broke away from his
former army friend, Major General Yakubu Gowan, who had become head of
the Nigerian government. Gowon denounced the secession and ordered an
attack on Biafra.

There was foreign involvement from the beginning. The Nigerian government received support from both the British and the Russians, each acting
from high policy reasons of its own. The British wanted not only to protect
their investments in Nigeria but also to discourage Russian penetration. The
Russians were drawn in by the possibility of winning friends and influence
among the new African military elites who were shaping the future of Africa.
Both insisted that they were acting for the benefit of their African brothers.
The French were sympathetic to the Biafrans, and probably gave them some
assistance. Washington officially proclaimed neutrality but donated relief
supplies, which were flown into Biafra.

The war was savage. Millions of Biafrans were threatened by starvation
from the blockade of the region by the federal government, despite the efforts
of the International Red Cross and other charitable organizations to airlift
food and medical supplies. By early 1969 the Biafran territory had shrunk to a
tenth of its original size. The secession movement failed and Ojukwu fled to a
friendly country.

The distressing civil war in Nigeria was symptomatic of the collision between nationalism and tribalism throughout black Africa. The perpetuation of national monstrosities was bolstered by the Biafran tragedy. Here, as well as elsewhere, nationalism revealed its propensity for encouraging conflict. There were no limits to the color of nationalism—it could be black as well as red, white, blue, or green.

The Urge to Negritude

A comparative analysis reveals that the desire for cultural identity is strong in building any nationalism. Just as the Grimm brothers sought to strengthen the sense of Germanness through research in linguistic paleontology, so did Africans turn to their past in search for cultural amalgams.

Closely related to the old tribalism is a new movement called Negritude, dedicated to the revival of the African personality as well as a corresponding rejection of Western values. To its spokesmen it is a conscious beginning of an African renaissance: an avowal for Africa and liberation from the European paradigm. They would rediscover and awaken the best of African traditions.

The two leading advocates of Negritude are Ndabaningi Sithole, a native of Southern Rhodesia, and Leopold Senghor, the dean of African men of letters and President of the Republic of Senegal. Sithole raised the question: How much African is the present-day African?

There is a world of difference between the African prior to the coming of the white man and the African after Africa was occupied by European powers. There is therefore a sense in which an African is African, and a sense in which he is not African, just as there is a sense in which an American who has spent two-thirds of his life in Africa is and is not an American, and is and is not African. While the Westerners may be consciously Westernizing Africa, Africa is also unconsciously Africanizing them. The interaction between the West and Africa is producing a new brand of the African. That is, it is pushing the white-man-worshipping African into the background, and bringing into the foreground the African who does not worship the white man.[7]

Senghor, too, accused the European of viewing life from an analytical, exterior perspective, "seeking to utilize, conquer, and even to kill objects." On the other hand, he sees the African as looking for a sympathetic symbiosis with nature in order to understand it. The African personality, in his estimation, is something special. The African Negro is not affected by images unless they are rhythmic, "uniting sign and flesh, flesh and spirit, into one whole." Image and rhythm are the two fundamental features of the African Negro style. It is this urge of vital force that is expressed by the religious and social life of the African Negro, "of which art and literature are the most effective instruments."

I shall be told that the spirit of the Civilization and the laws of African Negro culture, as I have expounded them, are not peculiar to the African Negro, but are common to other peoples as well. I do not deny it. Each people unites in its own aspect the diverse features of mankind's condition. But I assert that these features will nowhere be found united in such equilibrium and such enlightenment, and that rhythm reigns nowhere so despotically. Nature has arranged things well in willing that each people, each race, each continent, should cultivate with special affection certain of the virtues of man; that is precisely where originality lies. And if it is also said that this African Negro culture resembles that of ancient Egypt, and of the Dravidian and Oceanic peoples like two sisters, I would answer that ancient Egypt was *African* and that Negro blood flows in imperious currents in the veins of the Dravidians and the Oceanics.[8]

The dignity and self-confidence of this passage recall the similar attitude of Western nationalists. Negritude is a way of expressing pride in indigenous culture, in the ancient grandeur. It is something more than a rationalization of a common defensive pattern to denote a community of interests. It is a deeply felt sense of self-esteem which firms the foundation of nationalism. Patrice E. Lumumba said it succinctly: "A free and gallant Congo will arise from the black soil, a free and gallant Congo—the black blossom, the black seed."

Prospects for African Nationalism

Black Africa has had more than its share of turmoil and bloodshed, from the Mau Mau terror to the Biafran tragedy. We have seen how the Congo and Nigeria, the two richest and most promising states, the brightest hopes for successful nationhood, were shattered by civil war. They were not alone in suffering the misfortunes of tribalism. At least twenty-eight of black Africa's thirty-four countries were ravaged by coups or serious disturbances.

The political picture is still one of confusion. Most African nations are handicapped by inefficient, ineffective, and uneven leadership. The first presidents and premiers were mostly freedom fighters who were skilled in guerrilla warfare but inexperienced in statecraft, a costly combination.

The story of Ghana illustrates the thorny path of nation building. The British bequeathed to the new state a workable civil service, an excellent legal system, and a free press. But within a decade a potentially viable democracy was transformed into a stultifying dictatorship. This transition was the work of Kwame Nkrumah, who, obsessed by vanity, regarded himself as a new Caesar. He made himself a leading spokesman for the Third World. He instructed his followers to address him as "The Conqueror,"

"His Messianic Majesty," "The Redeemer (*Osagyefo*)," and equivalent titles. He covered the land with monuments to himself as a portent of future glory. Ghanian schoolchildren began each day's study by reciting the litany: "Kwame Nkrumah is our Messiah. Kwame Nkrumah does no wrong." Making himself President for life, he eliminated his opponents, shackled the courts, and muzzled the press. He succeeded in destroying not only his people's freedom but finally himself. Under his regime Ghana's gold reserves dropped from half a billion dollars to nothing. "The Nation's Pillar of Fire" was overthrown in 1966 and settled in Guinea in aggrieved and conspiratorial exile.[9]

Other political leaders were not so fortunate. Assassination was the fate of the Congo's Patrice E. Lumumba, Togo's Sylvanus Olympio, Nigeria's Sir Abubakar Balewa, and Kenya's Tom Mboya. Others managed to remain alive under dangerous circumstances. Kenya's Kenyatta, father of his country and ruler since its independence in 1963, was stoned at Mboya's funeral. A Kikuyu, he threw opposition leader Oginga Odinga into prison and banned the tribal Luo-dominated party. He warned the Luos: "We are going to crush you into flour. Anybody who toys with our progress will be crushed like locusts. Do not say later that I did not warn you publicly."

Added to tribal animosities and weak leadership was continuing economic chaos. Independence did not bring the expected prosperity. Despite the plethora of natural resources, African countries are still burdened by desperate poverty. Black Africa has 221 million people, about 8 percent of the world's population, but only 1 percent of the world's gross national product. Its per capita income remains at an abnormally low rate: in Nigeria it is about $100 a year, not enough to guarantee the minimum needs of life. The Congo has its minerals, Zambia its copper, and Nigeria its oil, but little of this wealth filters down to the ordinary citizens.

Uhuru (Swahili for "freedom") was no panacea. Change brought independence, but the winds shifted. At first the white colonial masters were forced out, but civil strife and economic chaos brought them back, not as participants in government but as technicians and businessmen. British administrators and troops were replaced by traders and technical experts. Swaziland looked to London for financial support. French technical counselors swarmed over that part of black Africa formerly under French control: Senegal, the Malagasy Republic, and Chad. In the Congo the number of white Belgians dwindled from 100,000 to 20,000, but then rose to 40,000. They did everything from mining copper to training the Congolese army. The mines, though owned by the Congolese government, were operated under contract by a Belgian firm.

Only a confident, astrologically oriented Nostradamus would dare to predict the future course of African nationalism. The more modest prognosticator sees a choice of: (1) the solidification of a number of strong national states; (2) disintegration into tribal fragments; or (3) a combination of both. Africa is too far down the road of nationalism to turn back now. Tribalism, the chronic cause of Africa's ills, might be overcome through urbanization and its accompanying destruction of family and clan ties. Educated Africans and such leaders as Nigeria's Hamani Diori, Tanzania's Julius K. Nyerere, and Zambia's Kenneth Kaudda, while recognizing the positive aspects of tribalism, believe that it is possible to create an African community of nations. They see "tribalism" as a distasteful word, suggesting an atavism unnecessary in the modern world. What Africa needs, they say, is a transmutation of tribal loyalties to the larger loyalty to nationhood. They understand that submission to a central authority is essential for nation building.

A new order in Africa might emerge only after tribes and would-be nations alike have gone through many additional tests of strength. If Africa is to become modernized, it must find a substitute for tribalism. Perhaps it might transfer to the nation-state the ideas of order, authority, and belonging, but this is no guarantee that it will achieve the blessings of peace and security. In this confused picture what is clear is that, comparatively speaking, nationalism in Africa, similar to that in Europe, seems to offer relief from deep fears and some hope for the future. Beyond nationalism there is the prospect of more nationalism.[10]

Notes

[1] This idea was presented originally by Friedrich Meinecke in his *Weltbürgertum und Nationalstaat, Werke* (Munich, 1962), 5:9ff., and was developed by Otto Pflanze in "Nationalism in Europe, 1848–1871," *Review of Politics,* 28 (April 1966): 129–43.

[2] See Philip D. Curtin, "Nationalism in Africa, 1845–1965," *Review of Politics,* op cit., pp. 143–53.

[3] Jomo Kenyatta, *Facing Mount Kenya: The Tribal Way of the Gikuyu* (London: Secker and Warburg, 1953), p. 317.

[4] Tom Mboya, *Freedom and After* (London: André Deutsch, 1963), p. 64.

[5] Quoted in A. P. Merriam, *Congo: Background to Conflict* (Evanston, Ill.: Northwestern University Press, 1961), pp. 352–53.

[6] Elie Kedourie (ed.), *Nationalism in Asia and Africa* (New York and Cleveland: World Publishing Co., 1970), pp. 22ff. of the introduction.

[7] Ndabaningi Sithole, *African Nationalism* (Cape Town: Oxford University Press, 1959), p. 157.

[8] Leopold Sedar Senghor, ''The Spirit of Civilization, or the Laws of African Negro Culture,'' *The First Conference of Negro Writers and Artists* (Paris: Presence Africaine, 1956), p. 64.

[9] Nkrumah died of cancer in a Rumanian hospital in early May, 1974.

[10] See S. Kajaratman, ''Beyond Nationalism, More Nationalism,'' *Solidarity,* LV (1969), pp. 42-47.

13

The Mainsprings
of Asian
Nationalism

Schoolmates, rise up running to the
    front of the war of resistance!
Listen! The bugle of the war of
    resistance is sounded.
Look! The red flag of combat is flying.
We are following the Communist party.
Take up your arms!
We are defending the frontier of our
        motherland till death.

—Graduation Song in the People's
Republic of China

A Comparison of African and Asian Xenophobia

On a comparative basis, African and Asian nationalisms are similar in that both are directed with xenophobic intensity against the white man. Lured by the prospect of great wealth (raw materials in Africa, trade in the Far East), Western imperialists carved out most of Africa as colonial outposts and set up spheres of influence in Asia. This was accomplished with little or no regard for the feelings or rights of the exploited peoples. It was accompanied by what Albert Einstein described as the "native aggressiveness" of man, a trait that virtually placed man—a human animal—in the category of the bull and the rooster.

What Western imperialists failed to see was that Africans and Asians were subject to the same urge for economic and psychological security common to peoples everywhere. When the reaction came against imperialism, it turned out to be an explosive force directed against the pious "white man's burden." Western exploiters began to learn that the days of land-grabbing, false territorial contracts, expropriation of wealth, confiscation of trade, extraterritorial rights, and all the tricks and treatises of imperialism were numbered.

The nationalism in both Africa and Asia was motivated partly by an understandable desire to live as free men and in part by a recapitulation of European nationalism of the seventeenth and eighteenth centuries. The same kind of Western European libertarian drive affected a wide variety of former colonial peoples from Ghana to Indonesia. Like their white counterparts, the peoples of Africa and Asia wanted the blessings of freedom. They were equally influenced by the mystique of nationalism: they, too, would sing the national anthem and weep in the presence of the flag.

Nationalism came to the peoples of Africa and Asia through a combination of what the anthropologists call parallelism and diffusion in culture. On the one hand, the new nationalism arose parallel to European developments as a psychological need. In this sense it was an independent phenomenon. On the other hand, many of its forms, techniques, and symbols were diffused from London, Paris, Rome, and New York along routes traveled by African and Asian students. This coalescence of parallelism and diffusion, always tempered by contempt for the white stranger, served to give both African and Asian nationalism their distinctive temper.

Whether or not African and Asian nationalisms will follow a course similar to that of Europe—that is, a transformation from libertarianism to integralism—remains to be seen. Given the stubbornness of the human animal everywhere, the chances are that the same kind of aggressiveness that colored European nationalism will appear in both of these large continents.

The charming point has been made that "once home rule is secured, it remains to be determined who will rule at home."

The pertinent handwriting already appears on the old wall of the new China. Millions of impressionable children in Maoist China have been weaned away from traditional family loyalty to fanatical devotion to "the only orthodox Marxist state." Defense of the father has been succeeded by defense of the fatherland. And by that curious semanticism utilized by totalitarian ideologists, such "defense" can mean being drawn backwards across the borders of a neighboring territory "defended" by other nationalists.

The Core of Asian Nationalism

Asian nationalism was not afflicted by tribalism, the inhibiting factor of African progress. The relative uniformity among the vast ethnic groups of Asia is in contrast to the divisive African tribalism, but, as we have seen, the peoples of both continents have a deep fear of and contempt for the stranger. They hold fast to that xenophobia which forms one of the more durable elements of nationalism. The sentiment is especially marked in Asia, which is quite understandable: for centuries, Europeans who came to the Far East regarded the Asian as an inferior breed. They were a people who could not mix with Westerners, an attitude expressed precisely by Kipling:

> Oh, East is East and West is West, and never the
>   twain shall meet,
> Till Earth and Sky stand presently at God's great
>   Judgment Seat.

Behind this judgment was a long history of successive waves of Western penetration: from Marco Polo's stay at Kublai Khan's court in 1275, to the Dutch East India Company in Indonesia (1602–1798), to Robert Clive's expeditions in the mid-eighteenth century (which has been termed the turning point in the Eastern career of the English), to the marking of British, French, German, and Russian spheres of influence in China in the late nineteenth century. Asians resented these outsiders. To the peoples of Asia, whose cultural traditions often matched or surpassed those of their invaders, the attitude of foreigners was insufferably insulting.

When nationalism spread throughout Asia in the twentieth century, its principal component was a xenophobia directed against foreigners. One can well understand the meaning of independence to the Indonesian servant, who had been forced to prostrate himself and touch his brow to the floor before serving food to his Dutch master.

The first whites who came to Asia were accepted as equals, but the fraternization did not last long, especially after fortresses began to out-number trading posts. Friendship declined and suspicions grew. The Indian Mutiny of 1857–1858 was a turning point. Originally a rebellion by the Bengal Army, the incident led to what amounted to a civil war. There were several motives: resentment against British reforms of ancient Indian insti-tutions, fear of forcible conversion to Christianity, and the issue of car-tridges greased with cow fat (which angered Hindus) or pig fat (which offended Muslims). There were many atrocities. British troops and their families, cut off at Cawnpore, were taken prisoner amd murdered. After the defeat of the rebels in July 1858, the India Act transferred the administration from the East India Company to the British Crown.

The Indian Mutiny left a heritage of resentment throughout Asia. Arnold Toynbee recognized the cause: "Every contact that the East has had with the West has been one of aggression by the West." Asians looked upon colonial-ism in all its manifestations as an evil that should be brought to an end. They wanted no more subjugation, no more domination, no more exploitation.

Asian rebellion against Western control eventually took the usual political, military, and economic forms, but behind the deepening sense of xenophobia were cultural, religious, and psychological drives. Asians were infuriated by Western denigration of their culture as either barbaric, quaint, or puerile. Ignorant white men sometimes went to the extreme of attempting to de-asian-ize the Asians in favor of "superior" Western culture. To ease administrative problems, Westerners sought to impose alien languages upon Asian peoples. Students who dared to speak their own languages were chastised in subtle or direct ways.

This assault upon Asian culture ignored the truly priceless heritage of the Far East. The Chinese had given the world such inventions as printing, gunpowder, and the compass long before Westerners took credit for them. Asians possessed magnificent literatures and exquisite art forms. To call such people inferior because they had not mastered modern technology was clearly a manifestation of Western ignorance and callousness.

Wherever Westerners went in Asia they were set apart by Christianity. Although Western missionaries were sometimes successful in implanting the cross on Asian soil, they were more often than not rejected by Asians. An element of xenophobia existed here, too. Asians preferred their own reli-gions, which stressed systems of conduct, ritual cleanliness, caste arrange-ments, the exclusiveness of the holy man, and sanctuaries. They discouraged outsiders, just as the Christian, Jewish, and Islamic creeds tended to reject the "infidel." They preferred their own revivals—the Reformation in the West and the purification of Hinduism in the East.

Most important of all, perhaps, was the psychological aura of Asian xenophobia. Asian liberators urged their followers to refuse to become "like dumb, driven cattle or like the grass that is trodden down." They were quite willing to accept benefits from the West, but always on the basis of equality and without incurring the danger of adopting methods that would be prejudicial to their own interests. These were men who would accept Western institutions without sacrificing their own.

At the root of Asian xenophobia was always a psychological need for equality. Hence the bitter protests against the Westerner. It was expressed by Ho Chi Minh when he denounced the French who had driven Indo-Chinese peasants away from their villages: "In consequence of that the Annamese peasants were turned into serfs and forced to cultivate their own lands for foreign masters." This kind of denunciation was recapitulated throughout Asia. Ho Chi Minh also revealed a popular Asian cause when he excoriated the Catholic mission, "which secured for itself all those lands by using every imaginable and unimaginable method, including bribery, fraud, and coercion." True or exaggerated, this represented Asian thinking about the foreigner. The ultimate in resentment was expressed by Mao Tse-tung when he attacked the idea of "unconditional Westernization": "The national, scientific, and popular culture is the anti-imperialist culture of the people, the culture of New Democracy, the culture of the Chinese nation."

The Negative Quality of Asian Nationalism

If Africa's burden was negative tribalism, Asia's was negative nationalism. In its fear and its contempt for the foreigner, Asian nationalism was not only negative in nature but reactionary in orientation. This trend was recognized by the Asian scholar Theodore Hsi-En Chen of the University of Southern California: "From China to Indonesia, nationalism in Asia is totally negative: it expresses deep-seated hatred of anything resembling foreign control."[1]

It is a fair appraisal. The characteristic may be noted, in addition to China and Indonesia, in India, Pakistan, Ceylon, Burma, the Philippines, Korea, and elsewhere. There may be differences of degree, but the quality is the same. In the drive for nationhood, leaders proclaimed the glories of tradition and history while at the same time calling for expulsion of "the foreign devil." But once the emotionalism of independence wore off, there came serious problems: administrative inefficiency, political chaos, economic decline, and social disunity. Nationalist leaders revealed an inability to function beyond the soap box or the guerrilla hideout. Outworn slogans of the past were just not enough to solve the pragmatic difficulties of the present.

This process was similar to the course of African nationalism. Here, too, nationalism began as a liberating force, with a sense of progressivism at first replacing the latent hostility to foreign masters. But in one new Asian nation after another this positive quality began to disappear. The dynamism of liberation began to be replaced by a selfish regard for private interest and by indifference to the national welfare. Most new leaders were unable to progress beyond the rallying cries of anticolonialism. Once they had eliminated foreign control, they turned on one another and tried to divert attention from their own disastrous behavior by setting up false national goals, while continuing to beat the straw man of "neo-colonialism."

It is presumptuous for Westerners, staggering under their own load of problems, to lecture Asians about the deleterious effects of nationalism. The issue facing the new Asian nation is a struggle against itself, not against the old imperialist masters. Far-sighted Asians realize that the old colonialism has outlived itself and can no longer serve as the foundation for a creative nationalism. Rational long-term planning and mass political participation are indicated. Internal unity and discipline form the sine qua non of nation building.

Categories: Ideological and Pragmatic Nationalism

Any interpretation of Asian nationalism must recognize that the issue cannot be expressed in simplistic terms. There are invariably degrees and gradations in all the patterns of nationalism, in Asia as elsewhere. Asian nationalism is a loosely concerted movement, dedicated to promoting the interests of peoples who wish to assert national as well as Asian identity in the contemporary world. There are contrasting lines: some liberator-nationalists aimed to set up nation-states modeled on Western constitutional democracy; others rejected democracy in favor of a dictatorial order.

Outstanding in the Asian pattern of nationalism is the clash between ideological and pragmatic forms. The ideological nationalists tend to be totalitarian minded. They call for liquidation of colonialism, absolute power at the political level, nationalization of the economy, education, and culture, heavy stress on industrialization, and agrarian reforms. They are convinced of the virtue of their cause and allow no interference in their role as guardians of the national image. On ideological grounds, they denounce all opponents as neo-colonialists and imperialists and congratulate themselves as a newly emergent force that is blending nationalist, religious, and Communist forces. Typical apostles of ideological nationalism were Indonesia's Achmed Sukarno and Vietnam's Ho Chi Minh. In the Philippines, ideological nationalists launched the Movement for the Advancement of Nationalism (MAN).[2]

Alongside the voluble ideological nationalists are the lesser-known pragmatic nationalists—political leaders, administrators, and professionals who call for a strictly practical and scientific solution to the problems of nation building. Aware of their underdeveloped economies and serious social problems, they advocate continued relations with both the former imperialist countries and fellow Asians on the basis of national self-interest. They reject the fixed, unchangeable concepts of the ideological nationalists and recommend dedication to the national cause as dependent not on ideological slogans and a closed society but on current national self-interest in an open society.

Disputes between ideological and pragmatic nationalists are often bitter and abusive: they reflect similar quarrels throughout the world. Both see truth in their own approaches to complex problems and both denounce each other as narrow minded and opportunistic. Pragmatic nationalists accuse the ideologists of being Leninist oriented and advocates of a viewpoint that has demonstrated its bankruptcy. Ideological nationalists denounce the pragmatists as confused liberals who are unable to make tough decisions at a time when hard remedies are necessary for the common good. This intellectual confrontation reflects an Asian version of the global cold war and the clash between open and closed societies.

The counter-nationalists, another category, are closely related to the ideological nationalists. Dissatisfied with the formation of the nation-state, they are convinced that the road to the future is revolution. The Communist Chinese, who fall within this category, believe themselves to be the truly orthodox force against bourgeois, capitalist nationalism, the "true Leninist" society remaining after the desertion of Communist ideals. The Maoists, waving little red books containing the holy words of the leader, have turned out to be among the most rigid nationalists on earth.

Added to these special categories of Asian nationalists are the broad masses of citizens, who in their everyday life, education, and family milieu work in their own way to strengthen the national cause. In carrying out their obligations to the state these citizens provide the cement for the structure of the nation-state.

In Asia, too, nationalism is the prime political institution. It represents the usual quest for security in an age of political tensions, economic instability, social frustrations, and cultural awakening. Asian nationalism may take on slightly differing patterns in China, India, and Japan, but its general character remains much the same as its counterpart in Europe, Africa, or the Near East. Here, too, nationalism became a new religion, whether based on the old religion or not. Here, too, nationalist prophets declare nationalism as not merely a political program but "as a religion that has come from God."

Role of the Western-Educated Elite

The comparative historian sees another similar trend in the development of African and Asian nationalisms. The new national rulers, whether democratic or authoritarian, were caught between the promising ideals of independence and the hard realities of immediate needs. They were not inclined to reject completely all Western values. Intellectuals on both continents were well aware of the implications of Western progress. They were anxious to learn more about the secrets of Western technical efficiency. This is what "modernization" meant to them.

Education was the keynote, the means by which Asians and Africans could adopt Western ideas and cast them in an Asian mold. The students who went abroad for this purpose returned to become leaders of their own nationalist movements. They wanted liberation from the bonds of imperialism, but at the same time they would construct their new nation-states in the Western image.

In Asia the groundwork had already been prepared during the era of imperialism. Governmental and missionary schools and colleges gave insights into the European way of life, into Western languages, literature, history, and legal institutions. Oriental students were impressed by British freedom, the accent on individualism, and equality before the law. They understood the message of the American Revolution, with its approval of life, liberty, and the pursuit of happiness. They were just as much influenced by the sacred slogan of the French Revolution—Liberty, Equality, Fraternity. Surely there was no reason why these concepts could not be as valid for Orientals as for Europeans.

At the opening of the twentieth century, Asian students began to flock to European and American universities. Western educators encouraged large numbers of Asians to come to their educational institutions. The United States government declined to accept the reparations imposed on China by the Western powers after the Boxer rebellion in 1900 and instead used the funds to support Chinese students at American colleges and universities.

The list is long and impressive. Gandhi, Nehru, and Jinnah, leaders in the movement for the independence of India, were educated in the law in England. Osmena and Quezon were Filipino lawyers trained in the West. Thailand's Luang Pradit was a Paris-educated attorney. Ho Chi Minh was self-educated in Paris and Moscow. Tunku Abdul Rahman of Malaya and Lee Kuan Yew of Singapore studied at London and Cambridge. Soetan Sjahrir and Mohammed Hatta of Indonesia attended Dutch universities. A similar formation of an educated elite may be noted in Africa: Kwame Nkrumah and Nnamdi Azikiwe studied in the United States, Jomo Kenyatta in London and Moscow.

These were observant men, who saw how appeals to tradition solidified national sentiment, how devotion to the state was made the citizen's prime responsibility, how poets sang about the glory of the fatherland, and how patriots regretted that they had but one life to lose for their country. They were familiar with Rousseau's social contract, with Montesquieu's analysis of the spirit of legal institutions, and with Alexander Hamilton's project of a national economy. They knew how Bismarck unified the German national state, how Mazzini, Garibaldi, and Cavour stimulated Italian unity, and how Marx and Lenin proposed to change the world. They came, they saw, and they listened.

Once returned to Asia, this elite gave direction to Oriental nationalism. One of the dangers, from the viewpoint of their elders, was that Western-trained youths might decide that they had more in common with Europeans than with their fellow Asians. It was an unnecessary fear: most young Asians retained a strong sense of loyalty to their homelands.

In addition to this feeling of loyalty, the educated elite revealed a quality of pride and dignity necessary for national consciousness. The attitude was expressed with cool logic by Jawaharlal Nehru, successor to Gandhi as president of the Indian National Congress and Prime Minister of India after independence in 1947. In a talk delivered April 24, 1955, at a session of the Conference of Asian-African nations held at Bandung, Indonesia, Nehru spoke eloquently on the spirit of Asia. Despite his imprisonment by the British, he admired them as a people and held their institutions in high regard. His words earned respect everywhere:

There is yet another spirit of Asia today. As we all know, Asia is no longer passive; it has been passive enough in the past. It is no more a submissive Asia; it has tolerated submissiveness for so long. Asia of today is dynamic; Asia is full of life. . . .

We value friendship of the great countries and if I am to play my part, I should like to say that we sit with the great countries of the world as brothers, be it in Europe or America. It is not in any spirit of hatred or dislike or aggressiveness with each other in regard to Europe or America, certainly not. We send to them our greetings, all of us here, and we want to be friends with them. But we shall only cooperate in the future as equals. . . .

Are we copies of Europeans or Americans or Russians? What are we? We are Asians or Africans. We are none else. If we are camp followers of Russia or America or any other country of Europe, it is, if I may say so, not very creditable to our dignity, our new independence, our new freedom, our new spirit and our new self-reliance.[3]

Asian and Western Nationalism: A Comparison

Let us recapitulate briefly. Coinciding with the rise of nationalism in the West were critical economic changes. The Commercial Revolution, the expansion of the world's highway in the sixteenth century, and the Industrial

Revolutions of the eighteenth and nineteenth centuries meant the end of the medieval feudal-manorial economy. The West adopted a money economy and enshrined the machine as the key to production.

Along with industrialization came the revolutionary idea that politically the state and nation were one. The medieval international theocracy was replaced by a combination of nations existing by natural law. The people—not a hereditary monarch—were to bring legitimacy to the state.

Socially, nationalism in the West was identified with the bourgeoisie. The middle class formulated the doctrine of nationalism, supported it, and used it to bolster the bourgeois position in the hierarchy of society. The aristocracy took advantage of nationalism to maintain its ancient privileges. The peasantry accepted nationalist slogans with passive resignation.

Culturally, the idea of a distinct background—common traditions and historical heroes—took root among these Western people, who regarded themselves as homogeneous. Nationalism promoted the use of vernacular literatures and unique art forms.

Concomitant with these factors were the fragmentizing effects of the Reformation and the consequent nationalization of religion. Church and state were separated at the time of the French Revolution: religion began to play an inferior role in the apparatus of the state.

Finally, these breaches in the old order were sealed by psychological drives. The individual—the "citizen" of the French Revolution—no longer felt himself bound by the solidified society of the past. He became aware of the existence of his nation and the fact that he was a part of it. The broader unit gave him what he wanted most—security in a hostile world.

These broad trends and tendencies, historically pluralistic in nature, followed the lines of European expansion into the non-Western world. There was no deliberate design, no conscious distribution of nationalism. Asia and other continents were to feel the impact.

Economically, Asians were impressed by the success of the West in utilizing the machine. Once they had won independence, they would shape their industrial life on the Western model, while at the same time stressing their own heritage in the process of nation building. They would accept economic modernization but maintain their ancient cultural heritage. They would superimpose industrialism upon their predominantly agrarian economies while introducing agricultural reforms.

Politically, Asians were inclined to accept Western forms, especially in identifying the state with the new nation. There were, of course, variations in different parts of Asia, but the central fact was that political nationalism had won its way in the Far East.

Socially, again as in the West, one of the impulses for nationalism came from the bourgeoisie, a social class with some degree of leisure. Most Asian leaders were middle-class intellectuals. For support they drew on the lower ranks of society, especially those who had been educated in missionary schools; for revolutionary activism they depended upon the broad masses, workers and peasants who responded to nationalist slogans. One by one the layers of Asian society parallel with or below the bourgeois liberators accepted the new nationalism. Included were the lower middle-class white-collar workers, the urban proletariat, and the vast peasantry. This was similar to the story in Western Europe a century earlier, although the Asian experience was telescoped and considerably more rapid.

Pride in a common culture, typical of Western nationalism, existed, too, in Asia. The national heritage was glorified: scholars worked on national languages and literatures as a means of supporting the political objectives of nationalism.

Psychologically, the peoples of Asia felt the frustration of a paradoxical situation. At long last they had overcome alien imperialism and had achieved a sense of equality long denied them. But they were torn between the old and the new. This psychological dilemma explains in part the unevenness of Asian development, the constant crises, the spasmodic changes of leader-ship, and the air of discord and dissension.

A comparison of Western and Asian nationalism reveals the truth of Boyd C. Shafer's observation that "men are psychologically, racially, nationally at least as much alike as they are different." But apparently this has no effect on the continuing strength of nationalism. The Indian scholar Sir Rabindranath Tagore exempted no people from this fragmentizing of humanity:

The idea of the nation is one of the most powerful anesthetics that man has invented. Under the influence of its fumes the whole people can carry out its systematic programme of the most virulent self-seeking without being in the least aware of its moral perversion,—in fact feeling dangerously resentful if it is pointed out.[4]

Case History I: Big Brother Sukarno

The developing nationalisms in Asia and in Africa, were ordinarily not blessed with competent leadership. There was much charisma but little political genius. Charisma was the special quality of an Indonesian guerilla expert who led his people to liberation and then to near bankruptcy. Achmed Sukarno was born in 1901 in Surabaya, East Java, the son of a poor Javanese-Muslim teacher and a Balinese-Hindu dancer. The child was father to the man: the youngster, nicknamed Djago (Rooster) always wanted to be the dominant boy among his peers. At the age of 14 he came under the influence of a pioneer Indonesian nationalist named Tjokroaminete, who filled the lad's mind with resentment against Dutch rule. The young man was committed early to the cause of independence.

Sukarno studied at the Technical Faculty in Bandung, where he acquired an enthusiasm for politics. He made a serious investigation of the nationalist movement in India, especially Gandhi's policy of non-cooperation. Perhaps his country with its 100 million people scattered over 3,000 islands, could use a similar weapon. He became chairman of a study group devoted to that task. Although he took an engineering degree, he decided to become a full-time revolutionary.

In 1927 Sukarno founded the Nationalist Party. Within two years he was sentenced to prison for a four-year term. In 1933 he was rearrested and interned on the island of Flores, and later in South Sumatra. He was still in exile when the Japanese overran the Netherlands Dutch East Indies early in World War II. When the invaders offered independence in exchange for cooperation, Sukarno and his followers agreed to work with them. Although he was criticized by some of his countrymen, he was supported by the nationalists.

Sukarno was in deep trouble in Japan's collapse in 1945. On August 17, 1945, in a radio speech given with Japanese assent, he, together with Dr. Mohammad Hatta, declared Indonesian independence. Taking to the jungles, he led a brilliant four-year guerrilla campaign, which finally forced the Dutch out.

Grateful Indonesians proclaimed Sukarno *Bapak,* Father of the Country, the peerless leader who had spawned a new sense of national identity. He was venerated as a successful practitioner of Javanese magic and he was adored for his intoxicating rhetoric. He did everything he could to maintain his mystique as nationalist hero. He wore fancy uniforms and took the title "Great Leader of the Revolution."

As President, Sukarno stripped the warlords of their power, centralized the government at Djakarta, and installed democratic forms. He became one of the world's most publicized statesmen. His big moment came at the 1955 Bandung Conference, when he presented himself as a spokesman for non-alignment among the developing nations.

Sukarno fervently believed in the liberating effects of nationalism in Asia. When visiting Washington in May 1956, he delivered an address to the National Press Club in which he exalted nationalism as "a positive creed":

We of Asia are told that the troubles of our continent are due to nationalism. That is as wrong as saying that the world's troubles are due to atomic energy. It is true that there is turbulence in Asia, but that turbulence is the result and aftermath of colonialism and is not due to the liberating effects of nationalism. . . . You who have never known colonialism can never appreciate what it does to man. . . .

In any case, whether all the world approves or not, the fact is that nationalism and the liberation of nations are realities. . . . The new nations of Asia and Africa are recent additions to an adult family. The older members of that family must not be jealous of new arrivals.

The chief factor that these nations have in common is their nationalism and the concomitant release from colonialism. *To understand Asia and Africa, we must understand nationalism.* For us, it is the mainspring of action. This cannot be surprising to Western peoples, for the love of country, the spirit of patriotism, is a great element in life here also. . . .

I know that nationalism is today in many circles a suspect word and that it conveys ideas of chauvinism, of racial supremacy, and a dozen other ideologies that we reject. Those evil things are not nationalism, but distortions of nationalism. Do not confuse the distortions with the sound fruit. How foolish it would be to reject democracy because in some places and at some times democracy has been bent into shapes which are a perversion of the democratic ideal. Equally, how foolish it is to reject nationalism because it has sometimes been perverted.

This I know: We of Indonesia and the citizens of many countries of Asia and Africa have seen our dearest and best suffer and die, struggle and fail, and rise again to struggle and fail again—and again be resurrected from the very earth and finally achieve their goal. Something burned in them; something inspired them. They called it nationalism. We who have followed and seen what they built, but what they destroyed themselves in building—we, too, call their inspiration, and our inspiration, nationalism. For us, there is nothing ignoble in that word. On the contrary, it contains for us all that is best in mankind and all that is noblest. . . .

You cannot establish international bodies until nations have established their national identities. You cannot build supernational bodies without using nations as the foundations and the bricks and the keystones.

Therefore I say: Do not denigrate our nationalism. Try to understand and sympathize with it. It is at least a positive creed, an active belief, and has none of the cynicism and lassitude of less virile outlooks.[5]

In this speech Sukarno spoke contemptuously of "perversion of the democratic ideal," but within three years he himself dealt a crippling blow to Indonesian democracy. There had been a gradual political polarization between the Muslim Masiumi Party and the Socialists on the right and center against the powerful Indonesian Communist Party (PKI) on the left. In the confusion, Sukarno dissolved parliament, banned political parties, combined the premiership with the presidential office, and adopted an authoritarian system of "guided democracy."

Sukarno abandoned the democratic ideal, but he had no intention of deserting nationalism. To combine the quarreling factions in a national front, he announced a policy of *Natsokom* (Sukarno had a weakness for acronyms), joining *nat*ionalism, *so*cialism, and *com*munism. He was impressed by views of political change in the People's Republic of China.

In 1963, despite critical problems on the domestic front, Sukarno added an aggressive tone to his nationalism. Denouncing the formation of Malaysia as a "neo-colonial creation" of Britain, he began a policy of confrontation (*Konfrontasi*) against the new state. In violent outbursts he threatened to "crush Malaysia." In 1965 Indonesia withdrew from the United Nations and Sukarno turned to collaboration with Communist China. The issue brought him into conflict with Britain and made him an even more bitter critic of the West.

Meanwhile, "Bung" (Brother) Karno, economically illiterate and bored by administrative details, was falling into the trap of economic realities. He drained the national treasury in the confrontation with Malaysia. Expensive monuments and skyscrapers in Djakarta were left uncompleted for lack of funds. Sukarno's florid oratory and fervent slogans meant nothing in the face of $2.4 billion in foreign debts and one of the worst inflations endured by any country since 1945.

Economic troubles led to political eclipse. A cabal of non-Communist officers led by General Suharto, angered by Sukarno's softness on the Communists and fearful that Indonesia might become a satellite of Peking, struck back at an attempted Communist coup on October 1, 1965. The military smashed the coup and began a purge that took the lives of an estimated 300,000 Indonesians in one of the most terrible blood baths in history. Sukarno was forced out in favor of Suharto. Crushed by his fall from power, Sukarno died in June 1970. At his request these words were placed on a plain stone marking his grave: "Here lies Bung Karno, Mouthpiece of the Indonesian People."

Sukarno's career illustrates the uneven course of nationalism in the new countries of Asia. Under difficult circumstances he had led his country to independence, he had proclaimed its nationalism to the world, and he had pointed to the dangers of colonialism in a new guise. He saw nothing anachronistic about nationalism and he insisted that it was all-important for Indonesia. He did his best to harness political jealousies and irredentism. But the whole story was a sad tale of how the performance of a venerated liberation leader could degenerate into slapstick. His behavior was bizarre and eccentric ("I love my country, my people, women, and the arts, but most of all I love myself"). The father of his country was transformed into a playboy parent. The case of Sukarno illustrates how the developing nationalisms were burdened by inexperienced new rulers, who helped turn great expectations into deep disappointments.

Japan: The Legacy of Yukio Mishima

Japanese nationalism, as nationalism elsewhere, looked to the past for identity and commitment. In many ways it repeated the European experience combining romanticism and nationalism. European cultural romanticism was a reaction against the dictates of pure reason: it exalted faith and intuition instead of the intellect; it emphasized the imagination, emotion, and feeling; it looked back to the great days of order, security, and legitimacy. Above all, it saw the organogenetic conception of culture as the expression of a national soul.

European political romanticism linked up with the rising sense of nationalism. Patriot-scholars began to study national laws, institutions, and languages to prove the distinction of their own national life. The drive for German national unification, for example, was considerably facilitated by Fichte's sense of Germanism, the Grimm brothers' concern for the images of the past, Herder's divine mission for the German nation, and Richard Wagner's barbarian heroism—all inspired by romanticism.

Japanese experience underwent the same process of romantic sentimentalization ending in a quickened sense of nationalism. In this sense Japanese nationalism was something more than a revolt against the West; it had its own cultural roots and awareness of the past. Despite their yearning for modernization, the Japanese persisted in tracing their origin to the Goddess of the Sun. This kind of romanticism was closely linked with Shintoism. The most influential document in modern Japanese history was the Imperial Rescript on Education, issued on October 30, 1890, which gave official sanction to state Shintoism:

Know Ye, Our Subjects:

Our Imperial Ancestors have founded Our Empire on a basis broad and everlasting, and have deeply and firmly implanted virtue. Our subjects ever united in loyalty and filial piety have from generation to generation illustrated the beauty thereof. This is the glory of the fundamental character of Our Empire, and herein lies the source of our education. Ye, Our subjects, be filial toward your parents. . . .

The Way here set forth is indeed the teaching bequeathed by Our Imperial Ancestors.[6]

Japanese nationalism, similar to nationalism in Asia and Africa, emerged slowly and then developed swiftly. It took on an aggressive form in the twentieth century. The justification was that Japan was "a divine country ruled over by the Son of Heaven" and that "the Imperial Principle must be propagated over the Seven Seas." A conference held in Tokyo in June and July 1927, presided over by Prime Minister Baron Gi-ichi Tanaka, presented a summary of its work to the Emperor. Published by the Chinese in 1929, the so-called Tanaka Memorial was denounced by the Japanese as a forgery.

Whether genuine or not, the memorial had the distinction of summing up aggressive nationalist ambitions. This was the key paragraph:

The way to gain actual rights in Manchuria and Mongolia is to use this region as a base and under the pretense of trade and commerce penetrate the rest of China. Armed by the rights already secured we shall seize the resources all over the country. Having China's entire resources at our disposal, we shall proceed to conquer India, the Archipelago, Asia Minor, Central Asia, and even Europe. But to get control of Manchuria and Mongolia is the first step if the Yamato race wishes to distinguish itself on Continental Asia. Final success belongs to the country having raw materials; the full growth of national strength belongs to the country having extensive territory. If we pursue a positive policy to enlarge our rights in Manchuria and China, all these prerequisites of a powerful nation will constitute no problem. Furthermore, our surplus population of 700,000 each year will be taken care of.[7]

Forgery or not, the Tanaka Memorial accurately presaged events. Japan seized Manchuria in 1931 and established the puppet state of Manchukuo. Two years later she withdrew from the League of Nations. A critical moment in the expansionist drive came at Pearl Harbor. Nippon took on too great a task: Japanese nationalism was given finally a deadly blow at Hiroshima. Aware that they had made a serious error, the Japanese began to soften their attitude toward the dangerous ism that had brought them close to destruction. Like the Germans, they subjugated their guilt in an all-out effort to win economic supremacy. No more nationalism! It seemed to work. Along with the new attitude, the Japanese economic miracle matched the German accomplishment.

It was too much to expect that nationalism could be dead in Japan after World War II. That it was not permanently snuffed out was revealed by an astonishing incident on November 25, 1970. At 45, Yukio Mishima was Japan's best-known novelist, a contender for the Nobel Prize, and a skillful practitioner of the ancient martial arts. His mind was brilliant. His body, small but powerful, had been honed to a sharp edge by hours of weight lifting and fencing (*kendo*). To the public, he was an eccentric poseur whose behavior was outrageous but delightful.

But Yukio Mishima was a tortured soul. Absorbed with violence and death, he was a living example of the contrast between two Japanese forces, the spiritual and the worldly, the esthetic (chrysanthemum) and the martial (sword). Convinced that his people had deserted their national heritage, he deemed it necessary to revitalize the Emperor system "so that the nation will not decay and degenerate." Japan, he said, "must revive martial power, not for aggressive militarism but for the restoration of national pride and self-respect."

To the fanatical novelist-nationalist, idea without activism was nonsense. He organized a private army, the *Tate-no-Kai*, or Shield Society, "to protect Japan from Communism" and "to re-establish the rule of the Emperor." He attracted about a hundred young followers, who wore dashing olive-drab uniforms which he designed and who sang the marching song he composed. He convinced the authorities to allow his men to train with the national Self-Defense Forces (SDF), which he hoped one day would become "a true and honored national military force, when it awakens."

On that fateful day of November 25, 1970, Mishima and four of his trusted lieutenants met in downtown Tokyo, drew up a ringing manifesto, and posed in uniform for their final formal portrait. The five then went to the Lichigaya military headquarters, where Mishima was known, and were admitted to the presence of Lieutenant General Kanetoshi Mashita, commander of the Eastern Defense Forces. Suddenly, the surprised officer was taken hostage, as Mishima demanded permission to speak to the troops.

Hastily, some 1,200 soldiers were assembled in the courtyard. From a balcony Mishima, hoping to inspire an instant rebellion, harangued the men about "the spirit of the *samurai*" and demanded a change in the constitution so that "the nation could rearm." The SDF, he said, was "too spineless and corrupt to preserve the Imperial way." A few listened, but most were indifferent and some shouted back "*Baka!*" (fool). "Let us die together," Mishima screamed; but the soldiers laughed. Mishima then called three times: "*Tenno Heika banzai!*" ("Long live the Emperor!").

Furious, Mishima retired inside to the office. Almost immediately he sank into the required position and in ritual *seppuku* (ceremonial disembowelment) plunged a sword into his abdomen.[8] His chief lieutenant then completed the rite of *kaishaku*, after several ineffectual attempts, by slicing off Mishima's head. Kneeling, the executioner then followed his leader into oblivion by a second act of *seppuku* and *kaishaku*. The remaining three followers remained alive on Mishima's instructions, to act as witnesses for the public.

"An act of madness!" was the first reaction. "He must have been crazy!" said Prime Minister Eisaku Sato. Mishima's elderly father, grieving but proud, issued an apology to the public.

Contrary to expectations, the suicide was not quickly forgotton. The first sentiment of horror gave way and the people, impressed by Mishima's classic statement of sincerity and honor, were plunged into a mood of self-reflection. Perhaps there was, indeed, something wrong with Japanese society and the frustrated novelist was trying to bring it to their attention in time-honored form. The once critical Prime Minister, responding to public opinion, changed his attitude and now mentioned "respect for Mishima's motives." A eulogist at the funeral spoke gravely: "You loved the Japanese language and

Japanese classics. To love the language is to love Japan.'' Another orator, carried away, called Mishima's suicide "the most glorious event in the history of the world since Christ died on the cross.''

The eulogies were exaggerated, but the public was insatiable. The press turned out torrents of comments on "the *samurai* of 1970.'' The sale of ceremonial swords boomed. Mishima's short story and film *Yokuku* (Patriotism), in which he played one of the nationalist officers who committed *hara-kiri* after the unsuccessful army coup of 1936, were revived as classics.

Mishima's gory death revealed the staying power of a Japanese nationalism grounded on romanticism and long military traditions. Far from being eliminated, Japanese nationalism was re-asserting itself. Behind Mishima's appeal, such as it was, was the staleness of the new Japanese prosperity, a problem interestingly similar to that faced by nineteenth-century Britain, as well as to the vanishing of one set of values with nothing that appeared ennobling to replace it. The quintessential manner of Mishima's death appealed, furthermore, to those Japanese who were searching for a renaissance of national identity and for new values to replace the psychological depression and self-doubt following the defeat in World War II.

Mishima stunned his fellow countrymen as few others had in the twentieth century. For many, his ritual act was the deed of a genuine patriot who was seeking to revive the noble spirit of a people who had gone soft and materialistic. His selfless behavior would guide them back to *Yamato Damashii,* the old spirit combining the virtues of patriotism with the aesthetic realm of art and poetry.

Others dismissed Mishima as merely another discredited ultranationalistic hothead, like those who in the 1930s had been responsible for bringing the country close to ruin. Nevertheless, the case of Mishima revealed that in Japan, as elsewhere, nationalism has persisted as a deep-rooted political force. Aggressive nationalism culminated in Japan's defeat in 1945. Since then nationalism in Japan has had an ambivalent character. Along with her booming economy came a right-wing explosion of nationalism illustrated by the patriot Mishima.

Ferment of Change

Indonesia's Achmed Sukarno may have been a poor administrator, but he was an expert on nationalism. A fervent supporter of Asian nationalism because of its liberating quality, he nevertheless recognized that the future might belong to greater organizations than mere nations. He was even willing to admit that the increasing trend toward internationalism, toward supernational or supranational bodies, "is an encouraging sign of man's growing maturity." At the same time, on the ground of his own experience, he insisted that the nation must come first. On a comparative basis, Sukarno's thinking was similar to that of his fellow Asians, who also felt that Asians must establish their own national identities before international organizations could be created. First things first. One could not build without foundations, without bricks and keystones.

Asia, like Africa, is undergoing the turmoil of change. On both continents a new sense of identity is arising within the infrastructure, much like that in Western Europe several centuries earlier. There are many problems of birth—political, economic, and social—all intertwined and all causing herculean difficulties: clashes between political entities, divergent ideological pulls in the cold war between capitalism and communism, drives for economic gain, differences between rich and poor, and special psychological motivations.

The two outstanding facts of Asian nationalism are a polarity of development and a dichotomy of ideas, both of which cause difficulties that have not yet been resolved. The story of nationalism in Asia is a story of struggle for a viable compromise between the old and the new. It was not, as might have been expected, exclusively a reaction in defense of traditional cultures, though that was a major essential. Of equal if not considerably more importance was the adoption of Western technology and culture. The outcome was an increasingly secular and in part anti-traditional modernization. This was especially true in the Communist countries, but the same occidentalizing tendency may be noted in those nationalist states which rejected or were not affected by Communist ideology.

The movement toward nationalism in Asia was motivated universally by this clash between the old and the new. Results were uneven, depending mostly on the political circumstances of each country. But the important characteristic is this blend of respect for European politico-economic power and pride in age-old Asian customs, traditions, law, and religion.

At the present moment, Asian nationalism is in a state of flux, but it is growing. Here, too, the sense of identity, the sentiment of national consciousness, and the mood of exclusiveness form the matrix of nationalism. In Asia, as elsewhere, nationalism has grown out of the deepest needs and desires of men. Asians, too, search for identity, prestige, hope, and security. So universal is the course of nationalism that the developing peoples of Asia, as those in Africa and elsewhere, despite the existence of possible alternatives, have made the choice of organizing themselves as nation-states.

Notes

[1] Quoted in *Time*, April 9, 1965, p. 33.

[2] See José Velose Abuva, "Filipino Nationalism, Public Policy and Political Institutions," *Asia,* 9 (Fall 1967): 68–71.

[3] Quoted in George McTurnan Kahin, *The Asian-African Conference* (Ithaca N.Y.: Cornell University Press, 1956), pp. 73–75.

[4] Sir Rabindranath Tagore, *Nationalism* (New York: Macmillan, 1917), p. 57.

[5] Achmed Sukarno, "Address to the National Press Club" (May 18, 1956), *Department of State Bulletin,* 24, no. 884 (June 4, 1956): 937–39.

[6] Quoted in *The Japan Year Book, 1939–1940* (Tokyo, 1939), p. 633.

[7] *The China Critic* (Shanghai, 1931), 4:924.

[8] "From his childhood Mishima had been fascinated by pictures of *samurai* committing *seppuku,* European knights dying on the battlefield and, above all, St. Sebastian, his powerful body bound to a tree, dying of arrow wounds. . . . His last letter to me, written shortly before his death, stated that he had long wished to die as a *samurai,* rather than a man of letters. Undoubtedly this was true, but Mishima was not a *samurai.* He was a writer. . . . He made of his body a work of art, only to destroy it with a knife-thrust. Beauty and death, the two elements in the 'stream' of his flesh, demanded his suicide." Donald Keene in *The Times Literary Supplement,* August 20, 1971.

14

The Impulse to Messianism (1): American Nationalism

The far-reaching, the boundless future, will be the era of American greatness. In its magnificent domain of space and time, the nation of many nations is destined to manifest to mankind the excellence of divine principles; to establish on earth the noblest temple ever dedicated to the worship of the Most High—the Sacred and the True. Its floor shall be a hemisphere—its roof the firmament of the star-studded heavens, and its congregation a Union of many Republics. . . .

—John Louis O'Sullivan (1839)

The Meaning of Messianism

Messianism is the belief in the coming of an extraordinary individual or group that will mark a new stage of history and transform the human condition from misery and suffering into one of abundance, happiness, and peace. Messianic nationalism is a similar sentiment held by the people of a nation-state in the belief that their way of life is a superior one and should be adopted by others. "We are the inheritors of the future, for which the old, worn-out, declining nations can no longer hope."

The call of messianism is a phenomenon repeated through the course of history. It provided the motivation for the *levée en masse* voted by the French Convention on August 23, 1783, upon recommendation by the Committee of Public Safety. The electrifying decree was to enable France to bring the blessings of her newly found liberty to all Europe:

Let us state a great truth: liberty has become the creditor of all citizens. Some owe it to their labor, others their wealth, some their counsel, others the strength of their arms; all owe it the blood which flows in their veins. Thus all the French, men and women alike, people of all ages, are summoned by the *Patrie* to defend liberty. . . .

Men, women, and children, in requisitioning you the *Patrie* summons you all in the name of liberty and equality, and it designates to each of you according to his means the service he must give to the armies of the Republic.

Early Americans were quite certain that Europe had sunk into decrepitude and senility. An American yokel boasted: "We air a great people, and bound to be troublesome to them kings." Noah Webster's spelling book made it culturally official: "Europe has grown old in folly, corruption, and tyranny." With this condemnation of an aging Europe went a sense of American mission. "We are acting for all mankind," said Thomas Jefferson. American nationalism, similar to Imperial Russian and Soviet nationalisms, was to be suffused with messianic zeal.

The Substructure of American Nationalism

The new American nation was a product of the Enlightenment, with its accent on liberty, equality, and property rights. Constitutionalism and parliamentarianism were woven into the fabric of the new society. Close attention was paid to the liberal political ideas of the Englishman Locke and the Frenchman Rousseau. Sturdy individualists, intoxicated by the clean air of the New World, entered enthusiastically into the rough frontier life. There was a nation to be made, a nation with monarchy abolished, and aristocracy delegated to a lesser role.

America was born just as nationalism appeared on the European scene. Early Americans inherited their language, law, and culture from the Old

World, but they wanted to be different. They would mold the body of "that new man, the American." The process took place, indeed, outside the periphery of European nationalism. In the beginning of the American experiment there was no common territory: the original accent was on sectionalism, not nationalism. There was, indeed, a decided lack of all things common. There was no common religion: people of all faiths flocked to the New World. There were few common historical traditions among such diverse groups as the Germans in Pennsylvania and the English in Massachusetts. The thirteen colonies had no common culture nor any sense of common descent. Yet out of these divergent elements appeared a nation of many nations.

Once it crystallized, American nationalism took on five outstanding qualities: (1) libertarianism, based on the English experience; (2) egalitarianism; (3) an emphasis upon materialism; (4) a multi-ethnic character respecting diversity; and (5) a messianic tone.

From its opening stage American nationalism was identified with the idea of individual liberty. Leaders of the young nation insisted upon an independent existence based on the principle that all men are created equal and endowed with certain inalienable rights such as life, liberty, and the pursuit of happiness. At first greater emphasis was placed on this libertarian formula than on such attributes of nationalism as common territory, language, religion, descent, or culture. The unifying factor originally was a deep belief in the blessings of liberty.

The idea of liberty was inherited from England. It was formulated in the Declaration of Independence to meet a new emergency. The English concept of constitutionalism was appropriated, in slightly altered form, by the founding fathers, who would break away from "the pernicious labyrinth of European politics," create a new and better world, and thereby "vindicate the honor of the human race."

Closely associated with the libertarian quality of American nationalism was a spirit of egalitarianism, a belief in the equality of all citizens. Whereas in Europe a man's social position tended to be fixed, in the New World there would be equality of status as well as social mobility. Any man could travel the road from poverty to riches, and perhaps back again. If there were class distinctions, they were supposed to be indeterminate and temporary. Americans wanted no vestiges of restrictive feudalism and manorialism in their new society, even if they could not escape them altogether.

A third hallmark of the new society was materialism, but the new American was not inclined to admit it. He was careful to transform the idea of life, liberty, and *property* into the slogan "life, liberty, and *the pursuit of happiness*," but later he would even boast of the identification of property with happiness. Recruited primarily from the middle and working classes of

England and the Continent, early Americans wanted a society in which careers were open to talent. Their desire was strengthened by the Protestant ethic: Calvinists, Puritans, Presbyterians, and Quakers alike refused to regard worldly success as sinful but rather as a sign of God's grace.

As the infant nation grew, nationalism became imbued with material achievement. In the second half of the nineteenth century came a spectacular industrialization as the country was transformed from a farming into a great free-market economy. Industry welded bonds of steel. Once institutionalized, American national values were geared to economic and technological change. Calvin Coolidge was to describe the mood perfectly: "The business of America is business."

The fourth major characteristic of American nationalism was its multi-ethnic character. The new nation was forged out of miscellaneous human material. Europeans came in search of religious freedom: Puritans who had seceded from the Church of England settled in Massachusetts; Catholics came to Maryland; Quakers found their promised land in Pennsylvania; French Huguenots appeared in the Carolinas and Virginia; and German Mennonites and Moravians chose Pennsylvania. More peoples came in the nineteenth century: Poles fleeing the revolution of 1830; poverty-stricken Irish who left their homeland during the potato famine commencing in 1846; Germans driven out by the revolution of 1848; Swedes and Norwegians who yearned for more opportunities; and Mexicans, attracted by the lure of California. In the twentieth century came another vast wave from Eastern Europe: Slavs, Jews, and Greeks.

Intermarriage resulted in a hybrid American, patriotic and nationalist. Crèvecoeur, a transplanted Frenchman, saw the Americans as "a promiscuous breed which has produced the race now called American." The vast folk migration had resulted in an ethnic hodgepodge. "You cannot spill a drop of American blood," wrote Herman Melville, "without spilling the blood of the whole world." In 1888 James Bryce spoke about "the amazing solvent power which American institutions, habits, and ideas exercise upon the newcomers of all races." Nature, said Bryce, repeated on the Western continent that process of mixing Celtic blood with German and Norse strains which was begun in Britain a thousand years earlier.

In 1908 Israel Zangwill called Bryce's "solvent power" a "melting pot" and thereby triggered an argument among scholars that has persisted to the present day. Some reject the appellation as incorrect or misleading. However one takes the melting pot argument, it is said, the values continued to be Anglo-Saxon dominated. In twentieth-century testing, it was found that the melting pot did not melt very well at all. The argument is bolstered by reference to other, more important values. For example, there was the relative security of American life, a luxury not shared by Russia. And of

vastly more significance, so the argument goes, was the fact that modernization and industrialization meant economic muscle, which vastly expanded
the power base.

As Europeans continued to come to the New World, a debate began on the
desirability of immigration. The melting pot, it was charged, was "a crime
against nature." Racial hybrids would inevitably produce ethnic horrors.
The old immigrant, it was said, came from "a free energetic stock," such as
the British, German, and Scandinavian, but the "new" immigrant, backward
and unprogressive, came from the inferior Slavic, Latin, and Asian
sources.

At the beginning of the twentieth century, leadership in the school of
Nordic supremacy was assumed by two amateur anthropologists, Madison
Grant and Lothrop Stoddard, lawyers by profession, and Henry Fairfield
Osborn, professional paleontologist. These three, and their disciples, pub-
lished a mass of racial treatises concerned mainly with postulates on the
Nordic theory, a concept which George Bernard Shaw dismissed as "despic-
ably unscientific."

Building on Houston Stewart Chamberlain's *Foundations of the Nineteenth Century* (1899) and Count Joseph Arthur de Gobineau's *Essay on the
Inequality of Human Races* (1853), two of the most provocative books ever
written on the subject of race, Madison Grant published his *The Passing of
the Great Race, or the Racial Basis of European History* (1916), in which he
accepted wholeheartedly the doctrine of the superiority of the Nordic
"race." Failing to observe that if a great race passed, it could not have been
great at all, Grant nevertheless repeated the stock doctrines of European
Nordicists.

Grant's thesis was a combination of absurdities. The "Nordic race" is a
physically superior race with blond hair, blue eyes, tall stature, and a high
instep. ("A high instep also has long been esteemed as an indication of the
patrician type while the flat foot is often the test of lowly origin.")[1] Christ was
Nordic. ("In depicting the crucifixion no artist hesitates to make the two
thieves brunet in contrast to the blond Saviour. This is something more than a
convention, as such quasi-authentic traditions as we have of our Lord
strongly suggest his Nordic, possibly Greek, physical and moral attributes.")
In Grant's view, Negroes do not possess the potentiality of progress or
initiative from within, and even as slaves they enjoyed great privileges:
"From a material point of view slaves are often more fortunate than freemen
when treated with reasonable humanity and when their elemental wants of
food, clothing and shelter are supplied."

Grant reserved his most bitter attacks for the melting pot. New York, he
charged, "is becoming a *cloaca gentium* which will produce many amazing
hybrids and some ethnic horrors that will be beyond the powers of future

anthropologists to unravel." He warned his countrymen to learn the lessons of biology and keep their race free of inferior blood. "If the Melting Pot is allowed to boil without control and we continue to follow our national motto and deliberately blind ourselves to 'all distinctions of race, creed, or color,' the type of native American of Colonial descent will become as extinct as the Athenian of the Age of Pericles and the Viking of the Age of Rollo."

These views were endorsed by Henry Fairfield Osborn ("The Nordic race has given us the true spirit of Americanism") and Lothrop Stoddard ("A mongrelized offspring [is] a walking chaos, so consumed by his jarring heredities that he is quite worthless"). Apparently, such opinions had an effect on official Washington. A governmental investigation made by the Dillingham Commission in 1910 led to 42 volumes of pseudo science and distorted statistics aiming to prove that the "new immigrants" were far less assimilable than the old. The commission seemed to be hypnotized by the phrase "inherent racial tendencies."

Despite this vigorous activity for the restriction of immigration, only a small minority of Americans accepted the opinions of Madison Grant and his cohorts. Most Americans regarded ethnic pluralism in their democracy of nationalities as highly desirable. They believed that an ethnically mingled America could withstand the strains of her New World responsibilities. President Theodore Roosevelt expressed the popular will when he said "We must shun as we would shun the plague all efforts to make us separate in groups of separate nationalities. We must all of us be Americans, and nothing but Americans." The most popular American war poster in World War I was one by Howard Chandler Christy, depicting a young girl appealing to onlookers to buy Liberty Bonds and pointing with pride to a list of names:

AMERICANS ALL! Du BOIS, SMITH, O'BRIEN, KNUTSON,
CEJKA, HAUCKE, PAPPANEIKOPOLOUS, GONZALES, ANDRASSI,
VILLOTTO, LEVY, TUROVICH, KOWALSKI, CHICZANEVICZ

The Tenor of American Messianic Nationalism

Messianism was of special import as a quality of the American way of life. From its earliest days, American nationalism took on a moralistic tone of missionary zeal. Just as messianism offered an escape into the joyous future, so did messianic nationalism present the idea of a superior grouping of mankind ready to lead the way to a better life.

The Puritan stimulus was vital in the flowering of American nationalism. Calvin's theocratic radicalism called for the creation of a new Christian commonwealth with accent on democracy and liberty. English Puritans, too, regarded themselves as predestined to bring the blessings of liberty to other, less fortunate peoples. The idea was carried to the New World in the great emigration of 1628–1640, when some 20,000 English Puritans, disgruntled by persecution and fearful for their future, left home for the promised land. Accompanied by their livestock and imbued with an enthusiastic missionary zeal, they made 1,200 voyages across the Atlantic. Some English towns were half depopulated by the Puritan exodus.

Puritan ideas of freedom, thrift, and messianism became engrained American attitudes. As early as 1765 John Adams said: "I always consider the settlement of America as the opening of a grand scene and design in Providence for the illumination of the ignorant, and the emancipation of the slavish part of mankind all over the earth." Adams' view carried over into decades of American experience.

The Puritan contribution was one of many forces at work to create an American national image. The process was guided by those founding fathers who had "brought forth a nation." This was the first time in history that men had deliberately fashioned a nation: in the past, nations had simply grown as a product of history, religion, royal dynasties, or armies. The founding fathers were careful to provide the new nation with a historic past, tradition, and heritage, all necessary concomitants of nationalism. They combined the ideals of the Enlightenment with the legacies of Puritanism and English common law to mold an explicit American ideology.

Americans saw themselves as the great egalitarian, pluralistic society. As the elect of God, revealing their Puritan ethos, they were proud of their political achievements and their technological record. They had an unshakable faith in American righteousness. They were always on the side of democracy, justice, and liberty. They were experts in the myth-making of nationalism.

There are innumerable clues to the making of American nationalism. In 1774 Patrick Henry exclaimed to the Continental Congress: "The distinctions between Virginians, Pennsylvanians, New Yorkers, and New Englanders are no more. I am not a Virginian but an American." In 1776, several months before the signing of the Declaration of Independence, Peter Thatcher of Massachusetts issued a call to arms: "Upon our exertions depends the important question, whether the rising empire of America shall be an empire of slaves or of freedmen." In 1802, in his second inaugural address, Thomas Jefferson presented the Americans as a chosen people to whom God had shown His favor when He "led our forefathers, as Israel of old, from their native land and planted them in a country flowing with all the necessaries and comforts of life."

Already the missionary quality of American nationalism was coming through. On July 4, 1778, on the second anniversary of the Declaration of

Independence, David Ramsay of South Carolina glorified the destiny of the United States in nationalistic and messianic terms:

We have laid the foundations of a new empire, which promises to enlarge itself into vast dimensions, and to give happiness to a great continent. It is now our turn to figure on the face of the earth, and in the annals of the world. . . . Generations yet unborn will bless us for the blood-bought inheritance, we are about to bequeath to them. Oh happy times! Oh glorious days![2]

American nationalism came of age during the War of 1812, in a needless conflict with Britain. In retaliation for the American destruction of public buildings at York (Toronto), British troops fired the Capitol and White House in Washington. The incident outraged American sensibilities and quickened the sentiment of patriotism. Some successes, especially naval victories, gave Americans a new sense of pride and confidence. The war, said Albert Gallatin, renewed and reinstated the national feeling and character which the Revolution had given. "They are more American; they feel and act more as a nation; and I hope that the permanency of the Union is thereby better secured."

Additional stimulus to the solidification of American nationalism was the fact that men of different states had fought side by side and that troops from the American West, who had less attachment to their states and more to the nation, had won several battles. Westward expansion began, and the West was always national minded.

American messianism was distinctly a part of the movement west. In 1839 John Louis O'Sullivan, a Jacksonian Democrat, denounced foreign governments that were seeking to obstruct the annexation of Texas in order to check "the fulfillment of our manifest destiny to overspread the continent alloted by Providence for the free development of our yearly multiplying millions." He made a classic statement of American messianism:

Yes, we are the nation of progress, of individual freedom, of universal enfranchisement.Equality of rights is the cynosure of our union of states, the grand exemplar of the correlative quality of individuals; and, while truth sheds its effulgence, we cannot retrograde without dissolving the one and subverting the other. We must go onward to the fulfillment of our mission—to the entire development of the principle of our organization—freedom of conscience, freedom of person, freedom of trade and business pursuits, universality of freedom and equality.

This is our high destiny, and in nature's eternal, inevitable decree of cause and effect we must accomplish it. All this will be our future history, to establish on earth the moral dignity and salvation of man—the immutable truth and beneficence of God. For this blessed mission to the nations of the world, which are shut out from the life-giving light of truth, has America been chosen; and her high example shall smite unto death the tyranny of kings, hierarchs, and oligarchs and carry the glad tidings of peace and good will where myriads now endure an existence scarcely more enviable than beasts in the field.

Who, then, can doubt that our country is destined to be *the great nation* of futurity?[3]

That overriding sense of mission went into eclipse temporarily during the Civil War, when leaders and public alike were wholly occupied by the problem of maintaining the union in the face of Southern nationalism. ("Land of the South, imperial land! Mayst thou be blest and free!"—Alexander Beaufort Meek.) American messianism was revived in the 1880s in slightly altered form. The earlier phase of manifest destiny had been structured on a simple faith in American superiority; the new approach was linked with social Darwinism, which presented a "scientific" explanation for America's mission. The "fittest" would dominate and bestow the blessings of the American way on backward peoples. America would lead the way in remolding the world.

Josiah Strong, Congregationalist minister, saw it as the historic mission of the great Anglo-Saxon "race" in its American form to bear the ideas of civil liberty and spiritual Christianity to remote areas. Ralph Waldo Emerson endowed the sentiment with a high moral tone: "The office of America is to liberate, to abolish kingcraft, caste, monopoly, to pull down the gallows, to burn up the bloody statute-book, to take in the immigrants, to open the doors of the sea and the fields of the earth."

By 1900 Admiral Alfred Thayer Mahan was urging Americans to "look outward." Senator Albert Jeremiah Beveridge was making it plain that the Filipinos would prefer the just, humane, and civilizing government of the United States "to the savage, bloody rule from which we have rescued them." And President William McKinley was confessing that when he realized that the Philippines had dropped into our lap, "I am not ashamed to tell you, gentlemen, that I went down on my knees and prayed to Almighty God for light and guidance more than one night."

President McKinley was not the only one confused by America's mission. The Wilsonian task of making the world "safe for democracy" turned out to be a monumental disaster. But there were those who maintained a sense of certainty. In 1932 the publisher William Randolph Hearst made it official: "Today the most envied honor in the world is to be an American citizen!"

American messianic nationalism carried over into the era following the two world wars when the United States became the world's strongest power. The American notion of commitment, to see a heritage protected and expanded, was retained. It was declared official policy in John F. Kennedy's inaugural address on January 20, 1961: "Let every nation know, whether it wishes us well or ill, that we shall pay any price, bear any burden, meet any hardships, support any friend, oppose any foe to assure the survival of the success of liberty." Kennedy reiterated the formula in a speech delivered in November 1961: "To save mankind's future freedom, we must face up to any risk that is necessary. We will always seek peace—but we will never surrender. . . . We are Americans determined to defend the frontiers of freedom."

What may have been patriotic oratory for Kennedy became for President Richard M. Nixon a solemn course of action. When, after ten years in South Vietnam, Nixon sent American troops into Cambodia, he justified the move by this explanation, delivered at a news conference on May 8, 1970: "If . . . we withdraw from Vietnam and allow the enemy to come into Vietnam and massacre the civilians there by the millions, as they would, if we do that, let me say that America is finished insofar as the peacekeeper in the Asian world is concerned."

Some distinguished non-Americans were not impressed by this brand of American messianism. Gunnar Myrdal, who was to win the Nobel Prize for economics (1974), praised the foreign aid program as an expression of the American conscience, but at the same time he labeled it "perverted Puritanism"—doing something good in one's own interest. Arnold J. Toynbee was not only disgusted but alarmed:

To most Europeans, I guess, America now looks like the most dangerous country in the world. Since America is unquestionably the most powerful country, the transformation of America's image within the last 30 years is very frightening for Europeans. It is probably still more frightening for the great majority of the human race who are neither Europeans nor North Americans, but are Latin Americans, Asians and Africans. They, I imagine, feel even more insecure than we feel. They feel that, at any moment, America may intervene in their internal affairs with the same appalling consequences as have followed from American intervention in Southeast Asia. . . .

The roles of America and Russia have been reversed in the world's eyes. Today America has become the world's nightmare.[4]

Notes

[1] All quotations are from the 1918 edition of Madison Grant, *The Passing of the Great Race* (New York: Charles Scribner's Sons, 1918).

[2] Quoted in Max Savelle, "Nationalism and Other Loyalties in the American Revolution," *American Historical Review,* 67 (July 1962): 923.

[3] John Louis O'Sullivan, "The Great Nation of Futurity," *The United States Magazine and Democratic Review,* 6 (November 1839): 6.

[4] In *The New York Times,* May 10, 1970.

15

The Impulse to Messianism (2): Soviet Russian Nationalism

Whither are you speeding, Russia of mine? Whither? Answer me! But no answer comes—only the weird sound of your collar-bells. Rent into a thousand shreds, the air roars past you, as you are overtaking the whole world, and shall one day force all nations, all empires to stand aside, to give way to you!

—Nikolai Gogol (1842)

Comparative Messianisms

Messianic zeal can grip the most diverse social orders. It would seem that the differences between the United States and Russia during the course of their history have been so great that there is scarcely any possibility of a common political motivation. Yet so wide is the appeal of messianic nationalism that it has exerted a tremendous impact in both countries in their earlier and later stages. Americans and Russians alike are convinced of the excellence of their institutions, and they are quite willing to lend or bequeath them to other, less fortunate peoples. The Americans were certain of their role as missionaries of civilization. Similarly, the Slavophiles of Tsarist Russia were positive about their place in history. They believed that they did not have a divine mission in the past, but that now it was their turn and that the future belonged to them.

After 1945 the United States and the Union of Soviet Socialist Republics moved to the fore as the two most powerful nations on earth. Confrontation between the two resulted in a cold war, one of whose manifestations was the same kind of messianic zeal shown in both countries a century earlier. Advocates of the two political systems, ideologically at loggerheads, believed their own way of life to be far superior to the other. The United States represented an advanced stage of finance capitalism, the U.S.S.R. the first great experiment to implement the communism of Marx and Lenin. American statesmen and businessmen went to some pains to reveal the value of their democratic way of life. The masters of the Kremlin similarly sought to extend the blessings of Soviet ideology, both to contiguous countries and to such far-flung areas as Egypt, the Congo, North Korea, and North Vietnam.

The Impact of Slavophilism

There were antecedents for Russian nationalism. The imperialist expansion of the eighteenth century, plus strong hostility toward Poles, says something on that point. Yet it is fair to add that the system of unlimited absolutism showed few national traits before the nineteenth century. The court, army, and bureaucracy were often more German than Russian, and the nobility spoke French and adopted French manners. Added to this upper-class cosmopolitanism was the indifference of the vast, illiterate peasantry. Oppressed by serfdom, military service, and taxation, the peasantry had scarcely any sense of national consciousness. They turned to the Orthodox creed as a substitute for national sentiment. An educated native middle class, the strongest advocate of nationalism, scarcely existed.

Russian national consciousness was enhanced considerably in the atmosphere of hatred for Napoleon. To the great masses of Russia, the French conqueror was surely the anti-Christ, the satanic leader of the Roman Catholic West against Moscow, against the citadel of the true faith. Russians sensed their backwardness when measured against the West, but they felt themselves to be poor, oppressed Christians who one day would inherit the earth. They were "God's own people," unlike those Western barbarians, immoral and corrupted by materialism.

Even more significant in stimulating a sense of Russian national conscious-ness was the rise of the middle class. This development was accompanied by a policy of forced russification of the many national minorities. The peasants continued to live in poverty and misery, but they were given scraps of nationalist myths and bones of manifest destiny.

Slavophilic nationalism provided an inspiration for future action in the new myth-making. Virtually straight racism, Slavophilic nationalism hailed the superiority of the Slavs and everything indigenous to Russia, while condemn-ing anything of foreign origin as inferior and dangerous. The movement was stimulated by a rising sense of national consciousness due to successful wars against Persia (1826–1828) and Turkey (1827–1829), as well as the suppres-sion of the Polish uprising (1830–1831). Slavophilic nationalism attracted strong support among Russian university students, who appropriated the core of Hegelianism, geared it to their own structured society, and set it off on a different historical course. Idealistic students were certain that it was now the turn of the Slavs to assume the historical mission that had been denied them in the past.

Slavophilic nationalism took on a crusading tone in the nineteenth century. Holy Russia, "the first state in the world," would lead all the peoples on earth to the paradise of true Christianity. The lowly Russian serf, the preferred servant of God, would spread the gospel of social justice to all the inhabitants of this planet.

The overture was played even more by poets than by peasants. Fyodor Tyuchev put it in this image:

> The King of Heaven under the guise of a serf
> Has traversed and blessed thee,
> Thee my native land,
> Bowed down by the weight of the Cross.

"The Russian spirit," said Dostoevsky, "is that beauty which resides in the people's truth in our soil." In *The Possessed* the great novelist placed these words in the mouth of the revolutionary Shatov:

If a great people did not believe that the truth is only to be found in itself alone, if it did not believe that it alone is destined to save all the rest by its truth, it would at once sink into ethnographic material, and not remain a great people. But there is only one truth, and therefore only a single one out of the nations can have the true God. That is the Russian people.

The Slavophiles were intoxicated with a sense of mission. The Russians and the majority of the Slavic peoples, they said, became with the Greeks the chief guardians of the living tradition of religious truth. Orthodoxy was the destiny of Byzantium: the Russians on their part continued that high calling to be the chosen people. Prince Odoevsky professed himself saddened by the strange spectacle of Western Europe, where "opinion struggled against opinion, power against power, throne against throne." Western Europe, he said, was on the high road of ruin. The Russians, on the contrary, "are young and fresh and have taken no part in the crimes of Europe. We have a great mission to fulfill. Our name is already inscribed on the tablets of victory: the victories of science, art, and faith await us on the tottering ruins of Europe."

Russian nationalists claimed credit as the ones who had freed Europe and the world from Napoleonic despotism. They insisted that the intellectually bankrupt West had overemphasized the role of reason in human affairs and to its peril had ignored the power of emotion and feeling. Western empiricism meant only decadence; it had erred in wiping away the great traditions of the past and stupidly it had substituted experience for faith. From Moscow, the West appeared to be a barren wasteland. Russia, faithful to the national idea and to her mission, would reveal to the entire world the one humanity which she alone could bring. She would no longer be an empire—"she will be a world."

Nikolai Danilevsky, leading spokesman for Slavophile nationalists, maintained that the Slavs were a special species who formed one family, led by "Big Brother" Russia. They formed a determining element in the story of civilization. The stream of world history, he said, began with two sources on the banks of the old Nile. One, the heavenly and the godly, went over Jerusalem and reached Kiev and Moscow "in serene purity." The other, earthly and human, and split into two main streams—culture and politics—flowed over Athens, Alexandria, and Rome into Western Europe, "at times drying up, then again renewing itself with always richer waters." On Russian soil, he concluded, there had arisen a new spring, a socio-economic stream which satisfied the masses of people in exactly the right way. "On the wide surface of Slavicdom all these streams will join together to form a mighty sea."

The Russian Danilevsky, with his Slavic hero, and the American Josiah Strong, with his Anglo-Saxon giant, would have understood one another had they met for a glass or a cup of tea. Both were certain of the glorious mission of their homelands.

Marxist Revival of the Russian Mission

When nineteenth-century Slavophile nationalists spoke of Russia's mission they scarcely thought of the possibility of a fusion with Marxism. Yet Russian nationalist messianism was to be revived under the auspices of communism. The "God-ordained" nationalist mission of the Slavophiles was succeeded by the new nationalism of the Bolshevik state, appealing to "the necessities of history."

Marx and Engels had no doubts about the absolute accuracy of their analysis: it is the emergence of classes, economically determined, that accounts for change in human history. In 1848 they denounced nationalism as a capitalist bourgeois invention: nationalism, like religion, is a temporary phenomenon generated by the bourgeoisie as a spiritual weapon against the proletariat. It penetrates to the masses in a form of "false consciousness," disguising their true condition from them. At the end of the class war, nationalism will evaporate altogether. "In the national struggles of the proletarians of different countries [the Communists] point out and bring to the fore the common interests of the entire proletariat independently of all nationality."

To replace nationalism, Marx and Engels proposed in its place the internationalization of a world society. Their "scientific" pattern of history was opposed to the romantic nationalism of contemporary Slavophiles. They never dreamt that the society they envisioned would succumb to the same kind of messianic nationalism they detested.

Lenin similarly excoriated "bellicose bourgeois nationalism, which dopes, fools, and disunites the workers in order that the bourgeoisie may lead them by the halter. Whoever wants to serve the proletariat must unite the workers of all nations and unswervingly fight bourgeois nationalism, 'home' and foreign." The aim of socialism, Lenin said, "is the elimination of the fragmentation of humanity in petty states and the individualism of nations—not only the coming closer of nations to each other, but their merger or fusion."

The creed that nationalism, the reactionary bourgeois ideology, was doomed to extinction became dogma among Marxists of all shades. Lenin's shock and dismay may be imagined when in August 1914 virtually all the Socialist parties of the belligerent countries came to the side of the nationalist cause. His spirit revived at the time of the October Revolution, which he regarded as anti-nationalist. Indeed, the opening days of the Bolshevik regime witnessed a genuinely anti-nationalist sentiment.

The mood to denigrate nationalism did not last. The Russian Revolution and its aftermath contained an irrepressible nationalist component. The Bolsheviks soon proclaimed the Russian people as the true guardians of Marxism. Stalin sensed and took advantage of the temper. In the ensuing struggle for power, Stalin (supporter of socialism in one country) won against Trotsky (champion of permanent world revolution). Stalin would "serve the proletariat," but his first concern was for the proletariat of his homeland. As dictator, he destroyed all "nationalist deviations" inside Soviet Russia. Between 1936 and 1938 he purged the nationalities in a campaign of mass terror. He would have no "nationalist deviators," no "bourgeois nationalists," no "counterrevolutionary-Trotskyite-diversionist-espionage" individuals or parties in his state.

With cold-blooded efficiency, Stalin turned his country into the path of nationalism, a process he completed during World War II. To him, the issue was starkly simple: Soviet Russia was threatened with annihilation by capitalist power, and the only way to self-preservation was to unite national life in a mighty weapon. There was no time to depend on the good will of the international proletariat. The poet Nikolai Tikhanov presented the core of the argument: "National pride, hitherto buried in the hearts of the Soviet people, burst forth in a bright flame before the threat of enslavement and in the face of deadly danger." As elsewhere, nationalism proved to be an all-powerful sentiment.

By the end of World War II Stalin had implemented the most daring dream of nineteenth-century Slavophiles: he had united all the Slavs under Russian control and had extended the borders of the motherland to the Oder River and the Adriatic Sea. With that accomplished, the dictator in the Kremlin could now spread the Marxian gospel to all nations.

Stalin's appeal was to Bolshevik orthodoxy. His argument was precise: national boundaries are for the bourgeoisie nothing but market commodities. Real national unity could be achieved by the proletariat only through revolutionary struggle and by the overthrow of the bourgeoisie. The middle-class nationalist illusions of peaceful collaboration and the equality of nations under capitalism must be dispelled. Had not the Second Congress of the Communist International declared in 1920 that the Bolsheviks had to "carry out a policy of realizing the closest union between all national and colonial liberation movements and Soviet Russia"?

Stalin could now safely quote his own lectures of 1924 on nationalism outside Europe. At that time he had expressed his concern for "the scores and hundreds of millions of Asiatic and African peoples who are suffering national oppression in its most savage and cruel form." He had then described the national problem as transformed from a particular and internal state problem into a general and international one, ''into a world problem of emancipating the oppressed people in the dependent countries and colonies from the yoke of imperialism.'' Stalin was careful to quote Lenin again and again. He came to this conclusion:

> Leninism has proved, and the imperialist war and the revolution in Russia have confirmed, that the national problem can be solved only in connection with and on the basis of the proletarian revolution, and that the road to victory of the revolution in the West lies through the revolutionary alliance with the liberation movement: of the colonies and dependent countries against imperialism. The national problem is a part of the general problem of the proletarian revolution, a part of the problem of the dictatorship of the proletariat.[1]

Stalin emerged the victor in the clash between pan-Slavism and pan-Germanism. After 1945 he continued his purge of dissident nationalities inside the Soviet Union and at the same time gave free rein to Soviet messianism. He was able to dominate Poland, Rumania, Hungary, East Germany, Bulgaria, and Czechoslovakia in a new community of nations under Russian control. While denouncing Western bourgeois imperialism, he created an imperialism of his own. As the old powers liquidated their colonial holdings, he sent Russians into the vacuum. The Soviet Union would be the mainstay of the revolutionary movement all over the earth, and Moscow would be the fountainhead of a truly international ideology. Such was the import of a revived messianism under Soviet auspices.

Cracks in the Structure: Ukrainian and Georgian Mini-nationalisms

Russian messianism is beset by a formidable obstacle which presents a serious problem for the Kremlin. This is the persistent nationality problem. In Soviet Russia, as in Western European, there are energetic mini-nationalisms which call for independence and a national sovereignty of their own. By far the most challenging threat on the domestic scene is the nationalist movement in the Ukraine, Russia's life-giving black soil belt and the chief wheat-producing area. Moscow has no intention of relinquishing control of this vital *Herzland*. Hence the harsh attitude toward non-conformity, the purges of Ukrainian intelligentsia, and the continuing efforts to stamp out any vestiges of separatism.

The Ukraine, which lies in the southwest of European Russia, is about the size of France and has a population of roughly 43 million. The Ukrainians, second only among the Slavs to the Great Russians (Russians 55 percent, Ukrainians 18 percent), have developed their own sense of national consciousness. A large segment of Ukrainians, bitterly hostile to Moscow, thinks in terms of independence.

The history of the Ukraine is a complex story of an unending search for autonomy. After the dissolution of Kievan Russia, especially after the Tatar (Golden Horde) conquest in the thirteenth century, the center of gravity of Russian history shifted westward. By the middle of the fifteenth century, what is today the Ukraine came under Lithuanian and Polish control. The territory became Polish in 1569. A struggle began between the Russian Orthodox people of the Ukraine and the Catholics in the area. In the seventeenth century, militant Cossacks of the central Ukraine rose in rebellion and won independence from Poland. Russians from the north gradually penetrated into the territory and by the eighteenth century had captured the Black Sea shores from the Ottoman Turks. In the early nineteenth century, Ukrainians were as much dissatisfied with Moscovite as with Polish domination.

The leading apostle of emerging Ukrainian nationalist energy was the poet Taras Shevchenko (1814–1861). Because of his affiliation with the subversive Society of St. Cyril and St. Methodius, a secret pan-Slavic organization, he was banished in 1847 for ten years by the authorities. His most famous work, *Kobzer,* was a collection of romantic poems designed to stimulate Ukrainian nationalism.

In 1859 Alexander Herzen pleaded from his exile in London with both his fellow Russians and Polish refugees to recognize the right of the Ukrainians to independence. If the Ukraine, he said, recalls on the one hand Muscovite oppression, serfdom, absence of rights, and "the corruption of the knout," on the other hand she should not forget how she fared under the Poles. "What, then, if she wants to be neither Polish nor Russian? In my opinion this question is easily settled. The Ukraine should be recognized as a free and independent country."

Herzen's conception of "easy settlement" made no impression on Moscow. The policy of russification was intensified against both Poles and Ukrainians. Publication in the Ukrainian language was forbidden, and the ban was not lifted until after the Revolution of 1905.

The Provisional Government which came to power after the February 1917 Revolution granted Ukrainian autonomy and recognized the authority of the Ukrainian *Rada* (Council) over the central Ukraine. In December 1917, after the Bolshevik Revolution, the *Rada* issued a series of official acts and proclamations known as "universals." The independence of the Ukraine was proclaimed on January 22, 1918.

The Bolsheviks, however, had no intention of giving in to Ukrainian separatism. At first, in his struggle against the "Westernizers" in the Marxian camp, Lenin spoke in terms of encouraging the nationalities. The

Bolsheviks, he said, would respect the right of self-determination. But as soon as the Revolution was won, Lenin was faced with annoying claims of independence by the nationalities. He quickly dropped the slogan of national self-determination and made ready to smash any moves for separate identity.

Stalin was even more determined to complete the russification of the Ukraine. His great purge of the nationalities (1936–1938) exceeded in brutality the excesses of imperial Russia. He denounced the Ukrainians as "bourgeois-nationalist-deviationists." He sent Nikita Khrushchev to the Ukraine for the special task of purging its nationalist leadership. The Tsarist knout was succeeded by the Stalinist bullet.

When on June 22, 1941, Hitler's armies invaded the Soviet Union, Stalin urged the defense of Mother Russia in what he called "the Great Patriotic War." In the Ukraine, the invading Germans were at first hailed as liberators. Here was a perfect opportunity for the German *Füehrer* to take advantage of Ukrainian separatism, but instead, in a key blunder, he set up an iron-clad rule in the Ukraine. To him, the Ukrainians were merely another version of Slavic beasts. For the bewildered Ukrainians it became a simple choice between two dictators. Sensing that Hitler intended to enslave them, they returned reluctantly to their Russian union.

Ukrainian separatism was by no means stifled when the Ukraine was returned to Mother Russia. For several years after the close of World War II the Ukrainian Insurgent Army (UPA) waged a large-scale guerrilla struggle against Moscow in the Carpathian mountains. Since then the movement for Ukrainian independence has continued to gather strength underground. Ukrainian nationalists call for a "national renaissance because national feeling lives in the soul of every human being." The sentiment is supported by Ukrainians living in the United States, who speak of "deprived nationhood" and the "national Ukrainian organism."

Moscow reacted violently against the "ugly strain of nationalism," which the Communists had elsewhere in the world encouraged for their own ends. Ukrainian writers and activists were imprisoned, exiled, or executed. In 1972 Pyotr Y. Shelest was dismissed as Ukrainian party chief for having been too permissive about growing nationalism in the republic. His successor, Vladimir V. Shcherbitsky, began a severe criticism. In May 1974 he excoriated the Ukrainian press and radio, citing their "low ideological level, and denounced "the priority of local interests" as well as "national narrow-mindedness and conceit."

In late 1974 the attention of the world's press was drawn to the case of Valentyn Moroz, a young Ukrainian nationalist and historian in his fourth year of a fourteen-year term. This was his second prison sentence since 1965 when, at the age of 29, he was arrested on charges of anti-Soviet propaganda.

Accused of criticizing the Soviet state, he was confined to Vladimir prison near Moscow. Through a former Soviet political prisoner who had emigrated to Israel, Moroz sent this message to the outside world: "Tell them only this—I am kept with the insane. They are creating a constant hell for me. They are trying to drive me to the insanity of those with whom they locked me up. I cannot breathe."

The Ukrainian form was only one of the mini-nationalisms plaguing the rulers of the Kremlin. Soviet authorities found it quite as difficult to contain nationalist sentiment elsewhere, including the Baltic republics of Latvia, Estonia, and Lithuania, and especially in Georgia, one of the transcaucasian republics. Here, too, there was a trend by which nationalism tended to break out of the mild, approved mold of "cultural differences that are ethnic in form and socialist in content." In May 1972 there was published in Georgia a decidedly unorthodox historical study glorifying the independent and anti-Bolshevik state of Georgia before it was absorbed into the Soviet Union. The title was *Historiography of the Bourgeois-Democratic Movement and of the Victory of the Socialist Revolution in Georgia, 1877–1921*. The book was written by Ushangi I. Sidamonidze and sponsored by the Georgia Institute of History, Archaeology, and Ethnography. The author made little use of Bolshevik sources and relied primarily on the writings of Mensheviks, officially branded as enemies of the state.

In Moscow the Communist Party was quick to condemn the author, the house editor who had let the manuscript go through publication, and the academicians and petty officials who had endorsed the work. Sidamonidze was accused of representing Menshevik views "objectivistically"; that is, he had given them without subjecting them to the strongly critical treatment expected of all good Communist historians. He was punished by withdrawal of his doctoral degree. At the same time, he was required to recant his "political errors," after which he was allowed to retain party membership. Such is the fate of the mini-nationalist historian in the Soviet Union.

The Kremlin wants no invitations for dismemberment—from the Ukraine, from Georgia, or from its Jewish citizens. The self-described practitioners of internationalism desire no challenge to their own nationalism. It is an ironic commentary on human affairs that all the conditions that have made old-fashioned nationalism the most powerful of modern political forces, operate in high gear below the Soviet surface. Great Russian nationalism is accepted as highly desirable, but "minority nationalism" is condemned as abominable treason. Denunciation does not seem to have any effect on the persistence of the mini-nationalisms inside the Soviet Union. The aspirations of the non-Russian peoples have swelled in rough proportion to those of Third World nations. Some observers believe that it is not inconceivable that during the next several decades the nationality problem in the Soviet Union might become politically more important in the Soviet Union than the racial issue has become in the United States.

Away from Moscow Polycentrism

Soviet Russia is plagued currently not only by the obstreperous mini-nationalisms within her borders, but also by persistent nationalism in her string of subservient buffer states. Her expansion since World War II was due in large part to what she regarded as a critical security blanket problem. The men of the Kremlin deemed it a matter of life and death to protect their Great Experiment in a hostile world. For them the reluctance of the satellite states to accept Moscow's domination and any expression of total independence presented a danger of the first magnitude. This kind of thinking was at the root of Stalin's attitude toward the nationalities and the satellites. He wanted it both ways: at home he preached the desirability of Great Russian nationalism while at the same time suppressing any moves for independence among the nationalities; abroad, in contiguous territory, he demanded a safe form of internationalism directed by Moscow. The resulting conflicts were irrepressible.

The trend against Russian control in neighboring countries began as early as 1948 in Yugoslavia. It was no easy task to fit the independent mountaineers into the Russian mold. Josip Broz Tito, leader of the Yugoslav partisans in World War II, preferred to duplicate Communist institutions in his own way. A furious Stalin sent Tito a warning: "We think Trotsky's career is sufficiently instructive." It was clearly a death threat, but Tito was unimpressed. Supported by the majority of his countrymen, he took his country along a modified Communist road, permitting some elements of private enterprise, foreign investment, and privately owned agriculture. He added a tough foreign policy: Yugoslavia would be neutralist.

In facing down Stalin and proclaiming his own version of communism, Tito was the first nationalist rebel to challenge Russian messianism. In this unexpected confrontation, Stalin thought it best not to challenge Yugoslav independence.

The defection of Tito was crucial for the loosening Communist empire in that it stimulated disaffection elsewhere. Nationalism surfaced among the satellites after the death of Stalin. In June 1953, industrial workers rioted in Czechoslovakia and others demonstrated in East Berlin. The Russians quickly regained control of East Berlin by sending in armored tanks. They invoked the Warsaw Pact to legalize the stationing of troops in the satellites.

Destalinization in Poland and Hungary was accompanied by rebellion. The workers of Poznán, angered by harsh factory conditions, rioted on June

28–29, 1956, whereupon Russian troops killed a hundred of them and imprisoned a thousand others. Moscow attributed the incident to "imperialistic agents," but at the same time made sure to raise the living standards of Polish workers. A new Politburo was set up under Wladyslaw Gomulka.

The Hungarian uprising was even more serious. Disturbed by the ousting of Premier Imre Nagy in April 1955, Hungarian intellectuals began to call for their own brand of communism. Matyas Rakosi, with Moscow's blessing, attempted to revive the unpopular features of Stalinism, including collective farming, purges, and terrorism. Demonstrations led to revolt: the huge statue of Stalin in the Budapest city park was toppled by enraged rioters. When security police fired on the people, they stimulated the formation of revolutionary councils throughout the country.

The Russian response was a familiar ploy: they withdrew their troops as if defeated. But within a few days there were 200,000 men and 2,500 tanks and armored cars surrounding Budapest. The Hungarian bid for a free government was crushed. Janos Kadar, installed as the Soviet-sponsored Premier of Hungary, tried a policy of "conciliation with the people."

Rumania, too, became increasingly suspicious of Russian messianism. Under Premier Nicolae Ceausecu she escaped total domination: she walked out on Communist conclaves, recognized the Bonn republic, built trade links with the West, and declared her neutrality in the Moscow-Peking split. The bitter anti-Russian jokes heard in the cafes of Bucharest would have been impossible during the Stalin era.

World public opinion was fascinated by Czechoslovakia's brief but exhilarating attempt to reconcile communism with freedom. In January 1968 the hard-line Stalinist party leader Antonin Novotny was ousted. Alexander Dubcek, the new party boss, holding widespread public support, attempted to reconcile liberty, prosperity, and Communist ideology in one coherent slogan. He demanded that Soviet troops, on "maneuvers" in the country, be removed. Demonstrators became more bold, paying special attention to the final aria of Smetana's opera *Libuse:*

> My beloved Czech nation will not die
> It will gloriously overcome the terrors of hell—
> It will overcome.

At first Moscow, fearful of stirring nationalism in the satellites, retreated in its usual Pavlovian reaction. Then, in August 1968, several hundred thousand Russian troops, supported by tanks, invaded Czechoslovakia to throttle the "counterrevolution." "One must not wait," cautioned *Pravda,* "for the shooting of Communists and the appearance of gallows before going to the aid of the adherents of socialism.''

Communists throughout the world were bewildered by the invasion of Czechoslovakia. In unprecedented fashion, a large majority of the world's eighty-eight Communist parties refused to approve the Kremlin's action. It was finally made clear that the Kremlin regarded Czechoslovakia's experiment in liberalization as fatal to the Russian system created after World War II.

In May 1970 Leonid Brezhnev and Aleksei Kosygin flew to Prague, to be thanked by Gustav Husak, Czechoslovak Communist Party leader, for crushing ''the reactionary forces that wanted to take Czechoslovakia out of the socialist camp.'' Brezhnev praised the new twenty-year ''friendship and mutual assistance pact'' as ''appreciated not only by the people of our countries but also by the whole socialist community.'' The Brezhnev Doctrine was defined: the Soviet Union has the right to interfere in the internal affairs of other Communist countries. A key article stated: ''The support, consolidation, and protection of socialist gains, achieved at the price of the heroic efforts and selfless labor of each people, are a common international duty of socialist countries.'' Moreover, an attack against one of the parties would be considered ''as an attack against itself,'' necessitating ''immediate armed assistance.'' This implied that the Czechs would be called upon in the event of a war between Soviet Russia and Red China.

This was in effect a desperate attempt to shore up the threatened structure. Nationalism was playing havoc with Russian messianism. Even tiny Albania dared to oppose the giant. While Stalin lived, Albania remained a faithful satellite; but under Premier Enver Hoxha she began to strengthen her ties with Communist China and took Peking's side in the split between Moscow and Peking. At the world conference of eighty-one Communist parties held in Moscow in November 1960, Hoxha boldly criticized Khrushchev as ''a traitor to the Communist idea, a weakling, and a revisionist,'' and was excoriated by Khrushchev in return. The Soviet Union broke relations with Albania in December 1961.

Nikolai Bukharin had predicted that centripetal tendencies would one day unite world communism under the Kremlin banner. But the Marxist dream of total, supranational communism was not to be realized. The monolithic world has suffered progressive fragmentation. There was more nationalism than socialism in the new Russian empire. By the late 1960s there was no longer a Comintern, but there were many Communist states. It was obvious that nothing short of a military adventure could bring back the Communist hegemony imposed by Stalin.

The crowning blow to Russian messianism was the confrontation with Communist China. Mao and his comrades denounced Russian leaders as Red

Fascists, as "filthy revisionists," as traitors to the ideals of Marx and Lenin. The U.S.S.R., they said, is the "graveyard of Communism." It is "a colossus with feet of clay," and—the ultimate in name-calling—"a paper tiger." All this, responded Moscow, is "galvanic Trotskyism," "super-revolutionarism," "betrayal of the class interests of working people," and "militaristic psychosis." "By acting thus," complained *Pravda,* "Peking shows the imperialists that it does not intend to take concerted actions with the U.S.S.R. and other socialist countries against imperialist aggression. This stand doubtless encourages imperialist quarters to carry out their antipopular designs and plans."[2]

It is questionable whether Russian messianism or "social internationalism" or "the coming global socialist community" can survive these blasts of hatred from both Peking and Moscow.

Confrontation of Messianisms: The Cold War

Two nineteenth-century French intellectuals saw it coming. Alexis de Tocqueville, historian of American democracy, pointed to the United States and Russia as the great powers of the future. "Each of these," he said, "seems to be marked out by the will of heaven to sway the destinies of half the globe." Charles Augustin Saint-Beuve, literary critic, prophesied that "Russia, still barbarian," and "America, an intoxicated immature democracy, that knows no obstacles," are destined to divide the world: "One day they will collide, and then we shall see struggles the like of which no one has dreamed of."

It was accurate prophecy. These two aspiring giants among the nations, with their huge territories, rich natural resources, and energetic peoples, indeed became major contestants for world leadership, prestige, and power. Each believed in its own way of life, each was quite willing to bequeath it to the world. They clashed in the cold war, the East-West conflict pursued through power politics, economic pressures, and propaganda—but with no declaration of war.

On one side was a century of Russian messianism, both Tsarist and Communist. In the Russia of 1842, Nikolai Gogol proclaimed his country's mission: "Russia of mine, you are overtaking the whole world." He had no idea that Russia was speeding in a new direction toward communism, nor was he thinking of a fusion of Slavophilism with any other ism. Ten years later, Karl Marx was presenting the messianic message of revolution. The father of Marxism clothed his appeal in moral raiment: "Surprise your antagonists while their forces are scattering, prepare new successes, however small, but daily; keep up the moral ascendancy which the first successful rising has given to you, rally those vacillating elements to your side."

Marx's exhortation "You have a world to win!" were glorious words for Lenin and Stalin, molders of the Soviet state. They saw communism as the only salvation for suffering mankind. The new Russia must never abandon her basic goals: to remake man and to conquer the world. This was the historic destiny of the Russian people. By the laws of history and by their own actions, the workers everywhere would liberate not only themselves but all mankind—under direction from Moscow. Marxism was torn by heresies, sectarianism, and revisions, but Lenin and Stalin made certain that the only orthodoxy, the true gospel of communism, would always be grounded on the home soil of Mother Russia.

Soviet rhetoric was suffused with this air of certainty. "The war has shown," declared Stalin in 1946, "that the Soviet multinational state system has successfully stood the test, has grown stronger during the war, and has proved to be a completely vital state system. . . . The point now is that the Soviet state system has proved an example of a multinational state system where the national problem and the problem of collaboration among nations are solved better than in any other multinational state." In that same year Soviet Foreign Minister V. M. Molotov declared that "no great issues can be solved without the Soviet Union or without listening to the voice of our Fatherland."

Kremlin leaders made it their business to listen to "the voice of our Fatherland." By the very nature of their ideology they believed that victory is predetermined and inevitable. The promise was there: nothing less than global triumph. Everyone knew about the combatants: on the one side the Communist heroes ("anti-imperialist, liberating, democratic") and on the other the allied devils ("imperialistic, anti-democratic"). Appropriating the term "democracy" provided no semantic difficulties. The cardinal purpose of the capitalist camp, said Andrei Zhdanov in 1947, is "to strengthen imperialism, to hatch a new imperialist war, to combat Socialism and democracy, and to support reactionary and anti-democratic pro-Fascist regimes and movements everywhere." Zhdanov added that the anti-Fascist forces of the second camp are based on the U.S.S.R. and the "new democracies," a final boost for the Russian mission.

It was this Russian messianism that came into head-on conflict with the American sense of mission. Both possessed much of the same drive. American messianism progressed in several stages from the Puritan ethic to the "Manifest Destiny" of the 1840s, to the imperialism of the 1890s, to Wilson's idealism during and after World War I, to the dream of an American peace after World War II. It was not quite as clearly defined as the Marxist-Leninist mission, but it operated on the principle that its way was as rational as any in history.

The cold war between the United States and her allies and the Soviet Union and her allies began almost immediately after the close of World War II. It was a struggle not only for territorial control but also for the minds of men. Each side would be pleased to see its own ideology and its own special way of life extended to other peoples. It was in essence a clash between opposing messianisms.

Contributing to the outbreak of the cold war was Stalin's determination to bring into the Soviet orbit those neighboring countries which could provide Russia with a security belt. President Roosevelt had hoped that the United States and Russia would cooperate peacefully after the war, but it soon became apparent that such association could exist only as long as Stalin had his way in Eastern Europe. He would isolate Germany, support "friendly governments" in Poland, Hungary, Czechoslovakia, and Rumania, and encourage Communists in Yugoslavia, Bulgaria, and Albania.

After Harry S. Truman became President of the United States in April 1945, he slowly abandoned the policy of cooperation with the Soviet Union. He saw Stalin's hand behind a Communist uprising in Greece, although evidence now available reveals that Stalin, far from fomenting the movement, did his best to discourage it.

American policy took two forms: containment and liberation. The containment strategy of the Truman administration, expressed in the Truman Doctrine, the Marshall Plan, and NATO, was the opening American plan in the cold war. Its aim was to roll back the Iron Curtain.

The American approach was altered by John Foster Dulles, who became Secretary of State in January 1953. With his sense of the importance of moral force in international affairs and his confidence in the ultimate triumph of principles, Dulles called on American moral resources as an antidote to Soviet imperialism. Americans must go beyond containment: they must work for the "liberation" of those nations forcefully kept behind the Iron Curtain. Containment, said Dulles, was immoral, negative, and futile because "it abandons countless human beings to a despotism and godless terrorism which in turn enables the rulers to forge the captives into a weapon for our destruction." Even if the impulse for liberation from the Soviet grasp must come from within the states concerned, the United States, he said, "must sustain hope from without."

In sum, the cold war was, in effect, the outcome of two clashing messianic nationalisms. The issue is still not resolved despite signs of a cold truce and despite the "détente" promoted by American Secretary of State Henry Kissinger and Soviet Communist Party General Secretary Leonid Brezhnev in 1974–1975. One of the primary goals for Moscow was a firm agreement to put further limits on strategic nuclear weapons, particularly the multiple warheads knows as MIRV's. There were also attempts to find agreement on such lesser arms issues as a ban on underground nuclear tests of more than a certain magnitude, and a reduction from two to one in the number of anti-ballistic-missile sites allowed each nation under the 1972 agreement in the strategic arms limitation talks. A ten-year trade agreement proposed cooperation on economic, industrial, and technical matters, with free exchange of economic data and a hope for a long-term increased commerce between the two nations.

Translated into political terms, détente connoted a relaxation of tension. Skeptics refused to believe that there was any possibility of success. They do not see the United States sacrificing its nuclear superiority to maintain the Soviet connection, nor do they show any trust in Communist promises. It is fine to note the Moscow Circus playing at Madison Square Garden to great acclaim and to see American jazz artists receiving tumultous welcomes in Moscow, but underneath, say the skeptics, the two suspicious governments retain an unhealthy disrespect for one another. Each is convinced that its own way of life deserves primacy on this troubled planet. And each is motivated by its own overwhelming desire for security and by the resulting perfervid nationalism.

Notes

[1] From Joseph Stalin, *Foundations of Leninism,* reprinted in *Problems of Leninism* (Moscow, 1945), pp. 59–67.

[2] Quoted in *The New York Times,* May 19, 1970.

16

Macro-Nationalism: The "Pan" Movements

Pan-Africanism is the highest political expression of black power. It means one country, one government, one leader, one army, and that this government will protest for Africans all over the world whenever they face racial discrimination and economic exploitation.

—Stokeley Carmichael

A Broader Unity beyond Nationalism

The term "pan," from the neuter of the Greek *pas*, denotes "all." When used in combined form, it signifies the entirety of a diversified group, to imply a common bond of union between constituents (pan-American). Derivative nouns are formed together with the mischievous three-letter suffix "ism" (pan-Arabism).

There is a great deal of phoniness and expediency about the pan movements, but they nevertheless deserve our attention. Historically, they are essentially political and cultural in scope. They aim to go beyond nationalism and promote the solidarity of groups or peoples or nations bound to each other by geographical proximity, ethnic similarity, common or related languages, common history and tradition, or a combination of any of these. In the wider sense, the ancient Roman Empire, as well as the modern British Empire, were actually pan movements based on dominance by one special people.

In the more narrow and popular meaning, pan movements may be divided into pan-religious, pan-continental, and pan-national. In consonance with everything concerned with nationalism, all the pan movements are ill defined, vague, and imperfect, although they tend to resemble one another structurally. All are dedicated to one consuming goal: to overcome the strength of nationalistic particularism and at the same time combine similar national states into a greater order, consolidated by the consciousness of common interests.

Pan-religious movements such as pan-Christianity and pan-Islamism, comparatively speaking, seek to obliterate the borders of existing national states that conform to the same religious pattern. Pan-continentalism represents a similar emotional drive to a larger unity, but its unifying principle is geographical, not religious (pan-Africanism, pan-Asianism). In both cases there is a tendency to submerge lesser groups into larger combinations.

Pan-national movements, beginning in the nineteenth century, ran parallel to the growing national movements. The pan-national idea was grounded on the assumption that all members of one nationality—no matter where they live—should be included in one larger common group, the fatherland or the motherland.

One fact stands out boldly in any interpretation of the pan movements: similar to the mini-nationalisms in the structure of many contemporary national states, the macro-national pan movements have been uniformly unsuccessful. Not one can boast the achievement of settling the chaos of national particularism. Nowhere has there been any effective supernational or supranational state. There has been no drift backward to the old pre-nationalistic universalism, nor has there been any formation of a viable world federation of large pan-national groupings. The current national state—particularized and balkanized—remains triumphant, with all its anarchic tendencies.

From Slavophilism to Pan-Slavism

The oldest and most important of the macro-national movements was pan-Slavism, which called for the expansion of imperial Russian power by incorporating all other Slavic-speaking people, whether or not they agreed, in a Greater Russia. Pan-Slavism was grounded on Russia's "historic mission" to liberate all the Slavs in southeastern Europe from both the Habsburg and Ottoman empires and to maintain union under Russian control.

Historically, pan-Slavism was an outgrowth of the older Slavophilism, comparatively a more definite religious movement holding that the Russians were chosen by God to lead mankind to salvation. As the "truly Christian people," as the guardians of Orthodoxy, the Russians were supposed to be called to spread the Gospel to all countries, but particularly to the unique and superior brother Slavs.

The idea of Slavophilism was enunciated dramatically by Dostoevsky, who believed in God: "I believe in Russia. . . . I believe in her orthodoxy. . . . I believe in the body of Christ. . . . I believe that a new advent will take place in Russia. . . . I believe. . . ."

Pan-Slavism, the politicized version of Slavophilism, made its first appearance among the Slavs in Austria. Its first impulse came from the German Herder, who called attention to the folklore of the Slavs and, influenced by Rousseau, eulogized their agricultural life. German romanticism stimulated a similar Slav spirit.

Among the earliest advocates of pan-Slavism was the Czech historian Frantisek Palacký (1798–1876), who, fascinated by the past of his people, urged the union of all Slavs. The First Pan-Slav Congress, chaired by Palacký, met in June 1848 in Prague. It called for reform inside the Habsburg realm, and especially for the creation of a federation of equal peoples: Germans, Magyars, and Slavs. In any such combination, Palacký was sure, the Slavs would form a majority.

Soon the little Slavs of the Habsburg domains were overshadowed by their "big Slav brother" to the east. Russia's defeat in the Crimean War marked the change from religious Slavophilism to politico-cultural pan-Slavism. From then on the movement became the Russian equivalent of the intense nationalism developing in Western Europe. Under Moscow's auspices, pan-Slavism became synonymous with Russian imperialism.

The Little Slavs of the Balkans were not altogether averse to Russian leadership. The *Ausgleich* (Compromise) of 1867, which recognized the equality of Austrians and Hungarians but ignored the Slavs, made it clear to the Little Slavs that they had little to gain from Vienna. Consequently, they turned eastward for guidance and support.

Moscow was quite willing to be drafted. At the Second Pan-Slav Congress of 1867, which met in Moscow, Russia proclaimed her leadership of the pan-Slavic world. A Slavonic ethnographic exhibition advertised Slav unity. The Russians boasted that they would fight to liberate Rumanians, Serbs, Bulgars, and Greeks from the Turks. By the late nineteenth and early twentieth centuries, Moscow was in confrontation with the rival pan-German movement. Pan-Slavism would open the gates to Constantinople and the Straits—the eternal objectives of Russian foreign policy. Pan-Slavism had brought Russia into the Balkan maelstrom.

The most influential drumbeater of pan-Slavism was Nikolai Danilevsky, who in his book *Russia and Europe* (1869) wrote about the incompatibility between Slavic and Western civilization. He believed it to be the mission of the Russians to liberate and unite all Slavs as a preliminary step to the conquest of Constantinople and the Near East:

Whatever the future may bring we are entitled, on the evidence of the past alone, to consider the Slavs among the most gifted families of the human race in political ability. . . . Russia does not have colonial possessions, like Rome or like England. The Russian state from early Muscovite time on has been Russia herself, gradually, irresistibly spreading on all sides, settling neighboring nonsettled territories, and assimilating into herself and into her national boundaries foreign populations. . . .

First, as a *sine qua non* condition of success, strong and powerful Russia has to face the difficult task of liberating her racial brothers; for this struggle she must steel them and herself in the spirit of independence and Pan-Slav consciousness.[1]

Pan-Slavism under Russian auspices never became a governmental policy, but many officials were attracted by the program. Tsar Alexander III, though a champion of russification, showed little interest in it, but the ruling class enthusiastically approved it. A Slavic Benevolent Society, established in 1858, became the center for pan-Slav educational activities, and branches were set up in Balkan cities.

Intolerant and explosive, pan-Slavism turned out to be singularly unsuccessful. Despite the theory of a pan-Slav community of interests, in reality there was no close cultural affinity among the various Slavic peoples. Slavs were as hostile to one another as they were to non-Slavs. The promise of Slav unity was fictitious in the face of the rivalries between Poles and Russians, Ukrainians and Poles, Serbs and Bulgars. Membership in the Slavic branch of the human race did not seem to be a very important bond to most Slavs outside of Russia.

Pan-Slavism, then, turned out to be an instrument of Russian nationalism rather than a movement for the union of all Slavs. It lost its impetus after the failure of Moscow to dominate Bulgaria in the mid-1880s, but was revived in modified form at the beginning of World War I. Eventually it was absorbed by Communist messianism, which in 1945 began to implement the goal of uniting all the Slavs westward to the Oder and Adriatic under control from the Kremlin.

Eccentricities of Pan-Germanism

The rise of pan-Slavism may be compared with the emergence of pan-Germanism. In much the same way, German romantic nationalists were entranced by the unique excellence of the German language. Fichte ridiculed the English tongue: there was no trace of "true culture" in England because the language was unfitted for it. It was an important task, Fichte said, to give the whole world the benefit of the German language, by force if necessary. Those who did not or could not speak German were, of course, outcasts.

Fichte's thesis was accepted warmly by other German nationalists. Ernst Moritz Arndt proposed that the German fatherland include any place where German was spoken:

> Where is the German's Fatherland?
> Name me at length that mighty land!
> "Where'er resounds the German tongue,
> "Where'er its hymns to God are sung."
> Be this the land,
> Brave German, this thy Fatherland.

Fichte and Arndt were predecessors of pan-Germanism, the Teutonic counterpart of pan-Slavism. From its very beginnings pan-Germanism took on an eccentric pattern. Some idea of its nature can be gained from the serious proposal, made at the Frankfurt Assembly in 1848, that a representative of Germans resident in Paris be seated as a delegate. That extraordinary suggestion revealed the type of thinking motivating pan-Germanists throughout the life of the movement. Hitler's "brown network" was to encompass German everywhere, including butchers in Yorkville in the heart of New York and plumbers and carpenters in Rio de Janeiro.

In 1891 an association to promote German nationalism was formed at Frankfurt-am-Main, and three years later it assumed the name the Pan-German League (*Alldeutscher Verband*). One of its founders was Alfred Hugenberg, who later became the first director of the Krupp concern and then leader of the conservative German National People's Party. The first president was the colonial explorer and propagandist Karl Peters. The guiding spirit of the league was Dr. Ernst Hasse, professor of colonial politics at the University of Leipzig, a conservative, monarchist, and energetic nationalist. He gave vigorous leadership to the movement until his death, and was succeeded by the even more aggressive Dr. Heinrich Class. The latter regarded all pan-Germans as the "shock troops" for an expanded Germany.

The league was run by conservatives but it appealed to all classes—generals, industrialists, doctors, lawyers, editors, businessmen, farmers, librarians, orchestra leaders, chimney sweeps, and librarians. It was equipped with a staff of intellectuals. Membership grew slowly but steadily. In 1894 there were 5,742 members; by 1900 there were 21,261.

The Pan-German League turned out to be a kind of general staff for extreme nationalism. It dedicated itself to "a quickening of German national sentiment" and in particular to "fostering the racial and cultural homogeneity of all sections of the German people." It was worried about "general apathy" and by the obliteration of national sentiment. Other peoples, it said, defended energetically "the holy possession of their race," but Germans were consuming their energy in internal struggles.

To check the disintegration of national sentiment, the league in the opening section of its constitution proposed these four aims:

1. Preservation of the German *Volkstum* in Europe and overseas and its support wherever threatened.
2. Séttlement of all cultural, educational, and school problems in ways that shall help the German *Volkstum*.
3. Combatting all forces that check German national development.
4. An active policy of furthering German interests in the entire world, in particular the continuance of the German colonial movement to achieve practical results.

Expressed in slightly different form, the league had two aims: (1) union of all Germans in one huge pan-German state with Germany at its core and (2) claim to world rule by an enlarged Germany. In this way German nationalism would be extended into a global force.

As the guardian angel of German nationalism, the league took an active role in both domestic and foreign affairs. Ruthlessly anti-liberal, it regarded the democratic platform as treason. It called for rigid germanization inside the *Reich* of Poles in the *Ostmark,* Alsace-Lorrainers in the *Westmark,* and Danes in the *Nordmark.* It regarded the *Ostmark* as critically important, especially in view of the rising pan-Slav storm. It worked hand in hand with the H. K. T. Verein (the East Mark Association) for German supremacy in Posen and West Prussia, which was "nationally endangered."

For the Pan-German League, the Danes were quite as dangerous as the

Poles. It protested in 1898 when Danes in Schleswig-Holstein wanted to become subjects of the Danish monarchy. "It is high time that we finally show through energetic acts that we are masters in our own house and intend to remain so." The league charged that Danes were forcing Germans to sell their lands and that Danish youth was involved in a conspiracy against *Deutschtum*. "The German work of a generation is there, in spite of hard opposition and heavy losses. Let us hope that a change will not occur too late, that a system of political strength and justice, which has been the backbone of *Deutschtum*, shall break the enthusiasm of a foreign nationality."

Pan-Germans found that same "foreign nationality" in Alsace-Lorraine. The league demanded German training in all the universities and schools of the two provinces. It insisted angrily that "too much French is spoken in Alsace" and it demanded the abolition of two-language schools in both Alsace and Lorraine.

The pan-Germans were even more interested in foreign affairs. They supported German colonization and William II's "big navy" ("Our future lies on the seas!"). They were ready to give instant advice to the government in any of its external affairs. When insurrection broke out in Brazil in 1891, the Pan-German League urged Chancellor Caprivi to dispatch a warship to protect German interests there. In the same petition the league protested the von der Heydt rescript, which had prohibited emigration of Germans to Brazil. It was successful in having the decree repealed.

Strongly anti-British, pan-Germans feared that friendship with the island kingdom might curtail Germany's colonial opportunities and obviate the need for a large navy. They took the side of South Africans ("our blood brothers") in their conflict with England. During the Boer War they raised a special fund to enable Germans to leave the fighting areas. They published manifestoes lauding the Boers and sent telegrams of support to President Stephanus Johannes Paulus Kruger.

In every matter of foreign policy the pan-Germans were on the side of German nationalism. When in 1904 Britain recognized Morocco as "a proper sphere for French influence," the pan-Germans stirred the nation into protest. They hailed with delight the dispatch of a cruiser to Agadir in 1911 to protect German interests. No matter what the question—immigration, *Deutschtum* in foreign countries, diplomatic clashes with the great powers—the pan-Germans appealed for "German honor," for "Germany's place in the sun," for "a share of the world as a conquering nation."

Like pan-Slavism, this home-grown imperialist ideology had few successes to show for its energetic activities. Critics called it a dangerous, intolerant, destructive force which helped to lead Germany into the tragedy of two world wars. It never was able to unify masses of people not actually in communion with one another. In the long run, it never achieved its stated goals. Pan-Germanism inspired Adolf Hitler and provided nazism with its fanatical ideology, but the Fuehrer's proposed Thousand-Year Reich lasted exactly twelve years.

One German historian judged pan-Germans to be "schoolboys" and "idiots." Particularistic German nationalism, at a lower level, proved itself to be tougher than a proposed Greater German nationalism. Once again the larger pan movement proved to be less effective than the limited form of nationalism based on national states.

The Gymnastics of Pan-Turanism

Western pan movements had their counterparts elsewhere. Just as the pan-Slavic and pan-German movements sought unsuccessfully to enlarge nationalism by combining peoples of divergent cultures in a greater whole, so did pan-Turanism seek to unite such disparate groups as the Crimean Turks, the Azerbaijan Turks, the Ottomans, the Uzbeks, the Kirghiz, and all other fragments of Turkism into one pan-Turanian nation. Beginning in the twentieth century, pan-Turanism was originally a movement for national regeneration, but then it broadened its objectives. In much the same way as pan-Slavism, it tried to cut through several layers of cultures—in this case Islamic, Persian, and Arabic—to combine all Turkish-speaking peoples in one vast supranationalism.

Not the least motivating factor for the rise of pan-Turanism was the proximity of Russia. With an eye on the Turks living along the lower Volga, in the Crimea, and the Caucasus (all subjects of Russia), the pan-Turanists saw their movement as a weapon against Moscow. If Russia could use pan-Slavism in her struggle against Turkey and the Austro-Hungarian Empire, then the Turks had a sacred right to use pan-Turanism for a similar purpose. What was good for the Russian goose was good for the Turkish gander.

For four centuries the Middle East had been under the dominance of the Ottomans. There was increasing dissent inside the Empire at the beginning of the twentieth century. In Constantinople, students who had been exposed to Western ideas were humiliated when comparing European progress with Ottoman despotism and backwardness. Secret societies were organized to demand an end to the old tyranny and to support a dynamic new nationalism. The Young Turks (Committee of Union and Progress) survived suppression by Abdul Hamid and made their presence felt in the revolution of 1908, which overthrew the old dynasty.

The Young Turks refused to accept the traditional view that the Ottoman Empire was the creation of the house of Osman working in the cause of Islam. They presented a new idea—the Empire was rather the special achievement of the Turkish, or the Turanian, genius. Until this time "Turk" had been used

by the Ottomans to mean "yokel" or "rustic" or "peasant." The dissenters
wanted to endow the word with pride and dignity. Encouraged by the new
philology, they discovered that Turks, Mongols, and Seljuks were all
branches of an *Urvolk,* the people of Turan. The Young Turks now had a
mission to bring together all these peoples who had been cut apart by time and
circumstance. Out of this aim grew the movement of pan-Turanism, or
pan-Turkism.

It took some tortured reasoning to justify this kind of linguistic acrobatics
to unite the people of "kindred families." This became the lifetime task of
Ziya Gökalp (1875–1924), the pseudonym of Mehmed Ziya, a journalist,
sociologist, philosopher and nationalist. At the root of his thinking was a
glowing patriotism originally intertwined with religious sentiment. Gökalp
regarded the Balkan wars as a *jihad,* a holy war against Christians, a feeling
expressed in his popular "Prayer of a Soldier":

> My heart's desire are two: religion and Fatherland. . . .
> Our War is the Holy War, its end martyrdom. . . .
> Have mercy on Islam, take revenge on its enemies,
> Make Islam flourish, O God!

By 1914 Gökalp began to have second thoughts about his emphasis on religion. He was angered by the failure of the Ottoman government to declare
a holy war against the Allies. He was even more disturbed by the participation of troops from India and other Muslims on the side of the enemy, as well
as by the growing Arab revolt against the Sultan. He began to soften the
Islamic theme in his writings.

By the end of World War I Gökalp decided that a universal religious
pan-Islamism, the unity of all Muslims under one ruler, was a messianic hope
impossible of fulfillment. A theocratic ideology was fine, but to Gökalp it
stood squarely in the way of Turkish revival. Religious ties must be used to
strengthen the truncated Turkish state. Islam in Turkey must have a unique
Turkish character. There must be a revival of Turkish folklore, ancient
customs, and popular traditions, precisely the sort of romantic nationalism
projected in Europe by the German Grimm brothers, the Italian Mazzini, and
the Russian Pushkin. The overriding problem, said Gökalp, was to regain the
national self-confidence that had been shaken by the decline of Ottoman
power.

By this time Gökalp was convinced that the country of the Turks was not
Turkey or Turkestan but "the broad and everlasting land of Turan." The
pan-Turanian movement would re-create the glory of Attila, Genghis Khan,

and Tamerlane. Gökalp was not at all averse to twisting history to make his point:

> There is, in fact, a homeland of Islam which is the beloved land of all Muslims. The other one is the national home: which, for Turks, is what we call *Turan*. The Ottoman territories are that portion of Islamdom which have remained independent. A portion of these is the home of the Turks, and is at the same time a portion of *Turan*. Another portion of them is the homeland of the Arabs, which is again a part of the great Arab Fatherland. . . .[2]

In this somewhat awkward way, Gökalp attempted to establish the idea of a visionary overall pan-Turanism. This is further evidence to show that both nationalism and the pan movements seldom escape the traps of irrationalism.

Gökalp's pan-Turanism, artificial and impractical as it was, was not destined to last long. After the Bolshevik Revolution of 1917, the Soviet Union entered into an agreement with the new Turkey and promised equal treatment inside the U.S.S.R. for all Turks. Turkish leaders were inclined to abandon the grandiloquent aims of pan-Turanism and concentrated instead on the regeneration of Turkey proper.

The new Turkism represented a blend of liberal Ottoman nationalism and Turkish nationalism. It was personified by Mustafa Kemal, the founder of modern Turkey. Emerging from obscure origins, he became active as a Young Turk conspirator. A legendary hero in World War I, he subsequently organized his followers into the ruling Republican Peoples Party and rose to leadership of the new Turkish state, which was considerably more stable and healthier than the Ottoman Empire it succeeded.

Early in his career Kemal was profoundly disillusioned by the old Ottoman Empire, which he regarded as an obsolescent structure which could not be preserved. He rejected Ottomanism, pan-Islamism, and pan-Turanism in favor of a homogeneous Turkish state. In the presidential campaign of 1931 Kemal announced a six-point program: (1) republicanism, (2) secularism, (3) populism, (4) nationalism, (5) statism, and (6) continuous reform. He spoke of pan-Turanism as an attractive idea but he judged it to be impractical; he would, therefore, concentrate on the regeneration of Turkey proper.

Politically, Kemal could well have become the new Sultan, but instead he preferred a democratic republic. He abolished the old sultanate and caliphate. He retained the Islamic religion, but secularized it with bewildering speed. He replaced Muslim religious law with a legal code borrowed from the Swiss, and at the same time took a commercial code from the Germans and a criminal code from the Italians. His new state, he said, would have a populist foundation, but in reality he took on the mantle of what is sometimes called a benevolent dictator.

Kemal turned his energy in two directions: (1) to create a new Turkish nationalism and (2) to prepare the way for a thoroughgoing westernization. Nationalism became the real Turkish religion. In achieving his goal of a new national state, he was careful not to abandon the cultural aspects of pan-Turanism. He supported the glorification of the pre-Islamic past and attempted to create a "pure" Turkish language, purged of Arabic and Persian elements. He abolished the diffuse Arabic script and replaced it with a Latin-type alphabet, much of which he adapted himself. Supported by Gökalp, he turned the full force of propaganda in schools and the press to the revival of ancient Turkish culture. He urged his fellow citizens to adopt Turkish family names: he himself took the name Ataturk (Father of the Turks).

Kemal was convinced that the state should pursue "an exclusively national policy." When he spoke of national policy, he meant it in this sense: "To work within our national boundaries for the real happiness and welfare of the nation and the country, by, above all, relying on our own strength in order to retain our existence."

Further, to Kemal national policy meant the westernization of his country. To retain the respect of other peoples, "to expect from the civilized world human treatment," Turkey must throw off her medieval raiment and accept the advantages of Western civilization. His plan for a continuous social reform, collectively called *devrim* ("overturning" or "revolution"), was designed to loosen the chains of tradition and prepare the way for a thoroughgoing westernization and modernization. Hence his familiar reforms. He abolished religious schools in favor of civil education. He closed shrines, mausoleums, and dervish houses. He forbade polygamy and outlawed the wearing of the fez. He adopted the Western Gregorian calendar and decreed Sunday, instead of Friday, as a day of rest. He emancipated women and allowed them to mix freely in public with men—for the first time in Turkish history. By 1938 Turkey was a modernized, secular state.

Pan-Turanism had served its purpose as a stimulant for nationalism in Turkey proper. Once it had achieved a limited goal, it began to recede into the past. Gökalp's complex linguistic gymnastics could not possibly succeed in a multi-ethnic, multilinguistic, and multireligious empire. Like other pan movements, pan-Turanism could not combine the uncombinable.

Pan-Arabism

In contrast to pan-Turanism, pan-Arabism was more a national than an ethnic movement. Historically, the Arabs were both a tribal people and the conquerors of a huge empire. Only the triumph of Charles Martel at Tours in 732 A.D. halted the advance of Islam into Western Europe and assured the future of Christianity. For four hundred years the Arabs of the Middle East were subjected to Ottoman control. By the late nineteenth century they were assured equality, but the Ottomans never carried out their promises. A clash between Turks and Arabs was inevitable.

There was little evidence of Arab nationalism until the latter half of the nineteenth century. Both Arab nationalism and Zionism developed as cultural movements out of the activities of literary societies and were closely linked with attention to, respectively, the Arab and Hebrew languages. For decades both movements were kept alive in obscure little magazines by dedicated pioneers. In the early 1880s, Arab nationalists in Damascus and Beirut, who were demanding home rule in Syria, Lebanon, and Palestine, were subjected to intensive persecution by the Turks. In the early twentieth century, Arab nationalists were to come into conflict with the considerably better organized Zionists, who called for a Jewish national and social renaissance and reconstitution of the ancient kingdom of Israel. Both Arabs and Jews were affected by a burgeoning national egocentricity which gave the twentieth century much of its character.

Arab nationalism was a protest not only against Ottoman domination but European imperialism. In World War I, Lawrence of Arabia and other British agents worked with Arabs to overthrow the Turkish yoke. Freed from Turkish control, the Arabs suddenly found themselves mandated to the Western powers. For a long time the Arabs were crippled by inertia and indifference to both Turkish overlords and European bondholders. Then latent nationalism came to the surface, stimulated, as elsewhere, by awareness of Western experience, by the nationalistic ideals of pioneer intellectuals, and by propagandistic activists. Adopting the trappings, myths, and mythology of nationalism, the Arabs traveled the road from subjugation to emancipation to national consciousness.

There were two tendencies at work in the Arab Middle East: (1) the urge to centralization under pan-Arabism and (2) regional separateness. Unifying factors were Islamic universalism and the Arabic language. Arab liberation meant the formation of ten sovereign states with a population of 70 million living on four million square miles in the Middle East. But Arab religious and cultural affinity was not enough to assure political unity. The differences were accented even more by the discovery of oil in the Middle East and the resultant sway of economic nationalism. By 1975 Arab oil would change the complexion of the world's economy but it did little politically to unite the squabbling Arab states.

The strength of the nationalist ideal varied through the fragmented Arab lands. In some, intellectuals prepared the way for nationalism; in others, champions were to be found mostly in the military and the bureaucracy. In all, the institution of Islam remained in an uneasy position: on the one hand, the faith of Muhammad was opposed to the purely nationalist idea; on the other, it lent itself easily to national purposes.

Pan-Arabism found its charismatic hero in Gamal Abdel Nasser. Born at Beni Mor, Asyut Province, on January 15, 1918, the son of a postal clerk, Nasser as a young man took to the streets to demonstrate against the British. With other youngsters he chanted *"Ya-Azeez, Ya 'Azeez, Dahiya takhud al-Ingleez!"* (Oh, Almighty God, may disaster take the English!"), just as his ancestors from the days of the Mamelukes had sung *"Ya Rabb, Ya Mutajille, al-Uth-manli!* (Oh, God, the Self-revealing, annihilate the Turk!"). To youthful dissenters, only the name of the oppressor was different.

Dedicating himself to the cause of Egyptian nationalism, Nasser worked with the Free Officers movement for the overthrow of the Farouk government. In the ensuing struggle for power, he outmaneuvered the popular General Muhammad Naguib and became premier on February 1, 1954. His first move was to seek a populist foundation for his regime. He confiscated land from the wealthy landowners and turned it over to the poor *fellahin*. In the national elections of June 1956 he was elected to the presidency for a six-year term. From then on, until his death in 1970, he revealed a remarkable resiliency in holding on to the reins of power.

Nasser explained his goal in *The Philosophy of the Revolution:*

There are no limits beyond which we will not go. Our task is the removal of rock and obstacles from off the way. This is our only duty. The future and all its challenge is work that is open to all patriots with ideas and experience. This is a duty and a privilege demanded of them. We cannot perform the whole task. It is our cherished duty, our moment of historical responsibility, thus to bring our people at long last together, and meld them in units for the future—the future of Egypt—strong and free.[3]

These were stirring words, but Nasser envisaged Egyptian nationalism in purely institutional and political terms. He failed to understand that control of economic factors was necessary for responsible national leadership. The new Egypt had her nationalist image—flag, anthem, coins, stamps, even parliamentary institutions in the Western tradition—but Nasser, like Peron of Argentina, Sukarno of Indonesia, and Nkrumah of Ghana, was to find political slogans insufficient to meet economic realities. Behind the facade of Egyptian independence were all the miseries of the past. Nationalism had helped win independence, but it had not solved the pressing problems of exploitation, poverty, and illiteracy.

Nasser made the mistake of regarding himself not only as the spearhead of Egyptian nationalism but also as the head apostle of pan-Arabism. He declined to bind Egyptian nationalism in time and space. He insisted on one point of gravity: any truly national Arab government must bow to the suzerainty of Cairo. Anyone who resisted the "irresistible tide" of Egyptian leadership—be he Bourguiba in Tunisia, Chamoun in Lebanon, or Khalil in the Sudan—was to be regarded as a traitor and an agent of imperialism. As the first decisive step toward the goal of pan-Arabism, Nasser in 1958 set up the confederation of the United Arab Republic (Egypt and Syria).

Nasser found philosophical justification for pan-Arabism in a kind of tortured philosophical reasoning. Egypt, he said, was destined to play a "positive role" in the troubled Arab world. She was the center of three circles. The first Arab circle "is a part of us, and we are a part of it, our history being inextricably part of its history." The Islamic heritage took shelter in Egypt. This most important circle is closely linked together by a common religion. It is the center of Islamic learning—at Mecca, Damascus, Baghdad, and Cairo.

Nasser's second circle (enclosing the Arab circle) was the continent of Africa. "We cannot remain aloof. We are in Africa. We gave them their northern gate. We are their link with the outside world. We will never relinquish responsibility for it." Africa, said Nasser, was vital for Egypt: after all, the life-giving waters of the Nile flowed to Egypt from the heart of the continent.

The third great circle, circumscribing all the continents and oceans, was Islam, "the domain of our brothers in faith." Nasser saw all three circles surrounding Cairo, as indicating "a wandering mission in search of a hero." He modestly nominated himself: "We alone, by virtue of our place, can perform the role."

In this way Nasser claimed leadership of all ten sovereignties in the pan-Arab world. The contention was unrealistic, however, in the face of Arab fragmentation. It was too much to expect that Arab chieftains would heal their historic jealousies easily or that Arab oil barons would accept the domination of impoverished Egypt.

Pan-Arabism was beset by enormous obstacles, both internal and external. Like other pan movements, it was long on promises, short on performance. Once again we see a kind of historical Parkinson's law at work: each nationalism is sensitive to the limits of its own security, and tends to withdraw into its own borders at precisely that point when it fears for its sovereignty and when faced with the prospect of being absorbed into a larger pan-nationalism.

Embryonic Pan-Africanism

The newer pan movements recapitulated the experience of the older forms. Pan-Africanism aimed to become a supernational racial movement. From its beginnings it was primarily ethnic—it transformed tribal sentiment into racial consciousness. There was in it no sense of national communion, nor any common linguistic bond, but rather a resentment against the white man and his self-assumed burden. First and foremost pro-Africa and pro-African, the movement called vaguely for the africanization of politics, economy, and education. Most of all it projected what it believed to be a common African personality.

The idea of one supernational Africa stemmed originally from Negroes in the United States and the West Indies. The term "pan-Africa" was first used in 1900 by a West Indian barrister, H. Sylvester-Williams of Trinidad, practising in London, who called for a pan-African conference. There was little response. Without deep roots, the idea of uniting the peoples of Africa remained quiescent for a generation.

Pan-Africanism received its most important stimulus from W. E. B. DuBois, founder of the National Association for the Advancement of Colored People and an able scholar who was fascinated by the ancestral societies of Africa. At a time when American Blacks were embarrassed by "African primitiveness," DuBois called attention to the complex and sophisticated cultures of sub-Sahara Africa. On the assumption that blacks throughout the world should work together, DuBois convened four pan-African congresses in Europe and the United States between 1919 and 1927. The general theme which ran through all meetings was a demand for "the absolute equality of races" and an end to imperialistic exploitation.

The First Pan-African Congress met in 1919 in Paris with fifty-seven delegates from fifteen countries, and twelve of these representatives were from nine African countries. It called on the Allies to draw up a code of laws for the protection of African nations and to create a permanent bureau of the League of Nations to ensure African freedom. At Versailles, DuBois attempted unsuccessfully to reach President Wilson to plead for an internationalized Africa based on the former German colonies there.

Typical of DuBois' articulation of pan-African ideals was the manifesto of the Second Pan-African Congress (1921), at which he advocated intellectual leadership for the movement ("the talented tenth"):

The world must face two eventualities: either the complete assimilation of Africa with two or three of the great world states, with political, civil and social power equal for its black and white citizens, or the rise of a great black African state founded in Peace and Good Will, based on popular education, natural art and industry and freedom of trade; autonomous and sovereign in its internal policy, but from its beginning a part of a great society of peoples in which it takes its place with others as co-rulers of the world.[4]

Meanwhile, the fires of black nationalism were awakened by the Garvey movement, which promised a black nation in the African homeland. Marcus Garvey, born in Jamaica, a Negro of Koromantee stock, founded the Universal Negro Improvement Association in 1914 with the motto "One God, One Aim, One Destiny." He recommended the wholesale migration of American Blacks to Africa because "whites will always be racist" and the black man must develop "a distinct racial type of civilization of his own and work out his salvation in the motherland." In thus separating blacks and whites, Garvey won the instant approval of the Ku Klux Klan.

Under the guidance of its remarkable leader, the Garvey movement took on bizarre overtones. There were numerous slogans: "Renaissance of the Black Race!" "Ethiopia Awake!" "Africa for the Africans, at Home and Abroad!" The official flag was black (for Negro skin), green (for Negro hopes), and red (for Negro blood). The anthem was titled "Ethiopia, Thou Land of Our Fathers." Garvey founded a host of subsidiary organizations: the Universal African Legion, outfitted in blue and red uniforms; the Universal Black Cross, with a special corps of nurses; and the ill-starred Black Star Line. Garvey sang praises to the African past and insisted, in his African Orthodox Church, that God, Christ, and the Madonna were all black.

Garvey's propaganda attracted followers among West Indians and American Negroes. To DuBois it was "a poorly conceived but earnest determination to unite the Negroes of the world." In turn, Garvey denounced DuBois' "caste aristocracy" of college graduates as too arrogant to mean much to the average Negro. When Garvey was jailed on a charge of using the mails to defraud, the movement collapsed. DuBois' pan-African efforts also receded into the background.

Pan-Africanism was revived after World War II with the withdrawal of the imperialist powers from the great continent and the formation of new African nations. The first Conference of Independent African States was convened in April 1958 in Accra, the capital of Ghana. Eight nations (five from the Arab north) condemned colonialism, warned the French to get out of Algeria, condemned South Africa as racist and Portugal as imperialist, and urged the creation of a permanent machinery dedicated to African unity. The delegates set April 15 as Freedom Day and ended the conference with the hymn "God Bless Africa."

The guiding spirit at the Accra conference was Prime Minister Kwame Nkrumah of Ghana, who believed that only he could unite Africa. "I'm like the man who walked into Jerusalem two thousand years ago—and people followed." "This conference," he said, "is the most significant event in the history of Africa for many centuries." He appealed for African political unity. A loose confederation of economic cooperation, he said, would be deceptively time delaying. "It is only a political union that will ensure a uniformity in our foreign policy projecting the African personality and presenting Africa as a force important to be reckoned with."

The Second Conference of Independent African States met at Addis Ababa, Ethiopia, in 1960. Already there was increasing polarization in methods of achieving the goals of pan-Africanism. On the conservative side was the Monrovia bloc, consisting of the "Brazzaville Twelve" (all former French colonies) plus Liberia, Nigeria, Somalia, Sierre Leone, Togo, Libya, and Ethiopia. Favoring a community of African nations rather than a union ("Africans should respect one another's sovereignty"), the Monrovia bloc supported the principle of gradualism. It was pro-Israel, neutralist, with leanings toward the West, and it favored United Nations operations in the Congo.

Leaning to the radical side was the Casablanca bloc (Morocco, the United Arab Republic, the Mali-Guinea-Ghana group, and the Algerian rebel FLN), which convened in 1961 to coordinate its policies. More precisely pan-African than the Monrovia bloc, it was socialistic, anti-French (it criticized France for atom bomb testing), and was willing to cooperate with the Communist bloc. It condemned Israel and was pro-Lumumba in the Congo. It called for a joint military command, as well as an African economic and cultural community.

By 1963 the Monrovia and Casablanca blocs constituted the two poles of pan-Africanism. In that year the Organization of African Unity (OAU), consisting of thirty–two states, convened under the mediation of President Touré of Guinea to resolve the differences between the two groups. Nkrumah again pleaded for a strong central government, but the majority favored his opponents, led by Sir Abubakar Balawa, Prime Minister of Nigeria, and Julius Nyerere, President of Tanganyika. The result was an "association" rather than a federation or union of African states.

In this indifferent way, pan-Africanism reached the apex of its existence. It had won no glittering success. Despite the emotional exhortations of its advocates, there was little chance of a continental-wide union: the Muslim north was drawn to pan-Arabism, the tribal center to the south to pan-Africanism and its concomitant Negritude. Pan-Africanism helped somewhat to prevent the balkanization of the entire continent. Africa, however, remained in a ferment of change as the artificially created nation-states tried each in its own way to determine the political form in which the new African personality would clothe itself.

The Call for Pan-Asianism

On a comparative basis, pan-Asianism had considerably more historical experience behind it. The concept went all the way back to Genghis Khan, who at the time of his death ruled an empire stretching from the Yellow Sea to the Dnieper. In modern times, major attempts to re-create that great realm were made by the Chinese (''the Celestial Empire'') and the Japanese (''the Imperial Principle'').

Until World War I, however, pan-Asianism was little more than an unorganized tendency. After the war there arose the sentiment that Asians, despite their medley of divergent cultures, had a common destiny, as well as a common enemy in the imperialist powers. At this time the Russian Bolsheviks, enthusiastically expecting the world revolution, stepped into the picture by organizing a Congress of Oriental Nations at Baku in 1920. It was conspicuously unsuccessful—Asians wanted no help from Moscow.

In the twentieth century an increasingly aggressive Japan turned to the Chinese mainland as the first step to attaining what it believed was its rightful place in the sun. ''The world will realize,'' said the Tanaka memorial in 1927, ''that Eastern Asia is ours and will not dare to violate our rights. This is the plan left us by the Emperor Meiji, the success of which is essential to our national existence.''

Baron Tanaka was wrong: his country could well exist without the responsibility of controlling the East. After Japan's defeat in 1945, the Chinese Communists aspired to leadership of the pan-Asian movement. But other Asia nations, alienated by Chinese totalitarianism, were not especially attracted by the prospect.

The First Pan-Asian Conference, under the auspices of the Pan-Asia Society, was held at Nagasaki in 1926. Little was said about political affairs: the main subject of discussion was economic cooperation. Provision was made for establishing a permanent bureau at either Tokyo, Peking, or Shanghai. The Second Pan-Asian Conference was held near Shanghai in 1928. By this time irreconcilable differences had arisen between the Chinese and Japanese. Pan-Asianism was dwarfed in mutual recriminations.

Distrust and fear of the old imperialist powers brought Asians and Africans together at the Bandung Conference, held April 18–24, 1955. It was an impressive gathering, seeking to express something of the common spirit of the new (or reborn) states. The conferees represented varying points of view, but they gave their support to the fundamental principles of human rights as set forth in the chapter of the United Nations. They agreed that ''colonialism in all its manifestations is an evil which should speedily be brought to an end.'' The subjection of peoples, they said, to alien subjugation, domination, and exploitation "constitutes a denial of fundamental human rights." They declared their support for the cause of freedom and independence for all peoples, and recognized the equality of all races and nations, large and small. It was their "keen and sincere desire to renew their old cultural contacts and develop new ones in the context of the modern world."

It was easy to obtain unanimity on such high-sounding pronunciamentoes. The Bandung countries could even operate as a loose bloc in the United Nations. But on the wider problem of pan-Asian or pan-African unity, there was little enthusiasm or agreement. The new Asian states were overwhelmed with the necessity of dealing with disruptive forces inside their countries. At the same time, they were deeply involved in adapting themselves to a new and changing world. They were undergoing what has been called the second stage of nationalism. The first stages of independence—revolution and civil war—were past. Now the new Asian states were faced with choosing between Communist expansion and American containment. At the present moment, there are few possibilities of inter-Asian regionalism or operating within the larger scope of pan-Asianism.

Organized Pan-Americanism

Pan-Americanism is considerably older than either pan-Africanism or pan-Asianism. It is not exactly a pan movement in the sense of either pan-Slavism or pan-Germanism, but rather a *policy* originated by Latin Americans to preserve their own independence. Later it was promoted by the United States as a means of ensuring hemispheric unity. The First Pan-American Conference, at which there was no North American participation, was called in 1826 in Panama by Simón Bolívar. After 1890, a series of conferences was convened under United States sponsorship to seek continental cooperation in economic, cultural, and legal spheres. No supranationalistic ideology was involved, nor was there any expressed connection with the Monroe Doctrine.

The pan-American movement was handicapped from its beginning by serious distrust upon the part of those Latin Americans who regarded their cultural ties with Europe, especially Spain and Portugal, as stronger than those with the Yankee colossus to the north. They preferred to look to London for finance, to Berlin for military advisers, and to Paris for styles.

Latin Americans accused the United States of using the Monroe Doctrine to justify intervention in their affairs, to bolster dollar diplomacy, and to promote American imperialism. The resulting anti-Yankee sentiment was compounded of a mixture of Latin *dignidad,* envy, and sheer cussedness. It regarded the northern neighbor as an arrogant, brash giant whose spiritual values had been sacrificed in the pursuit for the dollar. It denied that the term

"America" should be monopolized by the United States. There are, it was said, four Americas, representing four historic zones, four experiences in search of self-expression: Hispano-Indian America, Portuguese America (Brazil), English America (the United States), and Anglo-French America (Canada). No one of these roughly equivalent areas was superior: each began its history at a different date and in different centuries.

That the United States has become the wealthiest and most powerful nation on earth is attributed by many Latin Americans to an undeserved stroke of good fortune. They pay little attention to the notion that the Monroe Doctrine may have prevented the partition of their continent among the imperialist powers, as in the scramble which carved Africa into a set of European outposts. While looking with disdain at the Yankee character, they express pride in their older cultural traditions. "The very names Cuzco, Otavalo, and Patzcuaro are as authentically of the America south of the Rio Grande as that of Boston is of the United States." A Brazilian or a Bolivian is as much an American as a New Yorker or a Philadelphian. Costa Rica was a part of America a century before the first Pilgrims landed at Plymouth.

On a 1958 good-will tour in South America, Vice-President Richard M. Nixon was spat upon in Venezuela by young hotheads. Following the incident, José Figueres, ex-President of Costa Rica, appeared before a Congressional committee and issued a blunt statement to the American people revealing why Mr. Nixon had been received in so unfriendly a fashion. It turned out to be a highly emotional revelation of Latin American pride, resentment, and hostility:

> . . . I must speak frankly, even rudely, because I believe that the situation requires it: people cannot spit at a foreign policy, which is what they wanted to do. And when they have run out of other ways of making themselves understood, their only remaining course is to spit.
>
> With all due respect for Vice-President Nixon, and with all my admiration for his conduct, which was, during the events, heroic, and afterwards, noble, I must explain that the act of spitting, vulgar as it is, is without substitute in our language for expressing certain emotions. . . .
>
> Of course, you have made certain investments in the American dictatorships. The aluminium companies extract bauxite almost gratis. Our generals, your admirals, your civil functionaries, and your magnates receive royal treatment there. As your Senate verified yesterday, some concessionnaires bribe the reigning dynasties for the privilege of hunting on their grounds. They deduct the money from the taxes they pay in the United States, but it returns to the country, and upon arrival in Hollywood is converted into extravagant furs and automobiles which shatter the fragile virtue of the female stars.
>
> Meanwhile, our women are raped by gangsters, our men castrated in the torture chambers, and our illustrious professors disappear lugubriously from the halls of Columbia University in New York. When one of your legislators calls this "collaboration to combat communism," 180 million Latin Americans want to spit.

Spitting is a despicable practice, when it is physically performed. But what about moral spitting? When your government invited Pedro Estrada, the Himmler of the Western Hemisphere, to be honored in Washington, did you not spit in the faces of all the democrats of America? . . .

We are not asking for handouts, except in cases of emergency. We are not people who would spit for money. We have inherited all the defects of the Spanish character, but also some of its virtues. Our poverty does not abate our pride. We have our dignity.[5]

Despite the sentiment shown in this unique dissertation on spitting, Washington had long made efforts to appease Latin Americans and promote better hemispheric solidarity. President Franklin Roosevelt's "Good Neighbor Policy" of the 1930s renounced any United States police role in the Caribbean, supported increased trade, and set up pan-American organizations to settle disputes. In 1948 the Organization of American States (OAS) was formed with twenty-three countries "to promote the solidarity and defend the sovereignty of members and provide through the Pan-American Union social, economic, and technical services."

Despite this type of organization, pan-Americanism remained a somewhat shaky structure. United States capital continued to hold an obtrusive place in the Latin American economy (its investment in the 1960s was close to 10 billion dollars, representing at least a third of all American investments abroad). Many Latin Americans regard this economic penetration as an intolerable form of neo-colonialism. A viable pan-Americanism under such conditions is scarcely to be expected. Here, too, a pan movement, even with careful organization, reveals its weakness as even a partial substitute for the prevalent forms of nationalism.

The Bankruptcy of Nationalism Extended

The pan-national movements originating in the nineteenth century may be regarded as extensions of nationalism. They attempt to promote a broader consolidation of peoples bound together by common languages, traditions, ethnic kinship, and geography. They vary considerably in origin and character. Some are genuinely national movements and others are dedicated to supernationalism, based on a common ethnical stock. Still others have a religious or continental connotation geared to a consciousness of common interest. Most of them are vague and ill defined in concept and purpose. All attract the attention of self-interested manipulators, either eccentrics or shrewd, self-seeking imperialists.

The pan movements stand midway between particularistic nationalism and the projected "pan" ideal of world federation. Critics who see nationalism as inevitably leading to the horrors of war believe that the best chance for peace is a global political union dedicated to the interdependence of all peoples. From this point of view the pan movements represent a step forward, beyond the anarchy of nationalism.

Unfortunately, however, while nationalism has become firmly rooted in the political and intellectual milieu of our times, the pan movements have been conspicuously unsuccessful in their objectives. The broader movement has not been able to temper nationalism nor has it deprived nationalism of the emotional appeal it has had during the last two centuries. By some unfathomable and perhaps unconscious method, each nation in the contemporary world seems to realize automatically the boundaries which give it security and then withdraws into its own territory at the point where pan-nationalism beckons.

The question might be asked logically: why discuss the pan movements at all in view of their lack of success? To this the embarrassed historian can only respond with the words of the mountain climber who was asked why he persisted in trying to conquer Mount Everest: "Don't know! Because it is there!"

Notes

[1] Nikolai Danilevsky, *Russia and Europe: An Inquiry into the Cultural and Political Relations of the Slav World and of the Germano-Latin World,* quoted in Hans Kohn, *Nationalism: Its Meaning and History* (Princeton: Van Nostrand, 1955), pp. 153–54.

[2] Quoted in Elie Kedourie (ed.), *Nationalism in Asia and Africa* (New York and Cleveland: World Publishing Co., 1970), p. 52.

[3] Gamal Abdel Nasser, *Egypt Liberated: The Philosophy of the Revolution* (Washington D.C.: Public Affairs Press, 1955), p. 77.

[4] W. E. B. DuBois, "Manifesto of the Second Pan-African Congress," *The Crisis,* 23 (November 1921): 10.

[5] José Figueres at *Hearings before the Subcommittee on Inter-American Affairs of the Committee on Foreign Relations, Second Session* (Washington, D.C., 1958), pp. 73–93.

17 Panaceas: World, Regional, and Continental

And they shall beat their swords into
    plowshares,
And their spears into pruning-hooks;
Nations shall not lift sword against
    nation,
Neither shall they learn war any more.

—Isaiah 2:4, Micah 4:3

The Search for Remedy

The "pan" movements are only one response to the problem of finding a way to replace the anarchy of particularistic nationalism. In most cases they merely project the ills of nationalism on a broader scale. There are several other major proposals: world government, regional military integration, economic union, and continental unity. Each seeks in its own way to make it easier for peoples to live together and to ease hostile environments. Each thus far has attracted enthusiastic sponsors who present their cure-alls with enthusiasm and confidence. Each has won a minimum of success.

The Goal of World Government

The problem is as perplexing as it is old. How to attain world government has occupied the attention of thinkers from Plato to Bertrand Russell. In 1625 the Dutch jurist Hugo Grotius issued his celebrated work *On the Law of War and Peace,* in which he looked for rational principles for regulating the relations between nations. In the early seventeenth century the Duc de Sully projected for his patron, Henry IV, a "Grand Design" for a European federation of fifteen states, which he visualized as "a Christian republic."

Many others offered utopian plans for peace—from the Königsberg philosopher Immanuel Kant to the Quaker William Penn, founder of Pennsylvania. The Hague Conferences of 1899 and 1907 were called to bring about "a possible reduction of excessive armaments which weigh upon all nations." Little was accomplished beyond setting "rules" for guerrilla warfare, prohibiting the throwing of missiles from balloons, the banning of suffocating gases, and forbidding the use of expanding bullets. Participating nations were exhorted to be kind to Red Cross nurses in time of war. It was all highly moral, but it was at the same time disappointingly ineffective.

Unfortunately, the moral sense of civilized man had not kept pace with his scientific genius. Eventually he set foot on the moon, but here on earth he continued to reveal incredible shortsightedness in the task of living with others in peace and harmony.

President Woodrow Wilson, after the traumatic shock of World War I, warned that unless a world organization was established to maintain the peace, there would certainly be another and even more catastrophic global conflict within a generation. An even more acute observation was made at the close of the Versailles Peace Conference when an anonymous German plenipotentiary, upon leaving the Hall of Mirrors, commented bitterly to a passing Frenchman: "*Au revoir!* See you again in twenty years!" He could not have been more accurate.

The critical task in 1919 was to create an international order in a milieu marked by such handicaps as discontent among the defeated nations, the victors' disillusionment, and the retreat of the United States into isolation. At least the attempt was made. Conceived by Jan Smuts of South Africa and promoted by Wilson until his death, the League of Nations was designed to be a world government responsible for handling the affairs of common concern to all nations. The preamble was explicit:

The High Contracting Parties, in order to promote international cooperation and to achieve international peace and security by the acceptance of obligations not to resort to war, by the prescription of open, just, and honorable relations between nations, by the firm understandings of international law as the actual rule of conduct among Governments, and by the maintenance of justice and a scrupulous respect for all treaty obligations in the dealings of organized peoples with one another, agree to this Covenant of the League of Nations.

The League failed in its assault on nationalism. True, it worked under severe handicaps. It failed to include the defeated nations in its original membership; it was shunned by the United States, whose President had brought it into existence. Winston Churchill would later claim that the League was ruined by the failure of the United States to take an active role in its affairs. The key technical weakness was article XVI of the covenant, which called for economic sanctions against aggressors but which did not provide for a military force to back up its decisions, the decisions of the League. There were other contributory factors: the survival of power diplomacy, the unwillingness of the major powers to disarm, and the lack of adjustment by the peace treaties to new conditions.

The League of Nations could boast of moderate successes in small decisions (the Aaland Islands, the Mosul boundary dispute, the Corfu question), but it was helpless when faced with major clashes (Manchuria, Ethiopia, the Spanish Civil War). The results were discouraging and the League could not halt the drift to World War II.

Another major attempt was made after World War II to set up an international order. On October 24, 1945, the fifty-one original members ratified the charter of the United Nations. Once again the objectives reflected civilized thinking:

To save succeeding generations from the scourge of war . . .

To reaffirm faith in fundamental human rights . . .

To establish conditions under which justice and respect for the obligations arising from treaties and other sources of international law can be maintained . . .

To promote social progress and better standards of life in larger freedom . . . .

Again there were small successes. In the age of decolonization, the United Nations was able on occasion to supervise the peaceful transition of colonial dependencies to statehood, where in the past such changes had been accompanied by guerrilla warfare and civil wars. The United Nations concluded an outer-space treaty and worked hopefully for control of pollution of the air and oceans. Most important of all, its forum provided a cooling-off place for clashing interests, for "jaw not war." It became a channel for serious international negotiation and quiet diplomacy. In the eyes of its enthusiasts it was a town meeting of the world, where admittedly a lot of time was wasted, but where much was done to maintain peace. At least, it tried to diminish nationalist ambitions while at the same time recognizing the core of values that each nation-state regarded as sacred and inviolable.

True, it engendered hopes, but the United Nations has given little cause for rejoicing. Its military arm was weak and ineffective. Recalling article XVI of the League of Nations covenant, the framers of the United Nations made provision for a military force when necessary, but there was no standing armed force. The United Nations was obliged to rely entirely on national contingents mustered in time of crisis and subject to withdrawal at any time. It had no power to control national armaments nor to enforce settlements. There could be no real foundation for peace as long as the great powers leaned to unilateral military action whenever they saw a threat to their own security.

The Security Council was immobilized by the power of veto, a major error in the original charter that nullified the ability of acting in an emergency. In the formative days at San Francisco the United States insisted upon including the veto—and then scarcely used it. The Soviet Union, also supporting the veto, has used it on more than a hundred occasions.

The General Assembly was handicapped by the influx of new nations. After the transition of African and Asian colonies to statehood, membership burgeoned to 130 countries, many of them little more than enlarged districts. Under the admissions policy, designed to provide universality, the votes of the small nations counted the same in the General Assembly as those of the larger powers. When Nauru, an 8¼-square-mile former Australian trust territory in the Pacific with 3,000 inhabitants, won statehood in 1967, it immediately applied for United Nations membership. It is an unfortunate fact that some of the new states allowed their hatreds to blind them to their obligations as members of a world organization. Under bloc voting, the mini-states could often control an important issue.

The major difficulty was the unwillingness of any nation, small or large, to relinquish even a small part of its national sovereignty to the global organization. The world is still plagued by rivalries between political ideologies as well as a gap between stated ideals and actual practice. In a 1970 speech at the

University of Chile, U Thant, Secretary-General of the United Nations, admitted it: "Although there is not a government in the world that does not profess, in its own way, to be peace-loving, it is still uncertain whether all nations have completely abandoned the state of mind that has so often led to war—the nationalistic urge to dominate and extend, by various means, their sphere of influence, and the conviction of the unquestionable superiority of their own particular traditions, forms, and way of life."

U Thant was not only defining nationalism in its dangerous form but recognizing its persistent existence. He repeated the theme on August 24, 1970, before a conference of World Federalists in Ottawa when he stated that the United Nations was undergoing a crisis of authority because too many member states used the organization to advance their own interests rather than solve world problem. "It is a crisis of commitment," he said. "Too many nations still regard the United Nations as peripheral rather than central to their foreign policies." Outmoded and unworkable concepts of national sovereignty should be scrapped, he said, if the effectiveness of the United Nations was ever to increase. "I do not criticize national pride . . . national pride is natural. I say only that the sense of belonging to the human community must now be added to and become dominant over other allegiances."

U Thant's complaint bears witness to a painful record. The United Nations did nothing about the Berlin blockade in 1948. It was silent in 1959 when Communist China appropriated Tibet, in 1967 when Egypt sent 40,000 troops and poison gas into Yemen, in the same year when a bloody civil war began in Nigeria. When the Israeli-Arab war exploded in June 1967, it was over before the members of the Security Council could finish their speeches.

Despite this sad performance, U Thant believed that the "common needs, aims, and hopes are bringing the developing countries closer and closer together at the United Nations and may well strengthen the Organization with a cohesive influence that it still greatly needs, particularly in view of the very serious, continuing differences among the great powers." He saw the future of the United Nations resting to a considerable degree with the small nations, "in their sense of responsibility, their independence, and objectivity; their dedication to the principles of the Charter; and, above all, their collective determination to help attentuate and bring an end to the dangerous tensions that have affected international relations so adversely during the last 20 years."

In 1971 U Thant resigned his office. For ten years the quiet Burmese schoolmaster had served diligently and devotedly in an almost impossible assignment. He was deeply committed to the cause of international cooperation, and surely it was not his fault that he left the world organization in considerably worse shape than he had found it—political as well as moral. For a decade he attempted to function in the poisoned international atmosphere of the sixties. He tried to intercede on behalf of peace in Southeast Asia, the Middle East, and elsewhere, but his was a weak voice crying in a jungle of conflicting nationalities. The career of U Thant provides elementary evidence of the difficulties encountered by peacemakers in the continuing age of nationalism.

It is a distressing fact that stability in the post–World War II world has been achieved not by the actions of the United Nations "as an indispensable instrument for attaining peace" but by the development of a nuclear balance of terror. Unmanageable mammoth or indispensable town-meeting-of-the-world, the United Nations has not been successful in lessening the strength of nationalism in contemporary society. The principles remain high sounding but the reality is grim as the United Nations enters its second quarter-century.

Nationalism and Regional Integration

Another challenge to nationalism was regionalism, or the organization of supranational communities on the framework of national states. Regionalism achieved a modicum of success in military and economic spheres. It attracted the attention of nations seeking security. Soviet Russia sponsored her own version of regionalism for a similar reason and as a means of countering Western moves.

It was comparatively easy to fashion military and economic integration, but there was little success in extending it into political combination. The reason is clear: neither military nor economic union means any real loss of national sovereignty. Statesmen are willing to work together for military advantage or economic gain, but they invariably stop short at the boundary of political unification on a supranational level. National integrity—yes; international integration—no!

The North Atlantic Treaty Organization (NATO) was formed in 1949 with the goal of preventing any further Russian expansion into Europe. It was designed as a countermove to Soviet Russian expansion. The Kremlin, taking advantage of the political vacuum in Eastern Europe at the close of World War II, penetrated as far west as she could. Composed of military elements from the armed forces of fifteen Western nations. NATO provides for a joint command, a common procurement system, and a unified air defense. It was, in effect, a warning to the Soviet Union that she had gone far enough. Late in 1968 Moscow was told that any intervention affecting the situation in Europe (such as interference in Rumania or Yugoslavia following the invasion of Czechoslovakia) would result in a grave crisis. In terms of diplomacy this meant: "This far, no farther!" In 1969 NATO announced its intention to establish a joint naval force in the Mediterranean in response to the Soviet buildup there.

Any estimate of NATO as a supranational organization must take into account diametrically opposed views of its value and effectiveness. To its sponsors, its very existence, no matter what its strength, acts as a brake on Soviet intentions to penetrate any available vacuum. To its critics, it is something of a bad joke. They are inclined to ask: What could NATO forces do if Moscow sent its armies on a sweep through Western Europe to the Atlantic? Nothing could be done, it is alleged with a touch of exaggeration, until appropriate resolutions were passed by Denmark's *Folketing,* Norway's *Storting,* and West Germany's *Bundestag,* as well as by the parliamentary bodies of a dozen other NATO nations—Belgium, Canada, France, Great Britain, Greece, Iceland, Italy, Luxembourg, the Netherlands, Portugal, Turkey, and the United States.

NATO was not without internal difficulties, most of which stemmed from de Gaulle's suspicions of the United States and his fear of American domination. The French strong man was engaged in a prestidigitator's feat in lifting the morale of a defeated France and grafting the mystique of *la gloire* on a second-rate power. He would train Frenchmen to lift themselves by their bootstraps. As far as NATO was concerned, he would take the initiative and raise American eyebrows in the process. Besides, he had never forgotten how Franklin D. Roosevelt had humbled him in the days when he bore the Cross of Lorraine almost alone. He withdrew French forces from NATO and forced removal of its headquarters from France. To de Gaulle there was no substitute for nationalism, nor for his own grand design of a union of European states under French leadership.

The response of the Soviet Union to NATO was the Warsaw Pact (Eastern European Mutual Assistance Treaty) between Russia and six satellites. In 1956 Moscow crushed Hungary's attempt to leave the bloc. In 1968 she led troops of all the pact members (except Rumania) into Prague, where Czech dissenters had dared to introduce a liberal regime. For the iron men of the Kremlin, any disposition to freedom inside the Warsaw Pact was the most dangerous kind of bourgeois counterrevolutionary claptrap.

Thus the regionalists of both NATO and the Warsaw Pact had their bouts with local nationalisms. NATO had to contend with de Gaulle's reversion to nineteenth-century nationalism, while at the same time the Russians had to take into account the winds of freedom stirring in Hungary and Czechoslovakia.

The Lure of Economic Union

Added to military integration is the proposal for economic union as a preliminary step to political integration. Anti-nationalist ideologists see history on their side: there is evidence that economic union generally precedes political integration. The free flow of goods, they say, is usually associated with political objectives. They point to the experience of the United States as a guideline. The founding fathers made the new country an integrated economic community with free movement of goods, labor, and capital inside its borders (see Hamilton's famous *Report on Manufactures*). This was contrary to the traditional European restrictions of high tariff barriers, quotas, and controls. American economic unity had led to the highest productivity in history. Surely, Europe would learn the lesson and undertake a similar procedure.

There were examples closer to home. The *Zollverein*, the customs union proposed by Friedrich List and appropriated somewhat brusquely by Prussia, was a critical step along the road of German unification. Perhaps European economic union would lead one day to the goal of a United States of Europe.

A shaky Europe was still in the process of recovery from the pounding of World War II when in 1952 the European Coal and Steel Community (ECSC) was created. Conceived by two French statesmen, Foreign Minister Robert Schuman and Jean Monnet, the ECSC had a twofold purpose: to bring about a reconciliation between France and Germany and to forge the basis of European political union. It would maintain a common market for coal, iron ore, and steel, harmonize external tariffs, and abolish discriminatory pricing systems. "Our Community," said Monnet, "is not an association of producers of steel and coal. It is the beginning of Europe."

Eurocrats were impressed. Had not advances in technology and communication eased the way to international cooperation? Reconstruction called for combined efforts. The old nation-state system, with its high trade barriers, was inadequate for the new age. On to economic union!

In 1958 a group of foreign ministers, led by Belgium's Paul-Henri Spaak and Holland's Johan Willem Beyen, created the European Economic Community (EEC), designed to fuse West Germany, France, Italy, Belgium, the Netherlands, and Luxembourg, with their 175 million people, into an economic unit in which goods, labor, and capital would circulate freely. The purpose was to abolish all internal tariffs and other trade barriers and to align external tariffs. "We are all aware," said Spaak joyfully, "of living in a great day in the history of Europe."

There was deep interest in Moscow. The Communist answer to the EEC was the formation of the Eastern European Council for Mutual Economic Assistance (CEMA), organized in 1956 for the integration of the Communist realm based on "a socialist division of labor," "a world socialist economy," and a polycentric authority in Moscow. (There was silence in Peking.) The Central American Common Market (CACM) and the Latin American Free Trade Association (LAFTA) similarly organized members in a loose economic confederation. These communities also believed that industrialization could proceed more rapidly in regional areas under special agreements. Asian economic union was delayed by interminable territorial disputes.

Originally, the British refused to join the Common Market on the ground that membership was incompatible with its Commonwealth ties. But later they feared the loss of their markets to the Inner Six. In 1960 the British combined with Austria, Norway, Portugal, Sweden, and Switzerland to form the European Free Trade Association (EFTA) with similar goals of tariff reductions and an increase of trade among its 90 million people. Sometimes called the Outer Seven, EFTA aimed at a lesser degree of economic integration than the rival bloc. It was originally organized, however, with a view toward eventual association with the Common Market. Generally, it was less of an economic success.

Disturbed by her gloomy trade position, Britain in 1965 applied for Common Market membership, only to be vetoed by France. To the stiff-necked de Gaulle the whole thing was simple: if there had to be a united Europe, economic or political, it had to accept French leadership.

The situation changed after the death of de Gaulle. Conservative Prime Minister Edward Heath, the most European oriented of Britain's leaders since Winston Churchill, supported his country's entrance into Europe. There was substantial opposition due to the Englishman's traditional insular distrust of all things Continental. Britons did not want to see their way of life transformed and they especially feared any loss of national sovereignty. Anthony Burgess described the fear: "England is to be absorbed, her own distinctive character sordined, and the end of a great Empire is completed in the bastardization of a great empire-building nation." In a Louis Harris poll taken in 1971, only 30 percent of Britons favored the Common Market while 49 percent were opposed. But in early November 1971, by a wide margin of 356 votes to 244 in the House of Commons, Britain agreed to join the Common Market effective January 1, 1973.

Eurocrats hailed this decision as on a par with Magna Carta, the defeat of the Spanish Armada, and Waterloo. The 82-year-old Jean Monnet, "Father of the Common Market," watched the vote from the gallery of the House of Commons and commented: "This is what I have been waiting for during the last 25 years. Now it is the turn of the youth of Europe." Chancellor Willy

Brandt of West Germany was almost as enthusiastic: "It is a great day for Europe." On the cliffs of Dover happy celebrants lit a bonfire to signal France that Britain was now rejoining Europe. There was no answer from the French side of the channel.

For Arnold Toynbee, who attributes many of the world's ills and much of its pain, misery, and frustration to anachronistic nationalism, the accession of the United Kingdom, Ireland, Denmark, and Norway to the six founding members of the European Community opens wide and promising horizons. Voluntary associations, he says, between sovereign states are rare enough to be historic, especially in Western Europe. The Community exceeds all previous voluntary European unions. The combined territories of the six were approximately coextensive with Charlemagne's and Napoleon's empires, both of which were put together by conquest "and, for this reason, were ephemeral." In contrast, the European Community "is a spontaneous association based on equality, and it therefore has good prospects of enduring." While the Community collectively does not yet mean the end of nationalism, in Toynbee's estimation it is destined to play an important role on the world's stage, "since no individual member has the capacity to conduct the full scale of operations required in a global society." The achievement, in his view, augured well for the future of the struggle against nationalism.

Yet, within a year the fanfare that accompanied economic enlargement of the European Community was transformed into dissonant chaos. In the face of Europe's cascading economic problems—inflation, the oil crisis, payments deficits, declining growth rates, extreme social discontent, and rising unemployment—European governments engaged in depressing recriminations. The French continued to deal with the Community as if it were a French colony. The Germans criticized the French for floating the franc and seeking to underprice German exports. The British resented German monetary policies. All European governments vied with one another in attempting to win special bilateral deals with the Middle East oil producers. There was much lip service about "transferring sovereignty" from national governments to the Common Market's Council of Ministers.

Enthusiasm for the Common Market waned. After the Labor Party triumph at the polls in the elections of October 1974, Prime Minister Harold Wilson called for a national referendum on whether or not Britain should remain in the Common Market. The political assumption was that, if Conservative Prime Minister Edward Heath had led the country into the Common Market with little improvement in the nation's economy, then the Labor Government might well escort it out of the European economic community.

The hoped-for transition from economic to political unity did not take place. Rolf Dahrendorf, one of nine EEC commissioners, admitted that the organization "is incapable of recovering the broad political vision of its founders." The hoped-for giant step for mankind will come only when economic union is transformed into political integrations. Does the political urge for union match the economic drive?

The United States of Europe

Do not, say the Eurocrats, look to the nationalism of the nineteenth century as a model for the new supernationalism of the year 2000. Rock-ribbed nationalism, they say, is the villain of European history, the devilish force that has contributed fuel to two global conflicts and has been responsible for the economic stagnation that bred Marxist and Fascist ideologies. That type of nationalism (as distinguished from the proper emotion of patriotism) has outlived its usefulness and has now become outmoded in civilized society. So say the Eurocrats.

The Eurocrats grant that the European idea, historically speaking, has never been fully applied. Excepting its existence as a part of the Roman Empire and for a brief time under Charlemagne, Europe was never physically one. Yet the urge for union, while varying in intensity, has never disappeared. Struggles for unity have invariably been self-destructive. Eurocrats have now reached a point where they feel unity to be necessary. They are confident that history is on their side.

Advocates of European unity point to the experience of Europe's "daughter," the United States, which found a proper balance between federal and states' rights and unified a vast area. It survived sectionalism in a fratricidal war. And it emerged from secular isolation in 1917 and again in 1941 to rescue her parent from defeat. The nation-states of Europe, too, say the Eurocrats, must learn this lesson and unite in a similar system. Frenchmen, Italians, Germans, Britons—all should no longer regard themselves as narrow nationalists but as citizens of the United States of Europe.

So argued a host of supporters for the European idea, from Count Coudenhove-Kalergi, founder of the European Parliamentary Union, to Eugen Kogen, organizer of the European Union of Federalists. Early stimulus came from two French statesmen, Aristide Briand and Edouard Herriot. In late 1929 Briand circulated to twenty-seven European governments a memorandum calling for European federation. Herriot, a member of the French Committee, became a traveling salesman for a unified Europe. "Public opinion," he said, "is ready to welcome an idea so generous and so full of promise for the future of Europe." Together with Coudenhove-Kalergi, he set out on a lecture tour, Coudenhove-Kalergi speaking in German and Herriot in French.

Briand's memorandum drew twenty-six replies, all approving "in principle." The memorandum stated clearly: "It is on the plane of absolute sovereignty and of entire political independence that the understanding between European nations must be brought about." Despite this assurance, there was an immediate controversy about the meaning of "sovereignty." Most statesmen who responded used such phrases as "national and historical considerations" in qualifying their attitude. Only the Netherlands appeared to be willing even to think about a limitation of sovereignty: "Clearly, however, this work of coordination cannot be successful unless States are ready to limit the exercise of their sovereign rights to some extent—as, indeed, they have already done by signing the Covenant of the League of Nations. A conception of sovereignty leaving no place for the voluntary acceptance of certain limitations of the powers of State should, in Her Majesty's Government's opinion, be ruled out as incompatible with the essential nature of international relations."

At a conference held in Geneva on September 8, 1930, Briand's proposal met with such strong opposition that on one occasion he closed his brief case and declared that he believed it useless to continue. Apparently the time was unsatisfactory in view of a combination of global economic depression, British isolation, and French occupation of the Rhineland. In 1932 Herriot resigned from the movement in a protest against Coudenhove-Kalergi's assertion that in order to achieve European unity Germany's right to rearm could not be denied. The entire proposal for European unity collapsed on Hitler's rise to power in early 1933: there was no room on the European stage for both Eurocrats and Nazis.

After Hitler's suicide the project for Europe was revived. Winston Churchill, who as His Majesty's chief minister had refused to preside over the liquidation of the British Empire, used his eloquent voice on its behalf. In November 1948 he opened a United Europe exhibition with a speech in which he discussed the constitutional form that a United Europe should take. "It may, of course, be argued," he said, "that a purely deliberative Assembly should develop into an irresponsible talking-shop, that it would be better to leave the work of European unification to be achieved through intergovernmental negotiation. This is not true. The Assembly will perform an essential task and one which cannot be performed by governments; the task of creating a European public opinion and sense of solidarity among the peoples of Europe."

Meanwhile the movement was endorsed by such respected statesmen as Belgian Foreign Minister Paul-Henri Spaak, French Foreign Minister Robert Schuman, Italian Premier Alcide de Gasperi, and German Chancellor Konrad Adenauer. All called for action to break down the bonds of nationalism. Most were vague on matters of procedure, but to Spaak it was simple:

"Progress toward integration could be achieved only by a new supranational authority previously exercised by the governments of individual states." Europeans, he said, must abandon the idea of national sovereignty. They must be willing not only to elect a European parliament but to accept its decisions.

The strongest voice was that of France's Jean Monnet. Convinced that a decisive breakthrough had already been made, he argued energetically for his vision. He saw a future Europe whose nations would be bound together by common interests, including economic and monetary policies, political institutions, and common defense and foreign affairs. It would not be exactly like the United States of America, which had emerged out of a somewhat different tradition. The people of the thirteen colonies spoke the same language and were ruled by the same system of law imported from the mother country. "I believe," said Monnet, "that the individual states in a united Europe will retain their own educational systems, cultural institutions, local criminal laws, and so on." But they would adopt a similar form of federalism that had worked so well across the Atlantic.

Monnet saw Europe as composed of proud and ancient nations, which clashed frequently in commerce and war. Somehow they had come to recognize the need for fusing a large measure of sovereignty in common European institutions. "The nations of Europe were always fighting against one another. The curse was the spirit of domination. France wanted to dominate. Germany wanted to dominate. The notion of equality is basic to peace. Nations must accept this notion. Our plan would have accomplished nothing if it hadn't had at its foundation the notion of equality."

Questioned as to whether Europe would unite "in time," Monnet replied that the key factor was necessity. "Union among men is not natural. Necessity is always required." He remained enthusiastic: "Nothing like it has ever been done before. The process of united European action may stumble at times, but it is forging ahead."

The structure was already there. In May 1948 some 750 European statesmen met at The Hague to set up a European Assembly. A year later the Council of Europe was formed, with its headquarters at Strasbourg. The purpose: "To protect human rights, bring European countries closer together, and voice the views of the European public on the main political and economic questions of the day." Provision was made for a Parliament, a quasi-legislative body, a staff of governmental representatives recruited from the national bureacracies, and an independent judiciary to arbitrate legal conflicts between national states.

The organization was impressive and the speeches were eloquent. The Eurocrats argued that the "melting" of national economies would eventually lead to political fusions. There was no intention, it was argued, of swallowing nation-states and turning them into provinces of a new superstate. On the contrary, all that was desired was to start a continuous process of unification while moving at a most cautious pace. The framework would be loose: each nation would preserve all that it considered necessary while increasing its influence in the European union.

A united Europe would thus fulfill its real destiny and would avoid lapsing gradually into sheer provincialism or satellization. "The European Idea," said Sir Gladwyn Jebb, "[is] the glorious conception of the United States of Europe—a new type of unity, an example to the rest of the world, a great hope for peace."

These were powerful arguments, but what about the nationalist counterthesis? The European idea did not allay the suspicions of those geared to the old nationalism. Opponents dismissed the Eurocrats as impractical idealists. No one was going to approve the dissolution of his homeland. Granted—nationalism in its arrogant form was evil, but the day was not yet at hand for the transfer of national rule to the Strasbourg Assembly.

The nationalist counterthesis was represented by the formidable figure of General de Gaulle. Preoccupied by the possible loss of national identity, de Gaulle opposed the European idea. If France was to be merged in a Greater Europe, he believed, the foundation stone would be threatened and the entire structure would collapse. Convinced that he himself was France, de Gaulle regarded himself as the old nation-state talking. He would never accept any limitation on national sovereignty from outside France. The nation-state was rooted in the sixteenth century and it would retain its independence. Knowing his countrymen well, he appealed to the old and powerful instinct of "historic nationalism." Frenchmen must look out for themselves, for no one else would do it. There was still relevance in the old saying that God Himself acts through the Franks—"*Gesta Dei per Francos.*" If there had to be European unity, let it be a "Gaullo-centric system" equating de Gaulle and France, a *Europe des États* which would be actually a "Greater France." As long as de Gaulle lived, he remained an obstacle to a viable United States of Europe.

De Gaulle was not alone in advocating the nationalist counterthesis. Others agreed that the nation-state could not possibly allow the slightest derogation of its right to do what it wanted to do. This conception is engrained in the minds of the majority of people in Western Europe (where the idea of the nation-state originated). They regard the nation-state as having had a long and splendid history. How could a Europe of totally independent states possibly function? What is the means of arriving at a common will among diversified peoples? Obligation to a European parliament would be intolerable because it violates the principle that, in the last resort, the will of an individual nation cannot be overruled except by force. For many citizens it was a clear-cut question: Shall I send my son out to die for the cause of Europe at the behest of foreigners?

The motive behind this thinking is obviously fear. The peoples of separate nations in Europe still feel it necessary to be in command of their own destiny. They do not want to be members of a European Community that might affect their own territorial integrity as well as their own distinctive national character. The fear instinct may be irrational, but it is there and it continues to hold a terrible primacy.

The matter of European unity always boils down to the issue of sovereignty—the heart of nationalism. As early as 1930 Léon Blum stated it succinctly in *Le Populaire:* "There is an insurmountable contradiction between the solemnly proclaimed intention to unite the states of Europe by a federal bond and the equally solemn engagement to preserve the national sovereignty." An additional paradox may be added: Is it possible that nations struggle to become sovereign states in order to surrender that sovereignty? Can one expect the succession states of Eastern Europe, still tasting the wine of independence, to relinquish voluntarily even a small part of that sovereignty they had worked so long to achieve?

In summary, the evidence shows that the goal of a united Europe, what its proponents call a "confederal structure," remains a fragile dream. National interests continue to dominate the European scene, in politics, in monetary affairs, and even in oil policy. There is much idealistic talk of the virtues of continental union but there is little will to move forward to political union. There is little agreement on what form a United States of Europe should take. The concept of national egoism remains much stronger than the desire to relinquish sovereignty in favor of union. The dream of European unity remains beautiful, the reality cold.

18

The Continuing Dilemma

For the moment it would seem that the bawling demands of nationalism are louder than ever, and while the leaders of the world talk incessantly about cooperation, consultation and the common problems of a distracted world, each grabs what he can for himself and his own people, and the whole machinery of time works blindly on, in disregard of the humble and the poor, and the *realpolitik* and the steam-roller advance of organized force not only prevail but, as Herbert Butterfield puts it, actually seems "to be blessed with the final favor of heaven."

—James Reston
The New York Times, Dec. 19, 1971

Farewell to the Nation-State?

The questions are critical for our times. Is nationalism receding or does it remain the linchpin of world society? Is nationalism archaic, unnecessary, and disappearing in favor of a growing internationalism? As always in human affairs, there are diametrically opposed opinions.

The argument on the pro side is familiar. The reasoning starts with a generalization: historical movements from their genesis have always had within themselves the seeds of their own destruction. Thus the nation-state and the nationalism that provides its cement are both undergoing changes in a new era of sophisticated technology and worldwide intercommunication. Nationalism, antiquated and obsolete, has outlived its usefulness. It has revealed in a hundred different ways its inadequacy to solve the problems of peace, poverty, and human misery. Like other historical phenomena, nationalism may seem on the surface to be as powerful as it has been in the past, but actually it is in the process of being superseded.

Let us break down the arguments of the pro side into component parts.

1. **Politically, the nation-state has lost its raison d'être.**   Far from meeting the crises of this planet's social order, the nation-state has compounded them because of its close affinity with militarism and violence. The modern nation-state was conceived originally as a means to assure security for a people with a sense of national consciousness who agree to act together to maintain their territorial independence. For several centuries it has played an important historical role in providing safety against the outsider—the foreigner. At the same time it was a generating factor of wars that have cost tremendous damage in life and property. The nation-state system provided few solutions for the problems plaguing mankind.

This argument has become increasingly popular among political scientists concerned with the concept of national sovereignty. They see a softening of the old hard shell of territorial and psychological boundaries. They attribute such environmental changes to two causes: the development of modern techniques and the consequences of economic and psychological factors. The rising interdependence of peoples, they say, is fundamental to contemporary political life—and unavoidable. They assert that all over the world the idea of the political nation is liable to be less and less persuasive in the face of increasing need for, and trends toward, international integration.

2. **Contemporary nation-states find it more and more difficult to distinguish between domestic and foreign policies.**   In the earlier days of nationalism, foreign policy was differentiated ordinarily from local and domestic matters, but now, with interpenetration and interdependence, national societies have

become permeated with the external environment. Under such an impulse, domestic and foreign policies tend to merge and to become dependent upon one another. The result is a heightened sense of international consciousness.

3. **The nation-state is no longer able to cope with the new problems of the current age.** The pro argument holds that if civilization is to endure on this earth its citizens must eventually contend with such critical problems as ecology, the pollution of the air, earth, and waterways, air travel, the production of food, communicable diseases—in short, the housekeeping of the globe. Such problems have been and are being attacked on the national level, but they cannot be solved exclusively by national effort.

4. **In today's nuclear age the nation-state can no longer protect its citizens.** Moreover, say the critics, nationalism is an ineffective political concept at a time when no government, large or small, can defend its people against nuclear attack. The reality of nuclear power has undermined the fundamental basis of the authority of the nation-state.

5. **The moral judgment of history is opposed to nationalism.** Here the critics of nationalism interpose a moral judgment. Philosophers and historians, they say, have long known that nations, like individuals, must face, in the long run, the consequences of their acts. In scientific terms, every force creates a counterforce, and herein lies the weakness of nationalism. It seems to work for a while by sheer utilization of power. But there is still a moral law of compensation in the world, and the moral judgment of history applies to the nation as well as the individual.

6. **Superimposed on political failure is the bankruptcy of economic nationalism.** The more powerful nation-states owe their higher standard of living to a set of economic relationships that tend to keep the smaller countries in relative poverty. When such affluent nations as the United States, West Germany, or Japan seek to promote economic well-being among the undeveloped or underdeveloped nations, they run the risk of dislocating their own domestic economies. Moreover, the old day of gunboat diplomacy, when the flag protected the national corporation, is finished. Now multinational corporations, always on the lookout for profits, find it financially attractive to cooperate with private international organizations.

7. **The trend fusing nationalism and internationalism is worldwide.** Nationalism is being submerged in a rising internationalism. The process is working at such a rate that the traditional elements separating nations from one

another—geographical, political, economic, legal, and psychological—are becoming increasingly thin, and in reality are in the process of dissolution.

The argument holds that large and small nations, both the old and the new, are becoming accustomed to the growing internationalism. Far from retreating into isolation after World War II, the United States felt compelled to encourage the recovery of Western Europe. Added to a measure of altruism in American foreign aid was a realistic policy of survival and security. There was, indeed, a cutback in foreign aid in November 1971, due to domestic economic difficulties, and further cuts were threatened in 1975, but—significantly—the program itself was not abandoned. A similar motivation may be discerned in the Soviet Union's penetration into any area where a political vacuum occurred or where there was an opportunity for Russian influence. After a dozen years of revolutionary glory, Fidel Castro became more and more dependent on the Russians, who furnished 95 percent of Cuba's oil and spare parts for her sugar refineries. Moscow provided at least a million dollars a day to keep the wheels turning in Cuban industry.

If further evidence be needed, the advocates of increasing internationalism speak of the United Nations force in the Congo and American involvement in Vietnam as proof of how strongly the domestic allocation of values has become affected by the international environment. Everywhere, they say, statesmen and politicians now find themselves thinking in terms far beyond the traditional constitutional structure of their nations. There are new international obligations under regional military agreements or economic communities. The result is that national goals tend to coincide more and more with international integration.

8. There is an indefinable psychological trend toward a new world order. Proponents insist that there is a clear psychological urge toward some kind of international organization, even though they cannot as yet define it. James Reston of *The New York Times* observes how, in a flurry of diplomacy, nations head for a new world order:

In the words of an old song, they don't know where they are going but they are on their way.

Seldom in recent years has there been so much diplomatic activity, most of it clearly directed at influencing the course of the trend. . . .

While nothing fundamental has been changed, while there are ugly and dangerous confrontations . . . and while monetary and trade relations are out of balance, it is clear that the nations are in movement again toward some new relationship. . . .

Nobody is saying that we are on the verge of a new world order, but the idea seems to be getting around that even the most influential nations cannot always do what they like without unacceptable risks. . . .

The nations are becoming a little less interested in settling their disputes by force of arms and a little more interested in cooperating in limited fields because it is in their selfish interests to do so.

They have to cooperate in fields of world aviation, health, communications, environmental pollution, trade, finance and drugs, for example, to avoid damage to their own people.

That is the reality that is very slowly making its way in the world as the capacity for mutual destruction increases. The philosophers have known it for generations and even centuries but there is now quite a lot of evidence around that governments are gradually adjusting to it.

They are finding changes painful, as always, and the old suspicions are not easily removed, but the process toward a different kind of world has started.[1]

The Phenomenon of Transnationalism

Those who challenge the centuries-old convention of distinct territorial units like to speak of nationalism as an outdated paradigm. A hopeful note for the future is projected by Lewis Mumford. To reach human stature, he says, at the present stage of development, each of us must be ready, as opportunity offers, to assimilate the contributions of other cultures. Those who belong exclusively to a single nation without any touch from the world beyond are not yet "full men." "Archaic man, civilized man, axial man, mechanized man, achieved only a partial development of human potentialities; and though much of their work is still viable and useful as a basis for man's future development, no more quarrying of stones from their now-dilapidated structures will provide material for building the fabric of world culture."[2]

In the place of nationalism, say the advocates of major change, is appearing, slowly but surely, a transnational or multinational network of business and industrial enterprises which operate above and below visible nation-state controls. Governments throughout the world, they contend, are losing their traditional influence over the transnational flow of people, money, and ideas. At the same time, great corporations, already quasi-governmental, have stepped in to allocate resources and privileges across the old national boundaries. Nationalism, they are certain, is being undermined by the new transnationalism.

The trend is seen as inevitable. Conglomerate multinational enterprises, such as IBM, IT&T, and Unilever, have assets larger than at least half the members of the United Nations. The annual profits of a multinational business firm such as General Motors exceeds the value of the gross national product (GNP) of most independent African states. Multinational enterprises control clusters of corporations of different nationalities, joined together by the parent company. Each is a part of a powerful, largely private transnational oligarchy which deals only at the top level with agencies of national governments. On occasion these huge transnational corporations may work to frustrate policies either of the home government or a host government for a corporation subsidiary. They are able to take advantage of high-speed communications and transportation services, as well as the economic magic of an instantaneous transfer of capital from one country to another.

Those who forecast the doom of nationalism in the next three decades say that even relatively wealthy countries can be subjected to the economic strength of conglomerates transcending the national image. Some even see a world in which a few hundred giant corporations will be responsible for a large percentage of world production. Following the lead of the giant multinational corporation, large advertising agencies and banks have been lured into transnational activity. Even labor unions in the West have turned to the problem of enhancing their bargaining position vis-à-vis enterprises organized multinationally. In self-defense against the giant corporations, labor has had to modify its image.

In summary, on the one side transnational enterprises are seen as potentially important forces for regional integration and eventually for global political integration. The multinational thrust is in process of bringing an end to middle-class society and the dominance of the nation-state. In the long run, such enterprises pose a threat to the old idea of national sovereignty. The transformation process of the multinational corporate phenomenon is irresistibly under way, and should accelerate in the remaining two and a half decades of the twentieth century. Expressed in historical terms, the phenomenon heralds the end of nationalism.

On the other side are those observers, among whom the present writer counts himself, who decline to become overly enthusiastic about the erosion of the state-centered paradigm of national sovereignty. Granted that there is growing awareness of the importance of multinational enterprises, the question is still open as to which is the more durable of the two institutions. First of all, the thrust of transnationalism remains economic. The experience of the Common Market is enlightening: members graciously accept the benefits of economic union, but they invariably freeze at the merest prospect of political union. In the same way, transnational oligarchies think primarily in terms of profit and not necessarily of political union. Power realties of world politics remain in the firm grasp of national states. Moreover, and this is a key factor, the international corporation always succumbs to nationalism.

Transnationalism has generated no popular movement to compare with the past and with the current psychological drives of nationalism and its corollary chauvinism and jingoism. The chances are that today those who feel their security to be at stake will turn to arms to defend the blessed fatherland. It is too much to expect them to serve in a mighty transnational army to defend the interests of Ford, Olivetti, or Shell Oil. Because transnational airlines in cooperation with governments control the prices of travel between countries does not mean that British and American airlines are ready to merge under one flag.

Granted that transnationalism is creating a new interdependence based on expanding economic intercourse in the contemporary world, it is unwise to exaggerate its effectiveness. It is possible that transnational enterprise, instead of bringing peace and justice, may actually increase economic conflict on a global scale. In pursuit of its objectives, the multinational firm encounters a fundamental obstacle in nationalism and in the structure of the nation-state. If anything, nationalistic resistance to outsiders is aroused by the activities of multinational enterprises. Business may become internationalized, but not the political order.

Whatever the prospects, the fact remains that transnationalism has not effectively decreased the vigor of persistent nationalism.

The Power of Parochial Consciousness

In contrast to optimistic views of the trend toward a world order is a belief in the continuing strength of nationalism. Those holding this attitude are not convinced that nationalism is disappearing or lessening in impact. They see an unbroken continuum. In an interview in late October 1971, Walter Lippmann, when asked about the survival of the contemporary state, replied: "For as long as we can see there will be large nation-states, and they will exist without being able to dominate other states."

The argument is clear-cut. If nationalism is in decline, it remains a fabulously strong invalid. What Burke once called "the moral essence" of nationality has become even more powerful than it has been in the past. The reality is that the system of nation-states remains essentially the same as it was in the last two hundred years. Certainly there have been changes of permeation and interdependence, but nationalism persists as the psychological binding force of contemporary peoples. It retains its vigor among the old established states and the newly emergent countries. After 1918 the political map was remade along national lines; after 1945 the process was extended on a worldwide basis. The earlier nationalism, dominantly European, became global. Far from weakening, nationalism has acted as an accelerating force in the efforts of the new nations to catch up with the older and more industrialized countries.

The crucial test is that people everywhere still regard nationalism as high in the totality of their experience. They continue to use the stereotypes and clichés associated with nationalism. They still make inexact, erroneous, or equivocal use of such terms as "nation," "nationality," "national character," and "patriotism." The patriot, whether in Milwaukee, Manchester, or

Moscow, continues to judge his own nationalism as good and desirable, that of others as bad and aggressive. His love of country is a many-splendored thing; that of others he dismisses as chauvinism and jingoism. "For me nationalism is a blessing; yours is obviously a curse."

For a time during the period of student demonstrations, it seemed that the younger generation was in rebellion against the symbols of nationalism. But those who rejected loyalty to the nation turned out to be a minority of dissenters. More, they tended to polarize sentiment to the point where their actions were regarded as a supreme insult to national welfare. These two news reports indicate the trend of reactions:

FACING THE MUSIC

LIMA, July 31 [1971] (Reuter)—Two young men who stayed in their seats when the Peruvian national anthem was played in a cinema on Peru's Independence Day were sentenced to a day in jail for "failure to respect patriotic symbols."

FLAG RIPPER
MENDS IN JAIL

WASHINGTON, Oct. 27 [1971] (UPI)—The United States Court of Appeals has ruled that a Virginia teenager must serve a 60-day sentence because he ripped a hole in a 6-inch American flag and wrapped it around his finger in a V-sign.

In a 2–1 decision yesterday, the court upheld the conviction of Thomas Wayne Joyce, 19, of Richmond, who had been found guilty of desecrating the flag on Jan. 20, 1969, the day of President Nixon's inauguration.

Judge George Mackinnon spiced his majority decision with five pages of sayings and legends about the American flag and added, "A little American flag is entitled to the same protection as a large one."

There is little doubt that similar incidents have taken place in all countries which jealously guard their national sovereignty—from Italy to Israel. The argument for retained nationalism holds for any nation. There may be local peculiarities, but the generating force of nationalism is always present. As evidence let us look for a moment at Brazil.

In contemporary Brazil a military-led populism appeals directly to nationalism. The sense of Brazilian national consciousness is boosted, even more than by any political ideology, by the game of football (American soccer). More than any other single factor, football helped to unite the huge, sprawling country, whose people seemed to resist national integration. Illiterate peasants in the hinterlands, who owned transistor radios, became one with the city slickers in fanatical support for the national team.

Introduced by the English into Brazil in the late nineteenth century, football became a national passion. With a flair for the game, Brazilians became outstanding in international competition, winning World Cup victories in 1958 and 1962. The entire nation became football crazy, hysterical in victory, crushed in defeat.

To Brazilian fans the national image is associated with football superiority. The regime was quick to adopt as its theme song a swinging, foot-tapping tune, *"P'ra frente Brasil!"* (Forward Brazil!), which is played at presidential reviews and other official occasions and endlessly repeated on radio and television. Slogans are taken seriously: *"Ninguem segura mais o Brasil!"* (No one will any longer hold back Brazil!) and *"Brasil conta comigo!"* (Brazil, Count on me!). Until his recent retirement, Edson Arantes do Nascimento, better known as Pelé and regarded as the greatest football player in sports history, was depicted in huge posters plastered all over the country. Hundreds of thousands celebrated wildly in the streets on news of a Pelé triumph. *"Rei Pelé"* (King Pelé) became a success symbol for every Brazilian kicking a homemade football on the street.

This display of Latin American temperament in sports madness is by no means unique. Others, also known as sophisticated peoples, have celebrated sports victories with similar outbursts of joy, and in much the same way have confused national prestige with triumphs in sports events.

The power of parochial consciousness is admitted even by those who see change in human affairs. Karl W. Deutsch, in considering nationalism and its alternatives, suggests that the whole thrust of the technological development of our time moves beyond wars and beyond the economic fences of nation-states. "It seems to push toward a pluralistic world of limited international law, limited, but growing, international cooperation, and regional pluralistic security communities. In a few favored regions these may even give place to regional federations, but this will be a slow development."[3] Such developments, in Deutsch's estimation, may get us through the valley of the shadow of death, and may preserve us, individuals and nations, for the next three or four decades, in which nuclear war is all too possible.

The key words in Deutsch's analysis are the "slow development" of possible alternatives to nationalism. That is, indeed, the fact. As a dedicated student of nationalism, Deutsch realizes that, despite recurrent predictions about its end or its coming sublimation, nationalism remains one of the strongest political and emotional forces of our time. On the surface, it may seem to have been made obsolete by the new technology, but actually it shows a surprising vigor and a perhaps still growing power. Deutsch would like to see beyond nationalism, but wherever he looks the possible substitute phenomena—internationalism of varying kinds—remain weak and ineffective. Thus the optimism expressed by Deutsch fades as he joins the rest of us pessimists who do not yet see across the political horizon a brave new world free from the bonds of a regressive nationalism.

Battle of the Isms: Nationalism Triumphant

To those disillusioned with such isms as communism, socialism, capitalism, fascism—all seem to be irrelevant in the face of rampant nationalism. In confrontation with other isms, nationalism has proved to be the more resilient historical movement. The sense of national identity retains its vigor as the twentieth century reaches its final quarter. Western imperialism, Soviet communism, and American influence take second place to the dynamism of nationalism.

Here, again, we see one of the many paradoxes surrounding nationalism. Imperialism itself was an expression of aggresive nationalism, yet nationalism in its liberating form was the deciding factor in the rejection of imperialism. European colonialism was grounded on the assumption that the backward natives, unable to govern themselves, would receive fair and just treatment from their foreign overlords. Imperial masters kept a rigid eye on the main goal, profits, but at the same time regarded themselves as benevolent paternalists who were bringing the blessings of civilization, efficient administration, and security to childlike natives unable to govern themselves. They looked on local liberators "with their veneer of Western culture" as false representatives of the people.

Liberating rebels made good use of national consciousness in throwing off the chains of imperialism. Colonial peoples, becoming more aware of themselves, refused to be subordinated any longer to outsiders. They much preferred to be governed by their own kind than by foreign administrators, no matter how efficient. They respected European progress, but they were not quite convinced about the superiority of Western civilization, the virtues of democracy, workable government, humane laws, and better education. Leaders for independence hammered away at the notion: We accept all your evidences of superiority, but we prefer self-government with all its dangers to servitude in tranquillity. Tom Mboya of Kenya put it bluntly: "Europeans, scram out of Africa!"

Two forms of nationalism were in collision—European aggressive nationalism and a localized liberating nationalism. One begat the other: the seeds scattered from Europe took firm root in African and Asian soil and grew into a resistant variety. European colonialists managed unconsciously to arouse a host of clamoring nationalisms. They never dreamed that they would see this proliferation of nationalisms in subjugated territories. The trend called for a recasting of the world structure.

A second major ism, communism, was made partly irrelevant by the new nationalism. After World War II it was widely believed that the new nations would move through nationalism in the direction of communism. To devoted Marxists it was a revolutionary certainty: the exploited masses everywhere, having nothing to lose but their chains, would unite at long last and overthrow the minions of capitalism. Thus would be fulfilled the prophecies of that gospel originating at an obscure desk in the British Museum in the late 1840s.

History has a curious way of reacting to either the *mission civilisatrice* of capitalist bankers or to the paper-perfect solutions of Bloomsbury radicals—it pays little attention. Karl Marx, for all his genius, was so absorbed by his discovery of class interests that he underestimated the human propensity for loyalty to the soil. Individuals everywhere are more certain of their territory—they walk on it and live on it—than of their class. Class interests can be ephemeral; but one can see and feel the land. To put it simply, nationalism in practice exerts a greater appeal than communism. Nationalism, comparatively the dominant ism, remains the mainspring of mass action. The point merits emphasis: both socialism and communism only make it when identified with nationalism.

The trend toward an older form of nationalism may be observed both inside and outside the Soviet Union. Current reports indicate that more and more Russians, their spirit crushed by the drabness of their lives, are turning to the past in revising the great historical experiences that form the stuff of nationalism. Churches are restored, ruined monasteries are rebuilt, and "psychological writers," including Dostoevsky, Turgenev, and Gogol, are brought back into fashion. Actually, this reassertion of the older form of Russian nationalism is close to that nineteenth-century concept proclaiming all things Slavic as superior to anything European. Edward Kennan, soviet-ologist at the Russian Research Institute at Harvard University, calls it "a conservative and anti-industrial movement that has enormous affinity for the old days, for peasants, for things unspoiled by politics." Most noteworthy of all, it is not Marxist in scope.

Indeed, there are those who wonder what (save rhetorically) the U.S.S.R. has to do with communism at all. From their point of view, the Soviet Union is, and always has been since its inception in 1917, a self-perpetuating elite's dictatorship and has never followed the path of Marx and Engels. This argument regards the current Soviet nationalism as merely another version of an already established Russian nationalism.

For orthodox Marxist ideologists in the Kremlin the consistent display of nationalism in Communist societies, both outside and inside the Soviet Union, has proved to be most embarrassing. In a kind of desperate reaction, they chose Nicolae Ceausescu, leader of the Rumanian Communist Party and regarded as the most loyal of Leninist-Stalinist followers, to make a doctrinal issue of the matter. In a report presented to the National Conference of the Rumanian Communist Party on July 19, 1972, Ceausescu denied that the nation is historically obsolete or that it is opposed to socialist internationalism. "With respect to the national problem in socialist conditions, we have to say that the victory of the new society has opened the way to achieving true national unity, to strengthening and developing the nation on a new basis. . . . Between national and international interests not only is there no contradiction, but on the contrary, there is full dialectical unity." This kind of mental acrobatics requires no comment from nationalism watchers.

If there has been a realignment of nationalism inside Russia, it may be compared with the ascendancy of nationalism over communism throughout the world. Marxian socialism did have an impact on the postwar world—almost everywhere socialist regimes were organized in the developing nations; but in the last three decades three countries have gone the whole Communist way. Nationalist movements in China and North Vietnam were headed by Communists who eventually took over control. Cuba's Fidel Castro, calling himself originally an agrarian reformer, led a successful revolution, and then after his triumph pushed his country into the Communist orbit. These were three victories for the cause of communism, but they scarcely meant world control for Moscow. In all three cases communism took a second place to nationalism.

The hoped-for monolithic unity directed from the Kremlin disintegrated primarily because it could not withstand the kinetic energy of nationalism. Virtually all the small nations within the Soviet sphere of influence dream of a revived national sovereignty. They still look for a synthesis of nationalism, socialism, and democracy in the European rather than in the Russian sense. Their status may be uncertain, but it is clear that they are unwilling to submerge their sovereignty as a sacrifice for the goal of world communism.

There are varying patterns inside the Soviet orbit, but everywhere the dominant factor is national consciousness. Five states enjoy complete sovereignty—two democratic states, Finland and Austria, and three Communist states, Yugoslavia, Rumania, and Albania. Finland is bound to the Soviet Union by a treaty of alliance; democratic Austria is neutral. Of the Communist states, Tito's Yugoslavia follows its own road to socialism; Rumania has regained her independence but remains a Communist state of the Soviet type; and Albania has turned to Chinese Maoism. Poland, Hungary, and Czechoslovakia, despite their yearning for freedom, have felt the discouraging weight of Russian tanks. For the Kremlin it is a dangerous loyalty at best.

The growing sense of détente is a concomitant of nationalistic yearnings. East European states now in the Soviet orbit may be expected to seek means to counter the threat of Moscow's intervention. The new Soviet empire is by no means a well-constructed edifice.

The undeveloped nations of the Third World, hoping to avoid entrapment in the cold war, are equally affected by that sense of national consciousness so obvious in the Communist sphere. They resist both sides—Soviet expansionism and American influence. But these Third World nations, despite common goals, find themselves unable or unwilling to act together. Afro-Asian states put on a show of unity in the halls of the United Nations, but they do not function well as a bloc or unit. Each nation, no matter what its size, is jealous of its sovereignty and does not intend to sacrifice even a small portion of its independence for the promised advantages of international cooperation. For such nations the nationalism responsible for the balkanization of Europe is essential to assure what they regard as freedom of decision and action. For them, too, nationalism has won the battle of the isms.

Late Signal: The Greening of Bangladesh

From millions of throats came the cry *"Jai Banglai! Jai Banglai!"* (Victory to Bengal! Victory to Bengal!) as Pakistan's eastern wing broke away to form a new nation. In the streets of Dacca tens of thousands danced deliriously and sang "My Golden Bengal!" In countless villages the green, red, and gold banner of Bengal was brought out from secret hiding places. Amid such celebrations was Bangladesh born in mid-December 1971. Historians were presented with a rare case of a mini-nationalism impelling the birth of a nation.

The rejoicing began again a month later when Sheikh Mujibur Rahman, called *Bangabandhu* (Friend of Bengal), was flown back to Dacca on a Royal Air Force Comet to receive a tumultuous welcome in an outpouring of public affection by huge crowds. The national hero, after having served nine months in a West Pakistani prison, was unexpectedly freed by Pakistan's new President Zulfikar Ali Bhutto, successor to General Agha Muhammad Yahya Khan. The 51-year-old Mujibur Rahman, leader of the independence movement, was touched with that fiery charisma familiar to observers of nationalism. He gave vent to his feelings in emotional tones:

I did not actually hear a radio or read a paper until December 27 [1971], although I had met Bhutto. But I knew, I understood what had been happening in my country even during my months in solitary confinement. You see, I know my people. I knew my forces. I know my organizational leadership; I knew my student front, and I knew they were fighting every inch of the way. I sensed what was happening all those months, though I was alone with nothing to do but think. I always knew my people were behind me. I knew that God would help me. I knew, too, that in the war between falsehood and truth, falsehood wins the first battle and truth the last. That's what kept me going. I never wept during all those months in solitary confinement. I never wept when they put me on trial. But I wept when I arrived back here and saw my wonderful *sonar Bangla* [golden Bengal].

Bangladesh, the object of Mujibur affection, comprises an area of 143,000 square miles in what formerly was East Pakistan. It ranks eighth among the world's 140 nations in terms of population (78 million). Despite Bhutto's efforts to cut down its international position, Bangladesh emerged as a sovereign state. Mujibur's goal was clear: "Ours will be a secular, democratic socialist state." As President, a post to which he had been appointed while he was still in a West Pakistani prison, he announced a provisional government, set up parliamentary forms, and brought his own Swami League loyalists into positions of power. His foreign policy was to obtain diplomatic recognition for his fledgling country. He called for membership in the United Nations and for aid in rebuilding the shattered economy. He knew well that the political stability of Bangladesh depended upon how well he could solve its economic dilemma (the per capita annual income was about $24). He knew also that the task was a heartbreaking one: continued poverty and hunger could lead to chaos, anarchy, and attacks by extremist factions on his government. The new nation was dealt a crippling blow by the great famine of 1974-1975.

The birth of Bangladesh reveals the continuing appeal of nationalism. It came as a shock to those who feel that in this age of intercommunication nationalism is receding. The crowds of Dacca, reacting in the traditional way, proved that the historical movement is far from its death throes.

At the same time, the greening of Bangladesh illustrates the potency of nationalism as both a unifying and disruptive force. Pakistan was set up in 1947 as a separate British dominion, carved out of British India as a Muslim homeland. West Pakistan, with its forest-clad mountains, was separated from East Pakistan, with its river valleys and extensive deltas, by 1,100 miles of Indian territory. Islam, the state religion and the faith of 80 percent of its inhabitants, was considered to be the unifying factor of Pakistan. The unity was symbolized by a flag of dark green with a white vertical stripe at the hoist and a white crescent with a five-pointed star in the center. With the flag was the Pakistani national anthem, "Blessed be the Sacred Land."

For a time the widely separated parts of Pakistan were united by a common hatred for Hindu India and rivalry over Kashmir, whose predominantly Muslim population was ruled by a Hindu prince sympathetic to India. But these common interests began to be threatened by disintegrative factors. Religious unity was strong but not quite as powerful as the sentiment of regional particularism. A contributory element was the tendency of the autocratic Muslims of West Pakistan to exploit their Muslim brothers in the east. In December 1970 Pakistan's first free nationwide elections resulted in an overwhelming mandate for Sheikh Mujibur Rahman. Angered, Yahya Khan sent West Pakistani troops to the east to reverse the mandate. The brutal behavior of these soldiers aroused worldwide indignation. The situation soon degenerated into nightmare: nearly a million Bangalis were slaughtered; 10 million refugees streamed across the border from March to November 1971 to seek safety in India.

Unable to absorb the tide of refugees (the cost was $700 million, of which about $250 million was contributed by foreign governments), India sought a way out. There were cries for war from both Islamabad and New Delhi. When Indian and Pakistani forces clashed, the United Nations attempted to stop the conflict. The Security Council was made helpless by Soviet Russia's veto, whereupon the General Assembly called for a cease-fire by an overwhelming vote of 104 to 11. The representatives of India, who had long irritated United Nations members by their lectures on "the moral duty of nations," paid no attention. The Soviet Union, which had repeatedly denounced Israel for its failure to heed United Nations resolutions, also turned away from the new appeal for peace.

The two-week war stimulated Indian nationalism. At its close, Prime Minister Indira Gandhi announced to both houses of the Indian Parliament that India would be the first to recognize Bangladesh. The members cheered Mrs. Gandhi's oratory: "The valiant struggle of the people of Bangladesh in the face of tremendous odds has opened a new chapter of heroism in the history of freedom movements. The whole world is now aware that Bangladesh reflects the will of an overwhelming majority of the people, which not many governments can claim to represent."

Every phase of the Bangladesh story reflects the power of nationalism in action—the precedence of national over religious ties, the growth of regional separatism, the role of a charismatic leader, Yahya Khan's frenzied attempts to maintain unity, Bangali joy in the creation of the new nation, the Bangladesh symbols of flag and nation, and the quick metamorphosis of "peace-loving India" implementing its national aspirations. It is a classic example of how nationalism retains its grip in our contemporary world.

The greening of Bangladesh is by no means a unique story. The successful creation of a new nation stimulated mini-nationalisms everywhere—from the Basques in Spain to the Kurds in Iraq. Several million Kurds in the Mideast have fought for independence successively but not successfully against Turkish, Iranian, Russian, and British rule, and now against Iraq. The Baghdad regime, under President Ahmed Hassan al-Bakr refuses a negotiated agreement with rebellious Kurds. The Kurds, under their leader Mulla Mustafa al-Barzani, accuse the regime in Baghdad of being under Russian influence and urge Washington to consider the large Kurdish population in Kirkuk, the site of Iraq's major oil fields. Here, too, the goals of a mini-nationalism win the attention of the larger nationalisms.

Notes

[1] *The New York Times*, September 9, 1971.

[2] Lewis Mumford, *The Transformations of Man*, World Perspectives series (New York: Harper, 1956), 7:247.

[3] Karl W. Deutsch, *Nationalism and Its Alternatives* (New York: Knopf, 1969), p. 190.

19 The Skirts of Nationalism

World government is possible. It is possible in our lifetime. We can and we will make it happen, and by so doing we shall achieve peace not only for our children but for our children's children, a peace that will survive to the end of time. . . . Those who wrap the skirts of nationalism around themselves are living in the dangerous past, and we cannot be satisfied with that because it has produced our present.

—Cord Meyer, Jr.
The New York Times Magazine, Jan. 7, 1973

The Apogee of Nationalism

Astrologers are refreshingly certain about their special gift for divining the future. Unfortunately, social scientists cannot boast of any similar ability to predict historical trends. As for the future of nationalism, anything might happen. It could go on *ad infinitum* as an accepted mode of socio-political behavior. In its aggressive form, it will most certainly make for further conflict between peoples. It might be moderated to the point where its cultural attributes would outweigh its capacity for political mischief. The nation-state might disappear altogether as the sovereign unit in world society and be replaced by some kind of viable organization. Perhaps Arnold Toynbee might be right in his prognosis: "The world is going to be united politically in the teeth of nationalistic resistance."

No nationalism watcher—including Toynbee—has any foolproof answers. All of us can agree with Toynbee in recognizing the familiar symptoms of potential catastrophe all around us. We know that nationalism has been the ruin of one civilization after another, that loyalty to the nation-state produces international conflicts, and that these become intolerable. We know that we are living in a high stage of nationalism with the earth divided into 136 nations. We know that science and technology have become global, spanning national frontiers. We can agree with Toynbee that the centrifugal tendency on the political plane runs directly counter to the centripetal tendency on the technological plane. And we know that of these conflicting forces, Toynbee expects technology to triumph over nationalism. But what we know most of all is that Toynbee, like the rest of us, has the capacity for being mistaken.

Whatever happens to nationalism, one thing is certain: like any other ideology it is subject to the process of historical evolution. As early as the fifth century B.C., pre-Socratic cosmologist Heraclitus of Ephesus recognized that, while the world is eternal, it is always in change. Everything flows; nothing abides. ("You cannot bathe twice in the same stream.") That includes nationalism, which is quite as resilient as any other ism. Its structure may remain the same, but its form may change even drastically.

In our comparative study we have seen this process at work. In the Western world the unified Christian commonwealth of the Middle Ages was succeeded by a system of nation-states. Early nationalism was libertarian, only to lose its original impulse and become integral in the nineteenth and twentieth centuries. Nationalism helped churn up the storm of 1914–1918 and it was a contributory factor to the resultant disintegration of mighty empires. It was the motivating force in the postwar treaties that lifted small, clamoring nationalities to the plane of sovereign statehood. It spurred the ambitions of Fascist dictators who talked *Lebensraum* and it was the generating force of the desperate opposition to them in World War II. After 1945 a host of new nations appeared on the world stage as the remaining old empires either declined or disappeared.

The new nationalism had a different complexion: the face was transformed but the body remained the same. It spread everywhere, thereby multiplying its capacity for mischief. The new nations, no longer living in dread of Western imperialism, began to be gripped by fear of one another's nationalism.

The sentiment is ubiquitous: while working on the new nations, it still retains its hold on the superpowers. The Kremlin uses force inside the Soviet Union to keep Ukrainians and other nationalities in line, while at the same time it smashes down efforts by Eastern European satellites to express their own sense of independence. The United States faces increasing political dissent inside its borders but there is little evidence to show that Washington is abandoning nationalism as a sovereign fact in American life.

The peril of xenophobic nationalism is proved, but it continues to exist everywhere. It is taken over in part by the revolutionary left, seeking to attain its goals through guerrilla warfare in the streets. It enshrouds itself in the mantle of Robin Hood, as witness the activism of the IRA in Northern Ireland, the FLQ in Quebec, the Basques in Spain, the Tupumaros in Latin America, and the Black Panthers in the United States. All regard themselves as warriors in the cause of national regeneration. Regarding the establishment as archaic, this new brand of liberating nationalists far too often shows little regard for the decencies of civilized behavior. For "the cause" they kidnap ambassadors, consuls, and businessmen, hold them as hostages against the release of jailed comrades, and on occasion execute their prisoners in retaliation, vengeance, or warning. They expect entrance into the history books as "nationalist liberators" on the ground that nationalism can excuse any kind of behavior.

Carlton J. H. Hayes called nationalism a blessing or a curse. As a blessing, it is close to the ideals of liberal internationalism—dedicated to peace, freedom, and security. This kind of nationalism makes for "the institutionalization of decency."

As a curse, nationalism is a philosophy of despair, a weapon for discord, confrontation, and war. There is nothing attractive about this form. Appealing to the emotions, it is not subject to rational argument. Tinged with exclusivity, it fears and hates the outsider while glorifying the patriot. Intolerant, it allows no dissent: it regards the traitor as the worst heretic of all. Too much of it remains a curse in contemporary society.

What can reasonable men do to facilitate the remodeling of nationalism? First is the necessity to purge it of its archaic contents. This requires recognition of past errors and a sensitivity to reform. The prognosis is not good. The human animal has revealed an infinite capacity for creative work, but he has been sadly deficient in the task of fashioning a workable social order.

Perhaps the answer may be found in youth, in Toynbee's words "the first human beings who have become citizens of the world besides being citizens of their respective countries." Perhaps the young, with their zeal and energy, will find a new kind of national consciousness free from the old flaws.[1] They may be the ones to realize that we live in a world dominated by new systems of technology and intercommunication and that we have outlived that kind of nationalism designed to cope with relatively simple societies on their way to industrialization. Youths might understand that no nation can be self-contained and sovereign in a world where all must work together for the common good. And they may be the ones prepared to sacrifice what have hitherto been considered eternal values.

It is painful to end on a pessimistic note. Despite the optimism of youth, there are few signs that a meaningful remodeling of nationalism is on the way. The reluctant conclusion must be made that nationalism (either capitalist or socialist) will persist into the foreseeable future. At this time the answer to the critical question What follows nationalism? must be—Still nationalism! Eurocrats and internationalists may argue otherwise, but the road to internationalism still lies through the rocky ground of nationalism. That seductive historical force—divisive, chaotic, anarchic—the cause of much trouble in the past—may present a slightly altered face, but it still retains its capacity for mischief. It is a sad fact that nationalism continues to work for the dehumanizing of mankind.

In a very real sense, the whole framework of nationalism falls within what may be called the sin of mystification, in which a rational approach to the problems of mankind is forsaken. Nationalism has proved to be stronger than any other ism, and even at this moment is responsible for dividing mankind into opposing groups separated by a highly emotional historical force. Perhaps the prejudices associated with nationalism will vanish as new generations reassess the old values which place flag and national anthem above all other loyalties. Perhaps not.

The terrifying power of nuclear weapons makes it certain that the nation-state is no longer able to provide security for its citizens. Today the capacity for destruction is so great that there exists a real possibility that the human race might be annihilated in a nuclear holocaust, leaving nothing but a burned-out, charred planet. It would seem best to start rethinking the problem of nationalism and what it means for life on this earth.

Notes

[1] Thomas Lee Hayes, chaplain to the several hundred men who make up the American deserter community in Sweden, reported that among the exile community there was a distinct challenge to nationalism and a commitment to a transnational experience. "While they remain Americans, they become *de facto* internationalists." One of the young Americans, Rick Bailey, spoke on Swedish radio: "We want to get away from the extreme nationalism and ideologies of both East and West." Sympathetic to their cause, Hayes added: "The notion of absolute nationalism, the premise on which such charges of un-Americanism rest, is so wanting in common-sense, not to say enlightened self-interest, that it is remarkable to see the hold it has on people. Without condition, the concept of absolute sovereignty—in the nation and in individuals—is the greatest enemy of world peace today." Thomas Lee Hayes, *American Deserters in Sweden* (New York: Association Press, 1971), pp. 163–64.

How much this attitude has penetrated into the main streets of the United States is problematical: no sociological survey as yet has measured the sentiment of American youth on loyalty to the symbols of nationalism.

Bibliography
and Recommended
Reading

Ten Basic Books on Nationalism

1. Baron, S. W. *Modern Nationalism and Religion*. New York: Harper, 1947.
2. Carr, E. H. *Nationalism and After*. New York: Macmillan, 1945.
3. Deutsch, K. W. *Nationalism and Social Communication: An Inquiry into the Foundations of Nationality*. New York: Wiley, 1953.
4. Doob, L. W. *Patriotism and Nationalism: Their Psychological Foundations*. New Haven: Yale University Press, 1964.
5. Hayes, C. J. H. *The Historical Evolution of Modern Nationalism*. New York: R. R. Smith, 1931.
6. Hertz, F. O. *Nationality in History and Politics*. New York: Oxford University Press, 1944.
7. Kohn, H. *The Idea of Nationalism*. New York: Macmillan, 1944.
8. Royal Institute of International Affairs. *Nationalism*. London: Oxford University Press, 1939.
9. Shafer, B. C. *Faces of Nationalism*. New York: Harcourt Brace Jovanovich, 1972.
10. Znaniecki, F. *Modern Nationalities: A Sociological Study*. Urbana: University of Illinois Press, 1952.

Bibliography

Acton, J. E. E. D. *Essays on Freedom and Power*. Boston: Beacon Press, 1948.
Ahmed, J. M. *The Intellectual Origins of Egyptian Nationalism*. London: Oxford University Press, 1960.
Akzin, B., et al. *La nationalité dans la science sociale et dans le droit contemporaine*. Paris: Sirey, 1933.
——. *State and Nation*. London: Hutchinson, 1964.
Alba, V. *Nationalism without Nations*. New York: Praeger, 1968.
Allport, G. W. *The Nature of Prejudice*. Cambridge, Mass.: Addison-Wesley, 1954.
Anderson, E. N. *Nationalism and the Cultural Crisis in Prussia, 1806–1815*. New York: Rinehart, 1939.
Antonius, G. *The Arab Awakening*. London: Hamish Hamilton, 1938.
Apter, D. E. *The Political Kingdom in Uganda: A Study in Bureaucratic Nationalism*. Princeton: Princeton University Press, 1961.
Ardrey, R. *The Territorial Imperative*. New York: Atheneum, 1966.

Arendt, H. *The Origins of Totalitarianism*. New York: Harcourt, Brace, 1951.

Armstrong, J. A. *Ukrainian Nationalism*. New York: Columbia University Press, 1963.

Assac, P. P. d'. *Manifeste nationaliste*. Paris: Plon, 1972.

Astesano, E. *Nacionalisme historico o materialismo historico*. Buenos Aires: Editorial Pleamer, 1972.

Aulard, A. *Le patriotisme française*. Paris: Chiron, 1916.

Bagehot, W. *Physics and Politics, or Thoughts on the Application of the Principles of "Natural Selection" and "Inheritance" to Political Society*. New York: Appleton, 1881.

Bailey, S. L. (ed.). *Nationalism in Latin America*. New York: Knopf, 1971.

Balandier, G. "Messianism and Nationalism in Black Africa," in *Africa: Social Problems of Change and Conflict*. Ed. P. L. Van den Bergh. San Francisco: Chandler, 1965.

Ball, W. M. *Nationalism and Communism in Eastern Asia*. 2d ed. Melbourne: Melbourne University Press, 1956.

Banfield, E. C. *The Moral Bases of a Backward Society*. New York: Free Press, 1958.

Barclay, G. St. J. *Twentieth Century Nationalism*. London: Weidenfeld and Nicolson, 1971.

Barghoorn, F. C. *Soviet Russian Nationalism*. New York: Oxford University Press, 1956.

Barker, E. *National Character and the Factors in Its Formation*. London: Methuen, 1927.

Barr, S. *Mazzini: Portrait of an Exile*. New York: Holt, 1935.

Barrès, M. *Scènes et doctrines du nationalisme*. Paris: Plon-Nourrit, 1925.

———. *The Undying Spirit of France*. New Haven, Conn.: Yale University Press, 1917.

Barzun, J. *The French Race: Theories of Its Origins and Their Social and Political Implications Prior to the Revolution*. New York: Columbia University Press, 1932.

———. *Race: A Study in Modern Superstition*. New York: Harcourt, Brace, 1937.

Bason, C. H. *A Study of the Homeland and Civilization in the Elementary Schools of Germany*. New York: Columbia University Press, 1937.

Bauer, O. *Die Nationalitäten Frage und die Sozialdemokratie*. Vienna: Volksbuchhandlung, 1924.

Bay, C., et al. *Nationalism: A Study of Identification with People and Power*. Oslo: Institute for Social Research, 1950.

Benedict, R. *The Chrysanthemum and the Sword: Patterns of Japanese Culture*. Boston: Houghton Mifflin, 1946.

Berelson, B., and Steiner, G. A. *Human Behavior*. New York: Harcourt, Brace & World, 1964.

Berger, M. *The Arab World Today*. Garden City, N.Y.: Doubleday, 1962.

Binkley, R. C. *Realism and Nationalism, 1852–1871*. New York: Harper, 1935.

Black, C. E. *The Dynamics of Modernization*. New York: Harper & Row, 1966.

Blum, R. (ed.). *Cultural Affairs and Foreign Relations*. Englewood Cliffs, N.J.: Prentice-Hall, 1963.

Bluntschi, J. K. *Theory of the State*. Oxford: Clarendon Press, 1887.

Boas, F. *Anthropology and Modern Life*. New York: Norton, 1932.

Borkenau, F. *Socialism, National or International*. London: Routledge, 1942.

Bossenbrook, W. J. (ed.). *Mid-Twentieth Century Nationalism*. Detroit: Wayne State University Press, 1965.

Boveri, M. *Treason in the Twentieth Century*. New York: Putnam, 1963.

Braunthal, J. *The Paradox of Nationalism: An Epilogue to the Nuremberg Trials*. London: St. Bodolph, 1946.

Brogan, D. W. *The American Character*. New York: Knopf, 1944.

Brown, D. M. *Nationalism in Japan*. Berkeley: University of California Press, 1955.

Brownell, W. C. *French Traits: An Essay in Comparative Criticism*. New York: Chautauqua Press, 1896.

Bryce, J. *Race Sentiment as a Factor in History*. London: University of London Press, 1915.

Buchanan, W. and Cantril, H. *How Nations See Each Other*. Urbana: University of Illinois Press, 1953.

Burns, E. B. *Nationalism in Brazil: A Historical Survey*. New York: Praeger, 1968.

Burr, R. (ed.). *Latin-American Nationalistic Revolutions*. Philadelphia: American Academy of Political and Social Science, 1961.

Buthman, W. C. *The Rise of Integral Nationalism in France*. New York: Columbia University Press, 1939.

Cantril, H. *The Psychology of Social Movements*. New York: Wiley, 1941.

Cantril, H., and Strunk, M. *Public Opinion, 1935–1946*. Princeton, N.J.: Princeton University Press, 1951.

Carter, G. *Independence for Africa*. New York: Praeger, 1960.

———. *The Politics of Inequality: South Africa since 1948*. London: Thomas and Hudson, 1959.

Chaconas, S. G. *Adamantios Korais: A Study in Greek Nationalism*. New York: Columbia University Press, 1942.

Chadwick, H. M. *The Nationalities of Europe and the Growth of National Ideologies*. Cambridge, Eng.: Cambridge University Press, 1945.

Chamberlain, H. S. *The Foundations of the Nineteenth Century*. Trans. J. Lees. 2 vols. London: John Lane, 1913.

Chenu, M. le B. *La ligue des patriotes*. Paris: Sirey, 1916.

Chong, S. L. *The Politics of Korean Nationalism*. Berkeley: University of California Press, 1963.

Clarkson, J. D. " 'Big Jim' Larkin: A Footnote to Nationalism," in *Nationalism and Internationalism*. Ed. E. M. Earle. New York: Columbia University Press, 1950.

Clough, S. B. *A History of the Flemish Movement in Belgium: A Study in Nationalism*. New York: R. R. Smith, 1930.

———. *France: A History of National Economics, 1789–1939*. New York: Scribner, 1939.

Cobban, A. *National Self-Determination*. London: Oxford University Press, 1945.

Coberly, J. *The Growth of Nationalism in American Literature*. Washington, D.C.: George Washington University Press, 1950.

Cohen, L. J. *The Principle of World Citizenship*. Oxford: Basil Blackwell, 1954.

Cohn, N. *The Pursuit of the Millennium*. New York: Harper, 1961.

Cole, C. W. *The Beginnings of Literary Nationalism in America*. Washington, D.C.: George Washington University Press, 1939.

Coleman, J. S. *Nigeria: Background to Nationalism*. Berkeley: University of California Press, 1960.

Commager, H. S. *The American Mind: An Interpretation of American Thought and Character since the 1880s*. New Haven, Conn.: Yale University Press, 1950.

Cottam, R. W. *Nationalism in Iran*. Pittsburgh: University of Pittsburgh Press, 1964.

Count, E. W. (ed.). *This Is Race: An Anthology Selected from the International Literature of the Races of Man*. New York: Schuman, 1950.

Coupland, R. *Welsh and Scottish Nationalism: A Study*. London: Collins, 1954.

Cramb, J. A. *The Origins and Destiny of Imperial Britain and Nineteenth Century Europe*. New York: Dutton, 1915.

Craven, A. *The Growth of Southern Nationalism, 1848–1861*. Baton Rouge: Louisiana State University Press, 1953.

Curti, M. E. *Probing Our Past*. New York: Harper, 1955.

———. *The Roots of American Loyalty*. New York: Columbia University Press, 1946.

Curtius, E. R. *Maurice Barrès und die geistigen Grundlagen des französischen Nationalismus*. Bonn: F. Cohen, 1921.

Dahl, R. A. *A Preface to Democratic Theory*. Chicago: University of Chicago Press, 1961.

Davidson, D. *The Attack on Leviathan: Regionalism and Nationalism in the United States*. Chapel Hill: University of North Carolina Press, 1938.

Definition and Classification of Minorities. Lake Success, N.Y.: United Nations Commission on Human Rights, 1950.

Delaisi, F. *Political Myths and Economic Realities*. New York: Viking, 1927.

Delos, J. T. *La nation*, vol. 1, *Sociologie de la nation*, vol. 2, *Le nationalisme, et l'ordre de droit*. Montreal: Editions de l'Arbre, 1944.

Demiashkievich, M. *The National Mind: English, French, German*. New York: American Book Co., 1938.

Desai, A. R. *Social Background of Indian Nationalism*. Bombay: Popular Book Depot, 1959.

Deutsch, K. W. *Nationalism and Social Communication: An Inquiry into the Foundations of Nationality*. Cambridge, Mass.: M.I.T. Press, 1966.

———. *An Interdisciplinary Bibliography on Nationalism, 1933–1955*. Cambridge, Mass.: Technology Press, 1956.

———. *Nationalism and Its Alternatives*. New York: Knopf, 1969.

———. *Political Community at the International Level*. New York: Doubleday, 1954.

Deutsch, K. E., and Poltz, W. J. (eds.). *Nation-Building*. New York: Atherton, 1963.

Dilke, C. *Greater Britain: A Record of Travel in English-speaking Countries during 1866 and 1867*. New York: Harper, 1869.

Dimier, L. *Le nationalisme littéraire et ses méfaits chez la français*. Paris: Correa, 1935.

Dingwall, E. J. *Racial Pride and Prejudice*. London: Watts, 1946.

Dominian, L. *The Frontiers of Language and Nationality in Europe*. New York: Holt, 1917.

Doob, L. *Patriotism and Nationalism: Their Psychological Foundations*. New Haven: Yale University Press, 1964.

Drinkwater, J. *Patriotism in Literature*. London: Williams and Norgate, 1924.

DuBois, W. E. B. *The World and Africa*. New York: Viking, 1947.

Duffy, J., and Manners, R. A. *Africa Speaks*. Princeton: Van Nostrand, 1961.

Duijker, H. C., and Frijjda, N. H. *National Character and National Stereotypes: A Trend Report Prepared by the International Union of Scientific Psychology*. Amsterdam: North-Holland Publishing Co., 1960.

Durbin, E. F. M., and Bowley, J. *Personal Aggressiveness and War*. New York: Columbia University Press, 1938.

Eagan, J. M. *Maximilien Robespierre, Nationalist Dictator*. New York: Columbia University Press, 1938.

Earle, E. M. (ed.). *Nationalism and Internationalism: Essays Inscribed to Carlton J. H. Hayes*. New York: Columbia University Press, 1950.

Easton, S. C. *The Rise and Fall of Western Colonialism: A Historical Survey from the Early Nineteenth Century to the Present*. New York: Praeger, 1964.

————. *The Twilight of European Colonialism: A Political Analysis*. New York: Holt, 1960.

Eban, A. *The Tide of Nationalism*. New York: Horizon Press, 1959.

Embree, J. F. *The Japanese*. Washington, D.C.: Smithsonian Institution, 1943.

Emerson, R. *From Empire to Nation: The Rise of Self-Assertion of Asian and African Peoples*. Cambridge, Mass.: Harvard University Press, 1960.

————. "The Progress of Nationalism," in *Nationalism and Progress in Free Asia*. Ed. P. W. Thayer. Baltimore: Johns Hopkins Press, 1956.

Emerson, R., et al. *Government and Nationalism in Southeast Asia*. New York: Institute of Pacific Relations, 1942.

Engelbrecht, H. C. *Johann Gottlieb Fichte: A Study of His Writings with Special Reference to His Nationalism*. New York: Columbia University Press, 1931.

————. *Revolt against War*. New York: Dodd, Mead, 1937.

Essien-Udom, E. U. *Black Nationalism: A Search for an Identity in America*. Chicago: University of Chicago Press, 1962.

Eulau, H. *The Behavioral Persuasion in Politics*. New York: Random House, 1963.

Eysenck, H. J. *The Psychology of Politics*. London: Routledge and Kegan Paul, 1954.

Ezcurra, Medrano A. *Catolicismo y nacionalismo*. Buenos Aires: Adsum, 1939.

Falnes, O. J. *National Romanticism in Norway*. New York: Columbia University Press, 1933.

Farmer, W. R. *Maccabees, Zealots, and Josephus: An Inquiry into Jewish Nationalism in the Greco-Roman Period*. New York: Columbia University Press, 1956.

Featherstone, H. L. *A Century of Nationalism*. London: Nelson, 1939.

Feit, E. *South Africa: The Dynamics of the African National Congress*. London: Oxford University Press, 1962.

Fels, J. *Begriff und Wesen der Nation: eine soziologische Untersuchung und Kritik*. Münster: Aschendorffsche Verlagsbuchhandlung, 1927.

Fichte, J. G. *Addresses to the German Nation*. Trans. R. F. Jones and G. H. Turnbull. Chicago: Open Court Publishing Co., 1922.

Figgis, D. *AE (George W. Russell): A Study of a Man and a Nation*. Dublin: Maunsel, 1916.

Foltz, W. J. *From French West Africa to the Mali Confederation*. New Haven: Yale University Press, 1965.

Fouillée, A. *Psychologie du peuple français*. Paris: Alcan, 1898.

Franck, T. M. *Race and Nationalism: The Struggle for Power in Rhodesia-Nyasaland*. New York: Fordham University Press, 1960.

Friedmann, W. *The Crisis of the National State*. London: Macmillan, 1945.

Friedrich, C. J. "Nation Building?" in *Nation Building*. Ed. K. W. Deutsch and W. J. Foltz. New York: Atherton, 1963.

————. *The Age of the Baroque, 1610–1660*. New York: Harper, 1952.

Fröhlich, D. *Nationalismus und Nationalstaat in Entwicklungsländern: Afghanistan*. Meisenheim: Hain, 1970.

Fyfe, H. *The Illusion of National Character*. London: C. A. Watts, 1940.

Gardner, E. G. *The National Idea in Italian Literature*. Manchester: Manchester University Press, 1921.

Gaus, J. *Great Britain: A Study of Civic Loyalty*. Chicago: University of Chicago Press, 1929.

Gershoy, L. *From Despotism to Revolution, 1763–1789*. New York: Harper, 1944.

Gerth, H., and Mills, C. W. *Character and Social Structure*. New York: Harcourt, 1953.

Gewehr, W. M. *The Rise of Nationalism in the Balkans, 1800–1930*. New York: Holt, 1931.

Gibbons, H. A. *Nationalism and Internationalism*. New York: Stokes, 1930.

Ginsberg, M. "National Character and National Sentiment," in *Psychology and Modern Problems*. Ed. J. A. Hadfield. New York: Longmans, Green, 1936.

———. *Reason and Unreason in Society*. Cambridge, Mass.: Harvard University Press, 1948.

Giradet, R. (ed.). *Le nationalisme français, 1871–1914*. Paris: Colin, 1966.

Glauert, E. T. "The Cultural Nationalism of Ricardo Rojas." Ph.D. dissertation, University of Pennsylvania, 1962.

Glyn, A. *The British: Portrait of a People*. New York: Putnam, 1970.

Gooch, G. P. *Nationalism*. New York: Harcourt, Brace and Howe, 1920.

Gorer, G. "National Character: Theory and Practice," in *The Study of Culture at a Distance*. Ed. Margaret Mead and Rhoda Métraux. Chicago: University of Chicago Press, 1953.

———. *The American People: A Study in National Character*. New York: Norton, 1948.

Green, A. S. *Irish Nationality*. New York: Holt, 1911.

Gross, F. *European Ideologies*. New York: Philosophical Library, 1948.

Groth, A. *Major Ideologies: An Interpretive Survey of Democracy, Socialism, and Nationalism*. New York: Wiley, 1971.

Grunebaum, G. E. von. *Modern Islam: The Search for Cultural Identity*. Berkeley: University of California Press, 1962.

Gyorgy, A., and Blackwood, G. D. *Ideologies in World Affairs*. Waltham, Mass.: Blaisdell, 1967.

Hahn, L. *North Africa: Nationalism to Nationhood*. Washington, D.C.: Public Affairs Press, 1960.

Haim, S. G. (ed.). *Arab Nationalism: An Anthology*. Berkeley: University of California Press, 1962.

Hall, C. H. *Patriotism and National Defense*. New York: Society for Political Education, 1885.

Halstead, J. P. *Rebirth of a Nation: The Origins and Rise of Moroccan Nationalism, 1912–1944*. Cambridge, Mass.: Harvard University Press, 1967.

Handelsman, M. *Rozwój narodowości nowoczesnej (The Growth of Modern Nationality)*. Warsaw, 1923–1926.

Hanham, H. J. *Scottish Nationalism*. Cambridge, Mass.: Harvard University Press, 1969.

Hankin, E. H. *Nationalism and the Communal Mind*. London: Watts, 1937.

Hapgood, N. (ed.). *Professional Patriots*. New York: Boni, 1927.

Hauser, H. *La principe des nationalités, ses origines historiques*. Paris: Alcan, 1916.

Hayashi, C. *A Study of Japanese National Character*. Tokyo: Shiseido, 1961.

Hayes, C. J. H. *Essays on Nationalism*. New York: Macmillan, 1926.

———. *France: A Nation of Patriots*. New York: Columbia University Press, 1930.

———. *A Generation of Materialism, 1871–1890*. New York: Harper, 1941.

———. *Nationalism: A Religion*. New York: Macmillan, 1960.

————. "Philosopher Turned Patriot," in *Essays in Intellectual History: Dedicated to James Harvey Robinson*. Ed. J. T. Shotwell. New York: Harper, 1929.

Hegedus, A. de. *Patriotism or Peace*. New York: Scribner, 1947.

Hegel, G. W. F. *The Philosophy of History*. Trans. J. Sibree. New York: Wiley, 1944.

Heimsath, C. H. *Indian Nationalism and Hindu Social Reform*. Princeton: Princeton University Press, 1964.

Henry, P. *Le problème des nationalités*. Paris: Colin, 1937.

Heyd, U. *Foundations of Turkish Nationalism: The Life and Teachings of Ziva Gökalp*. London: Luzac, 1950.

Higham, J. *Strangers in the Land: Patterns of Nativism*. New Brunswick: Rutgers University Press, 1955.

Hinsley, F. H. *Nationalism and the International System*. London: Hodder and Staughton, 1973.

Hobson, J. A. *The Psychology of Jingoism*. London: Grant Richards, 1901.

Hodges, D., and Abu Shanab, R. E. *NFL: National Liberation Fronts, 1960–1970*. New York: Murrow, 1972.

Hodgkin, T. *Nationalism in Colonial Africa*. London: F. Muller, 1956.

Hoffman, S. *The State of War*. New York: Praeger, 1965.

Holland, W. L. (ed.). *Asian Nationalism and the West*. New York: Macmillan, 1953.

Holtom, H. G. *Modern Japan and Shinto Nationalism*. Chicago: University of Chicago Press, 1947.

Humphrey, E. F. *Nationalism and Religion in America, 1774–1789*. Boston: Chapman, 1924.

Hunter, E. L. *A Sociological Analysis of Certain Types of Patriotism*. New York: Columbia University Press, 1932.

Huntington, E. *Mainsprings of Civilization*. New York: Wiley, 1945.

Hu Shih. *The Chinese Renaissance*. Chicago: University of Chicago Press, 1934.

Huxley, J. S. *Man Stands Alone*. New York: Harper, 1941.

Hyman, H. H. *Political Socialization*. Glencoe, Ill.: Free Press, 1959.

Hyslop, B. F. *French Nationalism in 1789 According to the General Cahiers*. New York: Columbia University Press, 1934.

Jaarsveld, F. A. van. *The Awakening of Afrikaner Nationalism, 1868–1881*. Cape Town: Human and Rousseau, 1961.

Jahn, J. *Muntu: The New African Culture*. New York: Grove Press, 1961.

James, D. H. *The Rise and Fall of the Japanese Empire*. London: Allen & Unwin, 1951.

Janowsky, O. *Nationalities and National Minorities*. New York: Columbia University Press, 1945.

Jaszi, O. *The Dissolution of the Habsburg Monarchy*. Chicago: University of Chicago Press, 1929.

Jespersen, O. *Mankind, Nation and Individual from a Linguistic Point of View*. Oslo: Aschehoug, 1925.

Johannet, R. *Le principe des nationalités*. Paris: Nouvelle Librarie Nationale, 1923.

Johnson, C. A. *Peasant Nationalism and Communist Power: The Emergence of Revolutionary China, 1937–1945*. Stanford, Calif.: Stanford University Press, 1962.

Johnson, J. J. *Political Change in Latin America*. Stanford: Stanford University Press, 1948.

Johnson, W. F. *The National Flag*. Boston: Houghton Mifflin, 1930.

Joseph, B. *Nationality: Its Nature and Problems*. New Haven: Yale University Press, 1929.

Joseph, F. M. (ed.). *As Others See Us: The United States through Foreign Eyes*. Princeton: Princeton University Press, 1959.

Judd, P. (ed.). *African Independence*. New York: Dell, 1962.

Justo, J. B. *Discursos y escritos politicos*. Buenos Aires, 1933.

Kahin, G. M. *The Asian-African Conference*. Ithaca, N.Y.: Cornell University Press, 1956.

―――. *Nationalism and Revolution in Indonesia*. Ithaca, N.Y.: Cornell University Press, 1952.

Kalijarvi, T. V. "Nationalism," in *European Ideologies*. Ed. F. Gross. New York: Philosophical Library, 1948.

Kammari, M. D. *The Development by J. V. Stalin of the Marxist-Leninist Theory of the National Question*. Moscow: Foreign Language Publishing House, 1951.

Kann, R. A. *The Multinational Empire: Nationalism and National Reform in the Habsburg Monarchy, 1848–1918*. New York: Columbia University Press, 1950. (2 vols., Octagon, 1964.)

Kardiner, A., et al. *The Psychological Frontiers of Society*. New York: Columbia University Press, 1945.

Kayser, E. L. *The Grand Social Enterprise: A Study of Jeremy Bentham in His Relation to Liberal Nationalism*. New York: Columbia University Press, 1932.

Kedourie, E. *Nationalism*. New York: Praeger, 1960.

―――. (ed.). *Nationalism in Asia and Africa*. New York and Cleveland: World Publishing Co., 1970.

Keith, A. *Nationality and Race from an Anthropologist's Point of View*. London: Oxford University Press, 1919.

―――. *The Place of Prejudice in Modern Civilization*. New York: John Day, 1931.

Kelman, H. C. (ed.). *International Behavior*. New York: Holt, Rinehart and Winston, 1966.

Kennedy, J. *Asian Nationalism in the Twentieth Century*. London: St. Martin's Press, 1968.

Kennedy, J. J. *Catholicism, Nationalism and Democracy in Argentina*. Notre Dame, Ind.: University of Notre Dame Press, 1958.

Kenyatta, J. *Facing Mount Kenya*. New York: Vintage Books, 1962.

Keohane, R. O., and Nye, J. S., Jr. (eds.). *Transnational Relations and World Politics*. Cambridge, Mass.: Harvard University Press, 1972.

Kindelberger, C. (ed.). *The International Corporation*. Cambridge, Mass.: M.I.T. Press, 1970.

King, J. C. *Some Elements of National Solidarity*. Chicago: University of Chicago Libraries, 1935.

Kinross, Lord. *Ataturk*. London: Weidenfeld and Nicolson, 1964.

Klineberg, O. *Tensions Affecting International Understanding*. New York: Social Science Research Council, 1950.

Kluckhohn, C. *Mirror for Man: The Relation of Anthropology to Modern Life*. New York: McGraw-Hill, 1949.

Kohn, H. *The Age of Nationalism: The First Era of Global History*. New York: Harper, 1962.

―――. *American Nationalism: An Interpretive Essay*. New York: Macmillan, 1967.

―――. *Force of Reason: Issues of the Twentieth Century*. Cambridge, Mass.: Harvard University Press, 1937.

―――. *The Mind of Germany: The Education of a Nation*. New York: Scribner, 1960.

————. *The Mind of Modern Russia: Political and Social Thought of Russia's Great.* New Brunswick: Rutgers University Press, 1955.

————. *Nationalism and Imperialism in the Hither East.* Trans. M. M. Green. London: Routledge, 1932.

————. *Nationalism and Liberty: The Swiss Example.* London: Allen & Unwin, 1956.

————. *Nationalism in the Soviet Union.* Trans. E. W. Dickes. London: Routledge, 1933.

————. *Nationalism: Its Meaning and History.* Princeton: Van Nostrand, 1955.

————. *Pan-Slavism: Its History and Ideology.* Notre Dame: University of Notre Dame Press, 1953.

————. *Prelude to Nation-States: The French and German Experience, 1789–1815.* Princeton: Van Nostrand, 1967.

————. *Prophets and Peoples: Studies in Nineteenth Century Nationalism.* New York: Macmillan, 1946.

————. *Revolutions and Dictatorships: Essays in Contemporary History.* Cambridge, Mass.: Harvard University Press, 1942.

————. *The Twentieth Century: A Mid-Way Account of the Western World.* New York: Macmillan, 1949.

————. *World Order in Historical Perspective.* Cambridge, Mass.: Harvard University Press, 1942.

Kohn, H., and Sokolsky, W. *African Nationalism in the Twentieth Century.* Princeton: Van Nostrand, 1965.

Kohn, H., and Walden, D. *Readings in American Nationalism.* New York: Van Nostrand–Reinhold, 1970.

Krabbe, H. *The Modern Idea of the State.* Trans. G. A. Sabine and W. J. Shepard. New York: Appleton, 1927.

Krehbiel, E. *Nationalism, War and Society.* New York: Macmillan, 1916.

Kroeber, A. L. *Anthropology: Race, Language, Culture, Psychology, Prehistory.* New York: Harcourt, Brace, 1948.

Kuhn, J., et al. *Der Nationalismus in Leben der dritten Republik.* Berlin: Paetel, 1920.

Lala, R. R. *Young India: An Interpretation and a History of the Nationalist Movement from Within.* New York: Huebsch, 1916.

Langer, W. L. *The Diplomacy of Imperialism, 1890–1902.* New York: Knopf, 1935.

Langsam, W. C. *The Napoleonic Wars and German Nationalism in Austria.* New York: Columbia University Press, 1930.

Lanternari, V. *The Religions of the Oppressed: A Study of Modern Messianic Cults.* New York: Knopf, 1963.

Laqueur, W. Z. *Communism and Nationalism in the Middle East.* London: Routledge, 1956.

Laski, H. J. *Nationalism and the Future of Civilization.* London: Watts, 1932.

Lasswell, H. D. *World Politics and Political Insecurity.* New York: McGraw-Hill, 1935.

Lasswell, H. D., and Kaplan, A. *Power and Society.* New Haven: Yale University Press, 1950.

Latourette, K. S. *The Chinese, Their History and Culture.* 3d ed. London: Macmillan, 1956.

————. *The History of Japan.* London: Macmillan, 1957.

Lattimore, O. *Nationalism and Revolution in Mongolia.* Leiden: E. J. Brill, 1955.

Lawrence, T. E. *Seven Pillars of Wisdom.* London: Penguin, 1962.

Le Bon, G. *The Psychology of Peoples.* London: T. Fisher Unwin, 1899.

Lee, C. S. *The Politics of Korean Nationalism.* Berkeley: University of California Press, 1963.

Le Fur, L. *Races, nationalités, états.* Paris: Alcan, 1922.

Legum, C. *Pan-Africanism.* New York: Praeger, 1962.

Lemberg, E. *Geschichte des Nationalismus in Europa.* Stuttgart: Schwab, 1950.

Lenin, V. *Critical Remarks on the National Question.* Moscow: Foreign Languages Publishing House, 1951.

Leroi-Gourhan, A. *Ethnologie d'union française: Afrique la Somalie française.* Paris: Pays d'Outre-mer, 1953.

Levitt, L. *Silent Surrender.* Toronto: Macmillan, 1970.

Lewin, K. *Principles of Topological Psychology.* New York: McGraw-Hill, 1936.

Lewis, B. *The Emergence of Modern Turkey.* London: Oxford University Press, 1961.

Lieber, F. *Fragments of Political Science in Nationalism and Internationalism.* New York: Scribner, 1868.

Linebarger, P. M. A. *The Political Doctrines of Sun Yat-sen.* Baltimore: Johns Hopkins University Press, 1937.

Linton, R. (ed.). *The Science of Man in the World Crisis.* New York: Columbia University Press, 1945.

———. *The Study of Man.* New York: Appleton-Century, 1936.

Lipset, S. M. *The First New Nation.* New York: Basic Books, 1963.

Locke, A., and Stern, B. J. (eds.). *When Peoples Meet: A Study in Race and Culture Contacts.* New York: Progressive Education Assn., 1942.

London, K. (ed.). *New Nations in a Divided World: The International Relations of the Afro-Asian States.* New York: Praeger, 1963.

Lovett, V. *A History of the Indian Nationalist Movement.* London: Murray, 1920.

Lowie, R. H. *The Origins of the State.* New York: Harcourt, Brace, 1927.

Macartney, C. A. *National States and National Minorities.* London: Oxford University Press, 1934.

Macdonald, R. W. *The League of Arab States.* Princeton: Princeton University Press, 1965.

Madariaga, S. *Englishmen, Frenchmen, Spaniards: An Essay in Comparative Psychology.* London: Oxford University Press, 1928.

Malik, H. *Arab Nationalism and British Imperialism.* London: Cresset Press, 1961.

Marraro, H. R. *Nationalism in Italian Education.* New York: Italian Digest and News Service, 1927.

Martindale, D. *Community Character and Civilization.* New York: Free Press of Glencoe, 1963.

——— (ed.). "National Character in the Perspective of the Social Sciences," in *Annals of the American Academy of Political and Social Science.* Philadelphia: American Academy of Political and Social Science, 1967.

———. *The Nature and Types of Sociological Theory.* Boston: Houghton Mifflin, 1960.

Masur, G. *Nationalism in Latin America: Diversity and Unity.* New York: Macmillan, 1966.

May, A. J. *The Hapsburg Monarchy, 1867–1914.* Cambridge, Mass.: Harvard University Press, 1951.

Mazzini, G., *The Duties of Man and Other Essays.* New York: Dutton, 1929.

Mboya, T. *Freedom and After.* London: André Deutsch, 1963.

McCaffrey, L. J. *The Irish Question, 1800–1922.* Lexington: University of Kentucky Press, 1968.

McDougall, W. *The American Nation.* London: Allen & Unwin, 1926.

————. *The Group Mind*. New York: Putnam, 1920.

McGiffert, M. (ed.). *The Character of Americans*. Homewood, Ill.: Dorsey Press, 1964.

Mead, M. *And Keep Your Powder Dry: An Anthropologist Looks at America*. New York: Morrow, 1943.

————. "National Character," in *Anthropology Today: An Encyclopedia Inventory*. Ed. A. L. Kroeber. Chicago: University of Chicago Press, 1953.

————. "National Character and the Science of Anthropology," in *Culture and Social Character*. Eds. S. M. Lipset and Leo Lowenthal. New York: Free Press of Glencoe, 1961.

Megaro, G. *Vittorio Alfieri: Forerunner of Italian Nationalism*. New York: Columbia University Press, 1930.

Meinecke, F. *The German Catastrophe*. Trans. S. B. Fay. Cambridge, Mass.: Harvard University Press, 1950.

————. *Die Idee der Staatsräson*. Berlin: Oldenbourg, 1928.

————. *Weltbürgertum und Nationalstaat*. Munich: Oldenbourg, 1928.

Métraux, R., and Mead, M. *Themes in French Culture*. Stanford: Stanford University Press, 1954.

Michelet, J. *Le peuple*. Paris: Didier, 1946.

Michels, R. *Der Patriotismus*. Munich: Duncker und Humboldt, 1929.

Mills, L. A., and Thompson, V. *Government and Nationalism in Southeast Asia*. New York: Institute of Pacific Relations, 1942.

Minogue, K. R. *Nationalism*. New York: Basic Books, 1967.

Mitscherlich, W. *Der Nationalismus Westeuropas*. Leipzig: Hirschfeld, 1920.

Miyakawa, C. S. *Protestants and Pioneers: Individualism and Conformity on the American Frontier*. Chicago: University of Chicago Press, 1964.

Morant, G. M. *The Races of Central Europe*. London: Allen & Unwin, 1939.

Morgenthau, H. J. *Politics among Nations: The Struggle for Power and Peace*. New York: Knopf, 1949.

————. *Truth and Power: Essays of a Decade, 1960–70*. New York: Praeger, 1962.

Morison, S. (ed.). *The American Style: Essays in Value and Performance*. New York: Harper, 1958.

Morris, J. *Pax Britannica: The Climax of an Empire*. New York: Harcourt Brace Jovanovich, 1968.

Mphahlele, E. *The African Image*. New York: Praeger, 1962.

Muir, R. *Nationalism and Internationalism: The Culmination of Modern History*. London: Constable, 1917.

Mumford, L. *The Transformations of Man*. New York: Harper, 1956.

Mussen, P. H., Conger, J. J., and Kagan, J. *Child Development and Personality*. 2d. ed. New York: Harper and Row, 1963.

Myrdal, G. *An American Dilemma*. New York: Harper, 1944.

Namier, L. B. "Pathological Nationalisms," in *The Margin of History*. London: Macmillan, 1939.

————. *1848: The Revolution of Intellectuals*. London: Oxford University Press, 1946.

————. *Vanished Supremacies: Essays on European History*. London: Hamish Hamilton, 1958.

Nasser, G. A. *Egypt Liberated: The Philosophy of the Revolution*. Washington, D.C.: Public Affairs Press, 1955.

Nanda, B. R. *Mahatma Gandhi*. London: Allen & Unwin, 1958.

Nehru, J. *An Autobiography*. London: Bodley Head, 1936–1953.

Neucherlein, D. E. *Thailand and the Struggle for South-East Asia*. Ithaca: Cornell University Press, 1965.

Nkrumah, K. *Ghana*. Edinburgh: Nelson, 1959.
———. *I Speak of Freedom*. New York: Praeger, 1961.
Noether, E. *Seeds of Italian Nationalism, 1700–1815*. New York: Columbia University Press, 1951.
Nordau, M. *The Interpretation of History*. Trans. M. A. Hamilton. London: Rebman, 1910.
Nordskogg, J. E. *Contemporary Social Reform Movements*. New York: Scribner, 1954.
Novicow, J. *L'Expansion de la nationalité française*. Paris: Colin, 1903.
Nu, T. (U Nu). *Burma under the Japanese*. London: Macmillan, 1954.
Nuseibeh, H. Z. *The Ideas of Arab Nationalism*. Ithaca: Cornell University Press, 1956.

Oakesmith, J. *Race and Nationality: An Inquiry into the Origin and Growth of Patriotism*. New York: Stokes, 1919.
O'Connor, J. *History of Ireland*. New York: Doran, 1925.
Okakura-Kakuzo. *The Awakening of Japan*. London: John Murray, 1905.
Oliver, D. L. *The Pacific Islands*. Cambridge, Mass.: Harvard University Press, 1952.
Oliver, R., and Fage, J. D. *A Short History of Africa*. Baltimore: Penguin, 1962.
Osgood, R. E. *Ideal and Self-Interest in America's Foreign Relations*. Chicago: University of Chicago Press, 1953.
Osterweis, R. G. *Romanticism and Nationalism in the Old South*. New Haven: Yale University Press, 1949.
Otero, G. A. *Sociologia del nacionalismo en Hispano-América*. Quito, 1947.

Paassen, C. van. *The Classical Tradition of Geography*. Groningen, The Netherlands, 1957.
Padmore, G. *Pan-Africanism or Communism?* New York: Roy Publishers, 1956.
Padover, S. K. *French Institutions, Values, and Politics*. Stanford: Stanford University Press, 1954.
Page, F. (ed.). *An Anthology of Patriotic Verse*. London: Oxford University Press, 1915.
Paprocki, S. J. (ed.). *Minority Affairs and Poland*. Warsaw: Nationality Research Institute, 1935.
Parkes, H. B. *The American Experience: An Interpretation of the History and Civilization of the American People*. New York: Knopf, 1947.
Partridge, G. E. *The Psychology of Nations*. New York: Macmillan, 1919.
Patai, R. *Israel between East and West*. Philadelphia: Jewish Publication Society of America, 1953.
Patterson, S. *The Last Trek: A Study of the Boer People and the Afrikaner Nation*. London: Routledge, 1957.
Perry, R. B. *Characteristically American*. New York: Knopf, 1949.
Petrovich, M. B. *The Emergence of Russian Panslavism, 1856–1870*. New York: Columbia University Press, 1956.
Phillips, C. H. (ed.). *Politics and Society in India*. London: Allen & Unwin, 1963.
Pillsbury, W. B. *The Psychology of Nationalism and Internationalism*. New York: Appleton, 1919.
Pinson, K. S. *A Bibliographical Introduction to Nationalism*. New York: Columbia University Press, 1935.
———. *Modern Germany: Its History and Civilization*. New York: Macmillan, 1954.
———. *Pietism as a Factor in the Rise of German Nationalism*. New York: Columbia University Press, 1957.

Pipes, R. *The Formation of the Soviet Union: Communism and Nationalism, 1917–1923*. Cambridge, Mass.: Harvard University Press, 1957.

Platt, W. *National Character in Action: Intelligence Factors in Foreign Relations*. New Brunswick: Rutgers University Press, 1961.

Pollard, A. F. *Factors in Modern History*. London: Constable, 1926.

Porter, J. *The Vertical Mosaic*. Toronto: University of Toronto Press, 1965.

Potter, D. M. *People of Plenty: Economic Abundance and the American Character*. Chicago: University of Chicago Press, 1954.

Pratt, J. "The Ideology of American Expansion," in *Essays in Honor of William E. Dodd*. Ed. A. Craven. Chicago: University of Chicago Press, 1935.

Pullen, J. J. *Patriotism in America*. New York: American Heritage Press, 1971.

Pulzer, P. G. J. *The Rise of Political Anti-Semitism in Germany and Austria*. New York: Wiley, 1964.

Pundt, A. G. *Arndt and the Nationalist Awakening in Germany*. New York: Columbia University Press, 1935.

Purcell, V. *The Revolution in Southeast Asia*. London: Thames and Hudson, 1962.

Pye, L. W. *Politics, Personality, and Nation-Building*. New Haven: Yale University Press, 1962.

Quaison-Sackey, A. *Africa Unbound*. New York: Praeger, 1963.

Radin, P. *The Racial Myth*. New York: Whittlesey House, 1934.

Raglan, Lord. *The Hero*. London: Methuen, 1936.

Raguvanshi, V. P. S. *Indian Nationalist Movement and Thought*. Agra: Lakshmi Narain Agarwal, 1959.

Rapaport, A. *Fights, Games and Debates*. Ann Arbor: University of Michigan Press, 1961.

Redslob, R. *Le principe des nationalités*. Paris: Sirey, 1930.

Reisner, E. H. *Nationalism and Education since 1789*. New York: Macmillan, 1922.

Renan, E. *Qu'est-ce qu'une nation?* Paris: Calmann-Levy, 1882.

Riasanovsky, N. V. *Nicholas I and Official Nationality in Russia, 1825–1855*. Berkeley: University of California Press, 1959.

———. *Russia and the West in the Teaching of the Slavophiles*. Cambridge, Mass.: Harvard University Press, 1952.

Rifaat, Bey M. *The Awakening of Egypt*. London: Longmans, Green, 1947.

Rigg, M. G. *Theories of the Obligations of Citizens to the State*. Philadelphia: University of Pennsylvania Press, 1921.

Ritchie, E. J. *The Making of a Maori: A Case Study of a Changing Community*. Wellington, New Zealand: University of Wellington Press, 1963.

Rogger, H. *National Consciousness in Eighteenth-Century Russia*. Cambridge, Mass.: Harvard University Press, 1960.

Rolfe, S. *The International Corporation*. Paris: International Chamber of Commerce, 1969.

Romein, J. *The Asian Century: A History of Modern Nationalism in Asia*. Berkeley: University of California Press, 1962.

Romier, L. *Nation et civilisation*. Paris: S. Kra, 1926.

Rondot, P. *The Changing Patterns of the Middle East, 1919–1959*. Trans. M. Dilke. London: Chatto & Windus, 1961.

Rosberg, C. G., and Nottingham, J. *The Myth of 'Mau Mau' Nationalism in Kenya*. New York: Praeger, 1966.

Rose, J. H. *Nationality in Modern History*. New York: Macmillan, 1916.

Rostow, W. W. "The National Style," in *The American Style*. Ed. E. E. Morison. New York: Harper, 1958.

Rotberg, R. I. *The Rise of Nationalism in Central Africa*. Cambridge, Mass.: Harvard University Press, 1965.

Roucek, J. S. "Regionalism and Separatism," in *European Ideologies*. Ed. F. Gross. New York: Philosophical Library, 1948.

———— (ed.). *Twentieth Century Political Thought*. New York: Philosophical Library, 1946.

Rutherford, P. (ed.). *African Voices*. New York: Grosset and Dunlap, 1958.

Ruyssen, T. *The Principle of Nationality*. Trans. J. Mez. New York: American Assn. for International Conciliation, 1916–1917.

Savelle, M. *Seeds of Liberty*. New York: Knopf, 1948.

Saveth, E. *American Historians and European Immigrants*. New York: Columbia University Press, 1948.

Sayegh, F. A. *Arab Unity*. New York: Devin Adair, 1958.

Schaffner, B. *Fatherland: A Study of Authoritarianism in the German Family*. New York: Columbia University Press, 1948.

Schalk, A. *The Germans*. Englewood Cliffs, N.J.: Prentice-Hall, 1971.

Schelling, T. C. *The Strategy of Conflict*. Cambridge, Mass.: Harvard University Press, 1963.

Schnee, H. *Nationalismus und Imperialismus*. Berlin: Hobbing, 1928.

Schneider, G. *Absonderung von allgemeiner Ursprung und Wesen d. Staatsideologie d. hist. Nationalismus*. Düsseldorf: Henn, 1973.

Schneider, H. W., and S. B. Clough. *Making Fascists*. Chicago: University of Chicago Press, 1929.

Schultz, H. A. *Nationalism and Sectionalism in South Carolina*. Durham, N.C.: Duke University Press, 1950.

Schuman, F. *International Politics*. New York: McGraw-Hill, 1948.

Scott, J. *Patriots in the Making*. New York: Appleton, 1916.

Senghor, L. S. *African Socialism*. New York: American Society of African Culture, 1959.

Seton-Watson, R. W. *The Rise of Nationality in the Balkans*. London: Constable, 1917.

Shafer, B. C. *Faces of Nationalism*. New York: Harcourt Brace Jovanovich, 1972.

————. *Nationalism: Interpreters and Interpretation*. 2nd ed. New York: Macmillan, 1963.

————. *Nationalism: Myth and Reality*. New York: Harcourt, Brace, 1955.

Sharabi, H. B. *Nationalism and Revolution in the Arab World*. Princeton: Van Nostrand, 1966.

Sharman, L. *Sun Yat-sen, His Life and Its Meaning*. New York: John Day, 1934.

Shepherd, G. W., Jr. *The Politics of African Nationalism*. New York: Praeger, 1962.

Siegfried, A. *L'Âme des peuples*. Paris: Hachette, 1950.

————. *France, A Study in Nationality*. New Haven: Yale University Press, 1930.

————. *Tableau politique de la France de l'Ouest sous la Troisième Republique*. Paris: A. Colin, 1913.

Silvert, K. H. (ed.). *Expectant Peoples: Nationalism and Development*. New York: Random House, 1963.

Singer, J. D. (ed.). *Human Behavior and International Politics*. Chicago: Rand McNally, 1965.

Sithole, N. *African Nationalism*. Cape Town: Oxford University Press, 1959.

Skendi, S. *The Albanian National Awakening, 1878–1917*. Princeton: Princeton University Press, 1967.

Smal-Stocki, R. *The Captive Nations: Nationalism in the Non-Russian Nations in the Soviet Union*. New Haven: College and University Press, 1960.

––––––. *The Nationality Problem of the Soviet Union and Russian Communist Imperialism*. Milwaukee: Bruce, 1952.

Smelser, N. J. *Theory of Collective Behavior*. New York: The Free Press, 1963.

Smith, A. D. *Theories of Nationalism*. London: Duckworth, 1971.

Smith, C. H., and Taylor, G. R. *Flags of All Nations*. New York: Crowell, 1946.

Smith, D. G. *India as a Secular State*. Princeton: Princeton University Press, 1963.

Smith, W. R. *Nationalism and Reform in India*. New Haven: Yale University Press, 1938.

Snyder, L. L. *The Dynamics of Nationalism*. Princeton: Van Nostrand, 1964.

––––––. *From Bismarck to Hitler: The Background of Modern German Nationalism*. Williamsport, Pa.: Bayard, 1935.

––––––. *German Nationalism: The Tragedy of a People*. Harrisburg, Pa.: Stackpole, 1952.

––––––. *The Idea of Racialism*. Princeton: Van Nostrand, 1962.

––––––. *The Imperialism Reader: Documents and Readings in Modern Expansionism*. Princeton: Van Nostrand, 1962.

––––––. *The Meaning of Nationalism*. New Brunswick: Rutgers University Press, 1954.

––––––. *Race: A History of Modern Ethnic Theories*. New York and London: Longmans Green, 1939.

––––––. *The World in the Twentieth Century*. Rev. ed. New York: Van Nostrand–Reinhold, 1964.

Stalin, J. *Marxism and the National and Colonial Question*. New York: International Publishers, n.d.

Stambrook, F. G. *European Nationalism in the 19th Century*. Melbourne: Cheshire, 1969.

Stannard, H. *What Is a Nation?* London: Royal Institute of International Affairs, 1945.

Starr, M. *Lies and Hate in Education*. London: Leonard and Virginia Woolf, 1929.

Stavrianos, L. S. *The Balkans since 1453*. New York: Holt, Rinehart and Winston, 1963.

Stocks, J. L. *Patriotism and the Super-State*. London: Swarthmore Press, 1920.

Sturzo, D. L. *Nationalism and Internationalism*. New York: Roy, 1946.

Sulzbach, W. *National Consciousness*. Washington, D.C.: American Council on Public Affairs, 1943.

Symmons-Symonolewicz, K. *Modern Nationalism: Towards a Consensus in Theory*. New York: Polish Institute of Arts and Sciences, 1968.

––––––. *Nationalist Movements: A Comparative View*. Meadville, Pa.: Maplewood Press, 1970.

Symonds, R. *The Making of Pakistan*. London: Faber, 1950.

Tagore, R. *Nationalism*. New York: Macmillan, 1917.

Talmon, J. L. *Political Messianism: The Romantic Phase*. London: Secker and Warburg, 1960.

––––––. *The Rise of Totalitarianism*. New York: Praeger, 1960.

Taylor, A. J. P. *The Course of German History*. New York: Coward-McCann, 1946.

Taylor, T. G. *Environment and Nation*. Chicago: University of Chicago Press, 1936.

Taylor, W. R. *Cavalier and Yankee: The Old South and American National Character*. New York: Braziller, 1961.

Tegnaeus, H. *Le héros civilisateur*. Stockholm: Victor Pettersons Bokindustri, 1960.

Temple, P. *Bantu Philosophy*. Paris: Presence Africaine, 1959.

Thaden, E. C. *Conservative Nationalism in Nineteenth Century Russia*. Seattle: University of Washington Press, 1964.

Thayer, P. W. (ed.). *Nationalism and Progress in Free Asia*. Baltimore: Johns Hopkins Press, 1956.

Thornton, A. P. *Doctrines of Imperialism*. New York: Wiley, 1965.

Tims, R. W. *Germanizing the Prussian Poles: The H-K-T Society of the Eastern Marches*. New York: Columbia University Press, 1941.

Tinker, H. *India and Pakistan: A Short Political Guide*. London: Pall Mall, 1962.

Tocqueville, A. de. *The Old Regime and the French Revolution*. Trans. S. Gilbert. Garden City, N.Y.: Doubleday, 1955.

Tolstoy, L. N. *Christianity and Patriotism*. Trans. C. Garnett. London: Jonathan Cape, 1922.

Tourville, H. de. *The Growth of Modern Nations*. Trans. M. G. Loch. New York: Longmans, Green, 1907.

Touval, S. *Somali Nationalism*. Cambridge, Mass.: Harvard University Press, 1963.

Toynbee, A. *The Western Question in Greece and Turkey*. London: Constable, 1922.

————. *The World and the West*. New York: Oxford University Press, 1953.

Treitschke, H. von. *Politics*. Trans. B. Dugdale and T. de Bille. London: Constable, 1916.

Trevelyan, G. M. *Garibaldi's Defence of the Roman Republic*. London: Longmans, Green, 1907.

Troncoso, O. A. *Los nacionalistas argentinos*. Buenos Aires: Ed. Saga, 1957.

Tucker, R. C. *The Soviet Political Mind*. New York: Praeger, 1963.

Tucker, R. W. *The Just War*. Baltimore: Johns Hopkins Press, 1960.

Turner, R. H., and Millian, L. M. (eds.). *Collective Behavior*. New York: Prentice-Hall, 1957.

Tutsch, H. E. *From Ankara to Marrakesh: Turks and Arabs in a Changing World*. London: Allen & Unwin, 1964.

Vakar, N. P. *Belorussia: The Making of a Nation*. Cambridge, Mass.: Harvard University Press, 1956.

Vambery, A. *Western Culture in Eastern Lands*. London: Murray, 1906.

Van Deusen, G. G. *Sieyès: His Life and His Nationalism*. New York: Columbia University Press, 1932.

Vanel, M. *Histoire de la nationalité française d'origine*. Paris: Ancienne Imprimerie de la Cour d'Appel, 1945.

Van Gennep, A. *Traité comparatif des nationalités*. Paris: Payot, 1922.

Van Rensberg, P. *Guilty Land: The History of Apartheid*. New York: Praeger, 1962.

Varela, A. H. *El nacionalismo y los obreros socialistas*. Buenos Aires: Padilla y Contreras, 1944.

Vattel, E. de. *The Law of Nations*. Philadelphia: Johnson and Co., 1865.

Vaussard, M. *Enquête sur le nationalisme*. Paris: Edition Spes, 1924.

Veblin, T. *The Higher Learning in America*. New York: Sagamore Press, 1957.

Vernadsky, G. *A History of Russia*. New Haven: Yale University Press, 1929.

Vinner, P. (ed.). *National Communism and Popular Revolt*. New York: Columbia University Press, 1957.

Vossler, O. *Der Nationalgedanke von Rousseau bis Ranke*. Munich: Oldenbourg, 1937.

Wade, M. *The French Canadians*. New York: Macmillan, 1965.

Wagley, C., and Harris, M. *Minorities in the New World*. New York: Columbia University Press, 1958.

Wallbank, T. W. *Documents on Modern Africa*. Princeton: Van Nostrand, 1964.

Wallerstein, I. *Africa: The Politics of Independence*. New York: Vintage Books, 1961.

Walworth, A. *School Histories at War*. Cambridge, Mass.: Harvard University Press, 1938.

Walzel, O. *German Romanticism*. New York: Capricorn Books, 1966.

Ward, B. *Five Ideas That Changed the World*. New York: Norton, 1959.

———. *Nationalism and Ideology*. New York: Norton, 1966.

Ward, R. E., and Dankwart, A. R. *Political Modernization in Japan and Turkey*. Princeton: Princeton University Press, 1964.

Warner, W. L. *American Life: Dream and Reality*. Chicago: University of Chicago Press, 1953.

Watson, F. *The Frontiers of China*. London: Chatto & Windus, 1966.

Weber, E. *Action Française*. Stanford: Stanford University Press, 1962.

———. *Varieties of Fascism*. Princeton: Van Nostrand, 1964.

Wecter, D. *The Hero in America*. New York: Scribner, 1941.

Weill, G. J. *L'Europe de XIXe siècle et l'idée de nationalité*. Paris: Albin Michel, 1918.

———. *Race et nation*. Paris: Albin Michel, 1939.

Weinberg, A. K. *Manifest Destiny: A Study of Nationalist Expansionism in American History*. Baltimore: Johns Hopkins Press, 1935.

Weinstein, H. *Jean Jaurès: A Study of Patriotism in the French Socialist Movement*. New York: Columbia University Press, 1936.

Wertheimer, M. S. *The Pan-German League, 1890–1914*. New York: Columbia University Press, 1924.

Whitaker, A. P. *Nationalism in Latin America*. Gainesville: University of Florida Press, 1962.

Whitaker, A. P., and Jordan, D. C. *Nationalism in Contemporary Latin America*. New York: The Free Press, 1966.

White, E. B. *The Wild Flag*. Boston: Houghton Mifflin, 1946.

Wilson, D. A. "Nation-Building and Revolutionary War," in *Nation-Building*. Ed. K. W. Deutsch and W. J. Foltz. New York: Atherton, 1963.

Wingfield-Stratford, E. *The Foundations of British Patriotism*. London: Routledge, 1939.

———. *The History of English Patriotism*. London: Lane, 1913.

Winslow, E. M. *The Pattern of Imperialism*. New York: Columbia University Press, 1948.

Wint, G. *Communist China's Crusade*. London: Pall Mall, 1965.

Wirth, L. "The Problem of Minority Groups," in *The Science of Man in the World Crisis*. Ed. R. Linton. New York: Columbia University Press, 1945.

Wiskemann, E. *Czechs and Germans*. London: Oxford University Press, 1938.

Woolf, L. *Imperialism and Civilization*. New York: Harcourt, Brace, 1928.

Wright, Q. *A Study of War*. Chicago: University of Chicago Press, 1942.

Wrong, D. *American and Canadian Viewpoints*. Washington, D.C.: American Council on Education, 1955.

Wuorinen, J. H. *Nationalism in Finland*. New York: Columbia University Press, 1931.

Wylie, L. (ed.). *In Search of France*. Cambridge, Mass.: Harvard University Press, 1962.

Yale, W. *The Near East: A Modern History*. Ann Arbor: University of Michigan Press, 1958.
Yurchak, P. P. *The Slovaks: Their History and Traditions*. Whiting, Ind., 1946.

Zangwill, I. *The Principle of Nationalities*. London: Watts, 1917.
Zeine, Z. N. *The Emergence of Arab Nationalism*. Beirut: Khayats, 1966.
Zenkowsky, S. A. *Pan-Turkism and Islam in Russia*. Cambridge, Mass.: Harvard University Press, 1960.
Ziegler, H. O. *Die moderne Nation*. Tübingen: Mohr, 1931.
Ziemer, G. *Education for Death*. New York: Oxford University Press, 1941.
Zimmern, A. *Nationality and Government and Other War-Time Essays*. London: Chatto & Windus, 1918.
Znaniecki, F. *Modern Nationalities: A Sociological Study*. Urbana: University of Illinois Press, 1952.

Periodicals

Abuva, J. V. "Filipino Nationalism, Public Policy and Political Institutions," *Asia*, IX (1967), 68–71.
Alba, V. "Mitologia del movimientio obrero: el nacionalismo proletario," *Cuadernos Americanos*, XIII (1954), 43–57.
Alis, J. I. "The Indonesian Language: By-Product of Nationalism," *Pacific Affairs*, XXII (1949), 388–92.
Allport, L. "The Psychology of Nationalism," *Harper's Magazine*, CLV (1927), 291–301.
Appel, K. E. "Nationalism and Sovereignty: A Psychiatric View," *Journal of Abnormal and Social Psychology*, XL (1945), 355–62.
Arendt, H. "Imperialism, Nationalism, Chauvinism," *Review of Politics*, VII (1945), 441–63.
———. "Race-Thinking before Racism," *Review of Politics*, VI (1944), 36ff.
Attwater, D. "Welsh Nationalism," *Commonweal*, January 27, 1939, pp. 374–76.
Atuna, J. G. "Vers l'expression américaine: le sens d'histoire et le nationalisme dans l' oeuvre de Ricardo Rojas," *Revue de l' Amerique Latine* (1928), pp. 481–90.
Ayala, F. "El nacionalismo sano y el otro," *Sur*, no. 242 (1956), pp. 5–10.

Barber, B. "Acculturation and Messianic Movements," *American Sociological Review*, VI (1941), 663–69.
Barbour, N. "Variations of Arab National Feeling in French North Africa," *Middle East Journal*, VIII (1954), 308–30.
Barzini, L. "*Risorgimento:* Historical Reflections on the Making of Italy," *Encounter*, XXXVII (1971), 29–38.
Basadre, J. "Why Nationalism?" *Americas*, I, no. 7 (1949), 12–14.
Beaglehole, E. "Character Structure: Its Role in the Analysis of Interpersonal Relations," *Psychiatry*, VII (1944), 145–62.
Bell, D. "The National Style and the Radical Right," *Partisan Review*, XXIX (1962), 519–64.
Berger, M. "Understanding National Character," *Commentary*, II (1951), 375–86.
Berlin, I. "The Bent Twig: A Note on Nationalism," *Foreign Affairs*, no. 1 (1972), 11–30.
Binder, L. "Pakistan and Modern Islamic Nationalist Theory," *Middle East Journal*, XI (1957), 382–96, and XII (1958), 45–56.

Boehm, M. H. "Nationalism: Theoretical Aspects," *Encyclopedia of the Social Sciences*, XI (1933), 231–40.

Bolwell, E. R. W. "Concerning the Study of Nationalism in American Literature," *American Literature*, X (1939), 405–16.

Brogan, D. W. "The Nationalist Doctrines of M. Charles Maurras," *Politica*, I (1935), 286–311.

Bruner, J. S., and Perlmutter, H. C. "Compatriot and Foreigner: A Study of Impression Formation in Three Countries," *Journal of Abnormal and Social Psychology*, LV (1957), 253–60.

Buber, M. "The Beginning of the National Idea," *Review of Religion*, X (1916), 254–65.

Buck, C. D. "Language and the Sentiment of Nationality," *Political Science Review*, X (1916), 44–69.

Bühler, C. "National Differences in 'World Test' Projection Patterns," *Journal of Projective Techniques*, XVI (1952), 42–55.

Cahnman, W. J. "Religion and Nationality," *American Journal of Sociology*, XLIX (1944), 524–29.

Carrillo Flores, A. "El nacionalismo de los paises latino-americanos en la postguerra," *Jornados*, no. 28 (1945).

Cashman, W. J. "Religion and Nationality," *American Journal of Sociology*, XLIX (1944), 524–29.

Cattell, R. B. "The Dimensions of Culture Patterns by Factorization of National Characters," *Journal of Abnormal and Social Psychology*, XLIV (1949), 443–69.

Child, I. L., and Doob, L. W. "Factors Determining National Stereotypes," *Journal of Social Psychology*, XIII (1943), 475–78.

Choulguine, A. "Les origines de l'esprit national moderne et Jean-Jacques Rousseau," *Annales de la Société Jean-Jacques Rousseau*, XXVI (1937), 9–283.

Cline, W. B. "Nationalism in Morocco," *Middle East Journal*, I (1947), 18–28.

Cole, C. W. "Jeremy Belknap: Pioneer Nationalist," *New England Quarterly*, X (1937), 743–51.

Corbett, P. E. "The Future of Nationalism and the National State," *Annals of the American Academy of Political and Social Science*, CCXVIII (1941), 153–61.

Coulton, G. G. "Nationalism in the Middle Ages," *Cambridge Historical Journal*, V (1935), 15–40.

Curti, M. "American Philanthropy and the National Character," *American Quarterly*, X (1958), 420–37.

———. "Francis Lieber and Nationalism," *Huntington Library Quarterly*, vol. IV (1941), reprint.

Curtin, P. D. "Nationalism in Africa, 1945–65," *Review of Politics*, XXVIII (1966), 147–53.

Dawn, C. E. "The Rise of Arabism in Syria," *Middle East Journal*, XVL (1962), 145–68.

Degler, C. N. "The Sociologist as Historian: Riesman's *The Lonely Crowd*," *American Quarterly*, XV (1963), 483–97.

Denney, R. "How Americans See Themselves," *Annals of the American Academy of Political and Social Science*, CCXCV (September 1954), 12–20.

Deutsch, K. W. "The Growth of Nations: Some Recurrent Patterns of Political and Social Integration," *World Politics*, V (1952), 168–95.

———. "The Trend of European Nationalism: The Language Aspect," *American Political Science Review*, XXXVI (1942), 533–41.

Doob, L. W. "South Tyrol: An Introduction to the Psychological Syndrome of Nationalism," *Public Opinion Quarterly*, XXVI (1962), 172–84.

Dupre, H. "Carnot's Nationalism," *South Atlantic Quarterly*, XXXVII (1938), 291–306.

Eisenmann, L. "Quelques aspects nouveaux de l'idée de nationalité," *Bulletin of the International Committee of Historical Sciences*, II, pt. 2 (1929), 225–33.
Elkin, A. P. "The Reaction of the Primitive Races to the White Man's Culture," *Hibbert Journal*, XXXV (1936–37), 537–45.
Elviken, L. "The Genesis of Norwegian Nationalism," *Journal of Modern History*, III (1931), 365–91.
Emerson, R. "An Analysis of Nationalism in Southeast Asia," *Far Eastern Quarterly*, V, no. 2 (February 1946), 208–15.
———. "Nationalism and Political Development," *Journal of Politics*, XXII, 3–28.
———. "Paradoxes of Asian Nationalism," *Far Eastern Quarterly*, XIII, no. 2 (1954), 131–42.
Endleman, R. "The New Anthropology and Its Ambitions: The Science of Man in Messianic Dress," *Commentary*, VIII (September 1949), 284–91.
Ergang, R. R. "Möser and the Rise of National Thought in Germany," *Journal of Modern History*, V (1933), 172–96.

Fallers, L. A. "Ideology and Culture in Uganda Nationalism," *American Anthropologist*, LX (1961), 677–86.
Farber, M. L. "The Problem of National Character: A Methodological Analysis," *Journal of Psychology*, XXX (1950), 307–16.
Finer, H. "Reflections on the Nature of Arab Nationalism," *Middle East Affairs*, IX (1958), 302–13.
Frey, F. W. "Socialization to National Identification among Turkish Peasants," *Journal of Politics*, XXX (1968), 934–65.
Friedman, W. "New Nationalism," *Fortnightly*, CLXIII (1945), 27–34.
Friedrich, C. J., "The Agricultural Bases of Emotional Nationalism," *Public Opinion Quarterly*, I (1937), 50–61.
Fyfe, H. "The Illusion of National Character," *Political Quarterly*, IX (1938), 254–70.

Gershoy, L. "Barère: Champion of Nationalism in the French Revolution," *Political Science Quarterly*, XLII (1927), 419–30.
Gilbert, G. M. "Stereotype Persistence and Change among College Students," *Journal of Abnormal and Social Psychology*, XLVI (1951), 245–54.
Gilliland, A. R., and Blum, R. A. "Favorable and Unfavorable Attitudes toward Certain Enemy and Allied Countries," *Journal of Psychology*, XX (1945), 391–99.
Gillin, D. G. "Peasant Nationalism in the History of Chinese Communism," *Journal of Asian Studies*, XXIII, no. 2 (February 1964), 269ff.
Gillin, J. "National and Regional Values in the United States," *Social Forces*, XXXIV (December 1955), 107–13.
Ginsburg, M. "National Character," *British Journal of Psychology*, XXXII (1942), 183–205.
Giuste, R. F. "La restauración nacionalista," *Nosotros*, IV, no. 26 (1910), 139–54.
Gorer, G. "The Concept of National Character," *Science News*, no. 18 (1950), pp. 105–22.
Guiart, J. "Forerunners of Melanesian Nationalism," *Oceania*, XXII, no. 2 (December 2, 1951), 81–90.

Handman, M. S. "The Sentiment of Nationalism," *Political Science Quarterly*, XXXVI (1921), 107–14.

Harrison, J. P. "The Confrontation with the Political University," *Annals of the American Academy of Political and Social Science* (March 1961), pp. 74–83.

Hayes, C. J. H. "The Church and Nationalism," *Catholic Historical Review*, XXVIII (1942), 1–12.

———. "Contributions of Herder to the Doctrine of Nationalism," *American Historical Review*, XXXII (1927), 719–36.

———. "Nationalism: Historical Development," *Encyclopedia of the Social Sciences*, XI (1933), 240–49.

———. "Two Varieties of Nationalism, Original and Derived," *Proceedings of the Association of History Teachers of the Middle States and Maryland*, XXVI (1928), 70–83.

Hollander, A. N. J. den. "As Others See Us," *Synthese*, VI (1947–48), 214–38.

Horowitz, E. L. "Some Aspects of Development of Patriotism in Children," *Sociometry*, III (1940), 339–41.

Hume, D. "Of National Character," in *Essays and Treatises*, vol. 1 (London, 1770).

Humphreys, E. M. "Welsh Nationalism and Its Background," *Fortnightly*, CL (August 1938), 146–52.

Hymer, S. "Is the Multinational Corporation Doomed?" *Innovation*, no. 28 (1972), pp. 10–18.

Ichheiser, G. "Some Psychological Obstacles to an Understanding between Nations," *Journal of Abnormal and Social Psychology*, XXXVI (1941), 427–32.

Inkeles, A. "National Character and Social Structure," *Antioch Review*, IX (June 1949), 155–62.

Jahoda, G. "Development of Scottish Children's Ideas and Attitudes about Other Countries," *Journal of Social Psychology*, LVIII (1962), 91–108.

Kajaratman, S. "Beyond Nationalism, More Nationalism," *Solidarity*, LV (1969).

Kilson, M. L., Jr. "The Analysis of African Nationalism," *World Politics* X (1957–58), 484–97.

Kirkland, D. "The Growth of National Sentiment in France before the 15th Century," *History*, XXIII (1938), 12–24.

Klineberg, O. "American Culture and American Personality: Some Methodological Considerations," *Journal of Social Issues*, VII, no. 4 (1951), 40–44.

———. "A Science of National Character," *Journal of Social Psychology*, XIX (1944), 147–62.

Kohn, H. "Arndt and the Character of German Nationalism," *American Historical Review*, LIV (1949), 787–803.

———. "Begriffswandel des nationalismus," *Der Merkur* (August 1964), pp. 701–14.

———. "The Eve of German Nationalism," *Journal of the History of Ideas*, XII (1951), 256–84.

———. "Father Jahn's Nationalism," *Review of Politics*, XI (1949), 419–32.

———. "The Genesis and Character of English Nationalism," *Journal of the History Of Ideas*, I (January 1940), 69–94.

———. "Nationalism," *International Encyclopedia of the Social Sciences*, XI (1968), 63–70.

———. "The Paradox of Fichte's Nationalism," *Journal of the History of Ideas*, X (1949), 319–43.

———. "Romanticism and the Rise of Nationalism," *Review of Politics*, XII (1950), 443–72.

————. "Twilight of Nationalism," *American Scholar,* VI (1937), 259–70.

Koht, H. "The Dawn of Nationalism in Europe," *American Historical Review,* LII (1947), 265–80.

————. "L'esprit national et l'idée de la souveraineté du peuple," *Bulletin of the International Committee of Historical Sciences,* II, pt. 2 (1929), 217–24.

Kracauer, S. "National Types as Hollywood Presents Them," *Public Opinion Quarterly,* XIII (1949), 53–72.

Krehbiel, E. "Nationalism," *Annual Report of the American Historical Association* (1915), pp. 219–22.

Lambert, W. E., and Klineberg, O. "A Pilot Study of the Origin and Development of National Stereotypes," *International Social Science Journal,* II (1959), 221–38.

Lawson, E. D. "Development of Patriotism in Children: A Second Look," *Journal of Psychology,* LV (1963), 279–86.

Lehman, H. C. "National Differences in Creativity," *American Journal of Sociology,* LII (1947), 475–88.

Lippmann, W. "Vested Rights and Nationalism in Latin America," *Foreign Affairs* (April 1927), 353–63.

Maehl, W. "The Triumph of Nationalism in the German Socialist Party on the Eve of the First World War," *Journal of Modern History,* XXIV (1952), 15–41.

Mandelbaumm, D. G. "On the Study of National Character," *American Anthropologist,* LV (April-June 1953), 174–87.

Marmorstein, E. "Religious Opposition to Nationalism in the Middle East," *International Affairs,* XXVIII (1952), 344–59.

Martin, H. "Nationalism in Children's Literature," *Library Quarterly* VI (1936), 405–18.

Mathiez, A. "Pacifisme et nationalisme au dix-huitième siècle," *Annales historiques de la Révolution française,* XIII (1936), 1–17.

Mayer, K. "Cultural Pluralism and Linguistic Equilibrium in Switzerland," *American Sociological Review,* XVI (1951), 157–63.

McGranahan, D. V. "A Comparison of Social Attitudes among American and German Youth," *Journal of Abnormal and Social Psychology,* XLI (1946), 245–57.

Mead, M. "Anthropologist and Historian: Their Common Problems," *American Quarterly,* III (Spring 1951), 3–13.

————. "The Application of Anthropological Techniques to Cross-National Communication," *New York Academy of Sciences Transactions,* ser. 2, IX (February 1947), 135–52.

Meltzer, H. "Thinking about Nations and Races," *Journal of Genetic Psychology,* LVIII (1941), 181–99.

Mosllenhoff, F. "The Price of Individuality: Speculations about German National Characteristics," *American Imago,* IV (1947), 33–60.

Mosk, S. A. "El nacionalismo ecónomica en la América Latina," *Revista de Economia Continental,* I, no. 4 (1945), 401–11.

Namier, L. "Pathological Nationalism," *Manchester Guardian* April 26, 1933.

Nye, J. S. "Multinational Enterprises and Prospects for Regional and Global Political Integration," *Annals of the American Academy of Political and Social Science,* CCCCIII (1972), 110–26.

Oncken, H. "Deutsche geistige Einflüsse in der europäischen Nationalbewegung des neunzehnten Jahrhunderts," *Deutsche Vierteljahrschrift für Literaturwissenschaft und Geistesgeschichte,* VII (1929), 607–27.

Palmer, R. R. "The National Idea in France before the Revolution," *Journal of the History of Ideas*, I (1940), 95–111.

Pauker, G. J. "The Study of National Character away from the Nation's Territory," *Studies in International Affairs*, I (June 1951), 81–103.

Pettigrew, T. F. "Personality and Sociocultural Factors in Inter-Group Attitudes: A Cross-National Comparison," *Conflict Resolution*, II (1958), 29–42.

Pflanze, O. "Nationalism in Europe, 1848–71," *Review of Politics*, XVIII (1966), 129–43.

Potter, D. "The Historian's Use of Nationalism and Vice-Versa," *American Historical Review*, LXVII (1962), 924–50.

Potter, M. "American Women and American Character," *Stetson University Bulletin*, LXII (January 1962), 1–22.

Riesman, D. "Psychological Types and National Character," *American Quarterly*, V (Winter 1953), 325–43.

———. "The Study of National Character: Some Observations on the American Case," *Harvard Library Bulletin*, XIII (Winter 1959), 5–24.

Rivlin, B. "Unity and Nationalism in Libya," *Middle East Journal*, III (1949), 31–54.

Robinson, J. H. "What Is National Spirit?" *Century Magazine*, XCIII (1916), 57–64.

Rogger, H. "Nationalism and the State: A Russian Dilemma," *Comparative Attitudes in Society and History*, IV (1962), 253–64.

Róheim, G. "The Psychology of Nationalism," *American Imago*, VII (1959), 3–19.

Rotberg, R. I. "The Rise of African Nationalism: The Case of East and Central Africa," *World Politics*, XV (1962–63), 75–90.

Roucek, J. S. (ed.). "Nationalistic Ideology and Goals," *Annals of the American Academy of Political and Social Science*, CCXXXII (1944), 25–115.

Savelle, M. "Nationalism and Other Loyalties in the American Revolution," *American Historical Review*, LXVII (1962), 901–23.

Saveth, E. N. "Race and Nationalism in American Historiography: The Late Nineteenth Century," *Political Science Quarterly*, LIV (1939), 421–41.

Schlesinger, A. M. "What Then Is the American, the New Man?" *American Historical Review*, XLVIII (1943), 225–44.

Schmidt, R. J. "Cultural Nationalism in Herder," *Journal of the History of Ideas*, XVII (1956), 407–17.

Shafer, B. C. "Bourgeois Nationalism on the Eve of the Revolution," *Journal of Modern History*, X (1938), 31–50.

———. "When Patriotism Becomes Popular," *Historian*, V (1943), 77–96.

Silvert, K. H. "Nationalism in Latin America," *Annals of the American Academy of Political and Social Science*, CCCXXXIV (March 1961), 1–9.

Simon, W. M. "Variations in Nationalism during the Great Reform Period in Prussia," *American Historical Review*, LIX (1954), 305–21.

Sirjamaki, J. "A Footnote to the Anthropological Approach to the Study of American Culture," *Social Forces*, XXV (March 1947), 253–63.

Skendi, S. "Beginnings of Albanian Nationalist and Autonomous Trends," *American Slavic and East European Review*, XII (1953), 219–32.

———. "Beginnings of Albanian Nationalist Culture and Education, 1878–1912," *Journal of Central European Affairs*, XII (1953), 356–67.

Smith, M. W. "Towards a Classification of Cult Movements," *Man*, LIX (1959), 8–12.

Snyder, L. L. "The American-German Pork Dispute, 1879–1891," *Journal of Modern History*, XVII (1945), 16–28.

————. "The Role of Herbert Bismarck in the Angra Pequena Negotiations between Germany and Britain, 1880–1885," *Journal of Negro History*, XXXV (1950), 435–52.

————. "Nationalistic Aspects of the Grimm Brothers Fairy Tales," *Journal of Social Psychology*, XXXIII (1951), 209–23.

Spindler, G. D. "American Character as Revealed by the Military," *Psychiatry*, XI (August 1948), 275–81.

Stagner, R. "Impact of War on a Nationalistic Frame of Reference," *Journal of Social Psychology*, XXIV (1946), 187–215.

Stagner, R., and Osgood, C. E. "An Experimental Analysis of a Nationalistic Frame of Reference," *Journal of Social Psychology*, XIV (1941), 389–401.

Sukarno, A. "Address to the National Press Club" (May 18, 1956). *Department of State Bulletin* XXIV, no. 884 (June 4, 1956).

Symmons-Symonolewicz, K. "Nationalistic Movements: An Attempt at a Comparative Typology," *Comparative Studies in Society and History*, VII (January 1965), 221–30.

————. "Nativistic Movements and Modern Nationalism," *Transactions of the Illinois State Academy of Science*, LIX, no. 3 (September 1966), 236–40.

————. "Studies in Nationality and Nationalism in Poland between the Two World Wars," *Bulletin of the Polish Institute of Arts and Sciences in America*, II, no. 1 (October 1943), 57–125.

Tannenbaum, F. "Agrarismo, Indianismo, Nacionalismo," *Hispanic American Review*, XXIII (1943), 394–423.

Tansill, C. C. "Nationalism: Historical Prelude," *International Law and Relations*, vol. IV (1935).

Van Den Bergh, G. "Contemporary Nationalism in the Western World," *Daedalus*, vol. XCV (Summer 1966).

Viekke, B. H. M. "Communism and Nationalism in South East Asia," *International Affairs*, XXV (1949), 149–56.

Virtanen, R. "Nietzsche and the *Action Française*," *Journal of Modern History*, XI (1950), 191–214.

Walden, D. "Race and Imperialism: The Achilles Heel of the Progressives," *Science and Society*, vol. XXXI (Spring 1967).

Wallace, A. F. C. "Revitalization Movements," *American Anthropologist*, LVIII (1956), 264–81.

Walters, R. S. "International Organizations and the Multinational Corporation," *Annals of the American Academy of Political and Social Science*, CCCCIII (1972), 127–52.

Windmiller, M. "Linguistic Regionalism in India," *Pacific Affairs*, XXVII (1954), 291–318.

Wirth, L. "Types of Nationalism," *American Journal of Sociology*, XLI (1936), 723–37.

Zernatto, G. "Nation: The History of a Word," *Review of Politics*, VI (1944), 351–66.

Index

F1